Developing professional-level langua

D0706995

DISCARD

This comprehensive book examines approaches to teaching students who aim
to make the leap from "Advanced" or "Superior" proficiency in a foreign
language to "Distinguished" or "near-native" ability. While there are copious
publications on classroom techniques and methods for lower levels of instruction, virtually nothing exists about this transition, which is vital for those who
intend to use foreign languages in high-level international arenas. Written by
leading practitioners in this area of foreign language teaching, this book aims
to fill the gap and assist those developing language programs that lead from
the "Advanced" to the "Distinguished" level.

- Divided into three parts which provide information on different aspects of
  teaching at this level:
  - theory of advanced language teaching
  - nine sample programs
  - description of highly advanced learners based on long-term experience
    and empirical research
- Presents programs in seven languages – Arabic, Chinese, English, French,
  German, Russian, Spanish
- Content is both theoretical and pragmatic

BETTY LOU LEAVER is Director of the Center for the Advancement of
Distinguished Language Proficiency at San Diego State University. She has
published extensively in the area of foreign and second language acquisition (theory, teaching, learning, research), Russian culture and linguistics, and
general learning theory.

BORIS SHEKHTMAN is President of the Specialized Language Training
Center, and Lecturer in the Department of Modern Languages at Howard
University. He has more than fifteen years of experience in teaching Russian
to Superior-level students and has also lectured on methodology and area
studies. Among his publications are books for helping students to improve
their linguistic and sociolinguistic skills.

Developing Professional-Level Language Proficiency

Edited by

Betty Lou Leaver

*Center for the Advancement
of Distinguished Language Proficiency
San Diego State University*

and

Boris Shekhtman

Specialized Language Training Center

CAMBRIDGE
UNIVERSITY PRESS

CAMBRIDGE UNIVERSITY PRESS
Cambridge, New York, Melbourne, Madrid, Cape Town, Singapore, São Paulo, Delhi

Cambridge University Press
The Edinburgh Building, Cambridge CB2 8RU, UK

Published in the United States of America by Cambridge University Press, New York

www.cambridge.org
Information on this title: www.cambridge.org/9780521016858

© Cambridge University Press 2002

First published 2002

A catalogue record for this publication is available from the British Library

ISBN 978-0-521-81657-1 hardback
ISBN 978-0-521-01685-8 paperback

Transferred to digital printing 2009

Contents

Notes on contributors

CLAUDIA ANGELELLI (Ph.D., Stanford University) is Assistant Professor at San Diego State University. Earlier she was a Lecturer in Spanish at Stanford, and Assistant Professor at the Graduate School of Languages and Educational Linguistics and Visiting Professor of Translation and Interpretation at the Monterey Institute of International Studies. She has also taught in Argentina, Peru, and Puerto Rico.
Her e-mail address is claudia.angelelli@sdsu.edu.

SABINE ATWELL (MA, University of Nevada) is Director of Tester Training and Education at the Defense Language Institute. Prior to that, she held positions as a teacher of German, curriculum developer, faculty developer, and language program manager. She earlier taught French and German at the University of Nevada, Reno.
Her e-mail address is atwells@pom-emh1.army.mil.

ELSAID BADAWI (Ph.D., London University) is Professor and Director of the American Language Institute (ALI) and Co-Director of CASA at the American University in Cairo. A member of the Presidential Council for Higher Education and the Higher Council for Arts and Literature in Egypt, he is advisor to many international organizations. His publications include *Levels of Arabic in Egypt* and *Dictionary of Egyptian Arabic.*
His e-mail address is badawi@aucegypt.edu.

RICHARD BRECHT (Ph.D., Harvard University) is Director of the National Foreign Language Center, Professor of Russian at the University of Maryland, and Visiting Professor at Bryn Mawr College. He has authored numerous books and articles and has received awards from a number of national and international organizations in the language field.
His e-mail address is rdbrecht@nflc.org.

HEIDI BYRNES (Ph.D., Georgetown University) is Professor of German/ Linguistics at Georgetown University. Her research focus is the acquisition of academic literacy by adult instructed learners. Her department has implemented an integrated content-oriented and task-based curriculum, using literacy and genre as constructs. She is currently writing a book on principles and practices for curriculum construction.

Her e-mail address is byrnesh@georgetown.edu.

TIM CAUDERY (Ph.D., University of Aarhus, Denmark) is Associate Professor at the University of Aarhus, where he has taught in the English Department since 1988 and where his main research interests are in the area of ELT. Previously, he taught English to adults in Sweden, and served as Director of English Studies at The English Institute, Nicosia.

His e-mail address is engtc@hum.au.dk.

ZITA DABARS (Ph.D., Indiana University), now retired, was Director of the Center of Russian Language and Culture (CORLAC), Friends School, Baltimore. She also was the Project Director and Co-Director of NEH/ CORLAC Institutes in Russian Language and Culture. Among her publications are a book on culture and three textbooks with accompanying workbooks (3) and videotapes (4).

Her e-mail address is zitad@aol.com.

CHRISTIAN DEGUELDRE (MA, Université de l'État à Mons, Belgium) is Program Head in the French Department at the Graduate School of Translation and Interpretation (T&I) at the Monterey Institute of International Studies. He has taught T&I in English, French, and Spanish for twenty years in the USA and Korea and has extensive experience in interpretation in over forty countries, including for many heads of state.

His e-mail address is cdegueldre@miis.edu.

MADELINE EHRMAN (Ph.D., The Union Institute) is Director of Research, Evaluation, and Development at the Foreign Service Institute, and Senior Associate, National Foreign Language Center. Her publications combine a background in applied linguistics with clinical psychology, e.g. the books *Understanding Second Language Learning Difficulties* and *Interpersonal Dynamics in Second Language Education.*

Her e-mail is ehrmanm@aol.com.

CATHERINE W. INGOLD (Ph.D., University of Virginia) is Deputy Director of the National Foreign Language Center in Washington, DC. Much of her career has been in higher education administration, including successive service as Language Department Chairman, Dean of Arts and Sciences, and Provost of Gallaudet University, and as President of the American University of Paris.

Her e-mail address is cwingold@nflc.org.

OLGA KAGAN (Ph.D., Pushkin Institute, Moscow) is the Director, Language Resource Program, and Coordinator of the Russian Language Program, UCLA. Among her jointly authored and edited publications are *The Learning and Teaching of Slavic Languages and Cultures*, *Uchimsya uchit'* (We Are Learning to Teach), *V Puti* (On the Way), and *Russian For Russians*.
Her e-mail address is okagan@humnet.ucla.edu.

CORNELIUS C. KUBLER (Ph.D., Cornell University) is Stanfield Professor of Asian Studies at Williams College. He was formerly Chair of Asian & African Languages at the Foreign Service Institute and Principal of FSI's advanced field school in Taiwan. He has written over forty publications on Chinese language and linguistics.
His e-mail address is ckubler@williams.edu.

EKATERINA KUZNETSOVA is a Senior Instructor at the Specialized Language Training Center. Prior to that, she served as Instructor of Russian as a Foreign Language at Saratov State University (Russia), Senior Instructor of EFL at Saratov Law College, and Instructor of EFL at Saratov State University, and as a translator for several organizations in Russia and the USA.
Her e-mail address is evpk@prodigy.net.

BETTY LOU LEAVER (Ph.D., Pushkin Institute, Moscow) is Director of the Center for the Advancement of Distinguished Language Proficiency at San Diego State University. She has served as Language Program Manager, NASA; President, American Global Studies Institute; Dean, Schools of Central European and Slavic Languages, Defense Language Institute; and Russian Language Training Supervisor, Foreign Service Institute. She has written more than 100 publications.
Her e-mail address is leaver@aol.com.

NATALIA LORD (MA, Fordham University) is Senior Coordinating Instructor of Russian at the Foreign Service Institute. She has also taught at Howard University. One of the two developers of the first advanced course to be taught at the FSI, she has worked with Superior-level students since the mid 1980s. Her publications include *Mark Smith's Diary* (a cross-culture textbook, 1985).
Her e-mail address is lordna@state.gov.

ELENA OVTCHARENKO (Ph.D., Leningrad State University) is Assistant Professor of Russian at George Washington University and Senior Instructor of Russian at the World Bank.
Her e-mail address is ovtcharenko@mail.msn.com.

BORIS SHEKHTMAN (MA, Grozny Pedagogical Institute, Grozny, Russia) is
President, Specialized Language Training Center in Rockville, Maryland,
and Lecturer in the Department of Modern Languages and Literature at
Howard University. Prior to that, he taught at the Foreign Service Institute
and earned the Una Cox Chapman Award for teaching excellence. He has
also lectured extensively in the USA and England.

His e-mail address is sbsltc@aol.com.

Foreword

In nations around the world, the study of a second or third language is the norm, often beginning in elementary school and continuing through secondary school and into the university. The result is that by the time they graduate from the system students often reach a degree of functional competence that enables them to use the language – often English – in their personal and professional lives. By contrast, in English-speaking countries like the United States, the study of Languages Other Than English (LOTEs) does not occupy a central place in the educational system, nor does it typically result in usable competence. The education system in the United States often struggles simply to justify and then provide instruction in LOTEs since the need for such competence is less obvious to US educational policy makers and to the general citizenry in light of the perceived status of English around the world.

Developments in recent times seem to be changing the situation in English-speaking countries, where globalization and immigration have produced a sea change with regard to language use and learning. If one takes the USA as an example, the need for language competence in the public and private sectors is dire, as demand is exploding and the supply is patently inadequate.[1] The problem is that the US educational system is simply not structured to meet current – let alone anticipated – language demand, as too few students study a LOTE for long enough to reach any level of functional competence (Brecht and Rivers, 2000). While a strategic solution to this problem is obviously warranted, the immediate need in the USA is for programming in schools, colleges, and universities capable of producing high-level language competency across a range of critical languages and relevant professions with a growing global practice. However, language educators in US schools, colleges, and universities have almost no experience in such programming, given the fact that to this point they have not enjoyed the luxury of working in a system that has students spending years studying one language. Nor are language educators in non-English-speaking countries necessarily of much assistance in this regard, for traditionally they have been able to rely upon an early start and rich extramural

---

[1] Examples of current shortfalls in language expertise in the USA were recently chronicled in a front-page article in the *New York Times* (Schemo, April 16, 2001).

exposure to produce competency in, say, English without needing to develop rigorous models of instruction and learning at the highest levels of proficiency (Theo van Els, personal communication, April 19, 2001).

The relative insufficiency of programming experience at the highest levels of proficiency has resulted in a significant dearth of knowledge about learning and teaching at these levels. The current volume begins to fill this void by providing, for the first time, a record of the literature on the subject of learning and teaching at the Superior/Distinguished level in ILR/ACTFL[2] terms, together with clear examples of best practice of the relatively few efforts in this area.[3] Such information is particularly valuable for program managers who are attempting to meet the unprecedented demand for high-level language programming instead of being concerned exclusively with beginning and intermediate levels of instruction, where significant experience and a growing body of research does already exist.

Indeed, researchers in second language acquisition (SLA) have focused mainly on classroom learning and learners at the beginning and intermediate levels and have devoted some attention to somewhat more advanced levels in immersion environments. Such research concentrations are understandable, given the fact that these environments and levels are where the students and the data are. However, the literature on SLA contains very little, if anything, about learners and learning at the highest, Superior/Distinguished level. Experience, though, tells us that, outside of the extraordinary, like the programs described in this volume, the few students who manage to reach true, high-level functional proficiency do so mostly on their own, with relatively little programmatic assistance and usually on the basis of a protracted stay in the country where the target language is spoken. The challenge, then, is to actually build language programs in our schools, colleges, and universities that can be relied upon consistently to produce students with this level of competence, whether the learning is in the classroom, in the study-abroad environment, or in a distributed education mode where learners are responsible for management of their own growing knowledge and proficiency.

Such programming involves unprecedented research and development challenges in learner diagnosis, in specification of learning tasks, in flexible and responsive programming especially for small classes and individual learners, and in assessment of attained competence. The current collection of chapters by authors with actual experience at this level is a necessary first step in providing teachers and program managers with emerging and fundamental information

---

[2] The commonly accepted metric in the USA is the Interagency Language Roundtable / American Council on Teaching Foreign Languages standard.

[3] In these chapters one can see instances of practice that is capable of such high-level programming, whether in government agencies, in private language instruction providers, in study-abroad programs, or in the extraordinary university language program.

they need to begin to understand the issues and to design and build such advanced-level programming. This volume also presents to the SLA scholarly community new directions for research aimed at meeting the need for empirical evidence concerning performance at this level and the learning tasks involved to reach it.

In spite of the growing acute need for expertise at the ILR/ACTFL Superior (and even higher) level, most language programs even in US colleges and universities are content to settle for ILR/ACTFL Advanced as a reasonable goal for students in their program. This is not surprising; it is even reasonable, given the fact that most students have had only a year or two of language before they arrive on campus and most will take little, if any, more before they graduate.[4] Nevertheless, it is time to raise the bar, to aim for higher levels of proficiency among graduates reliant primarily on formal educational systems. Such raised attainment is actually possible even in the USA because of the large numbers of heritage language learners enrolled in these institutions and in their language courses; because of the growing numbers of students with opportunity to study and work abroad; and because of the improvement of language programming particularly at the school level. These factors suggest that programs can in fact plan to build upon the proficiency of entering students and provide them by graduation with truly functional language skills. The current volume can begin to show the way, as well as serve to encourage the belief that the Superior/Distinguished level is attainable and even programmable in a formal educational system.[5]

If this volume indeed provides the information that managers, teachers, and learners need in order to pursue higher levels of language competence, and if it serves as a call to raise the bar in language programs, then it can render a vital service to the language profession, particularly in the USA and other English-speaking countries. I believe it does, and I believe it can.

National Foreign Language Center   RICHARD D. BRECHT

---

[4] See the Office of Educational Research and Improvement (OERI) and the American Council on Education (ACE) for the latest accounts of language, taking in US schools, colleges, and universities (Wirt [2001]).

[5] In the USA, the National Security Education Program in collaboration with the National Foreign Language Center has recently launched a national effort to establish a small set of university "flagship" language programs that are capable of graduating students in critical languages at the Superior Level.

Acknowledgments

Many people have contributed to the editors' ability to present these Superior–Distinguished programs in book form. They include teachers and administrators experienced in developing this level of proficiency who have shared not only information but also ideas with us. They include as well a large number of Level 4 language users, who have shared their learning experiences – challenges as well as successes. Unfortunately, not all to whom we are indebted can be named here.

We can, however, name a few who have helped in exceptional ways. Renée Meyer and James Bernhardt voluntarily read chapter after chapter and provided invaluable feedback both on content and on format. Also, three Cambridge University Press proposal readers gave marvelous suggestions for additions to the book – and we were fortunate enough to be able to follow through on most of these.

We have very much enjoyed working with Kate Brett, our Cambridge University Press editor. She, as much as anyone else, has made this book a reality.

Books would not come into being without significant behind-the-scenes support. Carl Leaver prepared all the graphics, and Fawn Leaver proofread the original manuscript. Many thanks to both of them.

Finally, we must also thank the authors. A number of them read each other's work and provided very helpful commentary. Editors cannot do the job alone, and in this case, the support of the authors was keenly felt and much appreciated.

For our readers who would like to know more about teaching at upper levels of proficiency, we have included information about how to contact the various authors. In addition, readers may interact with others teaching at this level, as well as find additional information, on a web page devoted to advanced SLA: www.mindsolutionsinternational.com.

The publisher has used its best endeavors to ensure that the URLs for external web sites referred to in this book are correct and active at the time of going to press. However, the publisher has no responsibility for the websites and can make no guarantee that a site will remain live or that the content is or will remain appropriate.

Part I

Principles, practices, and theory

1 Principles and practices in teaching Superior-level language skills: Not just more of the same

Betty Lou Leaver and Boris Shekhtman

Historically, few students achieve Superior and Distinguished levels of proficiency in any foreign language. In fact, relatively few courses even propose to bring students to the Superior level, at which students can expect to use the language professionally while having obviously less than native control of linguistic and cultural elements, let alone the Distinguished level, at which students begin to approach the level of an educated native speaker. (These levels are called Level 3 and Level 4, respectively, on the 5-level US government scale, which is presented later in this chapter.) For many years, there has been a tacit assumption among foreign language educators and administrators that language programs cannot be expected to bring students any further in the classroom than the Advanced High level. Consequently, few teachers have much experience in teaching students at the Superior level, yet there is a growing awareness of the need to do so. This book focuses on just that part of the language-teaching spectrum: successfully assisting Superior-level students to reach the Distinguished level. Its goal is to provide theory and successful models for teachers who find themselves faced with this task.

The direction from which we have come

In analyzing how best to teach students at the Superior level, it may be helpful to look at teaching practices in general. Specifically, what are the underlying philosophies of today's foreign language education (FLED), what are the theories of second language acquisition (SLA), what has research shown us about language learning, and what are the methods that guide our instruction – and how do these assumptions, ideas, knowledge, and practices influence the teaching of students at Superior levels of proficiency?

A paradigmatic overview

Since the early 1960s, foreign language educators have experienced a paradigm shift not only in their specialty fields but also across all sociological phenomena.

3

Given a world that has become interdependent, the replacement of an industrial society with a technological and service industry in most developed countries, and a change in educational philosophy (not once but twice), it is no surprise that foreign language teachers would be hard-pressed to keep up with the changing – and escalating – demands to produce increasingly more proficient graduates in a world where language skills now play more of a pragmatic than an academic role and where language teaching practices, as a whole, have changed substantively in keeping with the so-called "New Paradigm."

We did not reach this state overnight. Rather, a number of steps led to our current beliefs, knowledge, and methods in foreign language education. Each of these steps holds important implications for teaching Superior-level students. They include a changing educational philosophy in keeping with social changes, a natural evolution in teaching methods as a result of new linguistic research, a growing understanding of the psychology of learning, and the appearance of a new paradigm.

Educational philosophy

Educational philosophy is shaped less by research in learning and teaching and more by the sociological and political needs of a given society. In the USA, we have seen at least three educational philosophies: transmission (passing the canon from one generation to the next), transaction (developing problem-solving skills), and transformation (personal growth) (J. P. Miller and Seller [1985]). While there has been a historical, i.e., chronological, order to the appearance of these philosophies, all do simultaneously exist today. Table 1.1 compares the "pure" forms of each of these philosophies as typically reflected in language classrooms.

At lower levels of proficiency, contemporary foreign language programs in the USA tend to reflect principles and practices associated with the transaction philosophy. This philosophy is seen most frequently in industrial and technological societies (although, interestingly, many foreign language and other educational programs in European countries remain in the transmission mode). In transaction classrooms, students learn how to solve problems, innovate, implement ideas, and make things work: in short, to "do," as opposed to "know." The knowledge of facts loses importance, the assumption being that if students know how to use resources, they will be able to locate any facts needed. In practice, classwork tends to be pragmatic. In foreign language classrooms, that has meant task-based, content-based, problem-based, and project-based learning, as well as the use of activities, such as role plays, and an emphasis on notions and functions. The nature of a transaction philosophy causes educators to focus on assessing the student program and program success based on outcomes of the classroom. In foreign language classrooms, assessments have most frequently taken the form of proficiency, prochievement (proficiency tests that use only

Table 1.1

Philosophy	Transmission	Transaction	Transformation
Goal	To "know" (knowledge)	To "do" (skill)	To "create" (ability)
Theory	Mastery Learning (Bloom, 1968)	Experiential Learning (Dewey, 1938)	Humanistic Learning (Rogers, 1968)
Class work	Exercises, use of teacher-made materials	Tasks, projects, role playing, use of authentic materials	Self-directed study, student-selected materials
Home assignments	Written exercises	Projects, tasks	Research
Role of teacher	Knower	Facilitator	Advisor
Grouping	Whole class	Small groups	Independent work
Type of tests	Achievement tests	Proficiency tests	Self-assessments
Syllabus design	Form-based, theme-based	Notional–functional, task-based, content-based	Learner-centered

materials and topics that students have worked with in the classroom), or performance tests. The development of national standards (ACTFL [1999]) is yet another example of transaction. These standards, in principle, do not focus on a corpus of knowledge but on a range of skills although knowledge may be required in order to demonstrate skill.

At the Superior level of instruction, the philosophical framework tends to be quite different. Most effective Superior-level programs, to wit those described in this volume, combine elements of all three philosophies, from teacher-controlled development of automaticity to fully independent learning. The knowledge, skills, and abilities needed at the Distinguished level may be the catalyst for the unification of seemingly incompatible philosophies and for the reemergence of a focus on conscious knowledge – at this level not that of the canon but a much deeper and broader cross-cultural understanding, greater linguistic and metalinguistic sophistication, and omnipresent metacognition as the predominant learning strategy.

Linguistics and methods

Since the early 1960s, methods that treated foreign language as a mechanism for converting information encoded in one linguistic system into the forms of another linguistic system have been ever better informed by theory and research in both general learning and SLA. In very recent years, SLA has become a discipline unto itself, and non-applied linguistic theory and research has had a decreasing influence on English as a Second Language (ESL) and Foreign Language (L2) teaching methods.[1]

That does not mean, however, that FLED practices have become any less focused on learning needs at lower levels of proficiency, rather than considering an ultimate goal of near-native proficiency from the very beginning (see Byrnes, Chapter 2, for a more detailed discussion). As a result, few methods contain essential elements for teaching very advanced students, and many practices set the student up for increasingly retarded progress as s/he climbs the proficiency ladder. Table 1.2 depicts the evolution of methods in the USA; it describes representative methods and identifies, where applicable, the deterrents to developing near-native levels of proficiency (Level 4 [of five levels] on the US government scale) in the practices of each method.

As can be seen, no method to date has proved to be a perfect vessel for carrying students to Level-4 proficiency. It is not surprising, then, that each of the authors in Part II of this volume describes programs that are highly eclectic in nature. Course content and teaching practice are determined not by textbook design or teaching method, but by the specific needs of students. Further, since some teaching practices seem to set students up to fossilize at Levels 2 (Higgs and Clifford [1982]) and 3 (Soudakoff [2001]), and not only in grammatical accuracy but also in emerging sociolinguistic and sociocultural (and other) competences that never finish developing, a number of the chapter authors have instituted teaching practices in their programs aimed at remediation of problems caused by one or another teaching method, e.g., ingrained error and unsophisticated strategy use (especially the overuse of compensation strategies) associated with communicative methods and inexperience with authentic culture and materials typical of cognitive code methods.

Psychological research

As psychologists have learned more about the functioning of the human brain, foreign language educators have been given more sophisticated tools for determining appropriate methods for classroom instruction. Unfortunately, language educators have been slow to incorporate these discoveries into classrooms for two reasons: (1) the discoveries have not been framed in ways that relate directly to language teaching, and (2) they often question long-practiced beliefs. We present a few current neuropsychological findings here as examples. However, there are many more findings in the literature of neuroscience that have direct application to teaching any level of proficiency, including the Superior level, and these, too, warrant consideration by classroom teachers.

---

[1] Here we are talking about the relationship between theory and practice in the USA and not necessarily that found elsewhere. For example, in some European countries and in Eurasia in general, theory and practice are often distinct fields, whereas the trend in the USA has generally been to apply theory (linguistic or, especially, SLA) to the classroom.

Table 1.2

Kind of method	Description	Typical results	Activities	Deterrents to Level 4
Grammar–translation	Learning of grammar rules; practices L2 and checks comprehension of L2 through L1	Ability to read in L2 and render content in L1	Translation; written grammar and vocabulary exercises; decontextualized vocabulary learning	Lack of cultural context; emphasis on written skills over oral ones; emphasis on language usage over language use
Structural approaches	Stimulus–response approach to learning (e.g., Audio-Lingual Method, Direct Method)	Automatization of responses in known and rehearsed situations	Repetition drills; substitution drills for grammar and vocabulary; dialogue memorization	Underdeveloped ability to handle authentic and unexpected situations and materials
Cognitive code	Based on the understanding of language as a system of rules through deductive approaches to learning (e.g., Silent Way, MMC)	Understand and see linguistic systems (accuracy)	Grammar exercises; Q&A exercises with teacher-made reading/listening materials; communication via manipulation of forms	Slow development of oral skills; inexperience with authentic culture and its artifacts
Communicative approaches	Loose collection of methods (e.g., TPR, Natural Approach) oriented toward interpersonal communication	Ability to negotiate meaning (fluency)	Role plays; tasks; projects; cooperative learning activities; reading/hearing authentic texts	Overemphasis on strategic competence; underdeveloped precision and formal language proficiency

The first reference is to the work of Ojemann, a neurosurgeon whose experimentation with epileptics uncovered the fact that first and second (and foreign) language centers are not co-located and that cell distribution and density is dissimilar (Calvin and Ojemann [1994]). These discoveries would seem to have direct implications for two groups of language teachers: (1) those working with beginners using methods based on information from first-language acquisition (e.g., the Natural Approach) and (2) those working with Superior-level students who need to reach near-native proficiency. The former group might consider the significance of differing L1–L2 brain structures for assessing the validity of L2 teaching practices that emulate L1 language acquisition. The latter group might look at brain structure information obtained on coordinate and compound bilinguals to inform some of their own teaching practices. While there is not yet enough information to dictate teaching techniques, there is enough information to guide (or, rather, redirect) foreign language education theory.

We would also reference the work in memory research (Reiser [1991]) that has questioned long-held but erroneous beliefs and promulgated new models for the conceptualization of memory functioning.[2] Where we once thought that information was stored as wholes, then recalled, we now know several important things about memory that have direct application to learning foreign languages. Some of the most important are summarized below.

1. Information must pass through sentient memory. For language students, this usually means that unless they pay attention to *and* understand what it is they are seeing or hearing, input does not turn into intake.

2. Information is stored componentially in diverse locations (form, function, pronunciation, and context are not one category once language enters storage; even if vocabulary is lexicalized within a specific content or context). With syntax, morphology, and lexicon separated neural components, students may be able to negotiate meaning with gross grammatical error (Allott [1989]).

3. Stored information can be overwritten. For lawyers, this translates into un-reliability of eyewitness accounts (Luus and Wells [1991]). In the language classroom, this can translate into a special form of "forgetfulness": at lower levels, when students learn the past tense forms, present tense forms can sometimes become inaccessible; at higher levels, formal language, instead of becoming synonymous with other registers (and available as alternative expressions), can, upon occasion, replace those other registers, especially while the individual student's interlanguage is struggling with forms in free variation during development periods.

4. Reconstruction, rather than recall, is the process used by the working, or ac-tivated, memory. Therefore, teachers can expect students to make mistakes, which no amount of overt correction will prevent. (We are not talking here about errors – instances where students do not know the correct forms – which can be corrected through overt instruction and practice, i.e. develop-ing greater automaticity [see discussion below of acquisition of linguistic competence at the SD level]. Rather, we are talking about miscues and slips of the tongue that occur in native language speech as well as foreign lan-guage speech. Sometimes a piece of information – an individual morpheme or lexeme, for example – can become temporarily irretrievable and result in grammatically or lexically flawed speech, including sometimes lower levels of speech than one normally expects from students at the SD level.

---

[2] We refer readers who desire more details about contemporary memory research as applied to language learning and teaching to work by Stevick (1996).

5. Many noncognitive factors affect memory. These include diet, exercise, and biorhythm, among others.

We would be remiss not to mention the traditional dichotomies of memory types: procedural memory (based on repetition of physical actions, such as those needed to drive a car) versus declarative memory (based on the knowledge of facts), as well as the difference between episodic memory (based on the perception, understanding, storage, and reconstruction of specific events, as well as words and facts directly or coincidentally associated with those events) and semantic memory (based on the encoding of thoughts and concepts into words used in rules-based phraseology, the decoding of words used in rules-based phraseology into thoughts and concepts, and the reconstruction of phraseology). Much of the current debate over direct instruction (DeKeyser [1998]) centers around the promotion of the requirement of one kind of memory over another for language acquisition. Traditional teaching methods depend on declarative memory, Audio-Lingual Method (ALM) on procedural memory, and many contemporary methods on episodic or semantic memory or some combination of the two. In reality, direct instruction does have a place, as does incidental learning. "Teaching in front" can be as important as "leading from behind." Level 4 users report the importance of all these experiences and approaches in attaining Distinguished-level proficiency (Leaver and Atwell [this volume]). Methodological demagoguery of any type rarely works, and, more often than not, the kind of eclecticism needed is highly variable, depending on individual students or groups of students.

Concepts of communicative competence

In using the term, *communicative competence*, we refer to the concept proposed by Hymes (1971) and defined within a language-learning framework by Spolsky (1978). That concept is generally realized in the classroom as "the ability to communicate with native speakers in real-life situations – authentic interpersonal communication that cannot be separated from the cultural, paralinguistic, and nonverbal aspects of language" (Stryker and Leaver [1997a, p. 12]).

As the concept of communicative competence settled deeper into the collective consciousness of the FLED community, analyses of the components of communicative competence suggested that it was not a unified whole but a composite of subcompetences. Canale and Swain (1980) identified four such components: grammatical (or linguistic) competence (ability to comprehend and manipulate the lexical and grammatical structures of a language), discourse competence (the ability to understand and apply culturally appropriate text structure), sociolinguistic competence (ability to understand and use the social rules of linguistic interaction for a given society), and strategic competence (the ability to apply appropriate learning strategies for acquisition of new languages and for coping with unknown language).

Although the segmentation of the concept of communicative competence into components has limitations (Byrnes [chapter 2, this volume]), it does provide a framework in which to shed light on the varying needs of students, as they progress from Novice to Distinguished levels of proficiency. While all students at all levels of proficiency need to develop all components of communicative competence, students at lower levels (Novice through Advanced High) appear to need the compensation aspects of strategic competence most of all, especially if they are enrolled in programs that introduce authentic materials at early stages of instruction (Stryker and Leaver [1997b]). Superior-level students, however, usually possess a fair amount of strategic competence (which they need to change from mostly compensatory to mostly metacognitive) and, to a lesser extent, sociolinguistic competence, which they must continue to develop. What they may need is more attention to linguistic and discourse competence (Ingold [this volume]; Dabars and Kagan [this volume]), especially to formal language (Leaver and Atwell [this volume]), and to something beyond the Canale–Swain construct.

That "something" may be the social and sociocultural components suggested by Mitrofanova (1996) and colleagues. Social competence is described as the readiness to engage in conversation (and we would add that for Level 4 speakers, this usually means the ability to use the language comfortably under conditions of stress, illness, or fatigue) and sociocultural competence as the integration of cultural elements into language use.[3]

Another added component may also be emotional competence (Eshkembeeva [1997]). An important factor in communicating competently is being able to express one's personality in the foreign language so as to project one's true essence (characteristic of Distinguished levels of proficiency) and not one's adopted essence that results from cultural mimicry (typical of Advanced and Superior levels) nor an absence of unique personality that results from lack of linguistic skill (observed at Novice and Intermediate levels).

While all students need most of the components of communicative competence at any given time, there is a changing balance that occurs with proficiency gain. Figure 1.1 shows what we see as the relative balance of componential saliency along the continuum from Levels 0 to 4.

The Proficiency Movement

The push for proficiency – its definition and measurement – originally came from US government agencies, first and foremost among them the Foreign

---

[3] While some might argue that readiness to engage in conversation implies a personality characteristic (extroversion), not a language competence, and can at least make a *prima facie* case for their assertions, there is nevertheless some merit to considering the existence of social competence as a possible component of communicative competence. In fact there is more than some merit to this because many introverts develop social competence in the interests of other goals, such as language learning (Madeline Ehrman, personal communication, September 9, 2001).

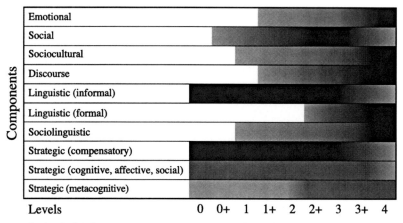

Figure 1.1 Need for an engagement of communicative competence components along the L2 learning continuum

Service Institute (FSI), the training arm of the US Department of State. The original intent in proposing language proficiency levels was to provide a means to identify, assess, and label foreign language skills with the goal of matching job requirements and employee capability. For the purpose of identifying and assigning labels for levels, an oral test, the Oral Proficiency Interview (OPI), based on skill descriptions, was designed (Frith [1980]). Thus, the Proficiency Movement by design was informed by testing approaches, which in turn and secondarily influenced teaching practices.[4] Table 1.3 summarizes the ILR levels under discussion in this volume – Advanced High, or Level 2+, through Distinguished, or Level 4. The ILR scale was developed as a way to quantify measures of quality. This becomes clear as one progresses through the various proficiency levels. It is not a matter of simply increasing the number of structures and vocabulary controlled – although that is part of proficiency – but of the way in which language is processed.

The Proficiency Movement formally began within academia at a meeting with James Frith (then Dean at the Foreign Service Institute), James Alatis

---

[4] An unfortunate outgrowth of this phenomenon has been the attempt by some teachers to "teach the test." In some cases, this means practicing the test format and the kinds of test items in multiple attempts to raise student scores. In other cases, this means designing a syllabus whose content is determined by test content. While on the surface, preparing students for a test may appear innocuous and one could even argue that a test that is truly a "proficiency" test cannot be "studied" or prepared for, the reality is that familiarity with test format, principles, and content can, indeed, put "prepared" students in a position to receive a higher score than equally proficient students who have not been prepared. The question of the tail (test) wagging the dog (teaching practices and syllabus design) has periodically been a hotly debated issue since the development of Oral Proficiency Interviews and other proficiency tests.

Table 1.3

Level	Listening	Speaking	Reading	Writing
2+	Understands social and work demands and concrete topics related to interests	Satisfies work requirements with usually acceptable and effective language	Reads factual, non-technical language, grasping main and subsidiary ideas	Writes with some precision and in some detail about most common topics
3	Understands all the essentials of standard speech, including technical aspects of professional field	Speaks with enough precision to participate in practical, social, and professional conversations	Reads a variety of authentic prose on unfamiliar subjects with near-complete comprehension	Prepares effective formal and informal written exchanges on practical, social, and professional topics
3+	Comprehends forms and styles of speech pertinent to professional needs	Accomplishes a wide range of sophisticated and demanding professional tasks	Comprehends a variety of styles and forms pertinent to professional needs	Writes in a few prose styles pertinent to professional and education needs
4	Understands all forms and styles of speech pertinent to professional needs	Speaks fluently and accurately on all levels pertinent to professional needs	Reads fluently and accurately all forms of language pertinent to professional needs	Writes professionally and accurately in a variety of prose styles

(Georgetown University), and heads of the American Associations of Teachers of various foreign languages and the American Council on Teaching Foreign Languages (ACTFL) in 1980, at which ACTFL agreed to accept responsibility for the OPI workshops for teachers that FSI had been conducting (Hancock and Scebold [2000]). ACTFL subsequently developed standards for academia accounting for the less intensive nature of most academic programs and the ensuing need for more categories at the lower levels of proficiency and fewer at the higher levels. Table 1.4 illustrates the relationship between the two scales and reflects the newly issued ACTFL guidelines (Breiner-Sanders *et al.* [2000]). The changes from the provisional guidelines issued in 1986 were the reconstitution of the two Advanced levels (Advanced and Advanced Plus) into three levels and the dropping of the proposed (but nearly never used) Distinguished level. For the purposes of this book, we have retained the earlier nomenclature in order to distinguish between students at Level 3 (which we refer to as Superior level) and those at Level 4 (which we refer to as Distinguished level).

Over time, the Proficiency Movement and the subsequent development of communicative approaches to teaching have focused on improving students'

Table 1.4

Level	ILR	ACTFL
5	Functionally Native Proficiency	Superior (formerly Distinguished)
4+	Advanced Professional Proficiency, Plus	
4	Advanced Professional Proficiency	
3+	General Professional Proficiency, Plus	Superior
3	General Professional Proficiency	
2+	Limited Working Proficiency, Plus	Advanced High
2	Limited Working Proficiency	Advanced Mid
		Advanced Low
1+	Elementary Proficiency, Plus	Intermediate High
1	Elementary Proficiency	Intermediate Mid
		Intermediate Low
0+	Memorized Proficiency	Novice High
0	No Proficiency	Novice Mid
		Novice Low

ability to use the foreign language rather than to know information about the foreign language. In most institutions that have moved from structural teaching approaches to communicative teaching approaches, student achievement has significantly improved (Corin [1997]; Klee and Tedick [1997]; Leaver [1997]; Stryker [1997]), as measured by performance on an Oral Proficiency Interview (OPI) or similar instrument.

Ironically, however, the very movement that introduced concepts of using language to achieve communicative goals spawned teaching practices that may be ineffective at higher levels while highly effective at lower levels. The authors of several chapters in this volume discuss this rather unexpected phenomenon and the reasons for it. We suggest that perhaps different attributes are needed for success at early levels of language study and success at much higher levels, a hypothesis embraced by most of the chapter authors, all of whom have worked with students at beginning, as well as near-native levels of proficiency.

Contemporary FLED

Given proficiency-oriented goals and a focus on the development of communicative competence, most FLED programs share a number of characteristics that differentiate today's cutting-edge programs from those of yesteryear. These characteristics include authenticity in task and language, a role for content, attention to learner differences, incorporation of elements of schema theory, use of higher-order thinking skills, and application of adult learning theory.

Authenticity. In ever larger numbers, language programs and teachers are turning to authentic materials (prepared by native speakers for native speakers) for use in the classroom at increasingly lower levels of proficiency. Some task-based programs have even used almost solely authentic texts from the very first day of language instruction (Maly [1993]). In Superior-level programs, authentic materials are essential and even unavoidable and are used in a number of ways: (1) text, discourse, and linguistic analysis; (2) source of expressions for acquisition; and (3) information. Truly authentic tasks (e.g., for journalism students, interviewing two statesmen on a controversial topic and preparing a balanced article for publication), as opposed to pedagogical tasks that make use of authentic materials but do not necessarily reflect real-life use of language (e.g., comparing articles in which the opinions of the two statesmen above have been reported), become more realizable at the Superior level. Nearly all the authors in this volume describe programs that require students to perform tasks while in training that closely resemble tasks they are undertaking or will undertake on the job. Some are advocates of a task-based approach to teaching; others simply find that language and job performance are often intertwined at the Superior level.

Content. Chaput (2000) points out that foreign language studies are the only university-level subjects that do not focus on specific content. At least, that was the case before the introduction of Languages Across the Curriculum (LAC) programs and other content-mediated communicative approaches. At lower proficiency levels, students benefit when new vocabulary and grammar is embedded in real content and real contexts. For students at the Superior level, language and content are inextricably intertwined by necessity.

The kinds of content in foreign language study vary tremendously at the Superior level. In all cases, a knowledge of literature and culture is unavoidable; even military institutions include reading and discussion of literature and learning about culture in their Superior-level programs. The Caspian Naval Academy's Russian program is an example. In this program, Red Army officers from Azerbaijan learned Russian through the study of classical literature with military themes, in addition to the use of actual military communications (Aliev and Leaver [1994]). Most Superior–Distinguished (SD) programs include content that is directly related to students' job needs, and that content can be scientific, humanistic, journalistic, diplomatic, or military, among many other options that are restricted only by the number of professions in which there is an opportunity for international employment – nearly any industry today.

Learner-centered instruction. In recent years, more teachers are beginning to understand and accept the importance of learner variables in the language acquisition process (Brown [1994]; Ehrman [1996]; Leaver [1998]; Nunan [1988]; Oxford [1990]), although program sensitivity to learner differences is not part of the New Paradigm *per se*. Learner-centered instruction refers to more than just understanding learning styles and developing students' repertoire of learning strategies. It also refers to accommodating students' needs and empowering students to be participants in the learning process. All of the programs described in this volume are learner-centered.

Today's study of motivation began with the suggestion that students can be motivated either integratively (desire to be part of the culture) or instrumentally (need for the language for professional purposes) (Gardner and Lambert [1972]). Although there appears to be a firmly held belief among many foreign language teachers that integrative motivation produces higher levels of proficiency, early empirical evidence suggests a more complex situation; in fact, instrumental motivation may be more frequently associated with the successful high-level acquisition of some languages (e.g., Americans learning Russian) and integrative with others (Europeans learning English) (Leaver and Atwell [this volume]). Other, more complex models, have been subsequently suggested, along the lines of various types of intrinsic and extrinsic motivations, that better delineate individual differences (for a discussion, see Ehrman, this volume); even so, no one form of motivation over another has been empirically shown to be a determinant for reaching Level 4.

Motivation, it now appears, is but one of many individual variables that influence the success of language learning. Anxious students can filter their language learning experience through such thick shielding that often immense amounts of comprehensible input result in limited intake (Horwitz [1988]). Risk-takers in terms of language learning progress more quickly and experience greater enjoyment than do their non-risk-taking peers (Beebe [1988]; Pellegrino [1999]). Within classrooms, many interpersonal and small-group issues can enhance or impair the efforts of any individual student in the "visible classroom" (the overt relationships) who reacts poorly to the "invisible classroom" (ubiquitous but covert group dynamics), to use the concept and terminology advanced by Ehrman and Dörnyei (1998), i.e., the significance of small-group dynamics and rapport may be greater than many teachers realize.

Again, the vast majority of research on these variables has been conducted on groups of students with mixed backgrounds and at lower levels of proficiency. In our seventeen-year experience in extensive and intensive work with Superior-level students, learners at this level, especially those studying in courses and groups, tend to have a different set of anxieties, most of which are more closely tied to linguistic aspects of job performance than to the intellectual risk-taking required of language learning in general. Some groups, such as teachers, however, may have group-specific affective impediments, as Dabars and Kagan (this volume) point out.

Schema. Schema theory has for some time informed communicative teaching practices. Although schema theory is often attributed to the New Paradigm, the first mention of schema is by Sir Francis Head (1920). By schema, Head refers to the background knowledge and sets of concepts that learners already possess. New information is understood via the concepts already acquired – or not understood due to lack of sufficient schema.

For foreign language students, content schemata, cultural schemata, and linguistic schemata are all essential for accurate communication. Research suggests that in many, if not most, cases, especially at lower levels of proficiency, lack of linguistic schemata is generally less an impediment than lack of content schemata in comprehension in both L1 and L2 (R. Gläser as cited in Hirsch [1987]). In fact, knowledge of content can help students fill in the linguistic gaps.

In the case of Superior-level students, both cultural and linguistic schemata are more extensive and more sophisticated than one finds in a beginning learner. For that reason, new content can be learned via already-possessed linguistic and cultural schemata, making many more authentic materials and situations accessible to Superior-level students. At this level, given the nature of tasks typically assigned and the precision with which they need to be completed, linguistic schemata tend to play a far more significant role than at lower levels of proficiency. Equally important is attention to sociocultural, sociolinguistic, and discourse schemata, as most of the authors in this volume point out.

Higher-order thinking. Bloom (1956) posited a hierarchy of thinking skills that he called a "Taxonomy of Educational Objectives." In this system, higher-order thinking skills (HOTS), such as analysis, synthesis, and evaluation create more powerful learning circumstances than do the lower-order thinking skills (LOTS), such as memorization, comprehension, and application. Although most language teachers nowadays, especially those who use task-based instruction

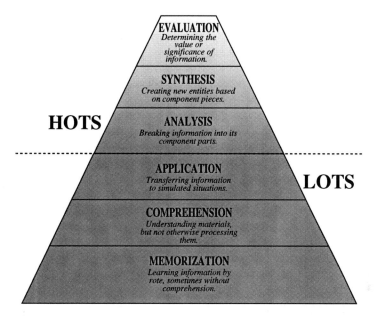

EVALUATION
Determining the value or significance of information.

SYNTHESIS
Creating new entities based on component pieces.

HOTS

ANALYSIS
Breaking information into its component parts.

APPLICATION
Transferring information to simulated situations.

LOTS

COMPREHENSION
Understanding materials, but not otherwise processing them.

MEMORIZATION
Learning information by rote, sometimes without comprehension.

Figure 1.2

as a method, incorporate higher-order thinking skills as a matter of course, we reproduce Bloom's hierarchy in Figure 1.2 for those who may not know it.

While higher-order thinking is the preference of many teachers at any level of proficiency, at the Superior level higher-order thinking is essential to students' learning – and, in our experience, is often demanded by students. By way of example, we cite the numerous programs presented in this volume, most of which incorporate higher-order thinking skills in the tasks and activities used in instruction.

Adult learning. In this volume, we speak exclusively about the adult learner. There is a clear reason for this: on the proficiency scales used, Level 4 / Distinguished proficiency clearly requires the linguistic maturity exhibited principally in the L2 adult population. In fact, a child, who has not achieved Piaget's formal operations (Piaget [1967]) and the requisite knowledge and experience, would not be able to speak at the equivalent of the Level 4 and beyond in his or her native language. To date, no study or test, to our knowledge, has shown a child at Level 4.

In working with adults, many foreign language educators recommend the application of students' knowledge and the personalization of questions and other tasks, in order to take into account adults' schemata, which are highly complex and sophisticated. Knowles (1990) suggests that adult students, unlike children, need to have control over their learning – much in the way that some foreign language educators over the past several years have advocated developing life-long language-learning skills in students (Brecht and Walton [1994]), designing learner-centered classrooms (Nunan [1988]), and empowering students to be in better control of their own cognitive processes and classroom behaviors (Oxford and Leaver [1996]). Learner-centeredness and personalization look very different at Superior levels than they do at lower levels of proficiency. Where lower levels might introduce open discussion, at Superior levels discourse assumes quite different traits, as described in various chapters in this volume. Teacher–student interactions change from master–apprentice to near-peers with the same mission (see, for example, Ehrman's discussion of Curran's theories on this topic in Chapter 12).

Interestingly, the myth that adult learners are less efficient language learners than children is being systematically debunked (Schleppegrell [1987]). Children who learn their first language to educated native levels can take up to eighteen years to do so. Further, children learning a second language in-country get far more hours on task with the second language than do adult learners, who, for the most part, are occupied with jobs and families where they use L1. A child's greater accuracy in phonetics due to lack of brain lateralization aside, the adult, with his or her greater number of schemata and limited time on task, may actually be the more efficient language learner. Regardless of which side of this argument a teacher supports, few would deny that adults need an approach to language instruction that differs from children's needs.

One of the major distinctions between children and adults – ultimately an impediment to adult acquisition of near-native skills in L2 – is the far greater number of L1 schemata possessed by adults. The result is the tendency of adults to subordinate L2 information to L1 schemata, following Piagetan theory that new information is acquired by linking it to already-known information (Piaget and Inhelder [1973]), a trait that allows for more rapid acquisition of the second language, yet at the same time creating an interlanguage that is neither L1 nor L2 but a learner's approximation of L2, usually based on L1 with varying amounts of L1 interference.[5] The obvious conclusion is that comprehensible input may not always be enough for adults since input, even when understood, can be interpreted in accordance with an interlanguage rather than the second language. The task of the Superior-level student is to replace a faulty interlanguage with an idiolect that subordinates itself only to the rules of L2.

A programmatic overview

Superior-level learning takes place in a variety of venues. A number of unique programs have been successful at developing Distinguished levels of proficiency.

---

[5] In cases where students are studying L3 and L4, interlanguage may also be based on other foreign languages, as well as the student's native language.

In this volume, we present programs conducted in generic foreign language classrooms and in-country settings. Both venues share many characteristics, and all programs depend on extensive in-country experience (or its equivalent, such as extensive interaction with the émigré community) and classroom learning. Most teachers of Superior-level students find that these students have usually already been in a country where their language of study is spoken (Leaver and Bilstein [2000]). In fact, for acquisition of some components of communicative competence, in-country experience or its equivalent appears to be necessary (James Bernhardt, personal communication, March 27, 1999).

Although the authors of the chapters in this volume have diverse opinions about the role of grammar in Novice through Advanced levels of instruction and how error correction should be handled at those levels, they are uniform in considering the development of accuracy and sophistication in grammatical expression to be essential in reaching Distinguished levels of proficiency. At Superior levels, the issue of explicit instruction versus implicit acquisition (VanPatten [1998]) is no longer the burning question that it has been at Novice and Intermediate (and even Advanced) levels. It is at the higher levels of L1 proficiency that elementary and secondary schools explicitly teach students the formal elements of language in keeping with the spoken and written norms of that society. Often, teaching Superior-level students boils down to identifying acquired inaccuracies and retraining for accuracy, along with the acquisition of formal registers (Kubler, Shekhtman *et al.*, and Caudery [all this volume]). Explicit instruction, in the experience of all the chapter authors, has been required to reach the Distinguished level efficiently, and each of the authors provides a rationale for explicit instruction at very high levels of proficiency (including authors who do not use much explicit instruction at lower levels of proficiency).

Classroom-based language instruction

Although some may insist that Superior and Distinguished levels of language proficiency cannot be achieved in the classroom, many Level-4 users who did not have instruction at the Superior level feel that such instruction would have been useful (Leaver and Atwell, this volume). The students in the programs described in this book, as well as other programs, have been able to reach these levels in the classroom; included in this volume are details of an immersion institute for German Teaching Assistants at Georgetown University (Byrnes [Chapter 3]), a course for improving language skills of students enrolled in Translation and Interpretation programs in French and Spanish at the Monterey Institute of International Studies (Angelelli and Degueldre), Chinese programs in China for students from the United States (Kubler), Russian courses in the United States that utilize the émigré community (Shekhtman *et al.*), a thirty-year-old reading program for foreign students in Cairo, Egypt (Badawi), a model for teaching writing (Caudery), programs for heritage speakers (Angelelli and Kagan), and a US-based program conducted eight times for teachers of Russian (Dabars and Kagan).

Technology-based instruction

Increasingly, the use of technology has provided a wide variety of opportunities for language teachers to adapt, augment, and supplement their classroom lessons. Homework assignments that require use of the Internet develop students' skills in navigating through authentic web sites in search of authentic materials for what is quite often an authentic search. The expanding plethora of technological support, however, like textbooks, nearly exclusively addresses students at lower levels of proficiency. While highly autonomous learners at the SD level can find many ways on their own to use the Internet to improve their linguistic skills, to our knowledge, no specific materials or programs have been developed with SD students in mind, with one exception: LangNet. The LangNet "Reading to the Four" Project is described by Ingold in Chapter 7 of this volume.

Toward an understanding of the Superior level for foreign language instruction

In teaching and supervising language programs at very advanced levels of instruction, we have noticed that a qualitative difference exists between teaching students at lower levels of proficiency and teaching Superior-level students. There is a clear difference also between the teaching and learning needs of any one student just starting out and that same student at the Superior level. At the lower levels, students need to acquire the basic linguistic system and some understanding of culture. At the higher levels, they need to acquire the uncommon, as well as the common, and the infrequent as well as the frequent, in linguistic, discourse, and sociolinguistic expression. Further, the emphasis on cultural appropriateness in the definition of higher proficiency levels presumes substantial interaction with native speakers, which is not a typical experience of basic and intermediate students. These needs and our experience lead us to suggest two characteristics that distinguish students at the Superior level of foreign language proficiency: linguistic experience and communicative focus.

Linguistic experience

Linguistic experience assumes that no student reaches the Superior-level classroom without prior language-learning experience and that this experience shapes that student's expectations for continued instruction. For that reason, Superior-level students typically have strong linguistic convictions. Their foreign language experience is rich and their range of strategies for classroom learning broad. As a result, their evaluation of instructor performance is frequently critical. This attitude can either damage the rapport in the classroom (when students are unused to or disagree with the teaching method) or significantly enhance it (when students recognize an individual teacher's skill). Affectively, these students often bring great goal orientation and perceive everything outside their specific area of interest to be distractive. Cognitively, Superior-level students bring a wealth of schemata to the learning task, but the nature of those schemata differs among students. Given these characteristics of Superior-level students, most Superior-level courses with which we are familiar allow students choices in content and/or adapt instruction to the specific learning needs of the students in the classroom.

Communicative focus

The term, *Communicative Focus* (CF), is introduced here by the authors in an attempt to provide a means for identifying levels of communicative effectiveness of the language itself. CF refers to the relative proportion of idea and language mechanics in the process of communication. For example, the native speaker communicates without conscious focus on language (i.e., the idea, or *what* the person wants to say, is of utmost importance). The native speaker, then, has high CF. In contrast, beginning students typically talk with pauses and difficulties, search for words, and deliberately think about the grammar they use (at the extreme, the idea may become inexpressible due to the emphasis placed on mechanics or *how* the person wants or can say something). These students have very low CF. As students gain in proficiency, their CF increases, and the balance of attention changes from mechanics to ideas. This is not to say that the language user with high CF never selectively chooses words or expressions. However, he or she does so under the full influence of the ideational and sociolinguistic–sociocultural (situational appropriateness) plane. (See Leaver and Atwell, this volume, for a fuller discussion.) Nor is this to say that the lower-proficiency language learner is unconcerned with the expression of ideas. However, the cognitive resources required for intelligible communication may prevent the learner from being able to say exactly what he or she means.

The significance of CF for students

The basic-course student focuses on *how* to say what he or she wants to communicate. For him or her, *how* is usually more important than *what*; in other words, the mechanical plane of communication is more important than the ideational plane.[6] Communication in such instances is viewed as a process of

---

[6] In fact, some well-intentioned teachers of beginning students, anxious to develop their fluency, may tell them not to worry about accuracy of content, just to say what it is that they know how to say, bending the truth to do so. While this might, indeed, build some kinds of fluency (or practice certain forms), it can lead students away from developing high CF.

stringing together linguistic units in a fashion that meets certain prescriptions or applies a set of lexicalizations to a known situation. In either case, the CF of the basic-course student is of necessity relatively low.

The Superior-level student already knows how to say what he or she wants to communicate. At this level, *what* is more important than *how*. In other words, the ideational plane becomes more important to the learner than the mechanical plane, choices related to which having developed into habits. His or her CF is correspondingly high. The high-CF student who is operating at the Superior level (Level 3) in focusing on the "what" or the ideational plane of communication may still exhibit relatively low levels of sociolinguistic and sociocultural competence.

Distinguished-level students have an even stronger ideational focus. At the same time, they have nearly full access to the mechanical aspects of the language, choosing to pay attention to language mechanics when they want to sound erudite, need to make a point very precisely (as is the case of people who must negotiate intergovernmental agreements), are talking with someone with lesser language skills but for whom the target language serves as the *lingua franca*, are preparing an article for publication, are giving a lecture to a group of native speakers, or are serving as a high-level interpreter or translator, among many situations in which precision in word choice and structure is essential.

At the highest levels, students have at their fingertips multiple correct structures to express the same idea, as well as a sense of how to build their own unique structures in pertinent situations, and are searching for phraseology, as well as discourse type, that will best meet their communicative need on a sociolinguistic, sociocultural, and emotional basis appropriate to the cultural situation and goal of their communication – or, in the case of translators and interpreters, that will best express the message, intent, and personality of a speaker or the innuendoes of a document. Thus, the words and grammar have become important again, but in the same way that they are important to the well-educated native speaker: how best to express oneself in order to convince, persuade, convey information, or achieve any other particular communicative need. On the receptive level, words also become important again, but in the same sense that they are important to the native speaker: a new word is a "find," intriguing, and, while not interfering with communication, attracts a moment of attention from the listener.

The influence of CF on instruction

An important part of developing communicative skills is providing students with more sophisticated and appropriate strategies than the ones they have used at lower levels. Such strategies are mostly metacognitive in nature, rather than purely cognitive or compensatory. Examples include planning and evaluation, as well as eliciting help in comprehending from a native speaker in natural and unnoticeable ways that do not impede the flow of thought, acting as an equal partner linguistically with native speakers, and entering and exiting a group discussion among native speakers appropriately.

Developing high CF typically requires that students acquire regular, irregular, archaic, and idiosyncratic possibilities of the linguistic system as it is used across a broad set of genres and in a broad set of situations. This demands attention in and outside the classroom to cultural appropriateness of expression, the elimination of acquired inaccuracies in structure and pronunciation, the development of greater lexical precision, work on text organization and other forms of discourse competence, finding a sense of self in expression (emotional competence), and increasing willingness to speak in a wide range of circumstances and situations (social competence).

Appropriateness of expression. With the exception of some heritage speakers, Superior-level students are no longer true foreigners, but they are not native speakers, either. They are in between. As such, they approximate, but do not equal, native speakers. On the one hand, they have the ability to comprehend many sociolinguistic and sociocultural references, including some nonstandard dialects and slang. On the other hand, they miss certain subtleties and nuances connected with those references and nonstandard speech elements.

Since language does not exist without context and context is cultural, a student whose foreign language is very good may still have communication problems due to an incorrect interpretation of his/her interlocutor's behavior. This is natural; there are many differences in accepted behavioral norms in various cultures. Even people with a shared native language can speak in different "tongues," as is the case for British and American English or for the many versions of the Spanish language. If differences among people with the same language can complicate communication, then differences among people with different languages and from different societies can be quite striking. In addition to purely behavioral differences, there are many communication problems that arise from cultural influences on the linguistic code. Cultural components of language influence its grammar logic, semantics, and idiomatic expressions. The social and political environment of a given society can penetrate language to such a point that many lexical units and phraseologies of that language are extremely difficult for a foreigner's comprehension.

Up to and through the Advanced-High level of proficiency, students do not need extensive and specific cultural information. They have a more essential requirement: to build a toolbox of the basic and intermediate structures of the foreign language while more often than not necessarily ignoring much of the language's richness and uniqueness. Moreover, they are not capable of receiving cultural specificity in the target language because their level of vocabulary is not extensive enough.

In contrast, sophisticated sociocultural and sociolinguistic information for Superior-level students is essential. While enrolled in a language program, students may receive this information and training through many channels: books and articles on intercultural differences, special sociolinguistic exercises, more attention to idiomatic contents of the language, organized or serendipitous meetings with native speakers, special tests, tasks, and study abroad or its equivalent. At this level, the need for development of sociocultural competence is a guiding principle for the selection of teaching materials.

At lower levels of proficiency, students' focus is on the standard features of language – and must be. Sensitivity to dialect and register can only be developed on the base of the standard language. At the Distinguished level, students not only understand dialectal difference but comprehend idiolectal differences, as well. As such, they display sensitivity to what idiolects say about a person's educational level, values, and general behavioral interactions and expectations. For example, the use of a more sophisticated word colors one's perception of a person, as does the use of coarse words or obscenities. Superior-level students also develop their own idiolect. This idiolect reflects social norms of the foreign culture, and by the time a given student reaches the Distinguished level, his or her idiolect reflects his or her own linguistic proclivities in any language. If students are erudite in their native language, they exhibit erudition in the foreign language. If they are descriptive in their speech in their native language, they develop culturally appropriate descriptive strategies in the foreign language. If they punctuate their native speech with humor and sarcasm, they punctuate the foreign language with culturally appropriate versions of the same.

Linguistic competence: sophistication and accuracy of structure. At the Superior level, grammatical accuracy is not a tautology, and grammatical fluency is not an oxymoron, as they often are at lower levels of language proficiency. Grammatical accuracy, without any doubt, is the most important element of high CF. Poor control of grammar is the main reason why students cannot concentrate on "what" to say and must deal with the "how" of communication. Superior-level students typically have an excellent theoretical knowledge of all parts of grammar: parts of speech, syntax, morphology, and sometimes even linguistic history. They do not need additional grammar explanation. They do not need an explanation of their mistakes: they know why they make them, and it is usually due to carelessness in applying the rules or a slip of the tongue. At the same time, they still do make mistakes because their automatic control of some grammar features is not good enough. So, although Superior-level students' grammar level does not inhibit adequate communication, it still troubles them, and sometimes, especially when they are under psychological pressure, lack of automaticity even lowers their CF.

Thus, an essential task for a language instructor when he or she begins to work with Superior-level students is to help each to: (1) identify the grammar features that have been learned but not acquired, (2) reacquire language features that have been acquired inaccurately, and (3) develop the essential sophisticated grammar structures that remain unfamiliar to him/her. For this reason, a diagnostic approach to teaching is essential. In establishing an appropriate grammatical diagnosis, it may help to consider that Superior-level students, in general, display three types of grammar patterns:

1. Automatic and correct;
2. Automatic but not correct;
3. Not automatic.

The first type means that a student can provide an appropriate pattern immediately and correctly and at the speed of a native speaker. DeKeyser (1997) suggests that this occurs when "declarative knowledge is turned into qualitatively different procedural knowledge" (p. 214) through quantity of practice.

The second type means that a student can provide an appropriate pattern immediately and at the speed of a native speaker but with a mistake (slip of the tongue) or error (feature incorrectly intuited). Sometimes, this results from overgeneralization (Logan [1988]) and sometimes from lack of focus on form (i.e. lack of knowledge) (Long [1988]). Knowledge, as well as memory, influences the decision-making process about grammaticality, and students who have focused on form have been shown to outperform those with no focus on form in transferring understanding of grammaticality to new situations (i.e. reducing error) (Robinson [1997]).

The third type means that a student cannot provide an appropriate pattern. There are many reasons for this, including not having seen the grammatical feature before, having developed interlanguage rules that do not match L2 rules, and a focus on mechanics over ideation, among other possibilities.

The diagnostic approach has three valuable features. First, it identifies the mechanism of fluency in foreign language. A student speaks fluently and readily when he uses only the first and the second types of grammar patterns. The less a student uses the third pattern, the higher his or her CF. Thus, the identification of three types of grammar patterns can guide teachers in improving students' CF through the appropriate selection of individualized exercises and activities.

Second, this approach defines the mutual tasks of a student and language instructor: to reduce the number of Type 2 mistakes, to make Type 3 patterns more automatic, and to introduce a specified quantity of new grammar patterns to a student. The fluency level of Advanced-High students, while by definition strong, depends to a great extent on the method used in their previous classrooms. Students trained in grammar–translation or cognitive code approaches to language teaching tend to sacrifice fluency for accuracy. Those raised on communicative approaches to language teaching tend to be "awfully" fluent – with "awful" referring to lack of grammatical control. Further, learning style preferences can influence the fluency of students at this level. On the one hand, students who, by nature, focus on the forest and miss the trees, especially those previously taught in communicative classrooms, may display more fluency than otherwise expected. On the other hand, students who see all the trees but cannot find the forest, especially those previously taught in grammar–translation environments, may have highly impaired fluency but strong accuracy.

Third, this approach contributes to the development of synonymous expression, which is essential to the development of Distinguished-level proficiency. Synonymous grammatical expressions are dependent on the possession of several automatic and correct ways to express the same thought, giving students a choice in which one they use. The process of selecting among synonymous forms becomes one that allows the student to display his or her personality (or emotional competence), situational sensitivities, and command of register.

Precision of lexicon. An essential and significant task for instructors of Superior-level students is to provide activities that promote the acquisition of an increasingly greater active vocabulary both in terms of quantity of lexical items and quality (sophistication) of expression. Attention now shifts to the formation of words and to the ability of students to determine the meaning of new words, not by using context as much as by using an already-developed understanding of the linguistic framework of the language – a sensitivity to the morphemes and syntagms of the foreign language, as well as an intuition of the multiple meanings of words and their correct (grammatical and cultural) usage.

Another crucial change lies in the storage of the words in long-term memory. For adequate progress toward a near-native goal, a Superior-level student needs to be acquiring a large number of new words consistently. A language instructor equipped with techniques that avoid reliance on direct memorization (i.e., reliance on repetition) and providing exercises requiring association makes the process of storage (and subsequent recall/reconstruction) easier for students.[7] There are many ways to do this, beginning with word games and finishing with preparation of professional reports on important topics. Several chapter authors provide examples.

---

[7] Although most textbooks still approach vocabulary via direct memorization, Terrell (1986) suggested that only vocabulary that is "bound" remains in memory and that binding occurs through subordination of meaningful new information to extant schemata, in essence repeating the claims of Piaget and Inhelder (1973). Psychological research (Atkins and Baddeley [1998]) also has found association to be more effective than repetition. Natural repetition that includes associations with context creates a form of "hidden" memory work, calling the memory into action without obvious dependence on the rote strength that underlies the former.

Discourse competence. Discourse competence at the Superior level means the ability to understand and construct full texts. At Distinguished levels, those texts can be very long manuscripts, as in the case of reading or writing books or dissertations. Professional redaction activity might also be expected from a Level 4 in limited environments. Discourse competence is needed both for handling lengthy texts, which usually have a different structure from the shorter texts used at lower levels of proficiency, and for producing texts that include all the communication management devices and discourse devices present in literary and professional texts produced by native speakers.

Students at the Distinguished level also differ from their Superior-level peers in their ability to handle formal and informal language and to switch back and forth with ease. Formal language is rarely developed through travel and living abroad. It comes, instead, from professional work abroad, enrollment in foreign degree programs, or L2 classrooms. Classrooms (as described in this volume) help students develop formal language by requiring in-class presentations (Angelelli and Degueldre, Dabars and Kagan), presentations to the émigré community and extensive internships with native speakers (Angelelli and Degueldre, Shekhtman *et al.*), and the preparation of articles or materials for formal or informal "publishing" (Caudery, Dabars and Kagan).

Emotional competence. Although nothing, as far as we know, has been written about the emotional component of communicative competence, as proposed and defined by Eshkembeeva (1997), nearly every Advanced-level student reports the acquisition of a new persona together with the acquisition of a new language. At the Distinguished level, however, something new appears to happen in many, if not most, cases: a blending of the previously separated native and target personalities and a stabilizing of behaviors, values, and responses across intercultural boundaries (Leaver and Atwell, this volume). This composite is generally accepted within either culture. In other words, while a student might have an English and a French personality at lower levels of proficiency (including through the Superior level), when students reach the Distinguished level, they have managed to coalesce both their personalities into one. The merger reflects the Distinguished-level student's true identity and is accurately perceived by speakers of both English and French thanks to the student's ability to use different (and culturally appropriate) behaviors and language in expressing that personality in each of the cultures.

Social competence. Social competence goes beyond simple willingness to enter into social and linguistic contact with another speaker of the target language.[8]

---

[8] Willingness to enter into communication has at least two sources: personality and social competence. In the former case, it is unrealistic to expect students to display behaviors in L2 situations that they do not display in L1 situations.

It includes the willingness and ability to enter into unexpected, as well as planned, contact – situations where control may well be out of the hands of the student. Examples might be honoring a request to make an unplanned presentation to a group and, more commonly, the need to offer an impromptu but elaborate toast at a formal gathering. It also includes exhibiting the same level of willingness as native speakers. Some cultures are more extroverted (or introverted) than others, and the Distinguished-level student "feels" this difference.

Distinguished-level students are also more likely than even Superior-level students to be willing to talk, even after a grueling day of work or under stress of any non-linguistic sort. The effort required to speak the foreign language at this level is hardly distinguishable from the effort required to speak the native language.

Where we seem to be going

As classrooms oriented toward the development of proficiency help students reach increasingly higher levels of communicative competence than in the past, it is likely that language programs will enroll more Superior-level students and, therefore, the need for teaching at this level will increase. Further, an increasingly smaller and more global world means that there will be an increasing need for higher levels of foreign language proficiency in future years than ever before. The issues that will be important to educating all students successfully at these levels will reflect the changes in teaching approaches at lower levels. These approaches will influence the ways in which teachers teach Superior-level students.

Issues in teaching at the Superior level

An educational philosophy of transaction has moved the goal of teaching from developing linguistic knowledge to being able to accomplish tasks, with or without a linguistic base. Unfortunately, many teachers of lower-level students argue over whether they should teach grammar when they should be asking how and when to teach it. Teachers who argue for the development of strategic competence over linguistic competence intensify the naturally occurring imbalance between these two components of communicative competence at lower levels of proficiency where language use is required in real-life or simulated real-life environments. As a result, more and more students appear to be reaching the Advanced level of proficiency without the strong grammatical base that is required to reach Superior and Distinguished levels. As a result, SD teachers often include lower-proficiency activities in the Superior-level classroom to make up for omissions in previous language teaching that now impede the development of higher levels of proficiency (Soudakoff [2001]). While Superior-level students can circumvent the need for well-developed discourse competence by following models (e.g., extant documents in the workplace), Distinguished-level students are often the officials who must draft these documents/models.

Nearly all SD teachers base their instruction not on a textbook but on authentic materials that often come from students' professional fields. While many students meet such materials long before they reach the Superior level, at lower levels of proficiency tasks usually require students to skim and scan in order to understand general meaning and obtain essential information for accomplishing a specific performance. At higher levels, understanding general meaning is more often than not a given, and the task focuses on form, genre, text organization, authorial intent, and interpretation of nuance, as well as overall meaning.

In working with authentic materials and texts, Superior-level students have to understand genre. Government protocols, for example, are prepared differently from business contracts. Additionally, Distinguished-level students have to understand cross-cultural differences in discourse. Therefore, selection of texts becomes broader at the Superior level, and students, for the most part, can use authentic texts for gaining new content knowledge, often without the need for pre-reading or pre-listening activities. Not only do these needs have an impact on instructional method and activities, but they also create a difficulty for teachers that occurs much more rarely at lower levels of proficiency: lack of textual resources. Sometimes, students can help locate authentic texts. In other cases, access to appropriate materials may be restricted. Further, because of the significant differences in thematic needs represented in each classroom, Superior-level instructors may not be in the same position to share materials among themselves as are teachers of students at lower proficiency levels.

Perhaps surprisingly, individualization becomes even more important in the Superior-level classroom than in classes for students at lower proficiency levels. Although learning styles may become less important, students already having developed skill at foreign language acquisition and, therefore, being able to be flexible in the style in which they take input, teachers need to know the background knowledge of their students, as well as their specific goals, for most students have become or are becoming rather specialized at this level.

Issues in staffing at the Superior level

Staffing Superior-level programs can be a challenge, as any administrator of programs at this level can attest. Teachers must be able to do all the things that teachers of students at lower levels of proficiency can do and know all the things that those teachers know. In addition, they often need specific content knowledge (or the skills and strategies to teach content in which they are not specialists), linguistic knowledge equivalent to an educated native speaker (or very close), contemporary knowledge of the target culture (implying a willingness to invest the time and energy that it takes to stay *au courant*), and good diagnostic skills.

Content knowledge

Because student goals at higher proficiency levels often focus on specific content – diplomacy, aeronautics, negotiation, business, social consciousness (for journalists), and interpretation skills, among many other possible specializations – programs are more often than not content-based. This can put an onus on the teacher, who often knows less than the students about the content area, including specific vocabulary. In fact, some teachers in programs that include both Superior-level programs and programs at the Novice, Intermediate, and Advanced levels of proficiency, elect not to teach the Superior-level courses because they consider their lack of content knowledge to be a handicap.

Those teachers without content knowledge who do teach at the Superior level have one of two choices, the same two choices that most content-based program instructors face: learn the content or rely on the knowledge of the students. Either approach is reasonable. Either approach works. Sometimes it is not possible for a teacher to learn as much information about the topic as is needed in order to teach the class because there is not enough time to do so. Other times it is not feasible for the teacher to learn the information because the topic is quite esoteric. In those instances, teachers need to be comfortable at accepting students' knowledge of the topic and providing the linguistic support for students to gain greater proficiency in the topic. While the content schemata may be high among students, most often the linguistic skill is not at the level needed. Teachers who find themselves in the position of having or wanting to teach a Superior-level course must decide which option they will choose.

Sometimes program managers are lucky. They find specialists in the content area who are also language teachers. This is absolutely the ideal. However, this is not the norm. Typically, the trade-off is language-teaching experience versus content knowledge, and each administrator must decide how best to staff his or her program, keeping this reality in view.

Linguistic knowledge

More important than content knowledge is linguistic knowledge. Since teaching at the Superior level requires direct assistance to students in improving their linguistic competence, as well as improving sociolinguistic and sociocultural competence, the former of which requires erudition in the target language and the latter of which requires erudition in the target culture, the obvious question is: can non-native speakers teach Superior-level courses? The teachers of most of the Superior-level programs presented in this volume are native speakers of the languages that they teach. In a very few cases, the courses were taught by very proficient, near-native speakers. The latter, however, have had direct access to native speakers and have most often taught with native speakers in a four-handed teaching situation. A successful exception is the program for teachers described by Dabars and Kagan. The comment made by an external evaluator who observed a grammar class taught to teachers in Russian by a non-native professor with nativelike language skills makes a case in favor of such non-native speakers as teachers at Superior levels: they serve as models and inspiration for students aspiring to reach the same level of proficiency.

Being au courant

In order to teach at the Superior level, simply being a native speaker is not enough. The teacher must be *au courant* with sociocultural, sociolinguistic, and a range of other aspects of life in the target culture, such as history, current affairs, politics, economics, and customs. Further, knowledge of the current jargon and slang among a variety of social groups is required.

Teachers can stay *au courant* only if they are interested in self-growth. Considering how little we still know about teaching at the Superior level, we are likely only to develop good programs and progress in theory if the teachers of these programs are oriented toward personal growth, change and progress in theory, and research in second language acquisition at the very advanced levels.

Diagnostic skills

Teachers at the Superior level must also have very good diagnostic skills. Teaching at this level is far more than enacting a particular method, more than good presentations, and more than group instruction. Rather, teachers must be able to focus on individual learners, determine their current proficiency levels not only on an accepted proficiency rating scale but also in terms of the relative development of the various components of communicative competence, and prepare individualized instruction that enhances all the components of communicative competence and strengthens any particular weaknesses in vocabulary and grammar. If there are affective or linguistic impediments to a student's advancement, Superior-level teachers must be able to identify them and find ways to overcome them.

Issues in testing at the Superior level

Tests at the Superior level must assess all the components of communicative competence, not just linguistic competence. For that reason, achievement tests are rarely used by teachers in Superior-level programs. If tests are used – and in many programs tests are not used – they are typically of the content-specific variety. Prochievement tests, hybrid achievement–proficiency tests using unfamiliar authentic materials about previously studied topics, have attained some popularity in recent years in programs for lower levels of proficiency that use task-based and content-based approaches to teaching, but are necessarily less common as classroom tests at the Superior level. More common are tests that require students to demonstrate their ability to use the foreign language to accomplish work tasks, i.e., work tests. As graduation requirements or proficiency level checks, often both global and specific proficiency tests are used. While specific proficiency tests are still very much unknown in the FLED profession, teachers at Superior levels are beginning to find that they do need some kinds of content-specific testing related to students' content area specializations in addition to the more traditional global proficiency test, such as the ILR or ACTFL test. The result is usually a test that is prepared by the individual teacher, although a few specific proficiency tests are beginning to be developed[9] and may serve as models for a wide range of specific proficiency tests used for students in Language for Special Purposes (LSP) programs, as well as those at Superior levels of study, in the not-so-distant future.

Because many Superior-level courses are LSP in nature, concentrating on a narrow range of topics, some teachers contend that these courses produce "hothouse specials," i.e., students whose language skills are at Level 3+ or 4 in a narrow content area but not across the board. However, it may be quite natural, as students approach native levels of language proficiency, for some content areas to be much better developed than others – and this parallels L1 development. Native speakers can handle some topics much more eloquently than others, depending on their areas of specialization, interests, experiences, social class, and geographic location.

Testing is needed not only for determination of accomplishment or current skill levels but also for placement, curricular design, and individualization. Nearly all the authors of this volume point out the importance to the development of an effective program of being able to diagnose student needs. Testing issues at Superior levels have been less researched than at lower proficiency levels, partly because of lack of subjects and partly because of the complexity of testing at that level.[10] If we are serious, however, about developing Distinguished-level skills in students, then we need a reliable and valid means of measuring those skills, not only in terms of global proficiency, for which the ILR OPI

[9] Examples include two tests developed by the American Council of Teachers of Russian: (1) to measure proficiency in Russian in financial matters, and (2) to measure proficiency in Russian and English in aeronautics and space communication. The former, a specific proficiency test developed for the International Monetary Fund, requires students to perform work-related tasks and scores the performance in accordance with the scoring criteria from the ACTFL test. The latter, a specific proficiency test developed for NASA, requires students to answer questions or make presentations related to space operations and scores the responses in accordance with the scoring criteria from the ACTFL test. The first test would also be considered a performance test, the second more a traditional proficiency test.

[10] At the time of this writing, the Defense Language Institute had just undertaken a comprehensive initiative to develop proficiency tests for identifying language users at Levels 3, 4, and 5.

appears adequate for the moment, but also in terms of diagnosing weak areas and assessing differences between global and specific proficiency.

Conclusion

The teaching of Superior-level skills is virgin territory. Few are attempting to accomplish it, although many more would like to. Therefore, there are more questions than answers, more theory than practice, and more anecdote than research in this area. The various chapters in this book attempt to begin to fill the void by providing models of successful programs.

As a profession, we need to consider a commitment to taking students beyond the Advanced level. In a world that is ever more frequently demanding near-native skills, our clinging to the tacit (and false) assumption that the Advanced-High or even Superior level is the limit to which we can teach students denies many students the chance to develop the skills they need for professional work because we, as a profession, fail to provide programs for them.

If we are to begin to bring students to the higher levels that a few in our profession have already demonstrated are possible, we need to develop an agenda to study the Superior-level student in greater depth. The editors and authors of this volume hope that the philosophies, experiences, and practices presented here will create an imperative to do so.

2 Toward academic-level foreign language abilities: Reconsidering foundational assumptions, expanding pedagogical options

Heidi Byrnes

Among the most enduring and pronounced disjunctures in American college foreign language (FL) programs is that between the lofty desire for students to attain upper levels of performance in a second language (L2) and realities on the ground. On the one hand, the ideal of upper-level L2 abilities – henceforth generically referred to as advanced second language (AL2) use[1] – is alive and well as indicated in departmental mission and goals statements and also in the profession's continued insistence on "near-native abilities" in candidates for faculty positions (Koike and Liskin-Gasparro [1999]). On the other hand, we know that the first few semesters at best enable students to acquire basic interactional facility in the L2 and that the subsequent content courses rarely even state appropriate acquisitional goals much less incorporate explicit instructional interventions that target AL2 learning.

However, a mismatch that may have been tolerable in the past may no longer be workable in the future, as external demands press in on the profession, with serious consequences for FL departments, including the outsourcing of language instruction, the dramatic reorganization of some departments, and even their closing (Schneider [2001]). For the real meaning to FL departments of the much-hailed globalization, the greater ethnic and linguistic diversity of nations, and the demands for more democratization around the world may not

---

[1] In choosing the generic reference *AL2* I face the dilemma that the profession lacks appropriate terminology for designating the level of language that is the focus of this chapter. I am reluctant to employ the terminology of Advanced Plus, Superior, or Distinguished that has gained currency through the ACTFL or ILR oral proficiency assessment rating scale for several reasons: (1) in nongovernmental educational settings and also in the second language acquisition (SLA) research community these terms carry strong associations with rating scales whose construct of proficiency has been subjected to extensive critical analyses (see Bachman [1990]; McNamara [1996]; Young and He [1998]); (2) these terms imply a priority for assessment-derived features of interlanguage while I am primarily concerned with L2 developmental and instructional issues; and (3) their impact in foreign language education (FLED) has been to privilege a particular system of assessment and a particular mode of language use, namely oral language, that is itself unnecessarily limiting of advanced L2 learning. I trust that the chapter will provide both sufficient elaboration and sufficient specificity to justify the otherwise awkward term *AL2* abilities.

simply be that societies require a multilingual citizenry but that this citizenry of the future requires upper levels of language abilities so as to be able to use an L2 competently in a wide variety of public and professional contexts and not only in private settings among family and friends. The question then becomes: how might college FL departments re-imagine themselves so as to be able to respond to the challenge of facilitating the development of AL2 abilities, a re-envisioning that would necessitate reflection about their nature, about actionable plans, and about viable and successful practices in support of reaching that goal?

I have begun to address these issues elsewhere by focusing on two areas of undergraduate education: curriculum and pedagogy. Specifically, I have advocated a focus on constructing curricula as carefully considered sequences of educational events, in contrast with mere aggregations of courses (Byrnes [1998]). I have urged reconstitution of college FL programs through integrated, content-oriented, and task-based curricula in order to replace the current split into "language courses" and "content courses," a program bifurcation which gives short shrift to the complex phenomenon of adult L2 learning (Byrnes [1999, 2000a]). Finally, I have recommended that college FL programs rethink their pedagogical practices by linking content and language form in a fashion that facilitates continued and balanced long-term L2 development in terms of accuracy, fluency, and complexity of language use (2001a).

Given societal demand for AL2 abilities, a focus on curriculum is justified for the following reasons: first, serious curriculum construction is inherently oriented toward fostering AL2 abilities; second, curriculum planning necessarily demands consideration of the long-term and intricately nonlinear nature of adult instructed L2 learning, as captured by the term *interlanguage*; and, third, any in-depth discussion of AL2 abilities requires that one reflect on how learners best reach them. Together, these issues require decisions on curricular sequencing and on suitable instructional interventions in order to avoid premature stabilization of interlanguage forms (Byrnes [2001b]; Byrnes and Kord [2001]; Doughty [1998]; Doughty and Williams [1998]).

In light of these considerations as well as my experiences and insights in conjunction with the comprehensive curriculum renewal project in my home department, the German Department at Georgetown University,[2] I begin by characterizing what I take to be the prevailing view of "advancedness" in foreign language education (FLED). Since I suggest that it draws on a theoretically and empirically insufficiently comprehensive understanding of the nature of language and language acquisition, I subsequently explore a profile for the advanced learner which might address these perceived shortcomings. On that

---

[2] This three-year project, implemented between 1997 and 2000 and entitled "Developing Multiple Literacies," is extensively documented on the department's web site: www.georgetown.edu/departments/german/curriculum/curriculum.html.

basis, I propose some principles for teaching the AL2 learner. My contribution in Part II of this volume reports on how these considerations informed an intensive eight-day immersion institute for graduate students of German. I conclude with observations that link the project of AL2 learning and use to larger educational concerns from the learners' and from the teachers' perspective and also to larger epistemological issues that, ultimately, pertain to the workings of civil society and, more deeply, to our self-understanding.

The advanced learner: Current assumptions and pervasive metaphors

The influence of the ACTFL Guidelines

Where the FL profession has considered AL2 abilities, it has done so largely under the influence of the ACTFL Proficiency Guidelines and their mode of testing oral abilities in the Oral Proficiency Interview (OPI).[3] Indeed, ways of imagining *any* advanced L2 abilities, not just speaking, essentially derive from that document and its associated practices. As a consequence, the profession has come to characterize advanced learners broadly in the following terms: they possess an ability to use language in paragraph and discourse length, to describe and narrate in different time frames, to address concrete and abstract topics, to support an opinion and hypothesize about non-present events, experiences, and issues, and can do so with only minor infractions against accuracy, with few violations of an expected level of fluency, and in a sociolinguistically appropriate fashion (see Breiner-Sanders *et al.* [2000]; also the introductory chapter of this volume, by Leaver and Shekhtman). Beyond that, the language abilities designated by "Advanced High," "Superior," and "Distinguished" on the ACTFL and ILR scales highlight the importance of the environment in which such language is likely to be used, namely diverse professional contexts that will require ever greater breadth, depth, and quality of expressiveness, and, consequently, greater cultural appropriateness and personal confidence, even including some aspects of dealing with dialectal variants as these characterize many linguistic-cultural groups.

Given the extent to which the above features have been naturalized in FLED and have become major guideposts for professional action (e.g., in K-12 curricular statements, as outcomes statements for collegiate L2 requirements, as specifying suitability or outcomes for study abroad, as graduation requirements), it is appropriate to query: what notion of language and of the AL2 learner is being projected, explicitly and implicitly, with these descriptors and, more generally,

---

[3] For a brief history of that connection and its influence on the notion of "near-native abilities," at least among collegiate FL faculty, see Koike and Liskin-Gasparro (1999).

with the proficiency framework from which these descriptors hail? Four aspects stand out.

An additive and componential notion of language

Language acquisition is essentially described as "more" and "better" incorporation of various separate attributes that make up language performance. Those attributes include, most particularly, grammatical and lexical accuracy, fluency, and also complexity, as well as sociolinguistic and pragmatic competence within a cultural context. A similarly additive dimension holds for length of utterance – from sentence, to paragraph, to discourse – and, implicitly, for contexts of use, private and public. In their approach, the Guidelines are reminiscent of the theoretical bases established at the beginning of the communicative turn in US L2 education by Canale and Swain's seminal article (1980). Their proposal analyzed language performance by way of four components – grammatical or linguistic competence, discourse competence, sociolinguistic competence, and strategic competence – and seemingly arrayed them in a hierarchical progression. It thus constituted a do-able challenge for the then dominant forms-focus in US FLED thinking as it shifted toward the newly advocated communicative orientation.

However, such an interpretation failed to understand that an emphasis on communication seriously challenged and even contradicted prevailing notions regarding the nature of language and language teaching. Perhaps it could not be otherwise, given the predominance of beginning and intermediate levels in US FLED teaching and research with its propensity to foreground formal accuracy and various compensatory and facilitative learner strategies. This was the usual sense given to Canale and Swain's strategic competence, despite numerous adjustments to that construct, particularly in the testing community (cf. Bachman [1990]; McNamara [1996]; Young and He [1998]). At the same time, discourse and sociolinguistic competence, the other aspects of communicative ability, received scant attention. Since few professionals had instructional experience at the advanced level, these terms retained their long-established additive meanings.

A privileging of the formal features of the language

It seems, then, that an additive and hierarchical notion of language acquisition is closely tied to an emphasis on formal accuracy. However, since competent language use quite assuredly does require accurate use of the lexicogrammar of a language, the issues cannot lie in the *that* of emphasizing accuracy but in the *how*. Specifically, an appropriate emphasis on formal features requires a larger frame of reference, permitting nuanced interpretation that provides a context for the occurrence of approximative forms and a basis for the creation and practice of instructional interventions. In my estimation, it is precisely this fundamental reconsideration of the nature and function of formal features within language use and their role and significance in L2 acquisition and pedagogy that the profession by-passed as it "implemented proficiency" in an astoundingly short time.

One can conclude that the "Proficiency Movement" brought about enormously beneficial changes, particularly in teacher education, pedagogical approaches, materials development, and assessment, even as it hindered an expansion of the profession's interpretive horizons. Let me provide just one example: one of the most enduring debates in communicative language teaching concerns the role of grammar. Almost inevitably, grammar is viewed in oppositional terms to communication that is encapsulated in the term "fluency," where fluency, in turn, is largely equated with temporal fluency (e.g., no unacceptable pausing behavior, no inappropriate level of self-correction and fractured syntax). As communicative language teaching gained wide acceptance, the two opposing sides made their own peculiar truce: both steadfastly affirmed that accuracy *and* fluency were necessary for language acquisition to proceed, a stance that could leave nearly everything in place, with communication *added* to it.

Though even the delimited assessment practice of the OPI provided ample evidence, discussion did not explore the deeper meaning of the phenomenon that both features of learner language, accuracy and fluency, are shaped by the nature of the tasks being performed, the kinds of meanings learners are attempting to convey, at what levels of formality toward their interlocutor, and within what communicative context (e.g., public or private). In other words, language performance at the very least is not entirely driven by abstract formal capabilities in and of themselves; it is also, in yet to be specified ways, influenced by situated and goal-oriented meaning conveyance. It is just this kind of nuanced specification that teachers require in order to develop their own rich understandings of the delicate and changing relationship between accuracy and fluency along the acquisitional path (Skehan [1998]). For with it they can make informed, situated choices so that students' language use at a time can continue to lead to language development over time, the heart of instruction that can foster learner development to AL2 abilities.

The dominance of interactive speech

While separate guidelines exist for all modalities, the speaking component became paradigmatic for how the Proficiency Movement was received in nongovernmental FLED. A direct consequence is the privileging of conversational (interpersonal) language in unmarked encounters among equals, rarely in marked formal events, and in pragmatic encounters, either of a factual, information-gathering nature or with a transactional goal (e.g., obtaining various goods and services). True, typically even adult learners initially acquire what J. P. Gee (1998) refers to as the primary discourses of familiarity among family and friends, generally within settings that are presumed to be known or at least highly predictable. However, by not referring to the unmistakable qualitative differences between these primary discourses and the secondary discourses of public life in a vast range of settings – not just "more and better" – the Guidelines do not explore the cognitive and semiotic needs and capabilities that characterize the AL2 learner (Halliday [1993]).

A more indirect but equally serious negative consequence is that the additive construct underlying the speaking guidelines strongly affected how FL professionals approached the other modalities. Accordingly, the reading guidelines were severely criticized early on for their disregard of the cognitive abilities (in L1) that the learner brought to the reading task, their assumption of a textual hierarchy according to a typology of texts, their insufficiently developed, even seriously misconstrued notion of comprehension, and, ultimately, their inappropriate pedagogical recommendations.[4] More recently, similar concerns have been raised, even for Novice and Intermediate-level learners, for writing development that "may not challenge the full writing potential of novice FL writers, especially if the language in question shares an alphabet with the students' native language" (Way, Joiner, and Seaman [2000, pp. 178–179]).

In sum, by referring to language primarily as oral, interactive language of familiarity, Guidelines-derived notions seem to have a tendency to *underestimate*, through their representations of the nature of adult L2 learning, the learners' acquisitional potential. This is a serious issue in and of itself. It is particularly consequential given the short time allocated within American FLED for attaining usable and, more important, upper levels of L2 ability.

The influence of assessment and particular assessment practices

As is well known, the proficiency construct was derived from assessment practices (for a brief overview, see Koike and Liskin-Gasparro [1999]). On an abstract level, the fundamental differences as well as the facilitative and detrimental connections between assessment and instruction are, of course, well known (Shohamy [1998]). In professional practice, however, an uncritical linking of assessment to goals setting, to curriculum construction, and to instructional practice amazingly swiftly foregrounded the latter, detrimental consequences. One way to undo these would be to see the implicational hierarchies used in much assessment, along with their breakdown of large performance categories into separate criteria, as reflecting highly specific interests and needs of assessment. By contrast, language itself, language learning, and language teaching are characterized by a host of facilitative and dynamic interrelationships that taxonomic treatments can all too easily conceal. Misinterpretations not only result in potentially less efficient L2 learning for individual learners. More seriously, they affect how the entire FL profession sets its sights, that is, what L2 abilities

---

[4] Representative of many of these criticisms is Lee and Musumeci (1988).

it believes instructed L2 learning can reasonably attain. Almost by definition, L2 classrooms have become deficitary environments which continually convey to their learners this message: if you want to acquire the L2, don't stay here but immerse yourself in the culture.

Naturally, the impact of that stance is the more detrimental and far-reaching the more we aim toward upper levels of L2 ability. For example, when some aspects of language use are characterized as discourse and sociolinguistic competence and these "advanced" abilities are deferred until after "mastery" of morpho-syntactic formal features, we disable L2 learners from experiencing their own evolving L2 use as predicated by meaning-driven choices, thus inherently discursive and socially constructed, and not merely a rule-driven, formal exercise of being "right."

Let me summarize where consideration of these four perspectives has led us. I have suggested that one reason for the impasse regarding AL2 learning is insufficiently robust assumptions about advancedness that build on an additive and componential notion of language. That notion, furthermore, is strengthened by a conceptualization of the relationship between knowledge, meaning, and language that has dominated Western philosophy and, by implication, linguistics since antiquity (see Christie [1989]; and the "General Orientation" in Halliday and Martin [1993]). In particular, the field has treated language as separate from knowledge and, in turn, knowledge as existing "out there" prior to and separate from language. As a result, most theorizing has constructed linguistic patterns distinctly and independently from individual and cultural knowledge, thereby enabling a focus on the interrelated system of signs, diachronically and synchronically investigated, that could be remarkably devoid of meaning, function, and use in a sociocultural context. Language thereby becomes a tool, an instrument, and being able to use a language, and, by implication, to acquire an L2, becomes a "skill." Focal attention can then shift from the sociocultural context of meaning-making and choices in the life world *through and with language* to accuracy *of language* in terms of an idealized norm. That norm, of course, refers to an abstract system of signs which itself is the result of a linguistic analysis that removes itself and its findings from a sociocultural context of human meaning-making. As Christie expresses the issue in the context of L1 education, this instrumentalist approach does not acknowledge "that the development of the desired mental skills is entirely dependent on the mastery of the linguistic patterns in which these skills are realized. Equally rarely is it acknowledged that 'knowledge' itself is constructed in varying patterns of discourse" (1989, p. 153). In other words, we have misrepresented both language *and* knowledge, a realization that confronts not only education and linguistics – particularly cognitive, functional, and sociolinguistics – but also philosophy.

To the extent that the Guidelines and their ILR predecessor and current companion constitute the FL profession's primary vision of L2 learning, they present a flawed understanding of the relation between language, knowledge, and culture, and also provide an insufficiently comprehensive and insufficiently sophisticated framework for teaching and learning. Insufficient and in need of reconsideration in particular is the profile of advanced learners. To varying degrees we, the authors of the chapters in this volume, realize and make reference to this fact. At the same time, our recommendations to counteract this legacy are fragile, inasmuch as we build on previous instruction that may well have been less than optimal, perhaps even detrimental to the goal of AL2 acquisition. However, their transitional status can also be seen positively, reflecting the profession's gradual ability to expand its imagination of what instructed L2 learning at all levels might be. In a reversal of customary practice, the following section explores possible avenues for that necessary reconsideration by using the AL2 learner as the point of departure.

Profiling the AL2 learner: an expanded conceptual base

The advanced L2 learner as a multicompetent speaker

As we reconsider how we might facilitate the attainment of AL2 abilities, we must first clarify the goals to which such learning aspires. At present, very advanced abilities have almost completely been understood in terms of the native speaker.[5] While that seems an innocent teleology, in reality the "native speaker" was imagined by way of a norm- and system-reference that bespeaks certain interests. For example, in the theory of transformational-generative grammar an idealized native speaker, wholly unperturbed by performance constraints, enabled statements about the nature of language which claimed not only descriptive but explanatory adequacy, a highly desirable designation in the pecking order of academic inquiry. In assessment practice and, by implication, within the FL profession, that native speaker is best known as the educated native speaker of the ILR/ACTFL Proficiency Guidelines from whom the learner who wishes to reach the top rungs of the hierarchical ladder should be indistinguishable.

Since the persistence of a "foreign accent" is the most readily identifiable obstacle to this lofty goal – after all, proficiency-tester lore has it that only

---

[5] For the remainder of my reflections I use the term *speaker* in a generic fashion to refer to the ability to use a language, native or otherwise. However, as the paper makes clear, efficient and effective language acquisition by adults requires the total integration of all modalities right from the start. More important, the potential for acquiring advanced abilities depends on increasingly greater emphasis on the forms of semiosis preferred in the secondary discourses of public life which, not surprisingly, are the forms of written language.

God and mothers create such speakers – a biological predisposition of human development captured by the critical period hypothesis holds remarkable sway. Although more recent research has suggested more nuanced interpretations for long-held research findings that seemingly precluded upper levels of performance in an L2 beyond the critical period (see particularly Bialystok and Hakuta [1994]; Birdsong [1992, 1999]), two assumptions about L2 learning persist: first, that such indistinguishability should, indeed, be the goal for L2 learning; and, second, that L2 learning involves, indeed requires, a virtual effacement of the learner's L1 abilities and predispositions.

Both assumptions have been subjected to extensive critique. For example, a theoretical clean distinction between competence and performance is already highly suspect from the standpoint of acquisition. Further, as Fillmore notes in light of variation in language behavior, "in a situation in which language use plays an essential role in a speaker's engagement in a matrix of human actions, however, the distinction [between competence and performance] seems not to be particularly helpful" (1979, p. 91). Finally, research by Birdsong (1999), Cook (1992 and 1999), and Coppieters (1987) indicates that non-native users can differ significantly in their underlying representations or grammatical intuitions about the L2, *even* when their performance is accepted by native speakers as being of native quality. Put simplistically, all L2 users, regardless of levels of ability, differ from monolinguals because they have an L1. This leads Cook (1992) to posit a "multicompetence" that recognizes not only the inescapable fact of L1 influence but, indeed, the desirability of a multicompetent individual as contrasted with an "ersatz native." Restating the goals of L2 learning in this fashion exposes the idealized goal of the native speaker, or of nativelike performance for the L2 learner, as at heart privileging monolingualism. The extent to which that is an interest of the nation-state which uses that ideology for identity, influence, and domination through language norms is worthy of some reflection, particularly at a time when the nation-state itself is being reconstituted.

Aside from reducing the potential for bigotry against non-native minorities (Valdés [1999]), these insights permit an important resituating of the goals of L2 instruction in terms of the L2 user as an "*intercultural speaker* . . . not an imitation L1 user" (Cook [1999, p. 203]) or, worded differently, as a multicompetent user of an L2 in his or her own right (1992). Attenuating, perhaps even reversing, the previous characterization of non-native speakers as defective or failing, we can see them as engaging in multiple interpretive border crossings and forms of translation precisely because they have an outsider perspective (Kramsch [1997]). Far from an insignificant play with words, such reconsiderations open up numerous programmatic and pedagogical possibilities, including, in a curious twist, the possibility of improving the educational support for L2 learners to acquire AL2 abilities at a higher rate and level of success than has heretofore been the case.[6]

How might knowledge/content and language be related to our concern with the AL2 learner? I begin to answer this question from the perspective of language processing as cognitive grammar explicates it. The subsequent section explores the possibilities of a genre and literacy approach. I conclude with remarks about the notion of cognitive fluency on the one hand, and about variation, identity, and voice on the other, where all these aspects are intimately related to the notion of choice in L2 use.

Linking knowledge and language – thinking for speaking

Key to a linking of language and knowledge is the nature of meaning. Refuting the objectivist tradition which excludes "ideas" or "concepts" from analysis, Langacker and other cognitive grammarians (as contrasted with cognitive linguists and cognitive scientists like Fodor) focus on cognitive phenomena (Langacker [1987, 1988a, 1988b]). These are explicated in terms of conceptualization, which includes both intellectual as well as sensory, emotive, and kinesthetic sensations. Part of overall psychological organization rather than separate from it, language is at its core a symbolic system, with its grammar not best described in terms of generativity, as though the expressions of language were a fixed algorithmic set that responds to conditions of logic and truth, but as a symbolic resource which speakers use as part of their general categorizing and problem-solving abilities. Thus, important notions are those of "construal" or "imagery," that is, interpretive and situated meaning-making, since "the semantic value of an expression does not reside solely in the inherent properties of the entities or situation it describes, but crucially involves as well the way we choose to think about this entity or situation and mentally portray it" (1988a, pp. 6–7).[7]

This approach evokes a number of consequences. First, since semantic structure is not universal but in important ways language-specific, we must find ways of deeply engaging learners in situated meaning-making that enables and requires them to draw upon the full body of their native speakers' knowledge and cognitive abilities, most particularly their interpretation of what Langacker

---

[6] As its title, "Developing Multiple Literacies," indicates, the desirability of such a multicompetence provides the ideational frame of reference for the reconceptualized undergraduate curriculum of the German Department at Georgetown University.

[7] A particularly interesting discussion and application of these issues to advanced language learning in the lexicogrammatical sphere of prefixed German verbs is that by Sprang (2002, in preparation), who locates her study of advanced learners of German within this framework and, accordingly, plans her instructional interventions around an explicit link between the potentialities of concept formation and the acquisition of complex language forms.

calls the "usage event" which leads to an utterance. In processing their L2 utterance they make choices regarding the preferred or most appropriate construal of the situation, drawing on the resources provided by the formal inventory of the L2, which, of course, permits variant possibilities (Chafe [1998]). In other words, contrary to past practice, well-formedness or, to use our preferred term, "accuracy," is not exhausted at the form level nor is it an absolute. The essential incorporation of the situation of use forbids that interpretation, as does the nature of language as a symbolic resource that offers highly conventionalized, nonetheless diverse meaning-making possibilities through semantic, phonological, and symbolic units.

For example, the same objective circumstance may be expressed in quite different ways:

(e) Russia invaded Afghanistan;
(e') Afghanistan was invaded by Russia.

These two phrases constitute a significant semantic contrast rather than being relegated to the status of a mere, almost whimsical, syntactic transformation (example taken from Langacker [1988a, p. 7]). In each case, the speaker chooses to foreground and emphasize a different aspect of the entity or situation being described. In a given context, one or the other may be more appropriate and more "correct," or simply more what the speaker intended to convey.

Second, grammar and lexicon, semantics and pragmatics, semantics and grammar, and literal and figurative, idiomatic, or metaphorical language are difficult to distinguish meaningfully. Specifically, despite a long tradition of the centrality of syntax and, correlatively, of lexicon as "really an appendix of grammar, a list of basic irregularities" (Bloomfield [1933, p. 274]), neither the dichotomous distinctions nor the autonomous components are justified as they stand. Indeed, while symbolic units (e.g., in "grammar" or "lexicon") do have conventional values, what Langacker calls "compositional values," these typically underspecify the contextual value they have in a given utterance, the way they are actually understood in use. There is always a gradient between what remains "outside" of linguistic expression, that is, what is "contextual" or "non-compositional," and what is actually expressed in language. On the expressive plane, we encounter yet another continuum, inasmuch as "the symbolic units characterizing grammatical structure form a continuum with lexicon: while they differ from typical lexical items with respect to such factors as complexity and abstraction, the differences are only a matter of degree, and lexical items themselves range widely along these parameters" (Langacker [1988a, p. 19]).

Finally, well-formedness or "accuracy" is also neither an absolute nor primarily a matter of the form level. Quite the opposite is true, a judgment that pertains less to the significance of formal accuracy and more to the speaker's conceptual meaning-making capacity and interests through the symbolic resources of a language. Therefore, a concern with learner centeredness might most appropriately be a concern with a learner acquiring the richness of the L2 system's symbolic resources rather than with learners "creatively" expressing personal meanings or applying their own learning strategies and styles, a frequent interpretation in FLED. A concern with accuracy might then be in terms of possible and acceptable learner choices within the nexus of intended meanings, available resources, and privileged forms of expression as the L2 speech community has evolved them.

Practical implications of such a shift for all L2 learning, but particularly for AL2 learning, become apparent in Slobin's crosslinguistic studies of online processing (1996a, 1996b, 1998). Just like cognitivist grammarians, he concludes that "thinking for speaking" (1996a, 1998) is shaped by the nature of the resources languages make available. Different from simplistic notions of linguistic relativity, linguistic determinism, or skill use, this research acknowledges that language resource potentials do influence, because of their degree of codability, how speakers encode particular events in online processing. For example, Slobin's explorations of motion events confirm a two-way distinction already posited in Talmy's extensive typology of languages according to various conceptual domains, such as aspect, change of state, action correlation, and event realization (1991): (1) verb-framed languages, in which the preferred pattern for framing motion events is the use of a path verb with an optional manner adjunct (e.g., "enter running"), and (2) satellite-framed languages, in which path is lexicalized in an element associated with the verb, leaving the verb free to encode manner (e.g., "run in") (Slobin [1998]). As a consequence, satellite-framed languages have a larger and more differentiated lexicon of manner verbs and use those verbs more frequently across a range of situations. Moreover, as the data were elicited through picture narratives, speakers' different gesture patterns provided evidence for different mental imagery and memory of descriptions of motion events, with satellite-framed languages devoting more attention to their manner dimension. Finally, beyond the sentence level, Slobin's investigation of translations of literary texts between Spanish and English (1996b) confirmed a preference in oral narratives whereby speakers of English, a satellite language, may devote more narrative attention to the dynamics of movement because of the availability of verbs of motion (often conflated with manner) while Spanish-speakers seem to be led (or constrained) by their language to devote somewhat more attention to static scene-setting. As a result, "the problem facing the Spanish translator . . . is whether or not to allot a separate clause to each of the path segments that are associated with a single verb in the English original" (p. 211). More precisely, the dilemma is this: "A faithful translation is either not readily accessible, due to lexical and syntactic constraints, and/or it would be too extended, thereby foregrounding materials that are naturally backgrounded in the original" (p. 210).[8]

Perceptive language educators have, of course, always known of the significant difference between the "packaging" of thoughts in languages and what thoughts are so packaged in the first place. Likewise, those whose education emphasized literature and careful textual analysis have been well aware of the different rhetorical preferences that engendered a different "feel" of a particular thought or entire narrative in different languages. From the standpoint of pedagogy, however, the challenge is how best to convey these insights to our learners. A first, somewhat uncomfortable conclusion might be that the frequent admonition that students should "simply think in the language" and not translate but work by intuitive feel is an insufficiently informed and inadequate way of supporting their desire to attain AL2 abilities, particularly in an instructed setting.

More specifically, we might follow Slobin's recommendation (1988) for a framework of thinking for talking and listening, thinking for writing and reading, thinking for translating, and listening and reading for remembering. One consequence would be to reconsider reading instruction in ways beneficial for the AL2 learner. As currently constituted, its principal instructional "metaphors" are scripts, frames, and schemata. However, these tend to overlook the intricate relationship between the conceptual and the lexicogrammatical formal linguistic level. As Kintsch (1988) shows, when scripts and frames are conceived in terms of a top-down predictive, expectation-based way of processing texts, which only resorts to bottom-up processing when it encounters unexpected difficulties, they are "simply not workable: if they are powerful enough, they are too inflexible, and if they are general enough, they fail in their constraining function" (p. 164). Instead, he proposes a *construction–integration* model that "combines a construction process in which a text base is constructed from the linguistic input as well as from the comprehender's knowledge base, with an integration phase, in which this text base is integrated into a coherent whole" (ibid.). Word identification is much more deeply embedded in discourse understanding than previously understood and knowledge that is eventually activated depends on the discourse context in terms of the "neighborhood" in the text, rather than in terms of a long-term memory net that exists separate from a discursive context. Once again, simply espousing a processing and communicative orientation is inadequate. What is called for is elaboration of the intimate relationship between language and the life world and a deep understanding of the nature of human semiosis, prototypically instantiated by language.

---

[8] A similar analysis, this time pairing English and German, is offered by Carroll (1997 and 2000). With a shift toward phraseology, Teliya *et al.* (1998) investigate the cultural infusion of lexical collocations in the context of Russian.

Genre as typified rhetorical actions in recurrent social situations[9]

At present, that relationship between knowledge and language is perhaps best explored in the new genre studies which begin with socially contextualized meaning-making as definitional for the human capacity to be a "languaging" species (Becker [1995]).[10] Among its most elaborated forms is that of systemic functional linguistics which underscores the symbiotic relationship between human activity and language. Its foundational assumption regarding language, ideas, and the performance of activities is that we must think "the very existence of one is the condition for the existence of the other" (Hasan [1995, p. 184]).

In line with the embeddedness of language within the life-world, Halliday proposes an explicitly social approach to language. To him, a functional analysis of language must seek to account for how language is actually used since "every text – that is, everything that is said or written – unfolds in some context of use . . . language has evolved to satisfy human needs; and the way it is organized is functional with respect to these needs – it is not arbitrary" (1985, p. xiii). Therefore, language is not a system of forms to which meanings are then attached, but "a system of meanings, accompanied by forms through which the meanings can be realized" (p. iv). In other words, the Saussurean dictum of the arbitrariness of the sign which has influenced so much twentieth-century thinking, including American structuralism, the grammatical system most frequently used in FLED, holds only in a general way with regard to the potentialities of human semogenesis for a range of construals of reality. It does not hold for the actual social practices of language use in a particular community.

To be able to serve human life, language must express two general kinds of functions: an ideational or reflective, which allows us to understand our environment, and an interpersonal or active, which allows us to act on others, where both of these metafunctions are held together and operationalized by a third metafunctional component, the textual. In this fashion, language creates a semiotic world of its own, a universe that exists only at the level of meaning but serves both as means and as model, or metaphor, for the world of action and experience. Where might the above-mentioned model of reality construed in and through language come from? In the most general sense, it arises from a social context with its acts of meaning and these are themselves occasioned by the need "for carrying out some **social action**, by co-actants in some **social relation**, placed in some **semiotic contact**. The meaning potential of language and its lexicogrammatical resources must be such as to enable its speakers to construe these important aspects of their social experience [bold-facing in original]" (Hasan [1999, p. 62]). Meanings in specific utterances are then the

---

[9] The following section follows the arguments in Byrnes (2001a).

[10] Becker uses this felicitous term to realign the privileged focus on language as a system in terms of an "attunement between a person and a context" (p. 9).

result of additional choices being made within a network of interlocking options that language, seen as a network of relations, makes available.

Closer analysis, particularly of the languages of literate societies, reveals the elaboration of two basic forms of semiosis that inhere in these semiotic practices. Halliday calls them the congruent forms of semiosis, the grammar of everyday life action and experience, which emphasize function, process, and flow, and the synoptic forms of semiosis, which emphasize stasis, structure, and "thinginess." Over time, the latter increasingly came to dominate in public and written language, thereby gradually reconstruing life from the primacy of doing and happening to a reality as object. In other words, the world is now experienced in metaphorical terms – as Halliday puts it, as a text – as a consequence of which dramatically different knowledge potentialities are created (1993).

The new genre studies recognize this by placing the notion of genre in the context of recurrent social situations (Berkenkotter and Huckin [1995]; Christie [1999]; Freedman and Medway [1994a, 1994b]; Halliday and Martin [1993]; Huckin [1995]; Hyon [1996]; Martin [1985, 1999]; C. B. Miller [1984]). Seen in this fashion, genres are the result of typified rhetorical action, which, in their totality, embody an aspect of cultural rationality. Genres arise as a result of particular conditions of speech and a particular function (scientific, technical, commentarial, business, everyday). They thus constitute "certain relatively stable thematic, compositional, and stylistic types of utterance" (Bakhtin [1986a, p. 64]). However, while Bakhtin's observations were largely conceptual, systemic-functional linguistics can draw on a powerful semantic analysis of the grammar of English, particularly with regard to the analysis of contexts of situation in terms of registers or genres. This analysis is based on the dimensions of "field" (the social activity that is taking place which often determines what we commonly refer to as its content), "tenor" (the relationship between the participants, including their roles and statuses), and "mode" (the part that language is playing in the situation, including the channel).

Within that framework, a number of broad concerns for AL2 can readily be addressed: first and foremost, the inherent cultural embeddedness of language use; second, the well-known tension in human language between centrifugal forces, which reflect the specificity of individual consciousnesses, and centripetal forces, whose shared center instantiates the possibility of communication within a cultural-linguistic community in the first place; and third, the well-known fact that, for very advanced learners, much like for native speakers, the ability to be full participants in the discourses of the L2 culture is a matter of practical command of the generic forms used in the given spheres, which both specify *what* can be meant in certain contexts and *how* it can be meant. As Bakhtin comments, observed shortcomings are "not a matter of an impoverished vocabulary or of style, taken abstractly: this is entirely a matter of the inability to command a repertoire of genres of social conversation, the lack of a sufficient supply of those ideas about the whole of the utterance that help to cast one's speech quickly and naturally in certain compositional and stylistic forms" (1986a, p. 80).

Finally, a particular advantage of genre studies that as yet remains unexplored for L2 learning in the USA[11] is its ready connection to concerns of literacy. As explicated for US L1 educational contexts by J. P. Gee (1986, 1990, 1998) and placed into larger societal issues by the New London Group (1996), literacy studies make a distinction that accords well with the two Hallidayan foundational types of semiosis. For example, in answer to the question, "What is literacy?" (1998), Gee distinguishes between "primary discourses" of familiarity that all of us acquire largely unconsciously in the process of socialization into our culture and social contexts and "secondary discourses" that "involve social institutions beyond the family . . . no matter how much they also involve the family" (p. 56). The ability to control such discourses is developed, often quite explicitly, "in association with and by having access to and practice with" what he calls the secondary institutions of schools, workplaces, stores, government offices, businesses, and churches (ibid.).

Together, this twofold discourse capability becomes the foundation of Gee's definition of literacy, the "control of secondary uses of language (i.e., uses of language in secondary discourses)" (ibid.). Its importance in an educational context that is largely dominated by essayist prose texts is heightened even more when one considers that in such texts

the important relationships to be signaled are those between sentence and sentence, not those between speakers nor those between sentence and speaker . . . A significant aspect of essayist prose style is the fictionalization of both the audience and the author. The reader of an essayist text is not an ordinary human being, but an idealization, a rational mind formed by the rational body of knowledge of which the essay is a part. By the same token the author is a fiction, since the process of writing and editing essayist texts leads to an effacement of individual and idiosyncratic identity. (Gee [1986, p. 736])

It is not difficult to see that the heavy emphasis in communicative language teaching on interaction and on oral language amounts to an extraordinary privileging of discourses of familiarity. By comparison, the desired secondary discourses of public life, particularly the discourses of the professions, the academy, and civil society, are largely disregarded. In so doing FLED runs the risk of seriously misrepresenting a key ability on the part of AL2 users, namely to make appropriate choices between two major forms of semiosis in an elaborated array of genres where the public genres often favor stasis-oriented over

---

[11] As Hyon indicates, within the Australian context this approach has been used primarily for L1 education, but also for adult English as a Second Language (ESL) education. I am also aware of some pre-collegiate uses for L2 pedagogy.

process-oriented thinking. Additionally, they are characterized by highly elaborated means of organizing the text itself at all its levels, in terms of theme and rheme, or givenness and new information, so as to assure efficient and effective communication with others who, more often than not, do not share one's own interpretive, and, that is, "textual," assumptions about the world (Halliday [2000]).

By contrast with this genre approach to AL2 abilities, much has been made of the AL2 learner's insufficient command of specialized vocabulary. However, in one of the most specialized environments, the natural sciences, Bazerman (1988) identifies the experimental report as one of the most remarkable *literary* accomplishments which, through its particular genre formation, was able to facilitate immense control over the material world in which we reside. At the lexicogrammatical level, Halliday and Martin (1993) single out the unique shift from verbal to nominal structures, what they refer to as "grammatical metaphor," as one of the key facilitators of our ability to see the world in a fashion that allows us to hold, measure, and experiment with it, as we remove it from the messiness of the singularity of any process in time and space and make it an object and thereby "objective." It is this shift in semiosis, a cognitive-linguistic phenomenon, rather than the acquisition of specialized vocabulary, that poses the most serious problems for competent command of scientific literacy.

Cognitive fluency, identity, and voice: the ability to make choices

To conclude this exploration of a new profile for AL2 learners I return once more to their ability to make situated meaning-making choices, best captured by Halliday's systemic theory of language as "a theory of meaning as choice, by which a language . . . is interpreted as networks of interlocking options: 'either this, or that, or the other,' 'either more like the one or more like the other,' and so on" (1985, p. xiv). AL2 users do just that: they make numerous interlocking choices regarding the topical focus and how that extends over longer discursive stretches in terms of certain genre requirements (the "field"), in the interpretation of and communicative significance of social relationships that are played out between the real or imagined communicative partners (the "tenor"), and, of course, on the lexicogrammatical plane. Altogether they are learning to deal with typified social action through and with language in response to recurring social contexts, a point that is well captured by the concept of genre which both facilitates and constrains communicative choice and thereby enables creative freedoms and the possibility for valid meaning-making (Freedman [1999]).

In particular, a message can be "either about doing, or about thinking or about being; if it is about doing, this is either plain action or action on something; if acting on something it is either creating or dealing with something already created" (Halliday [1985, p. xiv]). These choices are meaning-driven and occur within conventions of use that have high probabilistic values but which, nevertheless, show flexibility and variation. Only within this framed flexibility can individual voice and identity occur and be gained – not by being creative in a sociolinguistically non-recognizable fashion. In fact, access to the conversational forum, acceptance of one's contributions to it, and the ability to use the forum for one's interests and with one's own voice depend on a sufficiently elaborated knowledge of conventions of use in the first place. In this fashion, identity, through membership in a discourse community, and individual place and voice are acquired, differentially played out under different circumstances for different purposes, and maintained.

We can, however, also associate notions of choice with fluency, as Fillmore (1979) does when he lists various "fluencies" that pertain to choices at different levels of meaning-making, e.g., control of processes for creating new expressions; knowledge of the cognitive or semantic "schemata" for which the language has provided linguistic encodings, that is, of certain preferred knowledge schemata; knowledge of the various interactional schemata for conversations, including indirect forms of communication; knowledge of different discourse schemata, particularly the story; and knowledge of the appropriateness of certain registers and styles within certain social contexts. All these aspects are central to the kind of fluency we associate with AL2 use (Riggenbach [2000]).

There is yet another aspect to choice and fluency, highlighted by Pawley and Syder's (1983) seminal article, an early precursor to the current interest in phraseology or formulaic language, both as efficient processing and as instruments that mark culturally salient phenomena (e.g., Cowie [1998]; Gläser [1998]; Howarth [1998a, 1998b]; Pawley and Syder [2000]; Teliya *et al.* [1998]; Weinert [1995]). As they argue convincingly, a key puzzle for linguistic theory and for the learner is the dilemma between nativelike selection and nativelike fluency. The phenomenon to be explained is that many sequences that would be perfectly accurate from the standpoint of rule generalization are simply not among the preferred choices of a user community – "we don't say it that way" – which poses the challenge that learners need to learn much more than how to construct grammatically well-formed sentences. Crucially, they require access to an extended stock of lexicalized sentences and semi-lexicalized sequences as the community has developed them, as well as a refined awareness of the status of "rules," a continuum from fully productive rules of sentence formation and rules of low productivity. In other words, from the standpoint of processing, the L2 learner requires two types of processing capabilities, first, analytic and rule-governed approaches that guide online processing and help to enhance accuracy and, perhaps, push complexity, and, second, memory- and instance-based processing of a significant repertoire of language chunks that enhance temporal fluency (Skehan [1998]).

We thus arrive at this important descriptor of the AL2 user: (1) someone who is able to draw on a sizable repertoire of fixed or chunked language forms that will ensure the sociocultural appropriateness and acceptability of utterances while, simultaneously, enhancing their fluency, and (2) someone who also has a good command, including a significant level of metalinguistic awareness, of the meaning–form relationships that are encoded with various degrees of fixity and fluidity at the lexicogrammatical level, thereby giving the impression of fluent but also thought-ful, online, situated creation of meaning-ful language. Using Segalowitz's terms, such a speaker would be distinguished by both cognitive fluency which "refers to the efficiency of the operation of the cognitive mechanisms underlying performance" and performance fluency, "the observable speed, fluency, and accuracy" (2000, p. 202).

Principles for teaching at the Advanced level

From the previous discussion, I highlight four aspects for a pedagogy for AL2 learning: a cognitive focus on the learner; explicit genre-based teaching; modeling, coaching, and scaffolding; and task-based pedagogies. Though treatment of each of these areas inherently involves a critique of current practice, my greater interest is in how we might amend our thinking and our practices.

A cognitive learner focus

Since concepts and cognition are central to language use, we must find ways of engaging the learner cognitively. Beyond learner background, interests, and goals, the cognitive focus I intend arises from careful consideration of features of AL2 language use and ways of facilitating it for the learners. For example, assuming that professional-level use in a spoken environment is a goal, then extensive reading is called for, followed by carefully targeted speaking tasks that are based on a sophisticated awareness of genre and that elicit text-based understanding and interpretation of the text, thereby simultaneously enhancing content and language acquisition.[12]

Such genre-based, cognitively engaging language instruction requires us to confront a number of problematic assumptions about the AL2 learner, among them fossilization and the notion of limited processing capacity. Fossilization generally refers to "being stuck," as it were, in various areas of language form; rarely do we use the term to acknowledge that, not infrequently, we are also dealing with "fossilized" abilities with regard to meaning-making. In both senses of the word, however, we might be reaping what we sowed earlier on. Though we should proceed in this fashion from the beginning, at the very latest at the AL2 level we must engage learners cognitively-linguistically so they may

---

[12] See the report on an upper-level class focus on discourse and genre taught by Crane, in Byrnes, Crane, and Sprang (2002, forthcoming).

understand language and L2 learning as meaning-making through thought-ful choices through and with typified formal features. While such pedagogies would seem to address only macro aspects of L2 learning, my experience has been that a culture of attentiveness and thoughtfulness transfers as well into micro-level aspects of accuracy, including form-monitoring at the inflectional level, the concerns lists and memorization tend to address.

An approach of thoughtful choices would also require us to reconsider a second widespread assumption, that of learners' limited processing capacity, frequently interpreted as an either-or focus on meaning or form. Of course, human memory is limited. However, at the AL2 level there would be little further progress unless learners were, under carefully crafted pedagogical conditions, capable of attending simultaneously to both meaning *and* form in ways that differ qualitatively and quantitatively from earlier levels of ability. An instructional approach that is predicated on thinking for speaking explores and nurtures that possibility by creating pedagogies that foster awareness of intricate meaning–form relationships at various levels, from genre, to register, to the paragraph and lexicogrammatical level, arrayed on a gradient of cognitive processing rather than on formal difficulty. What Bernhardt and Kamil (1995) indicate for reading even at the lower levels, namely that we must get beyond conventional either-or understandings of a Linguistic Threshold Hypothesis alongside a Linguistic Interdependence Hypothesis, applies with particular force at the advanced level and in all modalities.

Explicit teaching

Reflection on AL2 learning should also enable us to overcome another unfortunate byproduct both of our programmatic emphasis on the initial stages of L2 learning and of the dictums of unsubstantiated "natural" methodologies. I am referring to the remarkable abdication of responsibility for devising explicit pedagogical interventions for AL2 learning. Held up against the constant foil of "naturalness" and "naturalistic acquisition," the scope of what classrooms can accomplish has, over time, seriously eroded. However, as Kubler (this volume) argues convincingly, we are coming to realize that, while an in-country experience leads to greater temporal fluency and a higher level of comfort, it does not in and of itself facilitate the qualitative shift in language use that AL2 abilities require.

Indeed, judging from the experience in L1 education that devotes years to enabling native-speaker learners to acquire a number of critical public genres in the L1 (e.g., writing a report, producing a summary, presenting a proposal), one should expect particularly thoughtful interventions to be required in the L2 context. A genre approach, in both oral and written genres, that includes such trajectories as "from private to public, from concrete to abstract, from sequential or descriptive to analytical and evaluative," using a range of topical areas, shows much promise. It uses to greatest advantage what the classroom can do particularly well, perhaps does exclusively, while offering what learners at this level need (for examples see Freedman and Medway [1994a, 1994b], and Jones *et al.* [1989]; also Christie [1989, 1999]; Martin [1985]). As noted, those "desired needs" are at a stratum between cognition and a *specific language*, therefore are generalizable only up to a certain point. For that reason, extensive engagement with, not merely comprehension-oriented exposure to, texts is crucial. When these texts are arranged in thematic units, they are particularly suited for facilitating the acquisition both of register- and genre-appropriate textual organization and also of the characteristic lexicogrammatical collocations of a particular genre and topical area.

A pedagogy of modeling, coaching, scaffolding

In line with the complex relationship between rule-governed and memory-based processing and the overwhelmingly context-dependent nature of language use, modeling becomes a particularly desirable pedagogical stance. To begin with, the fallback position of explaining language use according to rules is often not available because many of the phenomena that require refinement have not been appropriately analyzed in most languages.[13] Where they have, they tend to suggest fixed norms when contextualized choice is at play. Second, if learners are to be able to make good choices, they need to learn to make them in terms of goals and outcomes in contexts and with tasks that closely resemble the actual contexts of use *from the cognitive standpoint.* Thus, Collins, Brown, and Newman (1989) propose the concept of "cognitive apprenticeship" which is "aimed primarily at teaching the processes that experts use to handle complex tasks" (p. 457). By focusing on learning-through-guided-experience, that approach permits an externalization of processes that would otherwise remain internal and covert. It aims at reflection on the difference between expert and less expert task performance, on discussion and assessment of task performance, and on increasing the complexity of tasks as a consequence of greater cognitive and metacognitive abilities that come about through the alternation of roles between teachers and learners. All of these features foster attention, awareness, and internalization of cognitive processes, and success that itself bolsters motivation.[14] Again, modeling that creates high levels of saliency and, therefore, high levels of attention, can also help address flawed formal L2 use

---

[13] See, however, the functional grammars of English by Givón (1993) and by Martin (1992), and the new three-volume German grammar, also with a functional orientation, by Zifonun *et al.* (1997), all indicating the gradual shift, at least in theoretical circles, toward such forms of language analysis.

[14] See Sprang's contribution regarding the acquisition of complex lexicogrammatical features in Byrnes, Crane, and Sprang (2002, forthcoming), which uses careful modeling and scaffolding techniques.

at the local level of morphology and syntax for which we have otherwise pre-scribed rote learning. Most important, the classroom is no longer described as deficitary inasmuch as it does not emulate or replicate the "real world"; instead, it is a very real world of its own, with very real opportunities for enhancing learning, particularly AL2 learning.

A task-based pedagogy

My final pedagogical recommendation pertains to the notion of task, particularly the division into authentic and pedagogical task and the three characteristics of task difficulty, task complexity, and conditions of task performance as affecting language use and language development.[15]

The concept of pedagogical task was posited primarily as a way to bridge between the real world and the classroom by determining how instruction would prepare students to deal with that real world (see particularly Long [1998]). Typically, this propaedeutic function of pedagogical tasks was handled through identifying subcomponents of the full task and devising instructional contexts that would stage them in a fashion that held meaning and task accomplishment as central.[16] By comparison, the notion of task is likely to have greatest merit for AL2 learning in a more holistic sense, such that instruction would continually and richly endow the L2 classroom with the reality of "imagined textual worlds," the kind of cultural knowledge that characterizes adult literate members of the L2 society. In that case, the tasks performed by AL2 learners would hardly differ, in terms of cognitive-linguistic engagement, from those required in the L1 environment, where proposals are written for a business venture, presentations ending in question-and-answer periods are given at conferences, briefings about complex issues are prepared for superiors, and summaries of arguments, pro and con, are written for public debates.

Beyond the cultural situatedness, what the classroom lacks, of course, is urgency and motivation for the same level of personal investment. However, my experience is that very advanced learners are extraordinarily open to "imaginatively rehearsing" all of these "performances," precisely because they know them to be complex *and* necessary in the "real world." To the extent that such affective and intellectual engagement is, indeed, a critical component for the acquisition of public L2 literacies, the classroom setting can "become" a corporate training center where such abilities are practiced, or an office where key presentations are carefully planned and vetted with colleagues, or important documents are talked through, drafted, and critiqued.

---

[15] A good overview of issues can be obtained from Crookes (1986), and Crookes and Gass (1993), Doughty and Williams (1998), Long (1998), Robinson (2001), and Skehan (1998). The most recent book-length treatment is Bygate, Skehan, and Swain (2001).

[16] For an interesting extension of the notion of "task" into project-based teaching, see Turnbull (1999).

Thus, using "authentic tasks" is really only part of the story: the fuller story requires awareness of the kind of "imagined world" AL2 use requires and how to build that up with exquisite pedagogical finesse so that learners can take on, to the greatest extent possible, the roles, rights, and responsibilities they would have in these matters in the discourse community that otherwise performs such tasks in the real world. This is so since the genre-based language use we want to foster and facilitate – we have referred to that in terms of "field," "tenor," and "mode" – critically depends on such situated discursive authenticity. The horizon of instruction must be toward creating and upholding the virtual reality of those tasks, a project that is likely to be the more successful the more "context" can be created over an extended instructional period. After all, these role relationships and intertextualities require time to take on a life of their own so as to affect language use. The result: a virtual discourse community in the classroom.

While the above observations referred to task at the macro level, task also functions at the micro-level of psycholinguistic processing, through the concepts of task difficulty, task complexity, and the impact of task performance conditions (see especially Robinson [2001]; and Skehan [1998]).[17] In particular, (1) the notion of inherent task complexity and the identification of factors contributing to complexity addresses what are essentially cognitive burdens (e.g., familiar vs. unfamiliar; here and now vs. remote; concrete vs. abstract; simple retrieval vs. transformation); (2) the notion of task difficulty refers to individual learner factors, such as aptitude, confidence, motivation, and also proficiency level; and (3) task conditions affect the perceived difficulty during the performance of a task (e.g., time pressure, modality, language use, support, surprise, control, and stakes). As Robinson (2001) has found, "the complexity of tasks does exert a considerable influence on learner production . . . [which argues that] sequencing of tasks on the basis of their cognitive complexity is to be preferred over sequencing decisions based on task difficulty or task conditions" (p. 51). In turn, aspects of task difficulty and task performance can inform pedagogical decision-making in a particular classroom setting with its specific goals, specific learners, and specific considerations of the instructional sequence. For instance, is it the pedagogical intention that learners should reach toward new L2 capabilities or are they to shore up fragile existing ones by carefully refocusing their attention to fluency, accuracy, or complexity of language? In the end, as Skehan notes:

This perspective implies that in addition to having principles for the selection and implementation of individual tasks, sequences of tasks should also be examined for the cumulative impact that they will have. In this way, knowledge about task properties and implementation alternatives can ensure that the flow of tasks and their use is not going to make it more likely that unbalanced development will occur. (1998, p. 50)

---

[17] I have addressed these matters for their implications for curriculum and instruction in Byrnes (2000a).

In Skehan's words, the emphasis has to be that of "bridging the gap between ongoing performance and sustained development" since it is by no means clear whether "introducing focus on form *at a time* will have a beneficial impact on interlanguage development *over time*" (p. 293, emphasis in original).

Summarizing these issues, Skehan (p. 129) lists five principles for task-based instruction which would enhance the desired dual processing capacity: (1) choose a range of target structures; (2) choose tasks which recognize that some forms have a particularly high usefulness for expressing certain meanings; (3) select and sequence tasks to achieve balanced language development between accuracy, fluency, and complexity with their different processing requirements; (4) maximize the chances of focus on form through attentional manipulation; and (5) use cycles of accountability that reflect back on what was accomplished with certain pedagogical tasks. The explicit goal is *balanced development* in terms of accuracy, fluency, and complexity of L2 use.

Concluding reflections

Let me close with three points that place my interest in AL2 abilities into a larger context.

First, what is at stake can only be captured by a new and affirming stance toward language learning and teaching. However, the issue is not a simple-minded "we also contribute to students' intellectual formation," a stance that reveals a distressing scholarly insecurity and victim mentality. Instead, at stake is the possibility of a kind of "thoughtfulness," by both the learners and their teachers. Halliday points to the symbiotic relationship between meaning/knowledge and language as a social phenomenon. Slobin characterizes language processing itself as thinking for speaking. Noteworthy as well is the expanding discussion on the dialogic nature of meaning-making, a notion well explored by Bakhtin (1986b) and expanded to an understanding of texts as "thinking devices" or as generators of meaning (Lotman [1988]), to education (Wertsch [1990]), and to all aspects of moral life and public discourse (Taylor [1991]).

In the realm of L2 instruction, my concern with thoughtfulness turned to literacy and genre studies, focusing on goals and pedagogies. In terms of goals, this has been well explicated in the L1 context by the New London Group (1996). What needs to be added, given our multicultural *and* global environments, is the possibility for linking L1 and L2 in mutually enriching ways, in terms of multiple literacies, elevating to the socio-political environment what Cook (1992, 1999) argued on the individual level. At the level of pedagogy beyond the genre-based pedagogies that apply to L1 and L2 language learning, particularly insightful observations come from Readings (1996) who in his much-discussed analysis of "the university in ruins" devotes much attention to the need for a thought-ful pedagogy. Here we might wish to think of teaching and learning as "sites of *obligation*, as loci of *ethical practices* . . . Teaching thus becomes answerable to *the question of justice*, rather than to the criteria for truth . . . Teaching should cease to be about merely the transmission of information and the emancipation of the autonomous subject, and instead should become a site of obligation that exceeds the individuals' consciousness of justice" (p. 154).

Second, and expanding on the previous thoughts of dialogic inquiry, AL2 instruction must explore aspects of collaboration and joint construction. While collaboration is often thought of only as a flattening out of hierarchy, perhaps a more interesting interpretation of collaboration in the teaching context is that of "cognitive mentorship" alongside the already existing term "cognitive apprenticeship." It is an interpretation that would give real meaning to Vygotsky's notion of the Zone of Proximal Development which, unlike its frequent interpretation in terms of Krashen's comprehensible input, an intrapersonal and inaccessible phenomenon, is foundationally an interpersonal phenomenon and therefore to be performed overtly.

Finally, I am concerned with advanced language learning because it addresses the relationship of knowledge and language in terms of meaning-making in the life-world. In that project, it has much affinity with the interests of philosophical hermeneutics, as these have been most prominently explicated by Husserl, Gadamer, and Heidegger. In this day and age, AL2 must be of concern to FLED since advanced second language ability and literacy are, to a significant extent, based on the highly specific literacy of the natural sciences, with all the consequences that entails (Byrnes [2001a]; Halliday and Martin [1993]). We must come to understand the situated and interested provenance of that language use. More generally, we need to consider these matters for their larger societal implications, particularly for theory construction, but also in the context of the life-world as individuals understand it to make meaning of their lives and for the cultural praxis of societies (Heelan [1998]; Heelan and Schulkin [1998]). As Gadamer suggests, we might be able to address some of the greatest shortcomings of the modern proclivity for universal objectification of everything, including understanding language as a subjective tool for understanding, if we were to consider the possibility that "beings in the world" are disclosed by language, that there is a "'language of things,' which wants to be heard in the way in which things bring themselves to expression in language" (1976, p. 81). We might then be able to come to real self-understanding, which would include an understanding of the position of knowledge and the role of language in culture and human history.

Part II

Programs

3 Contexts for advanced foreign language learning: A report on an immersion institute

Heidi Byrnes

Among the many consequences of the communicative turn in foreign language education (FLED) we must count the demand for high levels of teachers' second language (L2) abilities where instruction is characterized by interactive communication and extensive engagement with authentic texts in all modalities, rather than by the conveyance of rule-governed formal knowledge. Although professional-level L2 performance had been a tacit and firm assumption, that confidence received a serious blow when, in conjunction with the Proficiency Movement, many states encountered acute licencing and recertification difficulties because teachers were not assessed at the mandated level, usually "Advanced" according to the ACTFL Guidelines. Higher education, too, has encountered this gap between desired L2 abilities for its faculty and reality, though it relegates these matters to the privacy, if not to say, secrecy, of the hiring process rather than to official assessment (Koike and Liskin-Gasparro [1999]). Taken together, the uncomfortable admission of insufficient competence of L2 instructors at all educational levels with its obvious implications for classrooms and the field as a whole, not to mention the deep disappointment and, at times, anger of the teachers and faculty candidates themselves, have led professional organizations to make the issue a priority in future planning.

For obvious reasons, graduate foreign language departments play a pivotal role in crafting solutions due to their educational interests and their responsibilities toward their non-native graduate students. Yet few devote explicit attention to developing such solutions, despite long-standing calls for incorporating aspects of advanced second language (AL2) learning into graduate education (e.g., James [1989]; Swaffar [1991]). Typically such efforts are thwarted by the privileged content demands as graduate programs prepare their students to become competent researchers and scholars, as well as by the pervasive belief, despite overwhelming counter-evidence, that academic L2 abilities should somehow have been acquired by students in their undergraduate studies.

Gradually, however, at the margins of FLED, creative action is being taken. This chapter reports on one such delimited, though, I believe, instructive, program, an eight-day immersion institute for very advanced graduate students of German who had been selected from a national applicant pool. Occurring during the summer of 1998,[1] the event itself was an explicit response to reports of worrisome German language abilities of non-native graduate students and possible actions the American Association of Teachers of German (AATG) might take (Byrnes [1996]). It reflects as well the context of efforts in my home department, the German Department at Georgetown University, to revamp its entire undergraduate program into an integrated content-oriented and task-based educational environment that explicitly targets upper levels of ability as its program goal. Over its three-year implementational phase, this project, entitled "Developing Multiple Literacies," yielded increasingly higher levels of awareness in faculty and graduate students not only about the nature of AL2 abilities, but also about pedagogical needs that must be met and opportunities that can be pursued in order to foster students' L2 learning to academic levels of performance.[2]

In Chapter 2 of this volume I began to lay out ways in which both of these areas might be addressed, in terms of a necessary reconsideration of foundational assumptions about AL2 abilities and about the advanced learners themselves and in terms of directions for expanding suitable pedagogies. In particular, I suggested and discussed four areas for enlarging available pedagogical options: (1) a genre and discourse orientation that cognitively engages learners through pedagogical interventions that continually draw attention to links between meaning and form at all levels of language use; (2) an explicit commitment to teaching the AL2 learner the features of major genres that characterize discourse in various public and professional environments, as contrasted with those that are prevalent in private familiar, interactive language use; (3) a pedagogy of modeling, coaching, and scaffolding that recommends itself for the macro generic aspects of AL2 language use that learners must acquire and also for diverse sentence-level phenomena, particularly an extensive repertoire of collocations at the lexicogrammatical level and fine-tuning of morphological and syntactic competence; and (4) a task-based pedagogy that situates task in two ways, into the larger context of the entire L2 class as an imagined textual community that can then motivate the culturally grounded language use that AL2 must target, and a pedagogical approach that is refined by awareness

---

[1] The institute took place from May 26 to June 2, 1998, on the campus of Georgetown University and was funded by the German Academic Exchange Service (DAAD) for a total of twelve students. It was the first and thus far the only time that this German government organization which otherwise focuses on faculty exchanges and graduate-level research funded an event that explicitly targeted the enhancement of upper-level academic German-language abilities of non-native speakers. Subsequently, the opportunity for repeating or expanding this pilot event encountered familiar resource cutbacks and questions of agency purview between the DAAD and the Goethe Institut which, traditionally, has addressed language learning, though, to my knowledge, never at this level of use.

[2] The entire three-year project is extensively documented on the Department's website, www.georgetown.edu/departments/german/curriculum/curriculum.html. It has been referred to in a number of publications, particularly Byrnes (2000a and 2001b), and Byrnes and Kord (2001).

of the consequences of task complexity, task difficulty, and task performance conditions.

To the extent that this chapter transfers those general considerations into the reality of a program and, even more, into the reality of the classroom, it constitutes a companion piece to that earlier chapter. In reverse, I address only those aspects of the institute that bear directly on the concerns of this volume, specifically the institute's overall goals, its application process and selection criteria inasmuch as they specify the situation of a particular AL2 learner group, its syllabus and instructional approaches as designed to respond to the learners' acquisitional profiles, and a selection of comments from participants that took the place of formal evaluation of their language abilities. Beyond the specifics of this discussion, however, I hope that readers will discern issues about AL2 learning that are broadly generalizable and perhaps also find solutions that respond to conditions in their own educational environments.

General goals

The institute explicitly targeted upper levels of language ability with a focus on the kind of language use that characterizes the academy from the standpoint of content and tasks. In other words, it assumed that the students, non-native students in graduate programs across the country, already possessed high German abilities in interactive spoken communication, most typically acquired during an undergraduate study-abroad period or, at times, through study at a German-speaking university during their graduate work. At the same time, it assumed that this broad general knowledge base had not been rigorously expanded into competent and comfortable use of the complex features of academic literacy in German, required for in-depth work with academic texts in reading, writing, and speaking, using a range of media. As a result, two general goals shaped the institute: first, the content goal of targeting those features in a range of textual genres and, second, the learner goal of increasing the participants' awareness of themselves as highly competent AL2 users of German who, nevertheless, must and, most important, can enhance their language use in certain strategic areas, both level-specific and highly individual. It is the latter goal that was extensively negotiated in the institute, between me as the sole instructor and the students and, in various configurations, among the students themselves. In the first part of this chapter I attribute this to the fact that the event was the students' first occasion for experiencing explicit instruction at this level. I attribute it as well to the short duration and intensity of the institute which inherently highlighted these issues, as compared with potentially less perceptible changes in performance related to language content. However, as excerpts from the extensive feedback in the appended material indicate, it is difficult to separate the two. To some extent, it is also unproductive to do so because the acquisition of AL2 language use demands intense affective and cognitive engagement on the part of learners.

Application process and selection criteria

The nature of the institute as one funded by the German Academic Exchange Service (DAAD), an organization sponsored by the German Government and known for its prestige graduate fellowships, the institute's demanding goals, and its time constraints required a complex and well-considered application and selection process. Specifically, the institute targeted L2 abilities that were already quite high but not so high as to exclude attaining tangible content and affective goals even within the short eight days of instruction. In a way, selection from among the applicant pool was a process of creating a workable lower and upper boundary that determined the institute's twelve participants, a nearly ideal group size both for the students and for me as the sole instructor. Thus, while the applicant pool itself flexibly defined the specifics of the participants' language abilities, the application and language assessment process had to be well conceptualized, rigorous, and well executed. Careful conceptualization was required due to the broad academic literacy goals the institute had set for itself right from the beginning, even as a range of performances within AL2 was a distinct likelihood. Rigor was essential because the targeted performance characteristics occur naturally only in highly specific task environments, and good execution was necessary because the applicants' language performance data had to be created in the context of each student's institution without compromising comparability.

In short, my goal in devising the application and assessment process was twofold: (1) to permit me to get an elaborated sense of the applicants' abilities as a basis for subsequent detailed planning of the institute in its content areas, pedagogical emphases, tasks, and instructional approaches; and (2) to form a group that would be able to work together coherently and supportively despite significant individual performance differences, while assuring that each participant would benefit maximally in the specific areas that were most in need of targeted attention.

Although those goals rendered the application/assessment process complex and made considerable demands on the students and also on me, all participants agreed that this approach contributed substantively to the success of the institute. I state this since these accomplished and competent graduate students, quite surprisingly, saw the requirement to read complex texts and to speak about them in a manner appropriate for a public event in front of a video camera as unusual in and of itself and also as a formidable challenge cognitively, linguistically, and performatively. There is no doubt that both the commitment of about 2 hours and 15 minutes to the actual assessment/application process, not counting making the necessary institutional arrangements with the advisor, facing the video camera, and accomplishing all tasks within the specified time limitations, and following instructions that I had carefully crafted for each task, discouraged some students from applying. However, despite initial bafflement, even misgivings, at the unusualness of this procedure (which revealed the fragility of students' comfort level with professional-level L2 use), all students agreed that this process contributed to the creation of the highly committed and motivated group of institute participants.

The application process targeted the following language abilities: (1) reading comprehension of a complex text, (2) writing a summary of the text, (3) formal academic speaking on the basis of that text in response to questions that I had provided, (4) a free-flowing personal narrative which gave information about their history of learning German, and (5) the actual letter of application for the institute.

For the textual basis that informed the first three tasks, I chose an article from *Die Zeit*, a highly respected German weekly, that dealt with the issue of how societies go about defining human death as they establish criteria for organ harvesting and transplanting. The choice reflected my assumption that none of the students regularly dealt with this topic in German, thereby assuring roughly even background knowledge conditions; at the same time, the topic is generally familiar nowadays. The text itself was unusually well structured, allowing and challenging students to use their awareness of rhetorical organization of a deliberative text that attempts to arrive at a carefully weighed public policy and the discourse markers that structure such genres. Thus, competent, analytical reading abilities could compensate for any content and language shortcomings and time limitations that applicants might encounter.

This integrated text-based approach gave me a sense of the range and depth – in terms of accuracy, fluency, and complexity – of the applicants' language abilities in reading, speaking, and writing. It enabled me not only to get an elaborated sense of students' abilities, particularly in the discourses of public life, but also to make my selection of institute participants with comparable evidence in tasks that are quite close to those that one encounters in "the real world." Having watched all video tapes, read all written materials, and taken extensive notes on student strengths and weaknesses, both for the whole group and for individuals, I selected the twelve participants, a relatively coherent, though diverse, group. My field notes also provided material for individual consultation with students at the very beginning of the institute. This was to assure that they could use the entire duration of the institute to work on those "problem" areas that I had identified from their performance profile.

Syllabus and instructional approach

It is impossible to detail the wealth of syllabus and instructional materials I prepared for the institute. The following information thus can be no more than an exemplar of the instructional approach I suggested in Chapter 2.

Topic selection

After soliciting topic proposals from the applicants, I chose the theme of higher education reform in Germany for its timeliness, inherent interest to American graduate students, wide range of textual materials, and deep cultural significance in the past and into the foreseeable future of the European, indeed global, context. It sparked lively discussion far beyond the texts themselves and a constant comparison between the students' individual situation and this country's decisions regarding higher education and those they detected in the German context.

Sequencing instructional events

The syllabus had a number of "slopes":

- from guided, highly specific text analysis of relatively short texts to extensive independent reading of longer texts;
- from public texts as the educated public reads them in *Die Zeit* to discipline-specific discussion, including preposterously dense language use in an official Goethe Institute document;
- from interviews and personal opinions to public political pronouncements such as the speeches by the former President of the Federal Republic, Roman Herzog;
- from whole-group work in class to small-group work outside of class on which students would subsequently report;
- from global comprehension to very detailed work with discourse organization, discourse markers, and semantic fields;
- from modeling a range of learner strategies for different tasks in different language modalities (e.g., reading, speaking, writing) to applying them independently;
- from a self-reflective individual focus on accuracy and complexity of language use to relatively unmonitored and spontaneous performance in lively debates where fluency, conversational management, and shifting identities and participant structures (e.g., holding the floor, overlapping, acknowledging others' contributions, on-the-spot shaping of intentions, role playing, appropriate dialogic listener behaviors) made high demands on student performance;
- from reading to increased writing and speaking;
- from careful analysis of one's own language use and learning styles and strategies (e.g., in the daily reflective learner journals) to assessment of group performance and progress.

Creating pedagogical tasks

In all tasks, the dimensions of accuracy, fluency, and complexity were handled flexibly under different task conditions, oral or written, planned or unplanned, with or without background knowledge, familiar or unfamiliar language material. This approach assured that every student could be directly engaged, could locate herself/himself at the highest possible level that met their global and specific expectations and goals for the institute and for a given task, and could constantly be challenged for a best performance, even while the overall atmosphere was non-threatening, supportive, congenial, and a lot of fun.

Establishing learner centeredness at the AL2 level

In a real sense, no one can "teach" such advanced learners and, in any case, it would be utter folly to assume that a one-week institute could have an easily discernible impact on performing in German when these students had been at this task for the better part of their lives – unless one condition were to be fulfilled: they must be able to understand pervasive characteristics of the advanced learner – strengths and weaknesses, learn to understand their own learner profile within such a conceptual framework, and start to develop approaches which they can subsequently enhance, continue to apply in different contexts, and observe in their language use under different task conditions. In this fashion, they can build a new foundation for themselves as developing users of the language, like any intelligent native speaker who has high demands for exacting language use would do. As their own comments in the institute evaluations indicate, this indeed was possible. For me, that is the most critical aspect – in fact, the central justification – for conducting such an institute in the United States and recommending similar events in the future.

As stated, commitment, motivation, and engagement on the students' part were critical qualities given the intensity and demanding level of the institute, not the least of its expectations being a voluntary language pledge of using nothing but German twenty-four hours a day for its duration, without exception. As it turned out, the participants themselves were very rigorous about upholding this promise, and all of them commented upon it as being an affirming cognitive experience as well as an affectively exhilarating experience that contributed invaluably to their sense of personal worth, accomplishment, and success.[3] Obviously, the institute could thereby explicitly span an enormous range of discursive practices, from the interpersonal, interactive language required when previous strangers find themselves working together intensely for a limited time, to the quotidian requirements of exchanging news and views in passing days, to complex issues as they arose during instruction. In this fashion, the institute was able to compensate in favorable ways for the fact that it was conducted not in a German-speaking cultural context but in the United States: it fashioned conditions that study abroad does not generally create precisely because it was

---

[3] An anecdote highlights this confluence of responses: as the group was sitting on the lawn one evening, some German visitors to the campus overheard their animated debating, in German, of an issue that had arisen in class, and approached them to determine what had brought them from Germany to study at Georgetown University!

able to integrate the range of performances that can occur within academic life, thereby nurturing the participants' ability to make sophisticated choices with regard to genres, registers, and personal styles (for details, see the discussion in Chapter 2).

Addressing this issue from the opposite perspective, I am unaware of any program in Germany that targets this level of language performance by learners of German and the specific needs of academic work at American graduate institutions. None of the summer courses at German universities do so, nor do the Goethe Institute offerings, if for no other reason than that they need to serve a range of participants who have very different learning goals, not solely academic interests. Also, when students attend German university courses they cannot expect to receive explicit instruction at this complex level of L2 literacy: this is neither the job nor the area of expertise of German professors, the subject-matter specialists in history or political science or even German literature. Thus, non-native speakers in a study-abroad context are often left to their own devices. Worse yet, they often feel patronized, frustrated, and offended at the same time, for they repeatedly receive comments for their excellent command of German, particularly for an American! A serious motivational and career-decision problem arises when those who are the ultimate gatekeepers in the profession in the USA judge them otherwise. Deep down, these students know that, unless highly competent professional support and personal effort is expended on this issue, they will never attain the high goals which they have set for themselves as part of their career aspirations.

Student comments

As with the instructional materials, it is impossible to present the richness of students' work and activities during the week. Nor is it easy to convey a sense of the camaraderie that developed among them, from the tentativeness of the first dinner to a farewell party on the next-to-last evening, to long evenings of conversations about their lot as graduate students and their future career plans inside or outside the academy, to a very provocative visit to the Holocaust Museum on Sunday, their only day off. However, to give a flavor of what was accomplished I include excerpts from responses to selected questions from the end-of-course questionnaire.[4] Of particular interest are the responses to question 7, "Name at least three things that you have learned that will help you strategically to improve and increase your command of German *in the future*," and to question 8, "In what areas of your use of German did the institute make a difference? Please be as explicit as possible about this change and how it came about." They can be found, along with some suggestions for improvement that address instructional issues, in the appendix of this chapter. Here, I provide only a brief summary.

---

[4] Extensive data were collected, both from the application process and throughout the institute. These await analysis.

With regard to question 7, students repeatedly remarked on their enhanced ability to work with texts, by relating general text organizational features to semantic and knowledge structures and to language form, where language form was increasingly understood as being located at the intersection of vocabulary and grammar, what systemic-functional linguistics terms the lexicogrammar. They also came to appreciate the multiplicity of processing strategies that would most enable them to emulate AL2 use: strategic use of chunked language, such as prefabricated sentence stems or entire phrases or metaphors, and also strategic generalization of "rules" of language that were now, increasingly, pragmatic/semantic rules that operate at the discourse level. In both challenges, they came to read texts considerably more carefully at many levels, all of which amounted to using texts as models for a diversity of language-learning interests. Finally, they clearly recognized that attention, awareness, and "thoughtfulness" on their part would be imperative if they were to progress further, a step that would ask them, once more, to leave the hard-earned comforts of an already high level of language ability in order to attain the added ability to choose judiciously and competently and to use various forms of semiosis in accordance with their intended meanings. Since all of them were either already engaged in language teaching themselves or anticipated being so engaged in the future, that level of reflection also led to new insights regarding their potential roles and responsibilities as instructors, irrespective of the educational level.

With regard to question 8, the differences they saw in themselves as learners, the responses often reflected a much higher level of confidence in dealing with complex German materials, a result that was particularly gratifying given the institute's short duration. In line with their heavy engagement with texts, they were beginning to see themselves as users of the language at the discourse level, rather than continuing their preoccupation with local morphosyntax, their presumed most serious and most obvious shortcoming. At the same time, that focus on discourse in no way made them oblivious to the continued need to address these language-specific features. On the contrary, it seemed to empower them to tackle these "nuisance" issues with a greater resolve and sense of being able to conquer them. Not surprisingly, reading comfort was considerably higher at the end. Here, too, the hoped-for nexus to speaking in accordance with public language-use requirements did, in fact, occur, enabling them to get a sense of voice, identity, and newfound joy in their tremendous abilities in German that was extraordinarily gratifying to them as learners and to me as their teacher–mentor.

Concluding programmatic considerations

Although the idea of conducting an immersion institute for non-native speakers in the home country rather than in the target-language environment initially seemed an undesirable oddity, there is good reason to consider it an appropriate and highly beneficial way of addressing the vexing problem of supporting the acquisition of very advanced L2 abilities. Of course, doing the same thing might bring about even better results if one were in-country. However, far from being a "natural" event, such a programmatic realization would have to be elaborately staged in the L2 cultural environment as well. In any case, it would be considerably more expensive and more demanding of time, always an important consideration with inherently cost-conscious American graduate students, many of whom are married and need to work over the summer.

Notwithstanding my positive assessment of what transpired in only eight short days, different programming formats should be considered, most especially an extension of the institute to two weeks, although probably not longer. This would enable the following desirable adjustments and consequences:

- staffing the institute with one additional instructor, an obviously highly desirable change which, however, would have to be accompanied by exquisite coordination between both faculty members so as to retain the beneficial integration of all aspects of the institute;
- reduction of the unusually heavy schedule, in terms of hours and intensity, which brought some participants close to cognitive overload and paralyzing exhaustion;
- creation of tasks for small-group work that could be carried forward over several stages and iterations, including self-generated strategies for task realization;
- multiple collaborative opportunities with participants who often have very different performance profiles, learning strategies and styles, and, hence, abilities to support the other participants in their learning efforts;
- opportunities for solidifying a performance feature that students were just beginning to understand and incorporate into their language use, generally in terms of accuracy and fluency;
- inclusion of a much greater variety of audiovisual materials, something that was not possible under the time constraints;
- independent research arising from the theme-based tasks;
- guided writing within a task orientation (with multiple drafts, peer editing and reviewing, revisions), increasing in length and with instructor feedback;
- more opportunities for extended, peer-critiqued, individual formal presentations in front of the class, inherently a time-consuming venture;
- reflection on and discussion of the pedagogies applied in the institute, in order to permit the participants to incorporate them into their own teaching at their home institutions and in their future careers in the academy;
- more individual consultation, involving specific diagnosis and progress reports over the course of the institute; and
- explicit incorporation of opportunities available in Washington for very high-level language use due to the presence of numerous agencies, offices, and businesses that require such abilities and language use.

From an instructor's perspective and with the benefit of some distance from the institute, perhaps my most important insight is this: the demand for instructional contexts that can foster further development of very advanced L2 abilities can be accommodated with remarkably few external requirements, perhaps a consequence of the negligible support we currently offer to such learners, but more likely the result of their extraordinary commitment to and their potential for attaining such levels of L2 ability when they have the opportunity to work within a conceptual and pedagogical framework that reflects an elaborated understanding of the nature of the relationship between language, culture, and knowledge as it is realized in elaborated forms of L2 literacy.

APPENDIX EXCERPTS FROM STUDENT EVALUATIONS OF THE ADVANCED LANGUAGE INSTITUTE FOR GRADUATE STUDENTS, GEORGETOWN UNIVERSITY, WASHINGTON, DC, MAY 26–JUNE 2, 1998

(All answers in sequence for each respondent; no spelling or punctuation corrections made.)

7. NAME AT LEAST THREE THINGS THAT YOU HAVE LEARNED THAT WILL HELP YOU STRATEGICALLY TO IMPROVE AND INCREASE YOUR COMMAND OF GERMAN *IN THE FUTURE*

I improved leaps and bounds this week. I have a plan for myself to learn a lot more of these semantic markers by heart and to practice them with German friends. I feel more self confident about my language skills, while I also see how far I have to go. My potential progress is clearer to me, as well as the limitations. I felt like this week was an excellent check-in and an excellent grounding experience. So much of graduate school is a kind of mild chicanery, in that it is simply assumed that we are completely fluent in this foreign language. Of course, that's never true. It was nice to be in a place where that was accepted and where we could work to get closer to that lofty goal.

1. Searching for discourse and semantic markers in order to break down a text into larger categories of meaning.
2. Combining reading and writing exercises in order to expand the comprehension of a text.
3. Using discourse markers in order to be able to speak more persuasively about a text

useful reading strategies, vocabulary-building strategies, and the need to SPEAK SLOWLY.

1. How to read for information (i.e. picking out the basic meaning of the text and not relying on minor details and anecdotes of the texts.)
2. Seeing and appreciating the workmanship in journalistic (or any for that matter) writing
3. Looking at authentic texts to model after instead of "reinventing the wheel"
4. Breaking beyond Just communicating and really trying to push my language to a new level

5. I've known this for a while, but I needed to be reminded of it again:] Every little thing I learn is one more step toward reaching my goal of fluency in German. It sounds hokey, but it's true.

1. Identifying rhetorical forms in a text. Reading strategically for understanding and not for detail.
2. The combination of rhetorical clusters and creativity in the use of new vocabulary.
3. The creation of a text matrix as a tool for text comprehension and acquiring new vocabulary. . . also as a help in the oral presentation of a text.

1. I learned how to use discourse markers and semantic fields to write and speak in German at a high level. These markers can and will really serve as *markers* in that they provide anchors when one is writing and, especially, speaking about difficult topics. I often become lost when speaking German at a high level and using such markers offers structure and control to speech.
2. I will be able to use the skimming and reading strategies in order to really understand difficult texts.
3. My vocabulary has increased because the practical exercises we used having moved many words from my passive to my active *Wortschatz* The ability to speak only German with my fellow students has also increased my vocabulary of colloquialisms and common expressions.

1. I've learned how to read more carefully by looking for clues (discourse markers) within the text that clarify what is happening not only conceptually, but also structurally.
2. Although my writing is still terrible, I now have some useful lists of words and phrases that will not only help me to write more effectively, but also more creatively.
3. I now know some specific weakness that exist in my spoken German that I can concentrate on repairing. The same lists of words/phrases that are useful for writing are also useful here. I've also developed some ideas of possible solutions for my writing and speaking problems.

1. Besseres Einsehen der Textstruktur
2. Erlernen des neuen Wortschatzes
3. Anschaffen der neuen Kenntnisse imbereich des deutschen Bildungssystems

1. Using discourse markers
2. Strategies for making sense of academic writing
3. Knowledge of the learning process, knowing how to recognize problems, work on solutions

I've learned that I can increase my German proficiency in ways that go far beyond a neo-grammarian approach. There are constant opportunities within the speaking, reading and writing required of me in this field to improve my German.

It will not happen by osmosis. Instead I must push myself to adopt vocabulary, expressions and constructions that I am normally in the habit of shying away from. I could study abroad, but without a starting point to begin systematic improvement of my German, any gains I would make overseas are going to inefficient. If I choose to study abroad now, I feel like I would be much more efficient and motivated to actively use the exposure to push my German to a more sophisticated level.

I feel encouraged to do that right now at home. Being with 12 other American graduate students in an American setting and speaking an enormous amount of very (for us at least) sophisticated German made me realize how much more I could be doing this back at my university.

I can not afford to remove myself from difficult, abstract discourse. I have to jump into the fray, so to speak, and constantly push to express myself without the use of anglicisms. Only then can I learn to speak about something rather than around something. That sounds like a platitude I might have gotten from the institute, but it's not – I have to confess I made that up myself.

How to go about "getting to the bottom" of a text – strategies in reading, writing and oral report preparation; new vocabulary – new means of expressing myself on a "higher" level

Reading strategies
professional vocabulary
how to write precis
how to overcome fears or at least keep trying to do so

8. IN WHAT AREAS OF YOUR USE OF GERMAN DID THE INSTITUTE MAKE A DIFFERENCE? PLEASE BE AS EXPLICIT AS POSSIBLE ABOUT THIS CHANGE AND HOW IT CAME ABOUT

Better able to speak on the academic level. Better able to write a precis. Better able to read newspaper articles on complicated topics. More self confident about speaking German in an academic setting among peers and mentors.

1. Willingness and ability to use German with other colleagues in the profession, both in relation to professional topics and general social situations. This came about through an anxiety-free setting and willingness of all the participants to engage in German about a variety of topics.
2. Confidence and willingness to engage more confidently and more in-depth with contemporary German material, e.g. newspapers, in order to gain a deeper understanding of cultural issues affecting German society today. Instead of reading for general understanding on a superficial linguistic level, the intense practice with complex texts, the practice with discourse markers, and the animated interest in the issues of the texts that was evident in the course inspires me to engage more complexly with the language and the issues of contemporary Germany.
3. A somewhat changed attitude towards the acquisition of new linguistic skills, i.e. moving away from semantic and sentence level approach to a larger, discourse and culture-based approach to understanding textual meaning and producing meaningful writing in German.

In all areas, but the most significant improvement was in my speaking ability, and the most useful thing I learned to do with regard to speaking was to speak more slowly and carefully. I also left the program a more careful reader, and I feel that I am likely to gain more from reading in the future thanks to the reading strategies and practice gained at the institute. I can see more clearly now how to improve my German through everyday reading, speaking and writing, and I understand better where these three areas intersect and how they can work together.

I feel I have become slightly more efficient in reading and writing. As mentioned before, I can spend a long time doing both, especially in German. Working under time limits, I believe, forced me to reach this efficiency. Furthermore, I found my speaking and writing is much conciser.

I'm sure my spoken German has improved, though I'm not personally aware of it. I would like to add that I don't think comparing the two videos is necessarily a fair indication of improvement in speaking, at least in my own case. Sorry to harp on this one (it came up in conversations, as well as in my learner-journal!), but I really believe the format of the first video created such an uncomfortable atmosphere that this was undoubtedly reflected in the spoken output.

But back to the positive things: Most important, the institute gave me the motivation to work toward enhancing my German. Though I have to admit I wasn't excited the entire week long, I now really am looking forward to seeing through with my own personal goals toward fluency (i.e. reading German books for pleasure, reading more newspapers, keeping in better touch with German-speaking pen pals, etc.) I realized again, as I hoped I would, that language is so much fun and such an important part of my own life and identity.

1) In the discussion or reading strategies, I was given a new approach to German texts, texts in general. I am now able to more effectively draw what is necessary from a text for my purposes.
2) I have learned to "fish" for expressions to enhance my written and oral expression in articles. My vocabulary has also been substantially extended
3) With the new understanding that I have attained of language learning in the advanced learner, i will now know where to concentrate my efforts to grow in my knowledge of the language and attempt not to sabotage myself with excessive self criticism

In reading, I have learned new strategies for understanding the structure and content of advanced texts. Additionally, the use of text matrices and the precis have taught me new ways of writing about difficult topics in an organized and structured manner. In speaking, the broadening of my vocabulary through intense instruction and conversation is clearly important.

This institute most directly helped my speaking and reading abilities by providing me with strategies about HOW one should read texts and then use those texts themselves to speak about them (to provide vocabulary, a context, a framework for discussion). We were forced to read carefully while searching for specific items within the text. I could feel myself automatically registering certain discourse markers as the week continued, a phenomenon reinforced by our restriction to one topic. No one had previously taught me how to strategically read and speak about a text and at this institute, I was provided tools to help with this problem.

Ich habe beschlossen, an diesem Semonar teilzunehmen, weil ich seit langem die Notwendigkeit spuehre, mein Deutsch auf ein anstaendiges Niveau bringen zu muessen, genauer gesagt, dorthin, wo es war, aber wegen des Fehlens der Uebung – nicht mehr.

Im Laufe des Kurses glaube ich einen grossen Schritt auf dem Weg zur Verbesserung meiner Sprache gemacht zu haben.

Es hat mir sehr geholfen, dass wir verschiedene Texte lesen und ihrer Struktur und dem Inhalt nach analysiere mussten. Besonders wurde es bemerkbar, als wir den Test am letzten Tag des Seminars belegen mussten, Ich habe sehr deutlich gespuert, das ich den Text, der mir auch vor ein paar Monaten angeboten wurde, anders gelesen und eingeschaetzt habe, und hoffentlich, richtiger analysiert. Das war mein Haupterfolg im Seminar.

I learned to communicate more effectively by becoming more comfortable with more complicated, formal structures of German. The stress on elegance and efficiency in communication helped me make more sense of texts that I might normally have been intimidated by and I learned to use many of the structures that I had previously only seen in print. To a large extent, this came through playing with the language and trying these structures on, so to speak, both in in-class discussion and assignments as well as in the constant German usage among the participants.

Specifically I think I've improved my use of the dative and genitive cases. Since one has to use these more in sophisticated, educated German, I also had to practice it more and use prepositions I normally wouldn't use.
– I am less hesitant to use or create compound nouns.
– I have a greater interest in hearing and using idiomatic expressions.
– I think before translating an English expression directly into German.
– I concentrate more on developing a larger base of synonyms.
– I try to construct sentences with more clauses, especially in my writing. This could be taken to an unwelcome extreme, but it's another way to practice the complexities of expressing several ideas at once in a foreign language
– I think more about the appropriate prefixes when using verbs.
– I speak slower, even if it kills me and the person listening. I'd rather say what I want to say in sophisticated German than give up and resort to not expressing myself fully in simpler German I am more comfortable with.

I would say that the institute made the most difference in my method of reading a text. Before the institute, I would have lost myself in all of the "little" details of the text, whereas now I understand where I need to place my focus. Having command of this skill has also helped me to write more quickly and concisely about complicated texts, something that will definitely help me in my studies in the future.

My writing skills have improved and my vocabulary has increased. The reason for this lies in reading of many texts and wonderful discussions about them.

SUMMATIVE ROLE PLAYS

- A lot of fun. We should have done a bit more of this.
- Very entertaining, an excellent synthesis of content and discourse strategies.
- Great fun! Preparation for this activity was a useful homework assignment, since it forced us to learn the language and opinions of our roles regarding a subject which (by this time) we knew quite well.
- I think the cassettes speak for themselves. We all had a great time performing the skits and taking on a new identity. In short, it was fun and forced us to reach out to new vocabulary that maybe our own personas wouldn't necessarily use in everyday situations. More of these in different formats would be good for future years.

- A rewarding and productive activity! I found the timing of it – half-way through the seminar – to be helpful as well. This activity allowed us and our teacher to see how much progress we had made in such a short time, if we had acquired new strategies, and if we were using these strategies in our oral expression.
- For me these were extremely important because I was able to use the discourse markers and semantic fields in a practical manner and because I was able to speak at a relatively high level of discourse without reading from a text.
- This is an activity that for me was the most enjoyable. I was worried about understanding my role, but once I was up in front of the class with my group, I relaxed and just had fun with it. Not only did I have to "teach" the others my position on the issues, but I had to pay attention and be taught by the others. What made this activity so effective is that it was fun and everyone really went all out in a humorful, yet knowledgable, way.
- Am meisten Spass gemacht, es war so gut wie der Hoehepunkt des Seminars
- Great cumulative, summing-up activity – and a lot of fun!
- Great fun. This exercise accomplished much of what the oral presentations did, but with an added benefit. Since we were able to take on another persona and adopt their argumentation, that left us with more time and energy to play with the language and adopt new expressions and vocab. Because it was also an interactive group setting there was less self-consciousness or pressure, thereby decreasing anxiety.
- This was a very creative way to pull together what we had learned and to have a lot of fun and laughs in the process.
- It was both fun and a big exam for me. I think, that I passed, at least for myself. During these role plays, we could use almost all the aspects of the foreign language use that we were talking about. It was a very good opportunity to use all the expressions and so on.

4 Bridging the gap between language for general purposes and language for work: An intensive Superior-level language/skill course for teachers, translators, and interpreters

Claudia Angelelli and Christian Degueldre

A person decides to become a language learner for a variety of reasons: to be able to read the literature of a given language in its original form, to travel and discover other cultures, to obtain a better understanding of the world, to meet people and be able to understand them, to increase business opportunities, to exchange ideas with colleagues and friends, to communicate better across language barriers. For most people, the goal is to be able to communicate. Others put their language knowledge at the center of their profession and become language teachers, translators, interpreters, or members of the diplomatic corps of their country.

The courses described here[1] were developed by the authors and taught at the Monterey Institute of International Studies from 1994 through 2000, following a 1993 pilot course in French. Since even Superior-level language learners encounter difficulties in using their language in a professional environment, the Spanish and French Summer Intensive Bridge courses were conceived with the goal of developing the proficiency needed to work professionally in the fields of teaching, translation, and interpreting. This goal differentiates them from Advanced-level summer courses for language enhancement (e.g., summer courses in Spanish universities for English-speaking teachers of Spanish).

The initial objectives were to bring students who had been accepted into the two-year Master's program to the proficiency level necessary to perform in the Translation and Interpreting (T&I) MA program and to offer professionals in the T&I fields the opportunity to enhance their foreign language abilities. Although many incoming students had lived in a country where their foreign

The authors thank William Hopkins and Catherine Ingold for their comments on an earlier version of this chapter. Their remarks served to inform the revision; any discrepancies that remain are our own.

[1] At some points in this chapter, features of the Spanish program are described, at other times features of the French program. Both programs contain all the features described for each of them. The various features are not described twice for lack of space.

language was spoken before they applied for admission to the T&I program, they had since had limited opportunity to maintain the foreign language at the same degree of proficiency achieved there. The goal, then, was to restore students' previous proficiency, improve lexical and structural precision and knowledge of the linguistic system, and develop the ability to perform at a Superior or Distinguished (SD) proficiency level even when under pressure.

However, from the very beginning, the possibility of a different course orientation became evident. To respond to students' desire to develop their language professionally, be it to teach, interpret, or translate, the courses evolved rapidly to include practical work on techniques and abilities that characterize the professional use of a language. The linguistic components were retained and complemented by others more pertinent to the T&I field. In this sense, the Bridge courses emphasized not only the skills needed to translate or interpret but also such other skills as analysis, active listening, reformulation of ideas – all within a monolingual environment. In this way, the Bridge course evolved to have a twofold goal for students: increased foreign language proficiency and acquisition of professional T&I tools. These goals can be replicated in diverse settings, wherever languages are used professionally at the SD level. Thus, the terms *translators* and *interpreters* used in this chapter can easily be replaced by *language professionals*, *language teachers*, *diplomats*, *foreign language lawyers*, and the like.

The students

The Bridge courses were simultaneously conceived as Superior-level language courses and as introductory courses in the skills of translation and interpreting. These goals were established to meet the needs of a very specific student body that planned to apply the results of language study to the demanding T&I professions. The skills, themselves, however, once acquired, provided students with the basis for working in any number of language-based professions.

Profile of Bridge students

Over time, the student body expanded beyond its original scope to include teachers, already-employed translators, and other professionals.

The participants were probably among the very best in their language class at the college level. Some were proficient in as many as four languages. Most had studied languages for many years, beginning in junior high school. Some were heritage speakers.[2] One common feature was that all students realized

---

[2] The term *heritage speakers* (HS) refers to speakers who have been exposed to the target language in the home and have not necessarily studied it or used it in an academic setting

that they needed more work on language *per se* to be able to use their language professionally.

The students had diverse backgrounds. Most of the students in the French and Spanish classes were English-speaking Americans. Some also came from other countries, among them Kuwait, Spain, Ghana, Kenya, Canada (French students), and Mexico and Cuba (Spanish students).

Students' learning experiences also varied. Students in the French and Spanish classes had usually learned their foreign language through textbooks and such traditional methods as grammar–translation or the Audio-Lingual Method (ALM). These students were accustomed to a teacher-centered learning environment where grammar occupied center stage. Others combined formal "traditional" studies with heritage traditions. Not all students were college language majors. Some were biology or physics majors with a minor or keen interest in languages. As a group, they were eager to learn and demanding in their expectations of teacher competence, preparation, and individualization. Both of these characteristics are in keeping with the student traits reported by the other authors in this volume. All of these elements contributed to the creation of an optimum learning environment.

Language needs

Students interested in becoming translators and interpreters usually enrolled in the Bridge course at the behest of the school's administration. During the admission process, all students take an Early Diagnostic Test (EDT)[3] to determine whether their level of foreign language proficiency is sufficient for T&I studies. The requirement for admission is an "acceptable level" of language proficiency and language control (consistent lexical precision and structural accuracy). Currently, determination of what constitutes this level is made by the professor assessing the EDT.[4]

Bridge-course students had often achieved language proficiency beyond the Advanced level. They had a solid command of grammar of the foreign language. They also had well-developed comprehension skills and a good understanding of the culture; they could take part in general conversations. In other words, their

(Valdés and Geoffrion-Vinci [1998]). Sometimes HS need to further develop the formal register that is acquired through academic studies and which they will need for professional work.

[3] The EDT consists of five parts for students with one foreign language: a 150-word translation from English to the foreign language; a 150-word translation from the foreign language to English; a 300-word essay in English; a 300-word essay in the foreign language; and an abstract in English of a 2-page English text. In 1998, an oral component was added for admission to the MA program.

[4] Although a foreign language testing expert assisted with test design and guidelines for test administration and scoring, the decision whether or not a given student needed to be recommended for the Bridge program was made by professional interpreters/translators (not Oral Proficiency Interview [OPI] certified foreign language testers) who applied their own judgment and experience in assessing test outcomes.

strategic, discourse, and sociolinguistic competence was high. However, they experienced difficulty in using the foreign language in, for example, a political or scientific discussion, when they had to be highly accurate and grammatically correct, and when nuances matter. When that happened, they felt their level of proficiency was not sufficient, and, indeed, their level of linguistic proficiency (as measured by lexical precision and grammatical sophistication) was not yet well enough developed to handle Distinguished-level tasks. (At the beginning of the Bridge course, many students frequently commented that they "used to be better" and were "losing their language.") They were, in fact, realizing the difference between language for general purposes, for which an Advanced level of proficiency is sufficient and language for professional purposes, for which a Superior (and often, in the case of T&I, even a Distinguished) level of proficiency is required. Put another way, they were moving from proficiency, or potential for real-life application, to performance, or actual job use (Child, Clifford, and Lowe [1993]), and that is precisely the "bridge" that the courses described here provided for them.

Skills

Students in the Bridge course acquired professional skills in a monolingual (immersion) mode. In this way, they enhanced their general foreign language proficiency as they worked on T&I skills.

Although few studies have been conducted on what specific skills are needed for T&I (Gerver [1976]; Gile [1995]), most professional translators and interpreters, as well as teachers in T&I programs, agree that the following skills are essential: linguistic competence (including accuracy); sensitivity to register; broad general knowledge; cultural competence (including cultural sensitivity and the ability to be a "cultural bridge"); analytical skills (e.g., active listening and the understanding of cause and effect relationships, subordination of ideas, and anticipation of what comes next in the discourse); quickness (or the mental agility to hear a message and instantly re-express it in the other language); memory (as a complement to note-taking, as well as for recall of terminology learned in preparation); an ability to abstract meaning from words (including reading between the lines and being able to handle culturally complex and idiosyncratically composed texts, which Child [1987, 1998] calls "Projective Mode"[5]); an ability to conceptualize (to create a mental representation of the ideas and concepts of the original message); public speaking and writing skills (translators often become *de facto* writers and co-authors); superior presentation;

---

[5] Child (1987, 1990, 1998) presents a text typology constructed from four levels, increasing in difficulty from Novice/Intermediate through Distinguished levels of complexity: orientational (texts that are bound to the external, concrete environment), instructive (texts that transmit factual information), evaluative (texts that respond to actual or perceived reality), and projective (texts that exemplify some unique aspect of the originator's thought).

and flexibility (a form of quickness characteristic of "adaptive performers" – those who display the "ability to adjust behaviors, focus concentration, and thrive in non-optimal work situations" [personal communication, Renée Meyer, March 28, 2001]).[6] Other skills might be added to the list. Interpreters and translators must have a natural curiosity, as well as the desire to communicate and to help people. Since interpreters and translators spend immense amounts of time accomplishing terminological research and preparation, they must have an inquisitive mind (Finlay [1971]). They must strive for perfection (and at the same time deal with the frustration of knowing they cannot reach it).

Affective variables

Like Dabars and Kagan (this volume), Bridge-course instructors noticed the presence of affective filters. Personality factors that get diluted in a regular course can become crucial elements in an intensive course, with its accompanying stress. Therefore, teachers worked to lower these filters by creating a positive atmosphere and a teaching approach of coaching and facilitating.

The program

History

The first Bridge course (French) started in 1993 as a pilot.[7] It had five students who wanted to become translators and/or interpreters. That course was highly successful, and a decision was made to expand the program to applicants in other languages. Spanish was added in 1994, later English and, on an *ad hoc* basis, Russian and Japanese. Table 4.1 shows the attendance of Bridge courses from their origin to 2000. As the reader will notice, the English course was the one with the largest student population, combining mainly Chinese, Japanese, and Korean students. French and Spanish enrollments remained stable during this

---

[6] The Department of Defense (DoD) has developed an eight-dimensional model for the High-End Language Analyst (skills, performance, knowledge): linguist, cultural expert, target expert, modern researcher, interpretive analyst, performance expert, master teacher, and adaptive performer (personal communication, Renée Meyer, March 28, 2001).

[7] It should be noted that some faculty felt that students should arrive with Level-4 skills. In some other cases, faculty felt that SD-level proficiency cannot be taught. This latter assumption finds a parallel in the experiences reported by other authors in this volume, in their case the implicit assumption that foreign language cannot be taught at the SD level but must come only from studying and living abroad. As mentioned in Chapter 1, the preponderance of Russian programs over those in commonly taught languages at the SD level reflects this belief; Spanish, French, and German programs could rely on Advanced students going abroad and returning at the Superior level whereas Russia was closed to Americans during the Cold War so that the higher levels of proficiency by necessity had to be developed in the classroom. Thus, Russian teachers were less likely to believe that high levels of language could not be taught in the classroom.

Table 4.1

Language	2000	1999	1998	1997	1996	1995	1994	1993
French	9	8	10	5	5	7	11	5
Spanish	8	7	8	8	8	8	5	-
English	29	26	26	24	26	17	14	-
Russian	-	-	2	-	1	-	-	-
Japanese	-	4	-	2	-	-	-	-

Statistics provided by the Registrar of Academic Records from the Monterey Institute of International Studies.

period. The Russian and Japanese programs did not share this fortune; enrollments were lower and not as stable in those programs.

The term *Bridge* was chosen because the course bridges a gap between language for general communication and language for professional applications (Angelelli [1996]). When students choose to work with a language, either by teaching, translating, or interpreting, proficiency, especially accuracy, at the SD level becomes critical. For this reason, the teaching approach to language at this level differs significantly from the one used for language instruction at lower proficiency levels, where the emphasis is more on the ability to communicate. At the Superior level, when a language is used for the purpose of translating, teaching, or interpreting, the expectation is almost "error-free" performance.

Administrative details

The Bridge courses were intensive in nature. Students attended 22.5 hours of classroom instruction each week. For each hour of classroom instruction, they were assigned 1–2 hours of homework. Upon successful completion of this course, at the undergraduate level they received four credits that were transferable to an MA degree and at the graduate level four credits that could be applied to the language requirements if they later changed their major to a different MA degree program.

Faculty

One of the difficulties faced in implementing the Bridge course was locating qualified pedagogues who would also understand the specific needs of using a language for a profession; extensive experience in T&I was essential, as well. Languages other than French and Spanish faced even greater difficulties finding instructors with those qualifications and, many times, the best solution was to put together a team to teach the course.

This approach worked. When asked what they considered the most valuable aspect of the Bridge course, students commonly replied that it was "the professors . . . they are professionals in the field and know just what aspects of our language skills we need to focus on."[8] The selection of appropriate faculty was, indeed, essential to the implementation of the type of program described here: student-centered coaching aimed at developing the skills, knowledge, and abilities to use the language in a professional environment.

Curriculum

The Bridge-course curriculum was established in two phases. Phase One was a needs assessment that determined the curricular objectives and course design. Phase Two was the actual implementation of the Bridge courses, which evolved over time.

Curricular objectives

Results of the needs assessment revealed shared requirements as well as differences between Spanish and French. In this sense, the approach to developing the Bridge courses differed from that of the regular courses in T&I, where all languages follow the same curriculum regardless of language-unique features. Table 4.2 illustrates some shared objectives.

Each language professor segmented the core curriculum into different units. The number and content of units varied by language. The common element was course duration: eight weeks at 22.5 hours a week for a total of 180 hours of instruction.

Implementation of the Bridge courses

Initial testing for Spanish
During the first five years, this course was optional for incoming T&I students.[9] During this time, there was a Spanish test in place to assure that the applicants to the Spanish Bridge course had the right linguistic level (Superior) to benefit from it, although an occasional Advanced-level applicant was admitted. Applicants to the Bridge course were tested orally and in writing. A telephonic ACTFL (American Council on the Teaching of Foreign Languages) OPI constituted the

---

[8] Hilary James, Bridge course – Spanish 2000.

[9] In 1998, the Bridge course became mandatory for candidates accepted to the MA program, with ultimate enrollment in the T&I program contingent upon successful completion of the summer Bridge course.

Table 4.2

Areas	Objectives	
Linguistic	(1)	Perform comparative analysis of similarities and differences between F/S and English grammar systems.
	(2)	Achieve vocabulary enhancement (field-specific).
Sociolinguistic	(1)	Gain exposure to different accents and language varieties used in the regions where F/S is spoken.
	(2)	Raise awareness in switching oral and written discourse from a formal to an informal register and vice versa.
Psycholinguistic	(1)	Understand the concept of multitasking and split attention.
	(2)	Gain information-processing skills in a monolingual mode.
Time management	(1)	Learn how to prioritize among tasks.
	(2)	Develop organizational skills to meet tight deadlines and to perform under pressure.
Information processing	(1)	Distinguish between main idea and subordinate ideas.
	(2)	Understand connections between ideas.
Research	(1)	Understand how to do terminology searches.
	(2)	Become familiar with monolingual sources in F/S.

oral test. The written test consisted of reading comprehension, vocabulary, and grammar sections. The reading comprehension section used general/scientific readings that paralleled in difficulty those used in the first two weeks of the course. The vocabulary section required applicants to define terms in their own words and to give synonyms and antonyms. The grammar section asked applicants to choose between options for ten items and justify their choice. For example, one item asked if the position of the adjective was correct and if so why:

Número 8:
  a) Las hermosas playas de Venezuela atraen a muchos turistas. (The beautiful beaches of Venezuela attract many visitors.)
  b) Las playas hermosas de Venezuela atraen a muchos turistas. (The beautiful beaches of Venezuela attract many visitors.)

Understanding the position of adjectives in Spanish discriminates between Intermediate High/Advanced and Superior students. At lower proficiency levels, it is common for students of Spanish to assume that adjectives are placed only after the noun. In item 8, both positions are correct, but they have different meanings. Item 8a states that all beaches in Venezuela are beautiful. Item 8b, by positioning the adjective behind the noun, indicates that not all beaches are beautiful. Some are, and some are not. Once the tests and EDT were passed, students were admitted to the course. Then the 180-hour journey began.

Spanish course syllabus
The Spanish course consisted of eight units: seven topical units and an introductory one. Unit themes included (1) Linguistic and Information-Processing Skills, (2) Science, (3) Technology, (4) Economics, (5) Politics, (6) Law, and (7) Translation/Interpreting/Teaching. The time assigned for each unit was approximately 22 hours, although they varied in content and degree of complexity. The only exception was Unit One.

Spanish Bridge-course materials
The Spanish Bridge course was taught with current authentic materials. A reader, a grammar reference manual, and two books (a play and a novel) were the mandatory texts for the course.

The reader contained articles from newspapers, journals, scientific magazines, book chapters, etc., illustrating each of the topical units. A large collection of videos and audiotapes was made available through the media center where students could check out audio materials with accompanying listening-comprehension exercises or watch videos in preparation for class discussion. Students were asked to locate the official web pages of various organizations (e.g., OEA: Organización de Estados Americanos) and electronic documents from various Spanish-speaking countries. These web pages and electronic documents served a dual purpose: they provided the content for the topical units (e.g., political speeches, organization by-laws), and they served as authentic discourse input for language in the sciences, law, politics, and other specific content areas. Materials were classified thematically, and students extracted specialized terms from them, on the basis of which they compiled glossaries, indicating country and register. For example, in a political text, the term *paro* in Spain refers to *unemployment*, whereas in Argentina it means *strike*. In their glossaries, students showed both meanings and indicated the country of use.

The grammar reference manual problematized grammatical concepts that are generally reduced to simple rules at the beginning/intermediate stages of students' acquisition of Spanish. For example, students were asked to read the reference manual's description of the use of the subjunctive mood. Then they were exposed to appearances of the subjunctive in authentic discourse (e.g., newspaper articles, speeches) and were encouraged to explore the similarities and differences between rules and usage.

A play and a novel were used to generate class discussions. The genre was chosen for affective reasons. Most students in American colleges are exposed to literary genre when they study a foreign language. So, using literature in the Bridge courses provided students with a sense of familiarity and security. The goal here, though, was not to perform literary analysis. Rather, the readings provided a basis for generating discussions and practicing discourse devices such as presenting and supporting an opinion, organizing an argument in linguoculturally appropriate ways, persuading, capitulating, and other elements of discourse competence expected at the SD level.

The play, *La barca sin pescador* ("A Boat without a Fisherman"), by Alejandro Casona, was the less demanding literary selection in terms of language. Since the play is based on universals of good and evil, most students were already familiar with the ideas and vocabulary, and it was easy for them to engage in class discussions. The play is divided into three acts, and it was used during the first three weeks of class.

The novel selected was *El amor en tiempos de cólera* (*Love in the Time of Cholera*) by Gabriel García Márquez. Even if college students have read works by Márquez, they are generally more familiar with *Cien años de Soledad* (*100 Years of Solitude*). *El amor en tiempos de cólera* is rarely read in Spanish in undergraduate programs. Once again, the focus with this material was not literary analysis but summarizing, expressing opinion, contextualizing, and comparing.

In addition to these books, students chose another two that they presented to the class individually. During these presentations, students worked on individual presentational objectives as they became experts on the chosen titles that they presented to their peers.

Representative Bridge-course activities

Every activity in the French and Spanish Bridge courses integrated a variety of abilities: reading, research, preparation, presentation, and the like. For example, the fourth week of the program in 2000 was dedicated to Science and Technology. This theme is obviously very broad and cannot be covered in just a few days (or 22.5 contact hours). The goal was to expose students to a more sophisticated terminology and more difficult concepts, for which they needed to do more research and read more reference/parallel documents. Topics included pollution and the protection of the environment, fish of the Amazon River, a car commercial with technical specifications, and energy-saving policies, among others.

During the "Science" week, students concentrated on scientific topics. For example, six to seven contact hours were devoted to the topic of marine biology and marine mammals (a topic that is particularly pertinent in Monterey, which boasts the country's largest aquarium). The students learned more about ocean life by listening to a tape, preparing and making a presentation, reading additional articles, preparing glossaries, and debating the pros and cons of a certain issue. For example, the interest in protecting marine mammals vs. the interests of the fishing industry is an emotionally charged issue in the Monterey Bay area and served as an excellent issue for debate.

The instructor also used less structured activities, such as crossword puzzles, to reinforce the acquisition of marine and marine-associated terminology. The lesson plan for marine biology can be found at Appendix A. The marine biology lesson contained three comprehensive activities (see Appendix A for specifics). These included a set of tasks associated with a videotape on Californian mammals, a field trip to the Monterey Bay Aquarium, and a report on the field trip.

The first activity required students to listen to a videotape on mammals in the California area. In the case of the French program, this was a 20-minute documentary from the Belgian National Television Network. The documentary describes the life of whales and marine mammals along the coast of California. The objective for students was to focus on technical terminology – in this case, the names of sea creatures and mammals. The speed of the video is natural speed, about 110 words per minute. There are naturally occurring pauses and, of course, the visual aids that accompany any video presentation. An anticipated difficulty was the use of new terminology and regional accents. Before students listened to the documentary, they completed a series of previewing activities. Some of these activities were typical listening-comprehension exercises, e.g., brainstorming probable content. Other activities were specifically geared to active listening for T&I, including the activation of relevant terminology. Following the previewing activities, students received a list of questions that they answered while watching the documentary. The questions followed the same order as the appearance of pertinent information in the video. Students were asked to write down their answers and to pay attention to the terminology and expressions used in the video as they did so. After students finished watching the video, there was a discussion of content. Students typically asked a number of questions related to verifying their comprehension of the video content. Usually, they brought previous knowledge and experience to bear on the discussion. At this time, the instructor's role is to keep the discussion flowing, bringing in expressions and new terminology from the video. At the end of the discussion, students review their responses to the questions distributed earlier. As a post-view activity, students were asked to write a summary of the video for diverse audiences. For example, some presented a report to a science commission, while others summarized an argument for an expert witness in a court. In preparing these summaries, students used the technical terminology embedded in the language of persuasion, description, and other forms of discourse.

The second complex activity in this lesson was a tour of the Monterey Bay Aquarium. Students were able to reinforce the information that they had learned from the video and in their research readings. They were required to make a presentation as "experts" on specific exhibits that they selected – sea otters, blue whales, kelp forest, etc. To prepare for that presentation and to make sure that they had relevant information, they were given a free visit to the Aquarium in advance of the "professional tour." On the day of the tour, each student made his or her presentation. (Frequently, when this activity was conducted, foreign tourists visiting the Aquarium listened to the students' presentations and asked questions, believing the students to be Aquarium docents for foreign visitors. This only highlighted the relevance of the visit for the students.) The three-hour visit to the Aquarium ended at a local restaurant for a debriefing. The students were then required to write a report of the visit.

The third activity in the lesson plan was the report itself. Students prepared a two-page report of their visit to the Aquarium. They were allowed to discuss any topic they chose, describe their impressions, or simply summarize the visit. Later, the reports were corrected and grammar, terminology, content, and style were evaluated and discussed.

Representative extramural activities

The success of an intensive course depends to a great extent on being able to diversify activities so that students are constantly motivated. A variety of supplemental activities were planned for each day of the Bridge course. Activities were repeated during the course, with modifications to reflect current topics. In this way, consistency in extracurricular and extramural activities was achieved. Activities included movies, information/library search, and field trips with subsequent oral presentations.

Movie nights. Every week two movie nights were organized to provide a different forum where students could keep working on the foreign language. Generally, a teaching assistant watched the movies with the students and facilitated a post-viewing discussion. Participation at the movie nights was optional but students welcomed them as opportunities to work on the foreign language in a less formal atmosphere.

Information search / library search. At the beginning of the second week of the course, the professor handed a list of 100 questions, ranging from "What is the age of Jimmy Connors?" to "What does the Japanese Diet consist of?" or "Who is Alois Mock?" The students had two weeks to find the answers. Prior to this assignment, the students would have already been familiarized with the library layout via a tour conducted by the library staff, with a special emphasis on the resources in the foreign language. The 100-question exercise had a dual role: help the students learn the library layout and resources and show them how to do research in an effective way. Each student kept a log of his/her research process in order to determine which resource worked best, which dictionary was most useful and which one was of no use at all, and which websites were worth visiting.

Field trips. Teaching language for special purposes must be very practical. Various field trips are organized every year during the course. Sometimes students become experts in local sites and give presentations. Other times students listen to experts present a topic and they take notes. Visits have pre- and post-visit activities that call for various skills, including researching terminology/content on a given topic, writing up a presentation, delivering presentations in front of an audience, taking notes of their peers' (or experts') presentations, summarizing, writing a report, etc.

Representative classroom activities
Readings. During the course, students were expected to read two books that they chose and read individually plus two books chosen by the professor and read by the whole group. The only condition imposed by the professor was that the books (reports, documents) not be translations. For each title selected, the students had to prepare a written summary. They were also expected to make an oral presentation in front of the class. This activity required students to do the following: (1) read something they enjoyed; (2) pay attention to vocabulary and grammar in writing the report; (3) analyze the message; (4) summarize the book's content; (5) use public-speaking skills in making their presentations; and, (6) justify their comments in discussions of the books with other students.

Crossword puzzles. Puzzles were used as a break from more strenuous exercises. The level of difficulty and the topics corresponded to students' work during a given week.

Dictation. Dictation is one of the most traditional activities of any language course. In the Bridge course, dictations were based on television or radio broadcasts (e.g., Charles De Gaulle's famous June 6, 1944 call to resistance). In addition to active listening, in taking dictation, the students had to make decisions about punctuation and spelling. Current articles read as a dictation by the instructor were later used for reading comprehension or to work on alternative phrasing of the original text as a mechanism for developing language flexibility and synonymy, aspects of language proficiency that many other authors in this volume (e.g., Leaver and Shekhtman, Dabars and Kagan) point out as distinguishing the SD level. The students later wrote summaries of the dictation and edited each other's work.

In the French Bridge course, De Gaulle's 200-word speech was used in the following manner: the professor announced the topic to prompt the students to talk about events of that time. Usually, some students had heard of that famous speech and could explain to the class the historical circumstances in which it was delivered (a call by General De Gaulle to keep fighting the German occupation in preparation for D-Day). The professor played the whole taped segment to be taken as a dictation once without stopping, a second time with pauses to allow the students to write it down, and a last time to allow them to check for mistakes. Then the students exchanged copies and made suggestions on their peer's copy. Finally, they received the transcript of the speech. A short discussion about specific grammatical or spelling points followed. The students were then asked to rewrite the speech in different ways and were divided into groups: one group of students was instructed to expand the text, using synonyms and fillers, while another had to do the opposite and try to be as concise as possible. These strategies are used in interpretation when it is necessary to emphasize a point that did not come across accurately the first time or to eliminate the repetitions in a convoluted speech. After working together for about 15–20 minutes, each group presented its work to the class for a final discussion.

Presentations. The value of oral presentations in developing foreign language proficiency, especially at the SD level, has been reported by a number of program administrators (Dabars and Kagan [this volume]; Leaver and Bilstein [2000]; Stryker [1997]). As in the courses at the Specialized Language Training Center (SLTC) that are described in this volume (Shekhtman *et al.*), formal presentations lasting 15–20 minutes were an important element of the Bridge program. The students chose a topic within the general theme of the week, completed the necessary research, discussed a first draft with the teaching assistant or the professor, wrote a final paper and presented it orally to the class. During the eight weeks of the course, the students also made shorter presentations on various topics and current events.

Results

From the comments of graduates from the Spanish and French Bridge courses over the years, one could conclude that the course has helped them enormously in reaching their professional goals. (Some of these comments can be found at Appendix B.) Among the students who entered the MA program in Translation and Interpretation, some changed careers and pursued an MA in Teaching Foreign Languages or Teaching of English as a Second Language and are currently pursuing teaching careers. Others use their bilingual skills as translators and interpreters in international organizations, in private companies (e.g., Mayo Clinic, McGraw Hill, Belgacom), or as translation managers in major translation agencies, as well as at T&I agencies, in the courts, and at community centers. In sum, regardless of the career path the participants decided to take, they succeeded in obtaining the linguistic proficiency and the professional skills necessary to meet the requirements of the positions that they currently hold.

Discussion

The previous sections illustrated how language learning at (and beyond) the Superior level for a specific purpose such as translation or interpreting can be facilitated. Clearly, working at the SD level is quite different from working with lower levels of proficiency. No deviation from those characteristics that define Superior and Distinguished levels of proficiency (especially including linguistic competence) is allowed. Elements of strategic competence, such as compensation strategies, that play an important role in language proficiency up to, and even including the lower ranges of, the Superior level of proficiency have no place in the work of the professional translator or interpreter. In T&I, accuracy is one of the greatest concerns. (Accuracy here not only relates to the transfer of meaning across languages – a typical belief within the T&I field – but also to the adequacy of word and structure choice with which such transfer is made, otherwise known as congruity judgment and defined by Child [1990] as "the ability to successfully match donor language features, characteristics, or forms to their most suitable receptor language equivalents" [p. 299]; of particular interest at Level 4 is the ability to render in parallel but accurate form the "shape" of the original text.) As discussed by Leaver and Shekhtman (this volume), linguistic, sociolinguistic, and analytical proficiency are essential at this level so that students may render an adequate translation or interpretation of a given text that does not feel like a literal translation or interpretation. Clearly, there is not only one accurate rendition of a text, since there are as many possible versions as there are translators and interpreters attempting them. However, most professionals agree about what constitutes a professional rendition and what represents the attempt of an amateur. Typically, the professional translation or interpretation is distinguished on the basis of language, word choice, register, style, flow of the text, and cultural sensitivity.

At the T&I level, students no longer use language simply for general communicative purposes. Rather, they work with the language itself, i.e., with its linguistic, sociolinguistic, discourse, and cultural components. Students need to monitor their production under pressure, incorporating into their performance various analytical skills (restructuring, hierarchical organization of ideas, etc.) used in their first language, as well as linguistic skills (circumlocution, paraphrasing) that they have acquired as foreign language learners at earlier stages of their linguistic proficiency.

During their journey to obtain their MA degrees in T&I, students are taught via a sink-or-swim methodology. T&I classes are not equipped to deal with language issues: the underlying assumption is that T&I candidates come to the task with the required proficiency to become translators and interpreters (Angelelli, 2000). There is no reference to the developmental stages of foreign language proficiency in the T&I classroom; nor is there any compensation for linguistic deficiencies. Language proficiency is taken for granted and T&I students spend four semesters acquiring the specific practice, principles, and strategies associated with professional work as a translator and/or interpreter. Students, therefore, have to be at least at the Superior level to navigate this type of instruction.

The fact that linguistic competence continues to develop at any level of proficiency and can be deliberately enhanced – a common belief among those experienced in teaching at the Superior (and higher) level – is not recognized by most T&I faculty. This is not surprising since most of them do not have a background in foreign language education. Generally, they are active professionals in the T&I field. This posits a dilemma for students who want to acquire T&I skills and cannot do so concurrently with improving their competence and performance in their first and second languages. Many students have found the Bridge courses highly relevant and even essential for developing the level of proficiency they required. (Excerpts from student surveys taken in the 2000 Spanish and French courses are at Appendix B.)

Implications

Eight years of experience with Bridge courses have revealed a number of implications for those who would like to establish language-enhancement courses or programs. These include a realistic consideration of the differing roles of classroom instruction and in-country experience, the background of the teacher, institutional integration of the program, marketing of the course(s), and community support.

A language-enhancement course or series at the Superior level could benefit language professionals as well as undergraduate and graduate students at the Advanced-Plus / Superior level. Generally, when learners reach a Superior proficiency level, the choices on how to update, maintain, or enhance their foreign language in their homeland are very limited. One obvious option is to spend a time abroad in a country where the foreign language is spoken. However, these learners have probably already been abroad at lower stages of their language proficiency. At the SD level, simply spending time abroad is not necessarily sufficient for their more specialized needs. They do not need just exposure; they need answers to questions and explanations that they can rarely get by simply being immersed in a language/culture. For example, many times

SD Spanish students wonder about the use of *de que* rather than *que* following certain verbs such as *pensar* (to think), *tener miedo* (be afraid of). This question often arises because they have heard some native speakers use *de que* and others not (just *que*). Students wonder if the preposition *de* is optional. They wonder if they can say, "Tengo miedo *que* la entrevista sea difícil" (I am afraid/concerned that the interview will be hard) or if they have to say, "Tengo miedo *de que* la entrevista sea difícil." Because native speakers do not necessarily know all the grammatical intricacies of the language they speak, students do not necessarily find answers to these questions just by spending time in an environment where the language is spoken.

Finally, linkages with the community are essential. In this program, participants are expected to become involved with the community (of the foreign culture/language) and learn from it in various ways.

Conclusion

This chapter described the conceptualization and implementation of Bridge courses in Spanish and French. Initially created to meet the linguistic needs of T&I MA applicants, the Bridge course expanded to enhance linguistic abilities of language professionals as well. From both a financial and administrative point of view, the Bridge courses have been a success. Students who would otherwise have been denied admission to the MA program were accepted, and they graduated. The very real need for such courses was evidenced in 1997/1998 when participation in the Bridge courses was made compulsory for the students who had not passed the EDT.

These courses can easily be replicated in other languages. They can also be taught for other professional purposes with minor adaptations.

A language-enhancement course, a course that can bridge the gap between language for general communication purposes and language for work, is one model of teaching language at the Superior level. It is motivating for both teachers and learners, and it is essential in encouraging learners to continue on the language-learning journey. Students see that there are goals they can still achieve, that there are answers to their questions and, most important, that they are empowered to be the search engines for finding their answers.

The Bridge courses taught for eight years at the Monterey Institute of International Studies constitute an example of how language taught at the SD level can serve to enhance the foreign language and provide the necessary tools to work with it in the T&I field. An array of classroom and extramural activities, coupled with the use of current and pertinent authentic materials, and the combination of instructors with language-education backgrounds and professional expertise in a given field constitute a recipe for success. Perhaps other institutions will find the models contained in this chapter of assistance in developing similar language programs. After all, students who must go out into the world tomorrow and use their language skills for real-life purposes that can, at times, be quite critical to the welfare of one or many deserve to have language instruction today that prepares them for this.

APPENDIX A SAMPLE LESSON PLAN (FRENCH 2000)

Theme: Science
Topic: Marine Biology

First activity: Videotape on California Mammals (20 minutes documentary, recorded on Belgian National Television Network).
　　Characteristics:
　　　　　　Content – Description of life of whales and marine mammals on and along the coast of California. Focus on technical terminology (names of sea creatures and mammals).
　　　　　　Speed: normal – about 110 words per minute, with pauses and visual aids.
　　　　　　Difficulty: terminology and accents.
　　　　　　Description of activity
　　　　　　Previewing activities:
　　　　　　brainstorming content, etc.
　　　　　　active listening and activation of marine terminology
　　　　　　Questions on video content; focus on terminology
　　　　　　Discussion of video content
　　　　　　Review of answers to questions
　　　　　　Written summary of the video for diverse audiences

Second activity:
　　　　　　Tour of the Monterey Bay Aquarium
　　　　　　Preliminary individual visit (in English)
　　　　　　Preparation of presentation
　　　　　　Professional tour / individual presentations
　　　　　　(Answering foreign tourists' questions)
　　　　　　Debriefing

Third activity: Field Trip Report.
Discussion of reports: grammar, terminology, content, and style

APPENDIX B EXCERPTS FROM STUDENT SURVEYS 2000 FRENCH
AND SPANISH BRIDGE COURSES

It was different in that it focused on the skills necessary for translation and interpretation work rather than only grammar and vocabulary. It was much more intense and fun. (French student)

It is more practical [than a pure language course]. The emphasis is on the use of press materials rather than textbooks. (Spanish student)

It is nothing like anything I had done before. Everything was geared toward practical understanding and usage of the language . . . We didn't review anything that didn't need it. (Spanish student)

[I was able] to dust off my French . . . Exercises involving building our knowledge of world affairs and French culture, learning to research and to prepare presentations on short notice, listening and memory exercises . . . all helped to prepare me for the career and semesters that await me. I must say that without this course my French would probably not have carried me through my first year of the program. (French student)

[U]sually courses can be teacher-centered, but there was a great balance between students and teacher. There was a lot of creativity put into the classes and thus, learning was fun. (Spanish student)

Overall, the skills we learned were practical and useful. The learning was put into real-life context. We didn't work on any artificial role-playing. (Spanish student)

5   Learning Chinese in China: Programs for developing Superior- to Distinguished-level Chinese language proficiency in China and Taiwan

Cornelius C. Kubler

The average lay person, if asked the best way to learn Chinese, would probably reply that one should go to China for a period of time and "pick up" the language naturally. For beginning students, learning Chinese in China is actually not the most efficient way to proceed.[1] However, once students have reached the intermediate stage, there is widespread agreement that the fastest and best way for them to continue their language studies is to spend a substantial period of time in a Chinese-speaking region in close contact with Chinese speakers.[2] In fact, it is questionable whether a non-native can attain Superior- to Distinguished-level (SD) proficiency in Chinese any other way.[3]

---

[1] The reasons why it is preferable for most beginners to start their study of Chinese in their native country include the following: (1) instructors in the students' native country are usually more familiar with the challenges facing beginning learners; (2) students there usually have a common native language and culture, making instruction more efficient; (3) if learners travel to China before they have attained basic proficiency in the language, they will initially be unable to take advantage of the main benefit of residence in China, i.e., interacting with the Chinese people in their language; (4) students may pick up nonstandard pronunciation and usage; and (5) students will learn words and grammar in the order of perceived utility to them rather than in the order that makes the most sense pedagogically.

[2] In the opinion of Dew (1994), "Intensive overseas study is essential for the attainment of high levels of Chinese language competence because that is the context in which (1) the student can devote full effort to language study; (2) the student can be exposed to the language in all of its varied uses, active and passive; and (3) maximum use can be made of the powers of reinforcement among the four skills" (pp. 40–41).

[3] Given talented students and sufficient resources, it should, in theory, be possible to bring students to the SD level in Chinese in the USA or anywhere else in the world. In practice, however, it is nearly impossible to achieve this in a non-Chinese environment, especially in the case of the oral skills. Because of the vast cultural and linguistic differences between Chinese and English, the student needs the culture for support. In this regard, it must not be forgotten that Chinese is one of the most difficult languages for native English speakers. The reasons include: (1) tones, (2) the enormous size of the vocabulary (due to the length and breadth of Chinese history and culture), (3) the great amount of linguistic and cultural variation across the Chinese speech area, (4) a paucity of linguistic and cultural cognates, (5) the large number of characters making up the writing system, (6) complexity of the characters, and (7) lexical and grammatical differences between speech and writing.

However, simply living in China will almost certainly not result in the acquisition of SD-level language skills. Everyone is familiar with the example of expatriates who have lived in a country five, ten, twenty, or more years but possess little or no real proficiency in the language. Then there are other longtime foreign residents who can manage daily affairs well enough and may think of themselves as possessing "near-native" proficiency but actually stick to the simplest vocabulary and grammar and, even then, produce few utterances that are not without a major or minor error. It is the thesis of this chapter that, to achieve SD-level proficiency in Chinese, students require a combination of long-term immersion in Chinese culture with an organized training program that systematically pushes them up the proficiency ladder, a thesis that finds resonance in several chapters of this volume (e.g., Chapter 3).

Current practices in teaching SD-level Chinese

The goal of this chapter is to identify and discuss the variables in learning and teaching Chinese at the SD level as they are reflected through current practice at a number of representative programs in China and Taiwan. In particular, an attempt is made to determine how these variables differ from just doing more of the same kind of learning and teaching that is done at the lower levels.

Description of the students

Student backgrounds

Based on the experience of many program directors and instructors, desirable qualifications for students aiming for the SD level include (1) advanced proficiency in Chinese at a solid Speaking Level 3 / Reading Level 3 (S-3/R-3) or higher, with oral and written skills as evenly balanced as possible; (2) evidence of strong language aptitude through prior successful, rapid learning of Chinese; (3) at least one year's residence in a Chinese-speaking region in daily contact with members of Chinese society; (4) substantial knowledge of Chinese culture and society; (5) in-depth knowledge of the student's field of specialization; (6) detailed understanding of the student's future job needs; (7) strong motivation for continuing the study of Chinese; (8) outgoing personality; (9) single status (or dependents who also speak Chinese); and (10) youth.[4] The more of these criteria a candidate for SD-level training meets, the greater the likelihood of success.

The bulk of the field's experience in bringing students to the SD level in Chinese lies in teaching native speakers of English who began their study of

---

[4] While specialists in language acquisition are still divided about whether there is a "critical period" for language learning, it is the experience of all the program directors and instructors with whom I spoke that, with rare exceptions, younger adults learn faster and better than older ones.

Chinese as adults. In recent years, increasing numbers of "heritage" speakers, i.e., Chinese-Americans who are native or semi-native speakers of Mandarin or other Chinese dialects, have been enrolling in university language classes. While these students often bring considerable strengths to their studies, some of them – having acquired all or most of what they know informally in a limited range of situations and registers – may find it difficult to add to their existing linguistic inventory the higher-level, more formal vocabulary and grammar associated with SD-level proficiency.

There are also non-native speakers of Chinese who may have learned and used Chinese informally in-country over a long period of time. Such speakers may be quite confident of their ability to use Chinese; they think they are very fluent but typically produce many fossilized errors and are limited in precision of vocabulary and range of topics (Higgs and Clifford [1982]; Vigil and Oller [1976]). In not a few cases, such speakers are at best S-2+, often with substantially lower reading and writing ability. These students are particularly difficult to bring to higher levels because they often feel their Chinese is perfectly adequate.

For both types of nontraditional learners described above, the first steps must include (1) convincing the student that accuracy and precision do matter; (2) convincing the student that educated Chinese do employ high-level, formal vocabulary and grammar on those occasions calling for them; (3) pointing out the student's errors and weaknesses; and (4) teaching effective study skills.

Student needs

Students aiming for the SD level in Chinese inevitably possess different strengths and weaknesses and have a variety of learning needs, including academic (e.g., studying at a Chinese university or conducting research in China) and professional (e.g., business, diplomacy, missionary work, or teaching of Chinese as a foreign language). As noted by other authors in this volume (see Byrnes [Chapter 3], Angelelli and Degueldre, and Shekhtman *et al.*), in order to teach students at this level effectively it is important to conduct a comprehensive assessment of each student's linguistic strengths and weaknesses on entrance into the program, as well as gaining a detailed understanding of the student's future language-related needs. This information should be communicated clearly to all of the student's instructors so they may design as relevant a curriculum as possible.

Description of the programs

A dozen major Chinese language programs in China and Taiwan that offer training through the SD level are described below. There are others besides those mentioned here, but these are the best-known and most representative. Unless a specific duration for the course of studies at a particular program is stated, it can be assumed that the program is for varying lengths of time depending on factors such as the learner's proficiency level on entrance into the program, the learner's rate of progress, and the amount of time the learner has available for training.

Associated Colleges in China (ACC)

ACC was founded by a consortium of American liberal arts colleges in 1996 in Beijing, where it operates at Capital University of Economics and Business. Distinguishing features of the ACC program include a language pledge, language practicum, Chinese host families, and a tightly organized schedule of extremely rigorous drill and exercise classes.

The ACC curriculum includes four hours of classes daily: (1) large-group lecture of about ten students, (2) small-group drill of five students, (3) two-person conversation class, (4) tutorial, and (5) independent study. Self-study is a very important component of the curriculum, with students expected to spend at least five to six hours every day in preparation and review. Course content for the advanced curriculum includes conversation, broadcast media, films, newspaper and magazine readings and discussion, modern Chinese literature, readings in history and culture, and Classical Chinese.

Each week students participate in 2–4 hours of language practicum, where they are assigned projects that require them to use Chinese with local citizens. The formats include on-site visits, interviews, surveys, and debates. Upon completion of a project, students make an oral presentation to their classmates and instructors and submit a written report. Comments from numerous US-based faculty who have visited the program as well as several years' worth of student evaluations attest to the fact that ACC is very effective in raising students' proficiency in formal speech and reading. One weakness, according to these faculty and the students themselves, is that the large amount of time spent in the classroom and in self-study limits students' opportunities for informal use of Chinese outside of the classroom, with the result that many students are not as fluent in informal Chinese as they should be.

American Institute in Taiwan (AIT)

AIT's Chinese Language and Area Studies School is an Advanced-level Chinese language program in Taipei operated for the Foreign Service Institute, US Department of State. Its students are US diplomats and other government personnel who need to attain professional levels of Chinese language proficiency. The majority of students at AIT enter with proficiency ratings of S-2/R-2 and hope to attain S-3/R-3 within a training period of eleven months. However, each year a small number of students who have previously achieved S-3/R-3 enroll for a special "Beyond Three" program that is designed to help students progress toward S-4/R-4.

A typical daily class schedule for students in the AIT "Beyond Three" program consists of three hours in small groups of two or three students plus two hours of tutorials. Class content consists largely of content-based instruction involving various aspects of Chinese culture (e.g., geography, history, literature) and Language for Special Purposes (e.g., politics, economics, agriculture). All students are encouraged to work on public speaking and Classical Chinese. Some students receive training in written translation (Chinese to English) and oral interpretation (Chinese to English and English to Chinese), while others take special classes in comprehension of accented Mandarin and reading of materials written in cursive script.

An important part of the training at AIT takes place outside of the classroom. Students are required to involve themselves in community-based activities – for example, delivering a series of lectures in their field at a local university or interviewing candidates in a local election and writing a report on their observations. Such activities are selected from students' areas of professional expertise and are designed to challenge them linguistically.

One major goal of the AIT program is to broaden the range of topics about which students feel comfortable speaking, since an important difference between Levels 3 and 4 is breadth in discussing higher-level topics. While Level 3 students typically are proficient in only one fairly narrow field, students aspiring to Level 4 must be able to discuss intelligently a wide variety of fields. There is also considerably greater emphasis on accuracy than at the lower levels; merely attaining the goal of successful communication is no longer considered sufficient. Consequently, much time and effort are devoted to correcting minor grammatical and word-choice errors. Another requirement is that students be able to adjust their speech for register, depending on their interlocutor and the occasion. Expanding students' lexical and syntactic repertoires is also critically important. One of the instructors' most important tasks is encouraging students to employ ever more sophisticated vocabulary and grammar in their speech.

According to the AIT Principal, a student's likelihood of attaining Level 4 in the skill of speaking and the skill of reading in eleven months depends on a number of factors including level and breadth of Chinese proficiency on entrance, language aptitude, and, of course, diligence. All "Beyond Three" students, but in particular those who enter with less than a solid 3 in any skill, are urged to attend Middlebury College's Chinese Summer School for two months of review and consolidation prior to arriving in Taipei. Nevertheless, not a few students in the AIT "Beyond Three" program conclude their period of training with a rating of 4 in only one of the two skills.

Beijing Language and Culture University (BLCU)
Founded in 1962, BLCU is China's premier institution for teaching Chinese language and culture to foreign students. With a faculty of about 700 and a

student body of over 3,000, BLCU has graduated more than 20,000 foreign students over the last thirty-eight years. BLCU offers foreign students courses of all lengths and at all levels, ranging from beginning courses of several weeks' duration to a comprehensive four-year curriculum that leads to a bachelor's degree in Chinese. The latter is divided by year and semester into required and optional courses.

In the third and fourth years of the four-year curriculum, which correspond roughly to the SD level, the required courses include listening comprehension, radio plays, advanced conversation, public speaking, newspaper and magazine reading, Chinese culture, Chinese society, Chinese history, business Chinese, composition, translation/interpreting, modern Chinese literature, Classical Chinese, and a practicum in Chinese society for which students are required to keep a diary and prepare both an oral presentation and a lengthy written report. Also required are special courses in vocabulary expansion that involve intensive practice of synonyms and antonyms, as well as courses in speed reading. The optional courses for third- and fourth-year students are art, calligraphy, folk customs, economics, linguistics, grammar, stylistics, history of Chinese–foreign cross-cultural exchange, "Chinese national sentiment," and Chinese word processing. While a large variety of courses is offered, all classes have twenty or more students, no opportunity for tutorial or small-group training being available.

CET/Beijing (CET/B)

This study-abroad program was founded in Beijing in 1982 and is now located at Beijing Institute of Education. Each year well over 100 students from a variety of different American colleges attend CET/B. The majority are at the beginning or intermediate levels, but there are also a small number of advanced students.

For the advanced students at CET/B, the daily schedule consists of four hours of classes in small groups of 2–4 students. The curriculum includes "7-minute mini-talks" on topics related to students' needs and interests, newspaper reading and discussion, modern Chinese literature, Chinese history, business Chinese, composition, and Classical Chinese.

A special feature of CET/B is a course on Chinese society where speakers from all walks of life are invited to address students about their life experiences, followed by questions and discussion. There is also a Chinese language and culture practicum where students travel to various sites of interest in Chinese society, interview Chinese people they meet, and then return to class to report – orally and in writing – on their observations. In cooperation with Boston University, CET/B also runs a program of internships at various Chinese and foreign enterprises that require the use of Chinese.

Another special feature of CET/B is that every student has the option of requesting a Chinese roommate, who not only lives with the student but also serves as tutor for some courses and participates in cultural excursions in and beyond Beijing. Some of the American students speak Chinese with their roommates while others tend to speak in English. Nevertheless, many students have commented that the roommate option is one of the strongest features of the CET/B program.

CET/Harbin (CET/H)

The CET/H program was founded at the Harbin Institute of Technology in Harbin in 1988. Unlike CET/B, CET/H was designed specifically for high-intermediate and advanced students, so all students are required to have Chinese roommates and take a language pledge. Locating a program for advanced students in a relatively remote city like Harbin is advantageous for a number of reasons, including the fact that there are far fewer foreigners and Western distractions and that local Chinese are often more eager to make contact with those foreigners present than the somewhat blasé residents of the capital city, Beijing.

The CET/H advanced curriculum consists of four hours of classes per day, five days a week. The first two hours are in small groups, studying subjects such as TV news, newspaper reading and discussion, modern Chinese literature, Classical Chinese, and composition. The third hour is a special "one-on-two" drill class, while the fourth hour is a tutorial.

The "one-on-two drill class," consisting of one instructor and two students, is designed to bring advanced students to a higher level by identifying and remedying, through the use of special drills and exercises, fossilized errors in pronunciation, including tones and sentence intonation. The tutorial, which involves intensive study of a topic chosen by students in consultation with CET and their home institutions, is designed to use students' academic or professional interests as a vehicle for enhancing their linguistic skills.

Instructors for the tutorials are carefully chosen from area universities or the local community for their content expertise. Besides studying with their instructors, students collect material through bibliographic research in libraries and through interviews, site visits, and surveys. The tutorials culminate in substantial written reports, which go through a series of drafts and rewrites, as well as several in-progress and final oral presentations before classmates and faculty. Recent tutorial topics have included environmental pollution, industrial policy, joint ventures, the Cultural Revolution, Chinese medicine, regional cooking, ethnic minorities, the role of women in society, and China's relations with various foreign countries.

Foreign Service Institute (FSI/B)

FSI is the US Department of State's facility for training diplomats and other government personnel in language, area, and professional studies. FSI's standard Chinese language curriculum, designed to help foreign-service officers attain S-3/R-3, comprises two years of full-time, intensive training: the first year in Washington, where the goal is to attain S-2/R-2 within ten months; and the second year at AIT (see above), where the goal is to progress from S-2/R-2 to S-3/R-3 within eleven months. A much smaller number of officers has the opportunity to receive a third year of training either at AIT or at a "Beyond Three" program in Beijing (FSI/B).

FSI/B was founded in Beijing in the mid 1990s and accepts each year a small number of officers who have previously achieved S-3/R-3, have already served at least one tour at a Chinese-speaking post, and have the desire and professional need to attain high levels of proficiency in Chinese. While the unofficial goal is to reach S-4/R-4 after about one year of training, the program is termed "Beyond Three" in recognition of the fact that, as different individuals progress to higher levels of proficiency, it becomes increasingly difficult to predict their rate of progress and highest potential level.

As at AIT, students are sometimes sent to summer school at Middlebury College for refresher training, so they may begin work on high-level materials immediately on arrival in Beijing. A resident FSI language-training specialist in Beijing coordinates each student's curriculum, many of the classes being taught at CET/B. Students at FSI/B generally take four tutorials daily as follows: (1) language course designed to strengthen the student's formal vocabulary and grammar; (2) language course designed to correct fossilized errors; (3) content course involving cultural literacy (Hirsch [1987]); and (4) content course in the student's field of specialization. While the two language courses are taught by professional language teachers, the content courses are taught by instructors with expertise in those areas.

Teaching activities include conversation, reading and discussion, role plays, and frequent short, prepared talks by students on a variety of topics, which instructors go over with a fine-toothed comb. As at AIT, some attention is given to strengthening students' ability in translation and interpretation. Students are encouraged to study Classical Chinese for its usefulness in raising students' levels. They are also urged to establish contacts in local society and to participate in university seminars or training sessions at local firms. Even though FSI/B is itself an in-country program, off-site activities lasting from a few days to a week or more are held at various locations in China so as to offer students opportunities for complete immersion.[5]

---

[5] FSI also offers "Beyond Three" courses in French and Russian. The curricula for both are to a large extent content-based, with modules on culture, geography, the media, and language for special purposes. In consultation with their instructors, students choose thematic topics, which form the basis for many of the classroom activities and assignments. Like the "Beyond Three" courses at AIT and FSI/B, the French and Russian courses require a minimum of S-3/R-3 for enrollment and are designed to graduate students at approximately S-4/R-4. Unlike the Chinese courses, the French and Russian courses are only about six months in duration and are conducted at FSI/Washington.

Hopkins-Nanjing Center for Chinese and American Studies (HNC)
HNC was founded in 1986 in Nanjing by the Johns Hopkins University and Nanjing University. Unlike most of the other programs discussed here, HNC is primarily content-based, offering a one-year program of graduate-level courses in Chinese history, sociology, culture, economics, and international relations. The faculty at HNC consists mostly of professors from Nanjing University; the students number approximately fifty international (mostly American) students and fifty Chinese students, all of whom are pursuing advanced degrees or preparing for careers in the public or private sectors. Although the international and Chinese students usually take different classes, they are paired as roommates and participate in joint educational and social activities.

All of the international students' classes, reading assignments, papers, and exams are in Chinese. The regular program consists of three content courses per semester, for which class size is approximately 15–30 students. Supplementary language courses, such as academic writing, are available on an optional basis to help students develop skills needed to succeed in their content classes. In addition, students may take for credit one course each semester at Nanjing University. More recently, an intermediate-level program has been created for students in Chinese studies who require additional language instruction to reach the level required for the regular program. Students in this track, which is offered only in the fall, take two intensive language courses and one specially designed content course, with the goal of being ready to join the regular program by the spring semester.

Titles of some recent courses at HNC are "History of the PRC"; "Chinese History: 1911–1949"; "Mao Zedong and the Chinese Revolution"; "History of the Cultural Revolution"; "Advanced Topics on Hong Kong, Macao, and Taiwan"; "Confucianism, Daoism, Buddhism, and Chinese Traditional Culture"; "Social and Intellectual Trends in Modern China"; "China in Search of a New Culture"; "Social Issues in Contemporary China"; "Chinese Women's Issues"; "International Relations Since the Second World War"; "China–US Relations in the Twentieth Century"; "Contemporary Chinese Foreign Policy"; "The Contemporary Chinese Economy"; "China's Financial Reforms"; "Reforms in China's State Enterprise System"; "Foreign Investment in China"; and "Trade Between China and Western Countries."

The more successful professors at HNC have adapted their teaching to the needs of the international students in a number of ways. For example, they may: (1) adopt a more engaging, student-centered teaching style that allows for questions and discussion; (2) provide students a detailed course syllabus at the beginning of the term, a concession that does not reflect common practice at Chinese universities; (3) prepare written questions for students to think about as they prepare the day's reading assignment; (4) put an outline of the day's lesson on the blackboard for students' reference during the lecture portion of the class; (5) write key words and phrases on the blackboard; (6) ask rhetorical questions and then proceed to answer them; (7) ask individual students questions to confirm comprehension; (8) use a fairly repetitive speaking style; (9) paraphrase difficult or rare terms; (10) translate specialized terms into English; (11) hand out supplementary lists of specialized terms; (12) avoid rare words and expressions; and/or (13) give students lists of topics from which final exam questions will be drawn.

Although classes at HNC are easier than regular Chinese university classes, numerous challenges remain for the international students. These include the following: (1) the pedagogical style of some professors is very teacher-centered, with long lectures and little discussion; (2) the Mandarin spoken by some professors has a regional accent; (3) some professors speak very fast, unclearly, or in a low voice; (4) the characters some professors write on the blackboard are very cursive; (5) some students are still unable to read quickly with good comprehension; (6) many students lack the ability to write well within reasonable time limits; and (7) a number of students possess insufficient content background in the subjects being studied.

HNC is the most comprehensive and successful content-based program in Chinese for non-native learners. Nevertheless, a number of challenges remain. Chief among these is how to raise students' proficiency levels in speaking. While listening-comprehension, reading, and writing ability usually increase markedly at HNC, speaking – in particular, the appropriate use of specialized terminology, aphorisms, and higher-level grammar – often does not. The problem is that there is insufficient opportunity for students to use the new words and structures to which they have been exposed in their own speech and receive corrections and guidance.

Another weakness often cited on student evaluations is that the language courses, which are taught as group classes of about eight students, fail to address the individual needs of students. Furthermore, the language courses need to be better linked to the content courses. Another concern is how to increase the amount of Chinese spoken by international students, since they normally speak to each other in English and are not required to speak in Chinese to their Chinese roommates. Related to this is the challenge of finding better ways to bring the international and Chinese students into greater contact.

Yet another problem is that although there is no doubt the adjustments made for the international students facilitate their learning at the initial stage, these same adjustments may eventually disadvantage students by sheltering them excessively. Finally, students at HNC have criticized some faculty members for catering in their teaching to the perceived interests of the foreign students, resulting in a skewed view of Chinese culture and society.

*International Chinese Language Program at National
Taiwan University (ICLP)*

Founded by a consortium of American universities as the Inter-University
Program for Chinese Language Studies in Taipei (IUP) in 1963, this program,
located on the campus of National Taiwan University, has over the last four
decades trained many of the current US academic and professional leaders
dealing with China. Although it was reorganized in 1997 as ICLP, when IUP
moved to Beijing (see below), the essence of the program remained the same
as before.

ICLP offers intermediate and advanced intensive ten-month training programs that enroll 35–50 students per year. The goal of the curriculum is to
enable students to achieve broad, independent competence in spoken and written Chinese for academic or professional purposes. Both modern and Classical
Chinese are taught. Although classes are divided into speaking and reading
classes, even in reading classes most of the actual classwork is oral in nature,
consisting of questions, discussion, and exercises based on what students have
read and prepared outside of class.

At ICLP there are four hours of classes daily, consisting of a mixture of
small-group classes of 2–4 students and tutorials. A substantial amount of class
preparation and self-study is expected. In the small-group classes, there are
intensive exercises designed to encourage students to use higher-level, more
formal grammar and vocabulary in their speech. For example, the instructor
may write a number of complex grammatical patterns on the board and ask
students to answer questions about their reading lesson, using those patterns.
In the tutorials, student and instructor discuss course material on a one-to-
one basis, addressing individual questions and targeting specific areas needing
improvement. Students may also audit classes at National Taiwan University.

*Inter-University Program for Chinese Language
Studies at Tsinghua University (IUP)*

The IUP, administered by the University of California at Berkeley and located
on the campus of Tsinghua University in Beijing, was designed primarily for
English-speaking graduate students who need to achieve high-level, broad competency in spoken and written Chinese for academic purposes. It is a continu-
ation in Beijing of the former Inter-University Program for Chinese Language
Studies in Taipei.

Classes at IUP, which extend over a nine-month academic year, typically
consist of three hours per day of small-group classes of 3–4 students and
one hour of tutorial. There are basically two types of classes: conversation
classes and reading/discussion classes. Even in the latter, the main classroom
activity is speech, based on the conviction that most character learning and
reading practice should be done out of class. Besides the twenty hours a week in

class, students are expected to spend an even larger amount of time in preparation and self-study.

The majority of IUP's advanced materials are developed in-house out of raw materials from the Chinese media and sources such as newspapers, magazines, television, film, academic writings, modern Chinese literature, law and business, public speaking, composition, and Classical Chinese. The curriculum can be adjusted, depending on individual students' interests and career plans. A guiding principle throughout is to foster students' ability to become independent, self-reliant learners and users of Chinese.

IUP maintains a language pledge on the premises. Housing is in dormitories for foreign students. Although IUP has made attempts to obtain permission to house students in dormitories with Chinese students, these efforts have not yet been successful.

Mandarin Training Center at National Taiwan Normal University (MTC)

The MTC was established in 1956 as an extension of National Taiwan Normal University. It is Taiwan's largest Chinese language-training program, with about 150 instructors, over 1,000 students, and more than 32,000 alumni throughout the world.

The majority of classes offered at the MTC are at the beginning and intermediate levels, but advanced training is available to qualified students. The standard curriculum is two hours per day, ten hours per week. Most classes are group classes of 7–10 students, though advanced students are eligible for one or two additional hours of tutorial each day.

The MTC advanced curriculum consists of radio and TV news, films, newspaper and magazine reading and discussion, modern Chinese literature, and Classical Chinese. Advanced students also frequently study the Taiwan Ministry of Education's junior high and high school Chinese language, history, and social studies textbooks.

Taipei Language Institute (TLI)

Founded in Taipei in 1955 to train American missionaries to the SD level in Mandarin and Taiwanese, TLI has since expanded to serve increasing numbers of non-missionary students from all over the world, in particular diplomatic and business personnel assigned to Taiwan, their family members, and foreign university students. There are currently over 1,000 students at TLI's five branch schools in Taiwan.

Courses at TLI, which may be full-time or part-time, typically consist of a combination of small-group classes of 2–6 students and tutorials. A rather rigorous audiolingual method is employed, especially at the beginning and intermediate levels. TLI has compiled many of its own materials but, beginning with the high-intermediate level, students are given the freedom to design their own curriculum based on current or anticipated job needs.

Classroom activities at TLI include drill, exercises, discussion, debates, and job simulations of all kinds. Missionary students at the upper levels read the Bible and other religious literature, practice delivering sermons, and role-play pastoral visits. Non-missionary students study newspapers, television news, modern Chinese literature, Classical Chinese, documentary Chinese, business Chinese, epistolary Chinese, and writing for academic purposes. With the increased democratization and liberalization of Taiwan, it is now possible to study mainland Chinese materials at TLI, even those printed in simplified characters.

US/China Links (USCL)

Founded in Qingdao in 1998, USCL is a training and internship program for Americans who plan, or have recently embarked on, careers in business or government involving China. Staffed and coordinated jointly by the Ohio State University and Qingdao Ocean University, this program is designed to provide students with the knowledge and skills necessary to sustain successful interaction within a Chinese context. Priority for admission is given to those applicants who possess intermediate to advanced proficiency in Mandarin. The curriculum consists of two months of study at the Cultural Training Institute at Qingdao Ocean University followed by a four-month internship.

The Cultural Training Institute is designed to impart to students an understanding of Chinese cultural expectations. Courses and activities are conducted largely in Chinese with professors, tutors, and other resources constantly accessible. The curriculum includes six components: (1) language clinic with individualized training on how to present oneself to a Chinese audience and how to manage one's learning of language and culture in China; (2) course on Chinese society and culture with training in techniques of cultural observation; (3) course on relationship-building in Chinese culture with performance-oriented exercises; (4) course on Chinese etiquette with practical training in how to conduct oneself in formal situations such as meetings, negotiations, and banquets; (5) course on Chinese corporate culture; and (6) practicum involving short-term participation in a local enterprise so students may practice implementing the tactics and strategies presented in their courses prior to embarking on their internships.

The internships, which may be arranged at joint ventures, national and international businesses, provincial and township enterprises, and development organizations are assigned according to participants' interests and abilities. Recent internships have been arranged at China Central Television, Jinjiang Hotel, Motorola (China), Sichuan provincial government, Tsingtao Beer Co., and Yantai Port Authority. Interns perform a variety of language-related jobs such as planning and implementing marketing campaigns for products, training service staff, and editing and translating English-language materials.

Curricular features of the programs

In developing language skills in Chinese at the SD level there is much, of course, that is still the same as at the lower levels. Students must still learn new grammar, new vocabulary, and new characters, and they still require guidance and correction by an instructor. However, there are also numerous differences from the lower levels.

Table 5.1 compares the occurrence of twenty-three curricular features that are characteristic of the SD level in the Chinese language programs discussed in the previous section. These features have been grouped into those that are related to training in spoken Chinese, those that are related to training in written Chinese, and those that involve curricular structure.

Spoken Chinese

Formal vocabulary and grammar

In Chinese there are tremendous differences in vocabulary and grammar between everyday colloquial language, as used by intimate friends chatting in a pub, and formal language, as used by educated Chinese in an academic lecture or political debate. At Level 4, students must be able not only to understand but also to use with a high degree of fluency the formal vocabulary and grammar of Chinese. Furthermore, they must be able to adjust their speech for register depending on their interlocutor and the occasion, and to organize their discourse using appropriate rhetorical devices such as verbal underlining, circumlocution, and transitions.

Radio, television, films

Radio, television, and films involve primarily non-interactive listening comprehension, though they can indirectly contribute to improvement in speaking. Listening comprehension of radio, TV, and films is difficult because, unlike conversation, there is neither the opportunity for the listener to negotiate the meaning of what he or she hears nor the possibility of managing the direction or speed of the communication.

Error correction

In a number of the programs described in this chapter, there are special classes designed to correct learners' fossilized errors. The reason for such error correction is that accuracy and precision are very important at the SD level. Major errors in grammar should no longer occur, but there may well remain minor errors in grammar and word choice.

One useful way to approach error correction is via the "five-minute lecture" (Kubler [1985]), where students prepare a brief talk on an assigned topic which the teacher records and then goes over with a fine-toothed comb, identifying and correcting all errors in pronunciation, grammar, and vocabulary. Student

Table 5.1

FEATURE/PROGRAM	ACC	AIT	BLCU	CET/B	CET/H	FSI/B	HNC	ICLP	IUP	MTC	TLI	USCL
(Spoken Chinese)												
Formal vocabulary and grammar	+	+	+	(+)	(+)	+	(+)	+	+	(+)	(+)	(+)
Radio, TV, films	+	+	+	+	+	+		+	+	(+)	(+)	
Error correction		+			+	+		(+)	(+)			
Word study		+	+			+						
Accented Mandarin		(+)										
Public speaking		+	+	(+)	+	+					(+)	
Interpreting		(+)	+			(+)						
Language for Special Purposes		+	(+)	(+)	(+)	+	+	+	+	(+)	+	+
(Written Chinese)												
Newspapers and magazines	+	+	+	+	+	+		+	+	+	+	
Modern Chinese literature	+	+	+	+	+	+		+	+	+	+	
Classical Chinese	+	+	+	+	+	+		+	+	+	+	
Cursive script		(+)										
Composition	+		+	+	+		+	(+)	(+)	(+)	+	
Translation		(+)	+			(+)						
Language for Special Purposes		+	(+)	(+)	(+)	+	+	+	+	(+)	+	+
(Curricular structure)												
Tutorials	+	+			+	+		+	+	+	+	+
Content courses	(+)	+	+		+	+	+	+	+	(+)	(+)	+
Practicum	+	+	+	+	+	+						+
Internship					+							+
Language pledge	+				+				(+)	(+)		
Chinese roommates				(+)	+		(+)					
Instructors with content expertise		+	+		+	+	+	+	+	+		+
Option for university classes		(+)	+		(+)	+		+	+			

A plus mark + indicates that a given feature is a major feature of the program's curriculum. A plus mark in parentheses (+) indicates that a given feature at least occasionally applies to the program, but to a lesser degree than those features indicated by a plus mark without parentheses.

and instructor then drill and practice the corrections, after which the student redelivers the talk.

Word study
At the beginning and intermediate levels of Chinese study, grammar patterns are considered primary and vocabulary secondary since vocabulary can always be looked up and "plugged into" the patterns as needed. At the lower levels,

paraphrasing is encouraged, the main goal being to get one's general meaning across. However, as one progresses toward the SD level, the individual words themselves gain in importance. At the superior level, the learner must know the exact meaning and usage of words – both common and rare, as well as synonyms and antonyms. For this reason, it is important to spend time on word study and vocabulary expansion, e.g., principles of word formation, common abbreviations, and aphorisms. Just as knowledge of Greek and Latin roots can help a reader of English understand unfamiliar English vocabulary, so can familiarity with Classical Chinese help a reader of Modern Chinese understand unfamiliar words composed of Classical Chinese roots.

Accented Mandarin

While standard Chinese – the national language, based on Beijing Mandarin – is now used widely throughout China, it is often spoken with pronunciation, grammar, and vocabulary that differ markedly from the speech of Beijing. This is one major reason why American learners of Chinese, who are typically exposed only to the standard Mandarin of their teachers, frequently encounter difficulties in listening comprehension when in China. Students aiming for the SD level should, like any educated Chinese speaker, be able to understand the gist of speech in any of the major regional varieties of standard Chinese such as Shandong Mandarin, Sichuan Mandarin, Shanghai Mandarin, Guangdong Mandarin, or Taiwan Mandarin.[6] Moreover, the ability to identify a speaker's place of origin from listening to her or his speech can be both useful and impressive. Comprehension of accented Mandarin and familiarity with the characteristics and distribution of the Chinese dialects is best attained through a combination of formal training in the classroom – including explanation and practice with tape recordings or live speakers – and informal experience living and traveling in China.

Public speaking

Fully half of the programs discussed in this chapter include training in public speaking in their SD-level curricula. The preparation and delivery of speeches to Chinese audiences can be a very useful experience for the non-native learner. An approach similar to the "five-minute lecture" discussed earlier can also be helpful. All foreigners who have spent time in China are familiar with commonly posed requests, such as "Please introduce yourself," "Tell us about your family," "Tell us about your work," etc. At a higher level, one could add such questions as: "Why didn't the USA allow China to join the World Trade Organization?"; "Why does the USA meddle in Tibet and Taiwan?"; "How do you apply for a

---

[6] The ILR descriptors contain, as part of the definition of Level 4, the following phrase: "can understand native speakers of the standard and other major dialects in essentially all face-to-face interaction."

visa to the USA?" etc. Much like the "islands" in the Shekhtman Method of Communicative Teaching (cf. Chapter 6), it can be most useful, reassuring, and impressive for non-natives to have at their command two or three dozen "canned mini-speeches" on likely topics that can be produced as needed, adjusted for the occasion.

Interpreting

At the lower levels frequent reference to English was avoided for obvious reasons. However, at the SD level, some training in interpreting – both Chinese–English and English–Chinese – is needed, since it is clear that many students will have a need to interpret and will be expected to interpret well. The ILR description for S-4 states: "Can serve as an informal interpreter in a range of unpredictable circumstances." Interpreting is not an easy skill to learn since, unlike when communicating one's own ideas, as an interpreter or translator one is obligated to convey the meaning of the original as precisely as possible. It is noteworthy that, of the programs discussed here, only AIT, FSI/B, and BLCU provide training in interpreting. (For a closer look at training in interpreting skills at Level 4, see Chapter 4 of this volume.)

Language for Special Purposes (LSP)

LSP can be defined as a specific variant of content-based instruction that develops language skills *per se*, is usually taught by foreign-language educators, and tailors the topics of language courses to those needed for work by enrolled professionals (Leaver and Bilstein [2000]). Here, LSP is taken to mean job-related training in spoken Chinese, for example, preaching a sermon or delivering a diplomatic *démarche*. In addition to its primary purpose of teaching specialized language, content-based, job-related language training can also serve to enhance student motivation and increase interest and involvement in the language course.

Written Chinese

Newspapers and magazines

Even though the level of most journalistic Chinese is more closely associated with Level 3 than with Level 4, it is still important for learners aiming for the SD level to continue reading widely in newspapers and magazines. At the SD level, the goal should be rapid reading of difficult materials (such as editorials, commentaries, and book reviews) with nearly perfect comprehension.

Modern Chinese literature

Due to the size of the Chinese vocabulary as well as variation in style ranging from relatively colloquial to very literary, modern Chinese literature is considerably more difficult for the foreign reader than newspaper Chinese. For both linguistic and cultural reasons, students aiming for the SD level should read as widely as possible in modern Chinese literature from the formative period of the 1930s to today.

Classical Chinese

At most of the programs discussed here, students aiming for the SD level study Classical Chinese. For the foreign student studying Mandarin, learning Classical Chinese is like learning "a foreign language within a foreign language" and could be compared to studying Latin along with Italian, or learning Old Norse in conjunction with Norwegian. Although challenging, acquiring an elementary knowledge of Classical Chinese is essential for two reasons: (1) cultural literacy in Chinese requires familiarity with Classical Chinese, which was the standard written language of China from the fifth century BC until the 1920s and is the language in which the great bulk of China's literature, history, and philosophy was written; and (2) Classical Chinese is very useful for raising one's proficiency in Modern Chinese since both formal spoken and, especially, formal written Chinese have been heavily influenced by it (e.g., aphorisms, formal speeches, newspaper editorials, instruction manuals, road signs). Finally, some familiarity with Classical Chinese is useful for the non-native in gaining credibility in Chinese society; nothing impresses native speakers more than a foreigner who can understand – or, even better, recite from memory – a few verses of Tang poetry or some quotations from Confucius!

Cursive script

When handwritten by educated adults, many of the individual strokes of Chinese characters are connected, there being dozens of conventional abbreviations for whole characters or character components. Students at the SD level in any language should be able to understand the general meaning of notes and letters written in reasonably legible cursive script. The ILR requirement for R-4, for example, states that the examinee "can read reasonably legible handwriting without difficulty." Very few foreign students of Chinese currently receive formal training in reading cursive script, yet it is often a major problem for them in Chinese society. (American students studying at Chinese universities have frequently related to the author their difficulties in trying to decipher the notes their professors scribble hastily on the blackboard, and US consular officers serving in China have complained that their training in Chinese often does not allow them to make sense of handwritten reference letters or politically sensitive notes which they may not wish to hand to their local Chinese assistants for translation.) The attitude of most Chinese language-instructors appears to be that students will gradually "pick up" the ability to recognize cursive script through exposure to Chinese society, but experience has demonstrated that an analytical approach during the training program can make later on-the-job progress much more efficient.[7]

Composition

Composition, which is a difficult skill to learn in any language, is especially difficult in the case of Chinese, due to the difficulty of writing the characters and the complexity and degree of divergence from spoken Chinese of Chinese literary conventions. Consequently, the development of a high level of proficiency in composition – such as the ability to compose business letters, formal reports, and essays – takes very much time. Moreover, the process can be demoralizing for students because it is difficult for them to avoid making many errors. Most teachers have found that it is more effective to assign frequent short papers at first, asking students to turn in early drafts and providing them with opportunities to incorporate the teacher's corrections, i.e., to teach composition as process writing. Some composition may also be done on computer, as is being done with increasing frequency in China itself. This approach can speed up the composition process by allowing learners to focus on composition *per se* rather than on the production of individual characters which is, after all, the most time-consuming factor in traditional handwritten composition. In any case, at the SD level, more should be done with composition than typically has been done before, both for its utility for the non-native living in Chinese culture and for the significant payoff in further raising reading proficiency.

Translation

At the lower levels of proficiency, most instructors purposely avoid large amounts of translation since it is important to study Chinese on its own terms without constant reference to English. However, at the SD level, some training in translation is appropriate, since many students will have occasion to prepare written translations from Chinese into English for the benefit of others.

Language for Special Purposes

Language training at the SD level typically includes a component in LSP (see above definition) involving job-related training in written Chinese. For example, this might consist of readings in economic journals or documents pertaining to maritime law. Due to the specialized nature of LSP materials, it is desirable to have on the faculty some instructors possessing content expertise in the subject areas studied.

---

[7] From 1981 to 1987, the author directed an SD-level Chinese language training program in Taiwan which included an optional six-month component in recognition of cursive script. Practical experience over the course of several years showed that those students who took the course were much more successful at reading handwritten documents during their tours in China than the students who took only the required reading courses in printed-style documents.

Curricular structure

Tutorials

At the lower levels of proficiency, the needs of students are similar, making group instruction the most efficient format. However, as students' levels rise and their needs begin to differ, there is an increasing necessity for tutorial training. Ideal for students aiming for the SD level is at least one hour of tutorial per day for error correction, training in public speaking, Language for Special Purposes, and preparation for practica or internships. In fact, the majority of SD programs described in this chapter provide at least one daily tutorial. Observation by the author of students at the few SD-level programs that do not offer tutorials suggests that they are often weaker in the active use of formal vocabulary and grammar as well as in the accuracy and precision of their speech.[8]

Content courses

At the SD level, a high degree of cultural competence is required, including familiarity with Chinese history, geography, and major works of literature. The SD-level student who is not familiar with historical references, famous quotations, or literary allusions will not only encounter difficulties in comprehension but also lack credibility in Chinese society. While Level 3 students typically possess advanced proficiency only in one fairly narrow field, students aspiring to Level 4 must demonstrate breadth in a variety of fields including, in particular, Chinese culture. Their goal must be to learn the content and associated language that any educated Chinese would know. For these reasons, it is essential that, at the SD level, a substantial portion of the classes be content-based (see Angelelli and Kagan, Dabars and Kagan, this volume, for a similar point of view regarding Russian and Spanish SD-level classrooms).

Practicum

Another feature common to many of the programs discussed here is practica or field tasks, which are designed to get students out of the classroom and into the society around them to use their language skills to accomplish various kinds of tasks. One of the biggest challenges facing in-country Chinese language programs is how best to take advantage of the resources of Chinese society and coordinate classroom learning with community-based activities. The practica or field tasks typically consist of four parts: (1) task assignment; (2) preparation in class with an instructor; (3) implementation, with an instructor observing silently; and (4) debriefing, with the instructor providing a detailed critique

---

[8] At the otherwise highly respected Hopkins-Nanjing Center (HNC), for example, although students' listening comprehension, reading, and writing levels increase markedly after a year of training, speaking proficiency increases more slowly. Based on personal observation and the comments of others, many students at HNC seem to be at about the S-2/R-2+ level on entrance and may reach S-2+/R-3+ by graduation.

followed by drills and exercises as needed. Research projects are also common. Besides standard bibliographic research in libraries and on the Internet, students may interview members of the local community or, when this is politically permissible, conduct surveys. Each student has a mentor on the faculty with whom he or she meets on a regular basis for guidance. Typically, a project will include the preparation of oral and written reports. The oral report may be divided into several parts: (1) an initial report to fellow students on the topic chosen and research plans; (2) an interim report; and (3) a final report that is presented to classmates, teachers, and invited guests, after which there is a discussion period led by the student. This is then followed by the writing of a formal research paper.

Internship

Internships, which are offered at two of the programs, are similar to long-term practica. For example, upon completion of three months of classroom language and culture training, a student may be placed for seven or eight weeks in a Chinese company, where he or she works a minimum of twenty-five hours per week and undertakes a daily language tutorial designed to integrate language study with the specific requirements of the work experience. Or again, after several months of special study, an American student might receive an assignment as assistant manager at a Chinese hotel, where he or she engages in customer relations work with guests and reports in Chinese to Chinese supervisors. Internships have great potential value for the student aspiring to the SD level. However, for an internship to be successful, there must be thorough preparation and, ideally, the chance for the student to "check in" with a language teacher periodically.

Language pledge

Four of the programs enforce a language pledge, either absolutely or while on campus, that obligates students to speak only in Chinese, whether with native speakers or non-native speakers. Although no empirical studies of the efficacy of language pledges have so far been undertaken, the consensus in the field of Teaching Chinese as a Second/Foreign Language is that a strictly enforced language pledge can dramatically improve students' fluency and listening comprehension. The benefit for developing high-level speaking skills appears to be more limited, however, since the types of grammar and vocabulary associated with Level 4 do not frequently come up in casual conversation.

Chinese roommates

Three of the programs have either a requirement or an option for Chinese roommates. However, only at CET/Harbin are the roommates required to speak in Chinese. At CET/Beijing and the Hopkins-Nanjing Center, the American students and their Chinese roommates themselves decide what language to speak. If Chinese is spoken, this can obviously be extremely beneficial for improving students' fluency and listening comprehension.

Instructors with content expertise

Content courses and courses in Language for Special Purposes involve specialized knowledge and related specialized language which a professional language teacher with a general education is not normally equipped to handle. Therefore, in SD-level language programs, it is important that both language pedagogy specialists and content specialists be represented on the faculty. Ideally, these two types of instructors should coordinate their instruction, but this is sometimes difficult to implement in practice. Since the combination of language teaching skills and content knowledge is rarely found in a single individual, it is sometimes advisable to hire promising college graduates in the content areas needed and provide add-on training in language pedagogy. For the reasons discussed here, many US government language-training programs deliberately hire content specialists, as opposed to a faculty composed exclusively of language instructors. At universities, subject-matter specialists can team with language faculty as a mechanism for providing training in LSP (see Shaw [1997]).

Option for university classes

A number of the programs offer students the option of taking or auditing classes at a local university. This can be very beneficial since, given the large number of non-natives present, the language programs themselves do not provide an authentic Chinese environment. After a certain point in a learner's progress has been reached, he or she needs to be weaned away from the sheltered existence of programs for foreigners. Attending university classes is an excellent way to improve one's knowledge of Chinese culture and society, make contacts among students and faculty, and increase listening comprehension (including of accented Mandarin) and reading ability (including speed reading and cursive script). However, as noted earlier, university classes by themselves are usually insufficient for developing high-level speaking skills. An ideal situation for some students might be attending a formal course of studies at a university, combined with one hour of speaking tutorial daily with an experienced language instructor.

Conclusion

In the past, very few Americans began the study of Chinese and, of those who did, only a small fraction ever progressed beyond the beginning stage. Whereas formerly it may have been considered admirable or unusual to possess an elementary knowledge of this difficult language, that is now clearly no longer enough. As ever more Americans and Chinese come into daily contact and China becomes an increasingly important player on the international stage, it is essential that more Americans learn Chinese to the truly advanced levels, where they will be able to use the language fluently for a full range of functions.

To accomplish this, it will be necessary for students to spend substantial amounts of time in a Chinese-speaking environment. As has been pointed out in the preceding pages, however, going to China for a period of time is by itself not enough. The most efficient way to attain high-level proficiency is by attending a well-organized, rigorous language-training program, like many of those discussed in this chapter, followed by a lengthy period of in-country residence, where one is in close, daily contact with native speakers in both formal and informal settings. Of course, each of the programs discussed here has its own strengths and weaknesses. To render these programs as effective as possible, it is to be hoped that administrators and teachers will take the issues discussed here into careful consideration, as they work to develop and improve their training programs.[9]

[9] I wish to thank the following for allowing me to interview them and observe classes at the programs for which they are responsible: Chang-Jen Chou (ICLP), Lea Ekeberg (CET/H), Ho Ching-hsien (TLI), Hong Gang Jin (ACC), Elizabeth Knup (HNC), Vivian Ling (IUP), Luo Ching (MTC), Thomas E. Madden (FSI/B), Charles Miracle (AIT), and Yin Xiaoling (CET/B).

6 Developing professional-level oral proficiency: The Shekhtman Method of Communicative Teaching

Boris Shekhtman and Betty Lou Leaver
with Natalia Lord, Ekaterina Kuznetsova and
Elena Ovtcharenko

The method proposed in this chapter, the Shekhtman Method of Communicative Teaching (SMCT), shares the strengths and advantages of contemporary communicative approaches: differentiation between language usage and language use,[1] goal-oriented teaching that focuses on proficiency outcomes, authentic language use in the classroom, authentic tasks, and so forth. However, unlike most communicative methods, the SMCT teaches Language (the linguistic system) on the basis of Communication (the use of the linguistic and paralinguistic systems in written and spoken interaction), incorporating aspects of both learning and acquisition.

The SMCT consists of two parts. The first part involves using communicative tactics to improve the strategic output of speaking. Many instructors intuitively teach some of these tactics as part of their lessons; however, they do not do so as part of a "system." Further, although this approach improves Communication, it does not teach Language on the basis of Communication.

The second part of the SMCT is based on using communicative tactics as a principle of teaching speaking and listening. Accomplishment of the latter requires the conversion of these tactics into a system of teaching guidelines, based not on Rules of Language but on Rules of Communication.

Speaking tactics for improving communication strategy

The term *speaking tactics* refers to the devices (including, but not limited to, Communication Management Devices [CMDs]) that allow students to manage, and where necessary or useful, take control of a speech event. In interaction

The authors acknowledge the contribution of John Caemmerer to earlier descriptions of the SMCT Framework that have informed the current chapter and thank him for his assistance. They also thank Robert Fradkin for reading an earlier version of this chapter.

[1] General reference is made here to deSaussure's distinction of *langue*, the knowledge of the structure of the language, and *parole*, the ability to use the language.

between a native speaker and a non-native speaker, the non-native speaker constantly performs dual activity in real time: keeping track of the ideas of both (or all) speakers as they evolve during the conversation and understanding and generating speech consciously through the manipulation of foreign forms, sounds, and word order. In other words, conversational interaction for the non-native speaker is Communication mediated by Language, i.e., formalized intercourse, since for the non-native speaker what to say and how to say it are two distinct and equally important aspects of the interaction. Moreover, sometimes (and, perhaps, even often) the content of the conversation depends not on what the non-native speaker wishes to express but rather what he or she is able to express in the foreign language – a situation that is diametrically opposite to that of the native speaker. The teaching of speaking tactics seeks to ameliorate this situation and assist in developing more balanced responsibility for communication between interlocutors who are native speakers and those who are not native speakers. Speaking tactics include: (1) answer expansion; (2) use of "islands"; (3) using questions to continue conversation; (4) adherence to the known; (5) simplification; (6) accepting mistakes; (7) embellishment; and (8) complication. The skillful use of these tactics can help students improve their oral communication quite rapidly (Shekhtman [1990]).

Answer expansion

This tactic is used when a native speaker asks a question. In response, the student gives the most verbose answer possible. The question asked by a native speaker can be considered to be an invitation for communication. Short, simple answers hinder conversation because they very quickly transform communication into interrogation, making both the foreigner and native speaker feel awkward. Moreover, when the native speaker becomes the "interrogator," it places a sharply increased "language load" on the foreigner, since one question follows another. It also results in placing the native speaker in complete control of the conversation. This position of control is uncomfortable for the native speaker, too; he or she feels that the communicative process is ineffective, strained, and unnatural. The native speaker feels that the foreigner does not know enough language for normal communication; the foreigner, in turn, perceives that it is very difficult to satisfy his/her companion. Both parties want to escape from this unpleasant predicament. Therefore, either the communication stops or, if the native speaker knows the native language of the student better than the student knows the foreign language, it reverts to the native language of the student.

The importance of this rule for a Superior-level student is explained usually not by the fact that he/she is unable to produce an expanded answer but by his/her unawareness of the necessity to control a process of communication depending on the situation and the type of communicator he/she is dealing with (passive communicator, conversation "hog," well-balanced communicator).

Use of islands

When a native speaker talks, the language flows easily, without any apparent effort on the speaker's part. It is not artificial; it is natural. For native speakers, speech is as natural as walking: they do not need to pay attention to how the walking is accomplished; they just walk. Speaking in a foreign language is quite different; it is like swimming. When foreigners speak, they do not walk, they swim. Foreigners have been thrown from their native habitat, as land is for humans, into an unfamiliar language environment, as if it were a large body of water. They know very well that if they stop swimming, they will drown immediately. Unfortunately, drowning occurs quite frequently. As fatigue sets in after a long period of swimming, swimmers lose their strength and efficiency and sometimes waste their remaining energy through panic. In the case of foreign language speakers, the tension that results after time in an unnatural language environment causes an increase in errors and a decrease in speed and confidence in the speaker's language. Communication-aware teachers encourage "swimmers" (students) to look for small islands upon which they can rest during a conversation in order to gather strength before continuing. Such an island for the foreign speaker can be a small, but very well memorized, much practiced, or frequently used monologue. The more such monologues the speaker knows, the more such "islands" are available when the need arises, the easier it is for him/her to speak/swim. In essence, even a native speaker has a number of such islands. These are the speeches in which the speaker sounds more effective and articulate than usual. These are stories that, as the result of much repetition, are more polished and impressive. These are formulas for expressing certain positions or conceptions about which the speaker has thought and spoken often. These are the speaker's speeches, lectures, "opening lines," and remnants from earlier training. The use of such islands helps the native speaker to express him/herself more precisely and eloquently. If islands can be so helpful to native speakers, what can we conclude about foreign speakers? For the foreign speaker, an island is salvation: it enhances the flow of conversation, affords a desirable break, and attracts the attention of the native speaker. The confidence of a foreigner in speaking can directly depend upon the number of islands he/she has in his/her command.

Islands have communicative value not only because they provide the speaker with the ability to shift quickly into fast and confident speech, but also because they supply a variety of grammatical patterns for successful application to different contexts and situations. For example, if one particular island contains a sentence such as "*literature* plays an important role in *society*," this sentence provides the foreigner both with an example of a basic grammatical rule and with a model that can be used in a different situation, such as "*music* plays an important role *in my family*." The most skillful use of a sentence pattern occurs when it is used not as a conduit for specific content, but as a template for use in situations that require similar communication. For example, a speaker can recycle the model, "This is one of my favorite books" as "Paris is one of my favorite cities," using known lexicon and parallel structures. There is a direct correlation between the degree of control a speaker has of an island and his or her ability and inclination to use it. There is little difference between having a poorly prepared island and no island at all. Only a fully automated island that is produced reflex can ease the foreigner past the pressure of the communicative exchange with a native speaker.

"When all else fails," explains Clines, a *New York Times* journalist, Russian student, and frequent visitor in Moscow, "there remains [an] . . . island . . . firm as a riff of Melville." (Clines, 2001, p. 3)

Such islands, in Clines's opinion, provide students with a sense of self-confidence and power in communication.

In helping students identify and develop islands, teachers need to try to ensure that the islands are small. Short, specific, "modular" islands have been found to be easier for the student to acquire and can be combined flexibly with one another as necessary. Islands are chosen on topics for which students have a practical application; it is difficult for a student to internalize and repeatedly use something for which he or she can envision no need. Students participate in constructing islands. The topics and language of islands must reflect the student's style and personality to assist the student in mastering the island. Teachers train students in island use through questions and answers, repetition, retelling, substitution, and singing so that a variety of stimuli trigger the island in the speaker's memory. Teachers find opportunities for students to repeat each island as many times as possible in order to enhance the process of storage of information into long-term and permanent memory, which requires, among other means of input, repetition over a period of time and in a variety of contexts, in order to improve transferability to new contexts. The ability to recite an island must become a reflex[2] for the speaker.

The SMCT Framework suggests two distinct categories of islands. The first deals with an individual's personal background and information, while the second provides information on less personal topics. Usually the second group of islands is more professionally oriented.

---

[2] Although the specific nature of islands and the ways in which they are used in language instruction may be unique, the concept of "ritualization" in learning is not new. To some extent, it was used in Audio-Lingual Methodology (Lado [1964]), by a number of textbook authors, (e.g., Lipson [1968]), and in studying other, non-language content areas, the most obvious ones being math and science.

With Superior-level students, teachers focus on the capability of each student to produce the island in any topic independently, quickly, and correctly. After the student produces the island, the teacher helps the student to make it linguistically and stylistically more appropriate. The student should see that working at the island improves his/her communication dramatically and prepares him/her psychologically and linguistically to deal with all possible questions in communication (Shekhtman [1990]).

Using questions to continue conversation

Another way that students can manage discourse is to conclude an expanded answer or island with a question to their interlocutor. This tactic permits students to control interaction with a native speaker, eliminates pauses from not knowing what else to say, helps the flow of conversation when an answer has been rather short, and permits students to avoid the questions of a native speaker that they cannot answer for linguistic reasons or to change the topic of the conversation when they do not feel secure.

Working with Superior-level students, teachers need to focus on how quickly (and correctly) students can ask the question; on their ability to ask all the types of questions existing in the target language including the most sophisticated ones; and their skillful use of questioning that is situationally pertinent. For this, teachers must ensure that students have a good command of the entire system of interrogative models of the target language.

Adherence to the known

Even in communicative classrooms, there is often a tendency on the part of students to translate mentally from one language to another. This tendency increases when students try to communicate in words and forms that they know in their native language but for which they do not know the equivalent words and forms in the foreign language. Use of the tool, Adherence to the Known, means that rather than translating grammatical structures of their native language into the foreign language word for word, students are encouraged to use the models of the target language.

Understanding the functioning of this tool requires understanding the dynamics of having access to two languages. There is a very interesting relationship between these two languages, determined by the extent of the foreigner's knowledge of the second language. If the foreigner knows the second language as well as he/she knows the first there may be no interdependency between the two languages, and the choice of one language or another is situationally determined. At lower levels of proficiency, however, the relationship between these two languages can become complicated. In this case, the foreigner, as he/she encounters deficiencies in speaking the second language, relies on the first language for help. The first language begins to dominate in this relationship because the foreigner constantly speaks the foreign language under the influence of the first. In his/her desire to speak the second language as well as he/she does the first, the foreign speaker tries to transfer the grammar structures of the first language into the second one, which quite likely has absolutely different morphology and syntax. As a result, the foreigner's speech sounds obviously non-native. (At lower levels of proficiency, as long as the native speaker understands the non-native speaker, this attribute is not necessarily a "failing." However, at professional levels of proficiency, it is, indeed, a "failing" and can often prohibit the non-native speaker from attaining his or her goal in undertaking the communication in the first place.)

Alleviation of this problem depends on understanding the nature of the grammar model being used by any given student. Grammar models consist of three types: (1) patterns that a student knows automatically and are correct in the target language; (2) patterns that are automatic but not correct; and (3) non-automatic patterns.

The first model is most frequently used by students because they do not experience any difficulties with this set of grammar patterns. Automatical-and-correct patterns allow students to avoid the process of translation and speak correctly, fluently and naturally. Such patterns are, in effect, ways of using grammar and vocabulary appropriately and even often in a personalized manner; to this end, they have evolved from declarative knowledge to procedural knowledge.[3] These models generally reflect *acquisition*, to use Krashen's (1985) terminology, or *automaticity*, to use McLaughlin's (1987).

The second model is used willingly and frequently by students. However, students have acquired faculty grammar patterns and, therefore, speak with mistakes, although their speech itself is fluent. The grammar mistakes rarely interfere with communication and over time become fossilized (Higgs and Clifford [1982]). (Fossilization is discussed in greater detail later in this chapter, as well as by Ehrman, this volume.)

---

[3] We refer to the classical definition of declarative knowledge as consciously controlled information (e.g., knowledge of facts and dates) and procedural knowledge as unconsciously controlled behavior/information (e.g., riding a bike, getting dressed). Some information can go from one category to another, as in dialing a new telephone number (conscious application; declarative knowledge) and automatically dialing (without thinking) a frequently called number (unconscious, automatic behavior; procedural knowledge). We claim that foreign language, too, can make this transition from conscious control to automaticity. Memory and cognitive processing research tells us that meaning is most often internalized exclusive of language (Damasio *et al.* [1990]). If students, then, are to develop language skills, they will need to make the molecular changes in their brain that are required for pattern storage, and this happens through association of a group of pieces (i.e. a set of phrases, probably within a context) over time; such a repeated association of stimuli has long been known to cause a persistent change in neurons (Damasio and Geschwind [1984]).

The third model contains grammar patterns that a student might know either passively (he can recognize and understand the model in an oral or written speech) or even actively, but it takes some time and effort to use them and that inevitably interferes with communication. This model generally reflects *learning*, to use Krashen's (1985) term, or are forms and lexica that have not yet been "bound" (Terrell, 1986).[4]

Adherence to the Known means that in the process of communication students are encouraged to use only models of a target language that are either automatic and correct or automatic and incorrect. In working with students, then, teachers have two contradictory assignments: (1) to develop students' complete confidence in the use of automatic models while preventing the use of non-automatic models, and (2) to encourage a student to make non-automatic models automatic, thereby reducing the number of models that are non-automatic for any given student.

Adherence to the Known in the native language is especially important for Superior-level students. Feeling secure in a target language, they tend to try to express themselves in the target language in as sophisticated and elaborate a way as in their native language thereby increasing the temptation to translate literally from the first language. This is because students are attempting to enter into Communication without incorporating Language. For foreign speakers, rapidly inventorying and selecting from the linguistic forms available to them to express a specific thought, idea, or intention, is perhaps the most important tactic for successful speaking.

Simplification

Using simplified models means that when presented with a thought or idea that is difficult to express, students express it as simply as possible and immediately. While this sounds easy, very few students do, or even can, use this tactic intuitively. Most need to be taught the tactic and given the opportunity to practice using it.

There are several reasons why simplification is needed as a tactic. Sometimes when we are talking about the need to discuss or resolve an important element in a companion's questions, we have to find special tools. For example, what if the foreigner needs to express something difficult, but important, and his language skill is not sufficient for the task? What should he/she do in this case?

---

[4] In Terrell's framework, forms and lexica, in order to be acquired, must be "bound" to something in memory. Sometimes, an "ah-hah" experience will immediately fill an information gap and, therefore, immediately "bind." In other cases, binding occurs through comprehension and association – much in the way that Piaget describes learning to occur: through the "tying" of new information to old information, building chains of knowledge. If there is nothing to "hook" the new information to, it is not learned, acquired, bound, or otherwise retained in memory.

What if the foreigner must transmit to the listener a valuable thought, which *must* be understood precisely? What sort of tools can help a person to convey an essential thought in a foreign language, without the special vocabulary and/or grammar needed to do so?

The mechanism of simplifying that SMCT uses consists of three levels of substitution: (1) substitution of a sophisticated or technical word for the most simple, easy-to-use, and general word (e.g., *give* instead of *endow* or *disperse*); (2) substitution of simple sentence structure for compound or complex sentence structure (e.g., *I am going to the theater tonight, following dinner with old friends whom I have known for many years* can be replaced with: *Tonight I am going out to dinner. I am going with friends. I have known them for a long time. After dinner, we will go to the theater*); and (3) substitution of complex grammatical structures with elementary grammatical structures (e.g., *The car was driven in a very careless manner by its angry driver* can become *The angry driver drove the car carelessly*).

Superior-level students typically know several ways to express the same thought (i.e., grammatical and/or stylistic synonymy). As a rule, they use the most difficult model that corresponds to their native-language level of complexity. If a student does not know this complex model automatically, he/she can retard and even ruin the communication. So, while working with the Superior-level students the main goal is to systematize the synonymy resources of a student, to identify the degree of automaticity of synonymy models acquisition, to encourage the use of the most automatic models, to make less automatic models more automatic.

Acceptance of mistakes

Acceptance of mistakes means never having to correct oneself in the process of communication. If a native speaker continues the conversation and does not ask the student to repeat what he or she has said, it means that the mistake has not impeded communication. In this case, self-correction interrupts communication rather than helps it.

In so doing, it is very important to differentiate between communicative and non-communicative mistakes. A communicative mistake is an error of word choice, grammar, or syntax that prevents the listener from understanding what the speaker intends to convey. A grammatical, syntactical, or lexical mistake that does not interfere with what the speaker intends to convey is not a communicative mistake.

In the SMCT Framework, teachers explain to students that in a real-life communication (or a learning activity imitating the real-life communication) they should correct only communicative mistakes and not worry about non-communicative ones – something that usually happens in the native language since native speakers also misspeak from time to time. This focus on fluency does not come at the expense of accuracy, but it does give students the opportunity to talk freely without worrying about mistakes.

A secondary, didactic purpose for doing so is to identify the linguistic models that belong to the level of automatic but incorrect models and to the level of nonautomatic and incorrect models, informing curricular design for any given student or group of students. Therefore, exercises where a student "enjoys" his/her mistakes are followed by exercises that are aimed at correcting the mistakes and transforming the model into an automatically correct one. At the same time, the SMCT Framework teaches students to control their mistakes in the process of communication. For example, the student is told that he will converse on a particular topic and be allowed to make no more than three mistakes. After the student has made three mistakes, he or she is stopped. The mistakes are corrected and practiced. This type of activity forces the student to be conscious of grammar while speaking. This is particularly needed by students who are fluent but sloppy. It is also needed by students with fossilized mistakes. The number of mistakes allowed in this exercise can, of course, vary.

Among the students who have reached the Superior level are two groups for whom the clear understanding and skillful use of this rule is especially important. In the first group are the students who hate to make mistakes and to be corrected. To avoid mistakes they use only the models that they know automatically and correctly. This makes their speech very clean but prevents them from improving and enriching their language, often keeping them from attempting to achieve the Distinguished level of proficiency. The second group of students, for the most part, pays nearly no attention to mistakes because they know that they communicate fluently in any situation. If not forced to concentrate on their mistakes, their speech remains inaccurate, and in some cases, because of fossilized errors, they may appear more like Advanced-level students than Superior-level ones. In any event, their lack of grammatical accuracy prevents them from reaching near-native levels of proficiency, no matter how extensive their cultural and lexical knowledge or discourse or sociolinguistic competence.

Embellishment

The embellishment CMD helps students to add natural discourse markers to their conversations. There are many phrases that comprise this type of CMD. These include phatic functions, such as exclamations and repetitions ("Oh!," "Right on!," "You bet!," "Uh-huh," "Yes, yes," "No, no," "Sure, sure"), pause fillers ("Well," "Let's say," "You know"), parenthetical elements ("In my opinion," "Of course," "Without a doubt," "On the one hand / on the other hand," "I'd say"), parenthetical sentences ("When I went to Paris – I was still in college then – I hardly knew any French"), rhetorical questions ("But, who really cares about that?"), guidance questions ("I forgot – What did you ask me?"), and synonymous apposition ("The boss, my supervisor, who is very strict – rigid and stern – confronted me, or more precisely approached me head-on and said – well, actually, hissed like a snake to me").

The embellishment rule also teaches students to expand conversation through providing additional information, such as the use of adverbial modifiers of time, place, or manner ("Yesterday," "Later on," "Nearby," "Far, far away," "Perfectly," "Loudly") or through emotional commentary using idiomatic expressions and cultural slang ("Stop joshin' me," "What's going down?" "Get off my back," "Get with it").

By employing these devices, the foreigner can decorate his or her conversation, making it more lively and natural. Moreover, this tool attracts the native speaker to the foreigner, intensifying the native speaker's feeling that the foreigner knows the language very well, and, in turn, increasing the foreigner's desire for communication. Conversation is no longer textbookish but quite natural.

In our experience, embellishment is an unusual tool because it is very easy to teach a student all of its elements in just a short time, but it is very difficult to encourage students to *use* it. Since speech in a foreign language is difficult and the most important goal for the foreign speaker is to take care of the main ideas of the discourse, attention to minor elements, such as discourse markers, additional information, and emotional commentary, is secondary. In other words, the foreigner first must concentrate on the main components of each sentence, rather than on the minor ingredients; this results in "textbook" language and is often seen at the Superior level, where speech is fluent and mostly accurate but far from natural. The SMCT Framework trains students to use this tool automatically.

Superior students often already know, either actively or receptively, many of the phrases they need to use the tactic of embellishment. They, however, are not accustomed to using this tactic, and, therefore, classroom exercises can both help them understand this tool and get them accustomed to using it. Once they are comfortable with the tool, acquiring additional embellishing phraseology is not difficult.

Complication

Complication, the opposite of simplification, requires sophisticated grammar patterns and is used in professional speech events such as briefings, oral presentations, oral position papers, press announcements, and the like. These are special kinds of monologic discourse that are important particularly (and usually exclusively) for students at Superior levels of instruction. They may, for example, include delivering a monologue reflecting the views of a particular social group: the government of a country, the leaders of an organization, a group of workers, and the like. In any oral presentation, the speaker talks without interruption for long periods of time. This makes the briefing an unusual mode of interaction, especially for a non-native speaker, since the audience cannot react to his/her mistakes, even if he/she does make some. This places a great deal of extra pressure on the non-native speaker, who must ensure that his/her language is clear and free of error, since his/her audience is not one person but a whole group of people, often journalists or important officials. The task is somewhat simplified by the fact that one can and should prepare a briefing in advance. This rarely solves the problem of making the language error-free, however. A briefing, therefore, is a mode of interaction that should be attempted only by those with a rather sophisticated command of the foreign language.

Another significant feature of the briefing is that it is complex in content and therefore, as a rule, it is also complex in form. Briefings usually address complicated issues and are often prepared in consultation with a group of colleagues or various information sources that in turn may themselves be quite complicated in form. For these reasons, from the point of view of form, i.e. grammar and vocabulary, the briefing is the most complex mode of interaction, since it frequently calls for the vocabulary and syntax of written language in a wide variety of styles and replete with jargon. For this reason, it is necessary for the non-native speaker to learn to use complex linguistic models in briefings even if he or she is not yet ready to use them in other types of communication.

A briefing is most effective when it offers a clear, logical exposition of a subject, a position, or a concept. This requires that the non-native speaker acquire a solid automatic command of discourse corresponding to the nature of the oral presentation.

Finally, it is important for the person delivering a briefing to prepare himself or herself to answer questions afterwards. Only a person who is extremely well prepared on the subject matter of a briefing will be able to handle with ease the kinds of questions that are often asked following the lengthy monologue portion of a briefing, since they are often unpredictable and may be quite complex. This poses an extremely difficult challenge for the person wishing to deliver a briefing in a foreign language. To prepare oneself for this it is absolutely essential to go through a series of specially organized practice sessions first in which one is made to use the entire arsenal of tactical devices to field complex, unexpected, and even provocative questions either by answering them or avoiding answering them, all without revealing any linguistic weak spots.

Since oral presentations belong to one of the most sophisticated types of communication and demand the highest level of language command, the speaker cannot confine himself or herself to simplified ways of expressing thoughts and attitudes. In fact, the content of a briefing is often rather profound, and the

Table 6.1

Speaking tactics	Classroom activities	Status (completed, started, not started)
Answer expansion	Questions: (I) What do you think about the Russian economy today? What forms of property are there in the USA? Do we have inflation here now?	
Use of islands	Preparation of an island: World Financial System	
Using questions	Preparation of questions to the Russian economist. The topic is the American dollar and the Russian economy.	
Adherence to the Known	Translation of sophisticated English sentences on economy into available Russian models.	
Simplification	The immediate transformation of sophisticated Russian economy jargon (spoken by the instructor) into student's available language.	
Accepting mistakes	Discussion on the topic of Russian economy, without error correction.	
Embellishment	Parallel talk–show: simple sentence – embellished sentences.	
Complication	Improvement of an announcement or text using target topic models.	
Real-life communication	Meeting with Russian economist.	
Text for receptive and productive vocabulary acquisition	Work with updated texts from Internet.	

is then asked the same question and must repeat the island. In this case, the opinion itself – and whether or not it agrees with the student's opinion – is inconsequential. The point is to develop the discourse for expressing opinions. Later, by analogy and the application of other tactics, students express their own opinions eruditely and accurately.

Using questions

In using this device, instructors develop students' ability to ask questions automatically without thinking deeply about the content. In this case, the ideas being expressed are not the main point. Rather, the point of the exercise is to develop question discourse. Any statement can be translated into a question very quickly through formalization and internalization. For example, the language instructor makes a statement, followed by an interrogative word, as in "The Canadian prime minister went to London on March 22; for what purpose?," to which the student responds, "For what purpose did the Canadian prime minister go to London on March 22?" Or, the language instructor says that he or she will be talking at length about some topic, but, at the very first pause, the student must ask three questions immediately and as quickly as he or she can.

Adherence to the Known

The objective of this group of exercises is to teach students to use only automatic patterns. For example, the instructor helps the student by modeling the student's own linguistic patterns. The student begins speaking on a theme and pauses to search for a word or slows down his speech indicating that he is struggling to find appropriate structures and vocabulary. The instructor interrupts with the words "you want to say that . . ." and then uses an appropriate model that the student already knows. (For this, it is imperative that the instructor knows which models the student has mastered.)[5] Throughout this exercise, the instructor demonstrates what the student can do – or rather what the student should do the next time. The student then repeats the story using familiar models and avoiding the painful search for something that is not yet under control.

In the event that four-handed teaching is possible, another variant of this exercise is for the two instructors to carry out a conversation on a topic after which two students repeat the conversation. In doing so, they do not repeat the conversation word for word but use the synonymous expressions that reflect the models of language and grammar/vocabulary that they personally possess. A secondary purpose of this set of exercises is to teach students to recognize when they are being tempted to translate, and to choose not to translate, but to transmit, ideas and expressions.

---

[5] The importance of knowing what students know and do not know cannot be overemphasized. It is a key element of the SMCT Framework.

Table 6.2

Function	Complete sentence	Simple sentence
Invitation	We would be delighted to receive you as guests in our home.	We would be very happy to have you stay with us.
Apology	I regret to inform you that it will not be possible for me to be present.	Unfortunately, I will not be able to attend.
Reassurance	There is little cause for alarm at present.	You need not be unduly concerned. (Or: Don't worry!)

Simplification

Often when Superior-level students encounter difficulty in expressing a conceptually profound, highly technical, or grammatically complicated idea, the simplification exercises they have practiced help them to resolve the difficulty. Communicative experience shows that students without this tactic tend to create communicative tension. There are a number of exercises that can be used to help students avoid this tension through simplification. One is to present the students with a very complicated sentence and ask them to simplify it. For example, the paired sentences in Table 6.2 show how this tactic can be used in a variety of situations, the first sentence being the more complex grammatically, and the second being one of several ways in which the sentence can be simplified.

Embellishment

Embellishment exercises help the students' language come alive, taking on personal coloration that is usually seen at the highest proficiency levels. A typical example is when the instructor asks the student to include introductory words in a paragraph or to turn a simple sentence into a compound sentence. Sometimes a competition can be held among students to see which student can make a given sentence or text the most eloquent.

Complication

Complication exercises help students raise their proficiency to a higher level, enrich their speech with more sophisticated patterns, and, for this reason, can be considered the most important tactic for Superior-level students. They are based on the language instructor's analysis of students' speech and consequent introduction of speech improvements, which students then automate.

This kind of exercise is critical for developing students' skills in preparing papers and oral presentations on professional topics. An example of complication

Actual Communication	*Complication*
You ~~are asking~~ me what ~~are~~ my impressions ~~on~~ the United States ~~after I came to this country. I will tell you that my impressions are very striking~~. The first three months I was in the United States I felt ~~myself~~ as if I ~~was~~ in ~~the~~ fairy tale. First ~~of all, what astonished me that I saw a lot of~~ people of different ~~colors~~ and races. On ~~one~~ street I saw Oriental, Black, ~~white~~ and they were walking, ~~talking to each other the same language~~. The second ~~what~~ struck me was the houses—neat, beautiful, small, surrounded with trees and flowers and without fences, ~~open for public to be observed~~.	You *ask* me what *were* my impressions *of* the United States *when I first arrived here.* *I can relate that my initial observations made a striking impression on me. For the* first three months I was in the United States, I felt as if I *were* in *a* fairy tale. First, *I was astonished to observe* people from *many* different *ethnic groups* and races. On a *single* street I saw Chinese, Black and *Caucasian* people walking *together and speaking the same language to one another.* The second *thing* that struck me was the houses—neat, beautiful, small, surrounded *by* trees and flowers and without fences, *in full public view.*

Figure 6.1

is shown in Figure 6.1. (This is an actual example of a Superior-level Russian speaker who was in the process of acquiring English at a higher level.)

Materials

Materials for the Superior-level student are highly individualized and based on the results of initial diagnosis. The SMCT uses a diagnostic instrument that identifies five elements.

The first element identified by the diagnostic instrument is the number of models that are automatic and correct, automatic but not correct, and not automatic. The number and kind of models are identified on a student card. (Note: simple grammar, i.e., that normally found in traditional textbooks – conjugations, declensions, and the like – is not tested but, later in the program, if the student makes repeated mistakes on some simple grammar points, those are also entered on the card.)

The second element determined is the student's tactical armament: how, for example, he can produce an expanded answer or what islands he has (i.e., can or cannot speak without preparation on specific professional topics, such as education or work requirements, using set and anticipated phraseology). This will show what tactics need to be taught and what do not.

The third element of diagnosis is to define the vocabulary reserve of the student. This is done through the testing of representative lexical items from various topical domains.

The fourth element is to determine whether or not the student possesses theoretical knowledge of target-language grammar, as well as grammar terminology in English. In addition, specific linguistic questions are posed. This is important for knowing how to prepare materials for that student.

The fifth element identifies listening skills. For this, the student is presented with a number of tests.

As a result, three factors are defined: what the student knows, what the student does not know well, and what the student does not know at all. Based on this information, a program can be designed and goals set for a specified course duration and subsequently adjusted to the specific tactics needed and exercises included, along the lines of those described above.

On the basis of the diagnosis, students receive copies of in-house prepared materials: exercises, teacher-prepared texts. Students also use authentic texts from newspapers and magazines. In addition, each student receives a set of cassette tapes. These tapes include texts prepared exclusively for the individual student. Class activities are recorded on them as well, creating a personal language-learning record for each student. Support materials include activities from textbooks that reflect particular linguistic items from the student's program, and, of course, students have access to dictionaries and other reference materials. Many excellent, appropriate, and current materials are also obtained from the Internet.

The experience with SMCT at the Specialized Language Training Center (SLTC) has essentially included only tutorial students. However, Superior-level students at the Foreign Service Institute were taught as a group, using an early version of this method. In this type of class, it is very important that students be at the same level. Since the Superior level of language proficiency represents a wide band of skills, in group situations cooperative learning and small-group (dyadic or triadic) instruction often improves instructional effectiveness.

Development of high CF

For Superior-level students, development of high Communicative Focus means, in part, making their automatic responses closer to the automatic responses of the native speaker – that form of communication that can help the student to express his or her ideas without effort and stress (McLaughlin [1987]). To develop high CF successfully requires increasing the level of automatic response of students. For this reason, the SMCT provides many exercises and opportunities for multiple repetition.

One exercise, called the "Washing Machine," is used for development of automatization and error eradication. In this exercise, the instructor converses with the student and corrects the student's mistakes. He also jots down those mistakes. When he has collected a group of them he asks the student to "wash his mistakes." The student must be able to produce the correct response automatically. When he is able to do so, the mistake is crossed off the list. When he continues to have problems, the phrase goes into the wash for a second cycle and, if needed, a third or fourth or fifth. The student's linen must be clean at the end of this work. If it is not, the instructor has overloaded the washer. It is better to have the student correct three or four mistakes completely, than ten incompletely. Typical instructor mistakes when conducting this exercise include overloading the washing machine, underloading it, not putting the wash in for the needed number of cycles, overwashing, and throwing in laundry that needs to be pretreated first. It is up to the instructor to make the washing cycle an effective one by adding in the right amount of detergent. The detergent helps the dirt be lifted off without as much need for friction on the part of the machine. Not all cycles need to be on the sturdy cotton setting – some require the delicate wash. Therefore, mistakes that require the delicate wash cycle should be included on the list. Too much heavy-duty washing of mistakes makes the student emerge from the mistake washer full of psychological wrinkles.

Among other important activities that are accomplished with Superior-level students is the pairing of each student with an émigré partner for completion of assigned tasks. These are primarily individual activities. Group activities include lecturing to émigrés, talking to them on the phone, joining them for dinners, and writing to them for specific information. This gives students the opportunity for multiple repetitions in a real-life environment, helping to solidify automatic-correct responses.

Implementation of the SMCT Framework

The SMCT Framework is used in its purest and most complete form at the SLTC, a private language school founded by Shekhtman in 1987. Among the students of SLTC are correspondents of the major news organizations, business executives, government officials, scholars, and other individuals whose work requires the ability to communicate in Russian. Most SLTC students have specific content-based work-related language-learning needs. Their entrance proficiency level may vary from 0 to 4+. It is those who enroll at Level 3 proficiency (Superior level) with a clear need to reach the Distinguished level, i.e., near-native levels of proficiency, that we present here. At SLTC, students work with native-speaker teachers exclusively.

SLTC programs for students are learner-centered. Advanced- and Superior-level students are encouraged to participate in the design and development stages through a structured interview following the placement test. Teachers take into consideration students' learning styles, which they determine through an optional questionnaire and observation; learning styles and their implications are discussed with the students. Learner-centered instruction also includes working with each student to determine his or her areas of interest which then comprise the subject-matter core of each course, and, as a result, sometimes extensively rewriting syllabi to fit an immediate professional need of a student. Teachers make students aware of the Shekhtman Method of Communicative Teaching

(SMCT), described above, that is used at the SLTC, and its underlying principles and concepts, with the goal of making them better learners.

All programs at the SLTC, including and especially courses for Superior-level students, are taught via SMCT. Students are placed in accordance with an SLTC-designed proficiency test based on the ILR OPI. Students also fill out a Student Self-Appraisal Form. An interview or questionnaire identifies the social or professional situations and contexts in which the student will communicate in Russian.

The SMCT Framework has also been used in other institutions. Many of the principles that underlie the SMCT were first developed and tested at the Foreign Service Institute (FSI) by Shekhtman and Lord in the Russian Advanced Course, a 6-month program for Superior-level students that aimed to bring these students to the Distinguished level.

Results

Testing is generally not required of students who attend the SLTC. However, within these limited confines, it is possible to confirm that informal testing, as measured on the FSI proficiency scale, has revealed better-than-average progress when compared to generally expected rates of progress for time in study as researched and proposed by FSI from the 1950s to the 1970s and revised very recently. (For a discussion of these rates of progress, see Leaver and Champine [1999].)

Students in the Russian Advanced Course at the FSI (1984–1989) were formally tested. All students who entered with the requisite proficiency (Level 3 / Superior) and took the full course did reach the target proficiency (Level 4 / Distinguished), and one student reached a Level 4+, as tested by the ILR OPI. (Note: an analysis of the demographics of the student body showed that the vast majority of those enrolled in the course had either spent time in the Soviet Union, spoke another Slavic language, or were married to a speaker of a Slavic language – a trend that seems relevant to all Superior-level language courses.)

Student reaction to the SMCT Framework, both at the FSI and at the SLTC, has been overwhelmingly positive. Student opinion at the SLTC has been systematically collected through student evaluation forms. Journalist students have also published their opinions in various magazines and newspapers. (Representative student comments are in the Appendix.)

Discussion

Although SMCT is used at all levels of instruction from beginner to Distinguished level, students at the Superior level display some unique characteristics, to which the method is sensitive. As a minimum, these include specific (and specified) goal-orientation and professional interests.

Superior-level students, for example, usually know what they want from the teacher. For example, a student might insist that he or she does not need to work on conversational skills in general but on the ability to discuss a particular topic, such as disarmament or environmental hazards. The SMCT is a good method of choice in such cases because the materials and topics used by the method can easily and fully correspond to the specific topical and functional needs of particular students.

Superior-level students also tend to need deeper and narrower Language development. With beginning students, vocabulary, grammar, and topical intro-duction is generally broad and superficial. This reflects the needs of beginning students to develop over time a broad base in Language and Communication. Superior-level students, however, already possess this broad base and need to develop deeper Language and Communication, albeit within narrower – and usually highly professional (i.e., work-related) – parameters. Here, too, the flexibility and student focus of the SMCT enable teachers to meet these kinds of specific and individualized student needs.

Interestingly, another phenomenon has been noticed with Superior-level stu-dents who are taught via the SMCT. These students are often capable of self-instruction. Once they understand the nature of the teaching guidelines, they often take over the application of these guidelines to their own learning. Thus, they begin to create their own islands or to find ways to practice new expres-sions (not-yet-automated) at any opportunity. Superior-level students are also very good at expressing their ideas through the linguistic models that they have already internalized.

SMCT instructors often teach the students how to use language instructors and native informants. In essence, the teaching guidelines are adapted for stu-dent use in helping other teachers, who are not familiar with SMCT, to begin to use its principles in meeting their learning needs.

Conclusion

The SMCT differs from other communicative methods in that it has created a mechanism for connecting language acquisition with communication strate-gies. By subordinating foreign language instruction to Rules of Communication rather than to linguistic rules, while simultaneously in no way diminishing the importance of Language itself, the SMCT maximizes students' time on task, generally allowing them to reach higher levels of proficiency in communication more rapidly than typically anticipated. As such, the SMCT presents a novel and successfully tested option for language teachers at any level – and espe-cially at the Superior level where so few models for teaching exist – that may presage a movement away from separating the concepts of language use and language usage and toward teaching Language on the basis of Communication.

APPENDIX REPRESENTATIVE STUDENT COMMENTS

To understand the "Shekhtman Methodology," you have to set aside traditional ideas about learning a foreign language. Most conventional foreign language teaching is built around rules of grammar, which are drilled into the student's head in a tedious and time-consuming way. In the equivalent of a Russian revolution in language approach, Shekhtman discarded the old system of old grammar rules, replacing it with his own new system based on "rules of communication" . . . Shekhtman's "rules of communication" are designed to build a relationship between a foreigner, who is learning a new language, and the native who is already in command of that language. Recognizing the inequality in such a relationship, Shekhtman works to close the gap, to level the playing field so that communication can flow more naturally. (Correspondent, *Newsweek*, and former White House Assistant National Security Adviser)

The strength and science of your methodology are uniquely effective, and I plan to tell the world. (Faculty member, Harvard Institute for International Development)

I have studied numerous languages (French, Spanish, and German) and this was by far the most effective language training that I have ever undertaken. (Former Deputy Assistant Secretary of Defense for Russia and Eurasia, US Department of Defense)

plung[es] a student up to his soft palate in the viscera of the language. (Columnist, *The New York Times*)

The attention to grammatical models and rules of communication was rigorous. The program, however, was unique in developing communicative skills and preparing me for the actual give and take of verbal interactions. In many teaching programs, the teacher does most of the talking. At SLTC, the student does the talking. (Correspondent, *The New York Times*)

7   The LangNet "Reading to the Four" Project: Applied technology at higher levels of language learning

Catherine W. Ingold

While multimedia language-learning opportunities, including those that are Internet-based, have proliferated in recent years, little or nothing of an instructional nature has been available for the highly advanced (SD) language learner. The "Reading to the Four" (R4) Project, currently being developed[1] for the LangNet website of the National Foreign Language Center (NFLC), is intended to begin filling this void.

The LangNet Initiative

The LangNet Initiative (Brecht and Walton, 1993) is a complex, many-faceted effort that shares expertise and learning resources in order to enhance and democratize access to effective language-learning opportunities. The project discussed in this chapter is a seminal component in that it addresses learning needs that are underserved in almost every setting – those of the most advanced learners of languages critical to the national interest of the USA, for whom pre-existing learning resources are scarce and often of poor quality.

Progressive development and elaboration throughout the 1990s of Brecht and Walton's proposed LangNet model led to a pilot project in four Less Commonly Taught Languages (LCTLs) and development of a first version of a website and database.[2] At that time, NFLC, in collaboration with more than a dozen national foreign language teacher associations, began to identify categories of learners in each of the languages whose needs were underserved, initially focusing on the academic sector. Editorial Boards, appointed by the associations, located

The author thanks William Rivers and Patricia Fisher for their assistance with this chapter. Rivers provided editorial assistance and historical information. Fisher provided some portions of the text, as well as the Spanish Learning Object.

[1] Some components of LangNet in a Proof-of-Concept format may be operational as early as September 30, 2002.

[2] Agencies and organizations that have funded LangNet efforts include the US Department of Education Fund for the Improvement of Post-Secondary Education, Ford Foundation, National Endowment for the Humanities, Mellon Foundation, and the National Security Education Project.

high-quality learning resources, which they catalogued in a searchable database. That database currently contains approximately 1,000 items, ranging from dozens in little-taught languages such as Tamil and Yoruba to roughly 400 in Spanish, with tags for specific learning needs, as well as bibliographical and acquisition information. Software, dubbed "LangNet 1.0," was a first-version user interface that quickly and conveniently retrieved resources appropriate to individual users' needs.

The LangNet initiative as a whole encompasses the range of proficiency levels from 0 to 4.[3] This chapter, dedicated to the R4 project, focuses on the Superior–Distinguished (SD) level.

The "Reading to the Four" Project

The LangNet R4 Project was commissioned by the US government to support its linguists and the specialists who train them in meeting demanding requirements for effective reading in critical languages. Initially, the four typologically different languages mentioned above (Arabic, Chinese, Hindi, and Spanish) were selected as prototypes, from which many other languages would follow. The project assumes that linguists using these materials are currently functioning at an ILR Level 3 or 3+ and will benefit from support in setting specific learning goals and in utilizing effective learning strategies with appropriately challenging texts in order to advance to the ILR Level 4. It does not assume that these linguists have ongoing access to instruction or mentoring in their language development, although many often do. The initial focus on reading reflects critical work requirements of many government linguists and is to be supplemented later by projects dealing with listening and, ultimately, speaking. The decision to address reading first also reflects the relative effectiveness of online learning environments for reading.

Using the basic methods and constructs of the LangNet initiative, the R4 Project will draft for each of the four target languages a set of descriptions of the most salient language features/behavior ("language-specific objectives" in the current LangNet terminology) that must be acquired to move from an ILR 3+ to a 4 in reading *in that language*. It will then use those language-specific objectives as the specification for collecting or developing online modules, or "learning objects," defined as a combination of a text or context (content object) and strategic activities (learning tasks that incorporate learning styles information), that linguists can use to develop their reading skills. The goal is not only to provide an admittedly finite group of instructional materials, but also to provide the linguists with guidance, through a Learning Plan, for reaching Level-4 reading proficiency.

---

[3] See Chapter 1 for a complete description and comparison of the ILR and ACTFL proficiency tests and the attributes of Levels 3, 3+, and 4.

Need for the Project

In a recently published report, Brecht and Rivers (2000) document the critical shortage in language skills facing the US government, "whose needs are of unprecedented scope and complexity" (p. xi). The problem is both quantitative – 831 students enrolled in Hindi in all of the nation's universities in 1998, 4,764 in Chinese, 1,158 in Arabic (Brod and Welles [2000]) – and qualitative. Using a language in the workplace generally requires, at an absolute minimum, an ILR rating of 2 or above in the required skills and modalities, with many tasks requiring a 3 and above. Yet data from the last quarter of the twentieth century consistently show that few US language learners acquire Advanced-level skills as an outcome of domestic foreign language study (Brecht, Davidson, and Ginsberg [1993]; Brecht and Frank [2000]). As an example, participants in National Security Education Program-sponsored Study Abroad, characterized by Brecht and Rivers as probably representative of "the best outputs of the university system in the United States" (p. 100) reached proficiency levels of Novice Low (Level 0) for Arabic and Portuguese, Novice High for Japanese (Level 0+), Intermediate Low (Level 1) for Chinese (Mandarin) and Russian, and Intermediate Mid (Level 1) for Spanish.

There are many reasons for the low outcomes from the education system. First, language study in the USA generally begins in the teenage years, often for a very short sequence of study; the significantly earlier start and greater number of hours of instruction devoted to languages in the European Community offer a striking contrast (Ministère de l'Education Nationale et de la Formation Professionelle [1998]). Second, lack of national curricula and standard text-books often creates articulation problems among levels (Brecht and Ingold [2000]; Byrnes [2000b]; Lange [2001]). Third, the percentage of US students, even language majors, who engage in study abroad is low: fewer than 3% of all US undergraduates participate in study abroad during the course of their postsecondary education, and fewer than 1% of all postsecondary students participate in study abroad each year (Hayward [2000]).

Small wonder, then, that federal agencies compete for an inadequate pool of language-competent job candidates; and often are unable, even when they fill positions, to hire at the level of proficiency required by the job. Moreover, none of the agencies routinely provides instruction nor routinely produces results above Level 3–3+. Given that situation, the current R4 Project both presents a particular set of definitional and methodological challenges and promises a much-needed, albeit partial, relief.

The underlying system

It is important to note that the organizational approach described below is provisional. Representative components only, not the full system, will be tested during the "Proof of Concept" period – approximately six months in duration.

The interface

In conjunction with the R4 and recent related projects, the NFLC has redesigned the LangNet user interface. The new interface is intricate and highly flexible in responding to user needs. It consists of a diagnostic assessment of language proficiency and learning style preferences, a database of Learning Objects, and a mechanism for generating an individualized Learning Plan.

For the diagnostic assessment portion of the interface, the NFLC team has drawn on two efforts. One is a tool for determining linguistic deficiencies and prescribing remedial strategic activities, developed and used at the Defense Language Institute (DLI). The other is the E&L (Ehrman and Leaver [1997]) test of cognitive styles for foreign language students, used principally at the Foreign Service Institute (FSI), combined with a self-assessment of sensory preferences (visual, auditory, and kinesthetic modalities).

Based on results from the diagnostic assessment, combined with student identification of preferred (or required) content areas, the interface then prompts the computer to calibrate, compile, and present an individualized Learning Plan, a document that provides a list of Learning Objects (described in detail below) and guidance in their use. Figure 7.1 illustrates how this interface works.

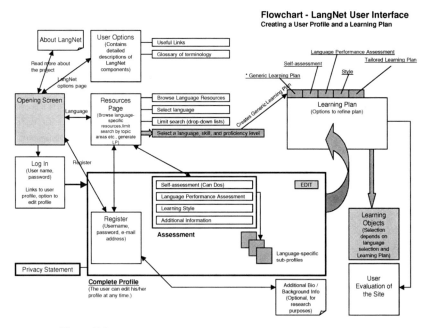

Figure 7.1

The Generic Learner Profiles (GLPs)

The system uses the overview statement of linguistic behaviors that characterize each ILR proficiency level, along with a significantly expanded list of associated Level-4 behaviors, developed through surveyed consensus of Level-4 language users and testers, as the basis for a set of Generic Learner Profiles (GLPs): one for each level and skill. Thus, there are GLPs for Reading at Levels 1, 2, 3, and 4, of which only the last is of concern to the R4 Project, and parallel GLPs will be developed in listening, speaking, and writing over time. These GLPs describe target behaviors (objectives) pertinent to all languages for each proficiency level, organizing them into as many as 10 functional categories. The GLP for Level 3+/4 Reading contains nearly 100 objectives. (A simplification [National Foreign Language Center, (2001)] is given in Table 7.1.)

General comprehension. The function category General Comprehension includes overarching objectives that derive from the ILR/ACTFL Proficiency Guidelines. The examples given in Table 7.1, as well as the remainder of the objectives, reflect the expectation that Level-4 readers will be able to understand nearly any text, no matter how sophisticated its structure or rare its lexis.

Strategic competence. This function category derives from the list of components of communicative competence suggested by Canale and Swain (1980). At this level, the nature of strategic competence appears to change, with much less emphasis placed on compensation strategies and a greater emphasis on planning strategies, as seen in the objectives in Table 7.1 (Ehrman, this volume; Leaver and Shekhtman, this volume).

Discourse competence. This function category is the second taken from the Canale–Swain list. Many Level-4 readers attending a May 2001 symposium on "Reading to the 4" organized by the National Foreign Language Center identified this set of objectives as critical for attaining Level 4, especially understanding of text organization and genre differences.

Structural competence. This function category includes part of the grammatical competence component proposed by Canale and Swain. At this level, readers are expected not only to have internalized the complete linguistic system, but also to understand a nearly endless range of archaic, dialectal, and obscure grammatical structures.

Lexical competence. This function category reflects the remainder of the Canale–Swain grammatical competence component, as it refers to reading. As with structural competence, readers are expected to understand a near-native range of archaic, dialectal, obscure, and invented lexical items.

Table 7.1

Function category	Objectives
General comprehension	understands all forms and styles of texts pertinent to professional, personal, and social needs on a par with the educated native speaker
	recognizes lack of comprehension
Strategic competence	plans approach to reading a text in advance, using logic and linguistic means available
	knows purpose and adjusts strategies accordingly
Discourse competence	understands most forms of discourse: persuasion, counseling, negotiation, conjectural materials, editorials, and literary spoofs
	recognizes erudite forms of discourse structures as erudite and interprets them accurately
Structural competence	exhibits complete understanding of grammatical structure, including many social and geographic dialects and many obscure, archaic, or, in languages where applicable, literary forms
	recognizes the difference between formal and informal writing styles
Lexical competence	understands a range of jargon: professional jargon, child language, "kitchen" talk, colloquialisms, and street language
	understands with near-complete accuracy any standard and commonly used lexical item, as well as many obscure lexemes
Fluency	holds new words, expressions, grammatical forms, and cultural and sociolinguistic information in memory while processing known information in order to absorb it from context or redundancy
	is aware when misreading occurs and is able to modify interpretation
Attentional focus	directs attention to intriguing unknown words and phrases
	directs attention to new ways of expressing ideas
Sociolinguistic competence	recognizes and understands professional, social, dialectal, age, gender, and country versus city registers
	recognizes appropriateness of forms of address for elders, children, pets, strangers, professionals, and others
Sociocultural competence	understands nearly all literary allusions in classical literature, popular literature, and interpersonal written communications
	reads beyond the lines, using knowledge of cultural and generational backgrounds for accurate interpretation
Emotional competence	infers personality attributes of the author
	understands emotional attributes built into the text (e.g., character intent in literary pieces)

Fluency. At lower levels of proficiency, the concept of fluency anticipates fluidity in reading; this can usually be accomplished with a singular, or linear, level of linguistic processing. At Level 4, however, attributes of fluency require multiple levels of linguistic processing, including holding new expressions in memory while processing known information. At this level, fluency also anticipates that students will be able to process most handwriting and nonstandard computer fonts.

Attentional focus. This category refers to those elements to which students pay the first and greatest attention. At Level 4, it is anticipated that ideas and mechanics can be processed simultaneously and that idiosyncratic ways of expressing thoughts will arouse curiosity and interest.

Sociolinguistic competence. The final component from the Canale–Swain list refers to readers' ability to recognize such socially bound elements as register, among other socially bound attributes of speech. Register for the Level-4 reader includes professional, formal, informal, social status, regional dialect, age, gender, and urban–country differences, as well as a wide range of slang, professional jargon, and acronyms.

Sociocultural competence. The ninth function category is an element of communicative competence suggested by a group of professors at the Pushkin Institute in Moscow (Mitrofanova, 1996) and defined as an understanding of "culture with a big C" as it is reflected in L2. At the 4 Level, objectives in this function category include the understanding of a wide range of literary, folkloric, political, and cultural allusions, as well as the ability to read between the lines of even sophisticated and idiosyncratic writings.

Emotional competence. The tenth and final function category is a component of language competence suggested by Eshkembeeva (1997) to mean the expression of individual identity in culturally appropriate ways. Although this function category is much more applicable to speaking, it does have a reflection in reading: the ability to understand emotional attributes built into the text (e.g., character intent in literary pieces).

Critical language features: the Language-Specific Profiles (LSPs)
The Generic Learner Profiles serve as the basis for the development of Language-Specific Profiles, which use the same organizational principle of proficiency level, skill, and functional category (competency), but describe the specific linguistic features that are salient as learners work toward a particular level of proficiency *in a particular skill in a particular language*. This distinction between generic and language-specific is intended to deal with the reality that

different language families present dramatically different challenges to English speakers in reaching a particular level of proficiency, with the critical language features for Level-4 proficiency in one language perhaps not being critical at all in another. For example, verbs play a minimal role in some languages but a relatively essential and complex role in others.

Learning Plans

Once the objectives (behaviors relevant to salient linguistic features) have been identified for the 3+/4 cusp in a particular language, the next challenge is to develop and make available learning resources that can be used by teachers and individual learners to develop those behaviors. One of the most innovative features of the LangNet Project is the development of a dynamically assembled Learning Plan for each user who requests one, personalized to the extent that user-provided information permits. User-provided information initially will include the target language, the skill targeted for development (initially, reading only), the ILR or ACTFL proficiency level of the user (based on prior testing, self-assessment based on behavior descriptions for each level, or completion of a "can-do" assessment), and (optionally) learning preference information.

With some or all of the information listed above, the query for a Learning Plan will provide a set of resources organized to assist the user (whether a learner or a teacher searching on behalf of a learner or group of learners). The resources include:
- texts (Content Objects) that provide a level of challenge consistent with the target level, including specific instances of the language features to which the language-specific objectives refer;
- Strategic Activities through which the learner interacts with selected texts in ways that are believed useful to develop the target behaviors identified in the objectives;
- Assessment Activities that either provide models of acceptable performance on the activities or suggest to the user ways to get feedback on his/her performance;
- pre-assembled Learning Objects consisting of one or more texts, Strategic Activities, and related Assessment Activities, addressing one of the objectives;
- other advice of a general nature related to crossing the 3+/4 cusp in reading in the target language, which may be related to learning styles, strategies for effectively working alone, and ways to increase opportunities for practice, among other possibilities;
- pointers to online sources of additional texts that present appropriate challenges.

Strategic Activities

Strategic Activities are language learning strategies embedded in a learning activity. They are selected to enable the user to interact with the text in ways that address one or more of the targeted objectives. They also provide examples to the learner of ways in which he can interact with texts in other situations, outside an instructional setting and outside the context of the LangNet system. This latter point is important because Level 4 requires, by consensus among those consulted in this Project so far, much more extensive reading than can be provided in any instructional system.

The Learning Object reproduced in Figure 7.2 (instructions have been translated into English) includes an example of a Strategic Activity related to one of the Level-4 objectives dealing with detecting and correctly interpreting rhetorical devices that convey author's spin and using the strategies of analysis, directed attention, and scanning/reading for detail.

Content Objects

Content Objects for this project on reading are specifically in the form of print-based materials. They are combined with Strategic Activities in order to produce a Learning Object that can be placed on an individual student's Learning Plan.

Content Objects most typically are texts, although they can also be contexts in which Strategic Activities are used. LangNet users will be able to browse Content Objects separately from the preparation of a Learning Plan if they so desire. For the Proof-of-Concept, content areas have been limited to geography, politics, economy, science, technology, society, culture, military affairs, and security issues.

Shown in Figure 7.3 is the Content Object of the "Author's Spin" Learning Object. This editorial has been used with other Strategic Activities to address other Level-4 objectives.

The challenges

The R4 Project has presented a number of important conceptual and practical challenges beyond those inherent in the overall LangNet Project. These include (1) finding experienced language users and teachers to inform the development process, (2) defining Level-4 behaviors and turning them into learning objectives, (3) selecting appropriate tasks, and (4) selecting relevant texts.

Finding experienced users and teachers to inform the process

A significant challenge for this project has been the identification of experienced Level-4 language learners and teachers of Level-4 programs to inform

II. Author's spin / Recursos retóricos (Highlight text)
Identify in the text at least five phrases the author uses to challenge the
credibility of the "intellectuals." After you make your selections,
compare them with the suggested answers.
Identifique en el texto por lo menos cinco frases con las que el autor
ataca la credibilidad de los "*intelectuales.*" Después de identificar sus
respuestas, compárelas con las respuestas sugeridas.
Feedback:
1. Quienes en Europa **sabían algo** sobre nuestro país,
2. Otros más enterados incluso podían saber que es el país productor
del café más suave del mundo o que es un importante exportador de
banano. **Pero apenas hasta ahí**.
3. Por eso no deja de ser sorprendente conocer el creciente interés de
tantos **centros de opinión**
4. cuando lo que ocurría era un cambio de escenario al trópico y del traje
de guerra de los protagonistas al **disfraz de inofensivos profesores**
5. estos **intelectuales** han escogido a Colombia como el último reducto
de sus batallas de la guerra fría,
6. No pocos ingenuos, sobre todo algunos periodistas y políticos, caen
en sus redes y se convierten en eficaces amplificadores de **una lucha
que ocultan hábilmente bajo el traje de los derechos humanos.**
7. Pero mientras esto para ellos es un capítulo más de la guerra fría,
librada desde sus escritorios y micrófonos, aquí es una confrontación

Figure 7.2

the process. First, there is no systematic testing done at this level outside the
US government. ACTFL, for example, tests only to the Superior level, and
although at one time in the past ACTFL did define a Distinguished level as
separate from and more advanced than the Superior level, for all practical purposes the Superior–Distinguished distinction is rarely, if ever, made. Second,
the number of Level-4 programs is extremely limited, and many, if not most, of
them are "Beyond Three" in objective, rather than "to four" – that is, they teach
students who are at the Superior level with the goal of helping them develop
their skills further but do not have a clear goal of having students achieve Level
4 (Ehrman, this volume).[4]

LangNet staff with Level-4 learning and teaching experience were an essential, albeit small, group that developed the original GLPs for Level 3+/4. In
addition, a small number of experienced users and teachers were found through
"snowball" searching; these few people were able to provide feedback and help
expand the GLPs and other aspects of the process.

---

[4] An exception to this is the Russian Advanced Course at the Foreign Service Institute, which,
from 1984 to 1988, routinely taught groups of students, enrolling at Level 3 and graduating six
months later at the established goal of Level 4 (Leaver and Bilstein [2000]).

Introducci n: El siguiente editorial del peri dico colombiano El Mundo incluye actividades de vocabulario con enf sis en figuras ret ricas.

I.   **Reading/ Lectura**

 **Miércoles 23 de mayo de 2001**

EDITORIAL

El último reducto

Desde Europa, un grupo de *intelectuales* de iglesias, universidades, ONGs y el arte, liderados por el Nobel portugués José Saramago, acaba de producir un documento pidiéndole a la *"opini n p blica internacional"* rechazar el Plan Colombia por su carácter militar, mientras en Oxford, por otra parte, culminó una reunión que también convocó a *intelectuales* franceses, alemanes e ingleses junto a la organización *"Di logo Interamericano por Colombia" (?),* para manifestar su inquietud por *"la derechizaci n del pa s, el crecimiento de las autodefensas y la desprotecci n de la poblaci n civil".*

Desde hace muchos años, cuando la guerrilla dejó de ser liberal para ponerse al servicio del comunismo, dirigida y auxiliada desde Cuba, el país viene sufriendo sus crecientes ataques, cada vez más inhumanos. Desde hace veinte años, nuestro país libra una dura lucha contra el narcotráfico, en un titánico esfuerzo que a veces parece llevarnos al agotamiento. Durante este tiempo, Colombia había estado sola. Quienes en Europa sabían algo sobre nuestro país, lo identificaban como el exportador de la cocaína que consumen los *yuppies* en Nueva York, Hollywood y las grandes urbes europeas. Otros más enterados incluso podían saber que es el país productor del café más suave del mundo o que es un importante exportador de banano. Pero apenas hasta ahí. Por eso no deja de ser sorprendente conocer el creciente interés de tantos centros de opinión por la suerte de este, uno de los tantos países del mundo que en la actualidad libran una confrontación interna.

La razón por la que una nación más de Sudamérica acaba por convertirse en el polo de atracción de intelectuales y ONGs, que tienden a calificarse como *"progresistas"* y se definen abanderadas de lo *"pol ticamente correcto",* hay que buscarla muy lejos de este trópico, en la historia que maravilló al mundo al comienzo de los años 80, cuando los reformistas, entusiasmados por Gorbachov e impulsados por Yeltsin, acabaron con el imperio comunista en la Unión Soviética, y abrieron las puertas al derrumbamiento del muro de Berlín y prácticamente lo que quedaba del comunismo como gobierno, dejando como único sobreviviente de la *pura doctrina* –algunos lo califican de dinosaurio– al comandante Castro. Con la apertura de la simbólica Puerta de Brandemburgo el marxismo-leninismo perdió su más importante batalla de la guerra fría en forma tan contundente que algunos proclamaron entusiastas *"el fin de la historia",* cuando lo que ocurría era un cambio de escenario al trópico y del traje de guerra de los protagonistas al disfraz de inofensivos profesores.

No es que estos *intelectuales* –entre quienes aparecen aguerridos defensores del marxismo desde el corazón del capitalismo, como la lingüista Noam Chomsky– estén muy preocupados por los colombianos que son asesinados cada año; tampoco por las decenas de pueblos que anualmente destruyen los guerrilleros con sus ataques con pipetas de gas y bombas; no creemos que lo que realmente les preocupa sea el acelerado empobrecimiento del pueblo colombiano, ni la pérdida de oportunidades económicas para este país. No; estos *intelectuales* han escogido a Colombia como el último reducto de sus batallas de la guerra fría, como se demuestra en el párrafo del comunicado de Saramago y compañía que reclama porque el Plan Colombia *"se dirige, sin duda alguna, al control de la cuenca amaz nica, afectando la soberan a de los pa ses que la integran".* Un fementido reclamo de quienes ven amenazado el brillante prospecto de extender la República del Caguán a la madre de las cuencas.

Y como estrategia para librar esa batalla final, estos expertos en la *combinaci n de todas las formas de lucha* han escogido la guerra de la desinformación, que arrasa sin vergüenza con cualquier asomo de verdad. Por eso hablan de *derechizaci n* y se atreven a seguir diciendo que la alternativa de nuestro país para el manejo de los cultivos ilícitos es *"la sustituci n sin el empleo de la guerra, ni aumentando los problemas de los desplazados".* No pocos ingenuos, sobre todo algunos periodistas y políticos, caen en sus redes y se convierten en eficaces amplificadores de una lucha que ocultan hábilmente bajo el traje de los derechos humanos. Pero mientras esto para ellos es un capítulo más de la guerra fría, librada desde sus escritorios y micrófonos, aquí es una confrontación bañada en sangre de inocentes, que se derrama en un país al que muchos de ellos no podrían identificar en un mapa. Por lejanos, inoportunos y aprovechados, preferimos, como los angloparlantes, decirles con alguna elegancia *"Mind your own business",* en lugar de disfrazar su batalla por su ideología en interés por un país que desconocen y pretenden explotar para su causa.

Figure 7.3

Defining Level-4 behaviors

Defining Level-4 behaviors was also a challenge. Although there are descriptions of Distinguished-level language performance, they are summative, general, and global in nature, not readily lending themselves to the development of objectives. The objectives, then, were determined in several ways. First, the descriptors for the ILR/ACTFL standards were deconstructed, categorizing them by the most salient of the competences enumerated above. Some cross-checking has been done at this writing with the C-2 level of the *Modern Languages: Learning, Teaching, Assessment. Common European Framework of Reference* (Council of Europe Modern Languages Division, 2001), but more extensive study of and comparison with the European work will be carried out later. (The ILR descriptors themselves, however, are particularly important for this project because the primary clientele, US government employees, must demonstrate proficiency through assessment instruments based on those descriptors.)

A next task was to determine which target behaviors, essential for Level-4 proficiency, present the greatest challenges to learners seeking to cross the threshold between 3+ and 4; and particularly to make that determination language by language. To that end, the Project gleaned information from teachers, learners, and examiners with Level-4 experience or attainments about (1) the nature of the greatest challenges and (2) what activities, both instructed and experiential, contributed to attaining Level-4 skill in reading. The language-specific teams used that information to identify a minimum of nine objectives (three from each of three function categories) that met the criteria of being level-appropriate, nontrivial for reaching Level 4, and susceptible to focused instruction and/or expert feedback. (It is worth noting that, across the four unrelated languages in the project, the function categories consistently chosen were general, discourse, sociocultural, and lexical competences.) It is expected that there will be changes and additions to these prototype objectives once they, and the Learning Plans and Learning Objects built on them, have undergone field testing and further study.

Selecting appropriate tasks (strategic objectives) for learning

Yet another challenge has been determination of the kinds of tasks or Strategic Activities that are appropriate for an online learning program that can be used both in the classroom and independent of it. Extensive reading, for example, does not lend itself readily to classroom activities; yet, that is one activity that all learners and teachers agree is required. Some alternative activities that are being tested in the Proof-of-Concept model include the teaching of strategies for use in extensive reading, making choices among heavily loaded terminology with multiple connotations (i.e., identifying the appropriate definition given a specific context and authorial intent), and the like.

Selecting relevant texts

The choice of texts for the lessons or Learning Objects to be presented in the Learning Plans is governed by the Language-Specific Objectives. The texts must provide appropriately challenging instances of the linguistic phenomena that, in the experience of the teachers and learners consulted, are salient for learners of that particular language moving from a 3 to a 4 in reading. The Spanish team, for example, has found a number of subtle and extremely well-written editorials on contemporary events in Latin America that make extensive use of socioculturally loaded terms and phrases based in current or recent political events or in popular culture within a particular country – which constitute a particular challenge for linguists not currently living in the country in question. To date, finding texts that are generally sophisticated and/or problematic, and searching through them for instances of challenges relevant to Level-4 objectives, has proved a more productive avenue than looking at texts for their overall level. Most texts tend to be a combination of relatively transparent and challenging passages, with few exhibiting most of the challenges addressed in the objectives.

Planned next steps

The first set of action items involves the completion of the Proof-of-Concept model. Underway are the preparation of Learning Plans based on Learning Objects (themselves the result of extensive efforts in developing Content Objects, Strategic Activities, and both Generic and Language-Specific Profiles with their respective sets of objectives) and creation of the computer interface. Several information-gathering and expertise-sharing seminars have been conducted, and more are planned.

Once the Learning Objects are in place for the Proof-of-Concept model, field testing will take place. In its earliest stages, field testing will be conducted in US government settings, as well as a limited number of academic venues. Spanish, for example, can be more readily vetted in an academic institution, thanks to the large number of Spanish programs available, whereas LCTLs, such as Hindi, have few potential users in academe unless, perhaps, one were to field test in other countries.

The initial products, then, will be the LangNet user interface and database of resources, including Learning Plans and Learning Objects at levels 3+ to 4 in Arabic, Chinese, Hindi, and Spanish, as well as learning plans and learning objects for 0+ to 3 in a variety of other languages. (Once fully operational, the R4 Project, like other LangNet projects under construction and/or proposed, will encompass over twenty languages.) These products are accompanied by a Procedures Manual (NFLC, 2001) that codifies the process and provides details of the products.

Following the appearance of these initial products, plans call for a quality review, language by language, conducted by the representatives of the relevant national foreign language associations. The process itself will be refined based on experience, field tests, and other kinds of feedback. The languages, skill areas, and proficiency levels included in LangNet will be augmented. The project itself is envisioned as a multistep, multi-year enterprise that is as much a process as a product, one that will require continuing refinement, seek continuing information from the field, and, it is hoped, provide a continually improving resource to the foreign language learning and teaching community.

Over the longer term, the plan is to build a much more comprehensive system of technologically mediated support for Superior/Distinguished learners that includes such features as a network of native-speaking mentors. Much work is needed in the short term, however, to assure that the system is user-friendly and efficient and that the quality of the content provided is universally high and appropriate to learner needs.

Conclusion

The LangNet Project is evolving so fast that one hesitates to document this particular stage in a book with prospects of a long shelf-life. Looking toward the future, one can imagine that the system will continue to evolve as more is learned about how these levels are attained and how a system such as this one can complement traditional instruction and unstructured experience – indeed, how such a system may help a learner weave together the disparate components that make up a language-learning career. What is particularly evident at Level 4, because it is attained typically after relatively extensive multi-year language learning and use, is that the particular complement of knowledge, skills, and attitudes that a language learner/user exhibits at any point is the product of an enormously complex interaction of the learner's uniqueness (cognitive, affective, social) and the particular mix of language experiences s/he has had. The result is the "snowflake phenomenon": no two learners have exactly the same skills and knowledge or the same set of strategies for learning and using languages. Moreover, because language is used to communicate all human knowledge, feeling, and experience, there is no way of constraining *a priori* the communicative demands that may be placed on an individual. The LangNet system must thus support the greatest possible range of personal requirements, and priorities can only be set based on the pre-definable needs of its known clientele.

In the case of the R4 Project, modest framing of the task is provided by the ILR descriptors. In the next few years, there will be an effort to develop global language-proficiency tests for US government personnel that are able to differentiate among the upper reading and skill levels of 3, 3+, and 4 in meaningful ways. The authors of the European Framework are actively encouraging the development of more focused frameworks (i.e., specific language proficiency) based on use requirements for specific jobs and content domains: these would be valuable in this context as well. Taken together, these two instruments might do much to guide further development of online SD-level language instruction and inform the ongoing continuous refinement of the R4 and related LangNet projects.

The ongoing research into how learners have attained Level 4 will help in providing an additional type of much-needed information: if these are the objectives that the learner needs to work on next, what can s/he do, and what can a teacher/mentor help her/him to do, to reach those objectives? Given the reality that many linguists working toward Level 4 lack access to formal instruction, that learners must bear much of the responsibility for deriving benefit from experiential learning opportunities, that curriculum for this level will in any case require extensive personalization to be effective, and that many of the language mentors available to these learners will not have training or experience as language teachers, the value is evident of an "expert system" that delivers web-based diagnostic assessment, tailored Learning Plans, Learning Objects complete with feedback, and guidance in how to learn effectively. The many participants in the LangNet Project from across academe and the US government are deeply committed to seeing this grand experiment reach its full potential.

8   In the quest for the Level 4+ in Arabic: Training Level 2–3 learners in independent reading

Elsaid Badawi

Arguments are made here that, in learning foreign languages, achieving independence at Level 2–3, particularly in reading, is a prerequisite for generating the power necessary for breaking away from the learning plateau characteristic of that level and continuing to Level 4 and beyond. Achieving such independence can, under the proper conditions, be realized through the effort of the learners themselves. The experiment in Independent Reading (IR) outlined below (which took place between 1970 and 1977)[1] was based on several considerations. Important among these were (1) the centrality of reading in foreign language acquisition, (2) the nature of Arabic as a polyglossic language, (3) the bi-polar competence of the educated Arab as the model for the educated foreign learner, and (4) a suggested strategy for learning polyglossic Arabic. The course on independent reading was taught at the Center for Arabic Study Abroad (CASA) as a part of a full-year program in Advanced Arabic to American graduates at the American University in Cairo. This chapter discusses that course within the following framework: (1) preliminary considerations, (2) the CASA program, and (3) a detailed description of the course itself.

Preliminary considerations

Centrality of reading in foreign language acquisition

Experience shows that adults seriously seeking to learn foreign languages to high levels of proficiency have had, as a rule, significant amounts of formal education, i.e., are either college graduates or undergraduates. For such people, the printed word will have become, at this stage of their development, of paramount importance in their pursuit of knowledge. The printed word, important to the already educated as, perhaps, the most effective and reliable tool for sustained

---

[1] The program changed executive directors after 1977. The IR course is still being offered with some inconsequential changes. However, the account given here is limited to the 1970–1977 period when the writer served as curriculum advisor for two years, then for five years as executive director as well.

learning (new subjects, new skills, etc.), is also significant in learning foreign languages. Experience also shows that foreign language learning methods mainly utilizing the spoken word have (in spite of their current pedagogical appeal) a limited, albeit important, role to play in the totality of learning the target language to high levels of proficiency. The Audio-Lingual Method, for instance, so strongly advocated and widely employed in the 1970s, may significantly help in putting the learners on their way to acquiring plausible and effective pronunciation and listening skills. However, it usually loses its edge beyond the elementary level when the need for vocabulary and structural wealth begins to grow.[2]

Even in proficiency-oriented approaches, in which all four skills are supposed to receive equal attention from learners, teacher examination of what actually takes place inside and outside the class indicates that in the case of those who have achieved high levels of proficiency *reading* seems to have been assigned the largest share of attention. Further, not only do adult learners come to the language-learning task as already printed-word preconditioned but also only the printed word, no matter how learned a company the learner may keep, is capable of providing the learner with material sophisticated enough to help her/him to internalize the multiplicity of possible social nuances.

In addition to the generic role it plays in the learning of Arabic, reading has special significance for the learning of this language, necessitated by the nature of Arabic as a polyglossic language (Badawi [1985]). (The most salient features of this situation in Arabic are given here in order to facilitate some of the arguments upon which this experiment in reading is based.)

The polyglossic nature of Arabic

Broadly speaking, the term, *Arabic*, embraces several language varieties, which can be classified into two major types. These are labeled by Ferguson (1959) as High (H) and Low (L).

H Arabic is a prestigious variety mainly used for written communication. It is variously termed, somewhat unsatisfactorily, *Classical*, *Literary*, *Written*, *Standard*, and, by Arabs, *Fusha* (the eloquent). Societal forces, mainly religious, have been helping to maintain for the H variety continuous intelligibility throughout the documented 16 centuries of its existence – from approximately two centuries before the birth of Islam in the 6th century AD to the present day – and continue to do so. Important for our purposes here is the fact that similar forces (including, recently, nationalistic ones) prevalent in all Arab countries throughout the successive centuries have helped to maintain for H what can be described as a "detached" existence, minimally touched by local geographical

---

[2] Out of curiosity I took an audiolingual course in absolute beginner's French at the French Centre in Cairo in the early eighties. Everything went fine for three weeks until with no warning the teacher asked us to take a dictation without ever having shown the class a printed word!

influences. The great concern of Arabs – in particular, of Moslems – has been, and is still, the arrest of natural language-change processes and the maintenance of perfect parallelism with the language idiom of the Koran, which, aided by the strength of religious beliefs, has met with remarkable, if not complete, success.

Passage of time, more than geographical changes, has had the greater influence on the H variety. As a result, we can predicate on a formal basis, in spite of the historically maintained intelligibility, a Modern H, a Classical H, and, also, a Medieval H. The most significant feature of H in learning/teaching Arabic as a foreign language, however, is that there has not been, at any point in the history of H, sufficient linguistic features particularly characterizing the geographical varieties in such a way as to enable us to establish what may be labeled as Syrian Modern Arabic, Egyptian Modern Arabic, Saudi-Arabian Modern Arabic, and the like, in the way linguists are able to distinguish among American English, British English, Ghanaian English, and other dialects.

Further, in spite of the historical nomenclatures, the three varieties that can be established for H are functional in contemporary Arab societies on a complementary distribution basis: Classical H mainly for religious functions for Moslems (non-Moslems generally use Modern H), and Medieval H principally for the voluminous literature of Moslem, Christian, Jewish, and other scholars of the Golden Era of Islamic Civilization. Both varieties are allocated space in the school curriculum throughout the Arab world and, in fact, are favored as writing idioms by many classically minded contemporary Arab scholars. However, because of the comparatively limited roles these two variants play in Arab societies they must be considered, at least, as marked varieties. Modern H, on the other hand, is the universal, unmarked, medium of contemporary learning and culture in Arab societies. Modern H is fully functional as a written medium, although as a spoken one it has only narrowly prescribed formal functions which are poorly carried out by halting performers. Reading of news bulletins on radio and television, which is always carried out through H, cannot be considered as speaking. The situations in which spoken Modern H is used as a necessary medium of communication between individual Arabs are conferences and learned gatherings of Arab scholars from different Arab countries. Oral performances in H, which vary considerably in the level of proficiency from one individual to the next, cannot be described as native ability. (In fact, some, on such occasions, substitute the H with Educated Colloquial Arabic.) Lack of sufficient geographic boundaries has caused Modern H to become known as Modern Standard Arabic (MSA).

L Arabic ("Ammiyya," i.e., vernacular or colloquial) is the medium of spontaneous oral communication. It varies markedly from one Arab society to the other to a degree where intelligibility, particularly in contexts removed from learned topics, may become seriously impaired. Syrian, Moroccan, Egyptian, and Iraqi colloquials, for instance, are independent mediums, each exhibiting its own structure, vocabulary, and semantics.

Because L stands in opposition, in the eyes of Arab societies, to H with all its religious and nationalistic affinities, it carries a social stigma and is regarded, even by some scholars, as having merely corrupted H features. Writing in L has been sporadically attempted. The introduction of the European-style theatre in Arab countries, particularly Egypt, nearly two centuries ago, provided grudgingly, if slowly, a respectable context for writing in L. Educated Arabs rarely write in their own brand of L even in personal letters, but when they do they often render the spoken words idiosyncratically. In this regard, writing in L parallels attempts to speak H.

The interaction between H as a written medium for learning and culture and L as a spoken medium of spontaneous self-expression resulted in the creation of Educated Spoken Arabic which, together with MSA, can be regarded (but is not readily accepted, particularly by the Arabs) as the living language of culture and education in the Arab world (Badawi [1985]). An important difference between H and L is that the former is the product of formal schooling whereas the latter is learned at home.

The bi-polar competence of the educated Arab as a model for the Level 4+ learner of Arabic

Now comes the question of where the foreign learner stands with regard to this language situation. If one agrees with Lado's (1964) premise, as I do, that in learning a foreign language the educated adult (except in some special situations) usually identifies with her/his counterpart in the target society, and given that the serious learner aims at gaining competence approximating, as much as possible, that of the educated native speaker, then the question may be answered by mapping out the totality of language skills an Arab adult is supposed to possess upon graduation from college. (I have chosen this approach rather than the somewhat fragmentary Arabic Proficiency Guidelines that fail to package L and H features together and posit features that are not possessed even by native Arabs.)[3]

Typically, a college-educated Arab possesses two sets of Arabic language skills: Active (A) and Dormant (D).[4] The main difference between the two sets is that A skills are the ones called upon to carry out normal daily tasks

---

[3] Specifically, the ACTFL Guidelines state that a "superior speaker of Arabic should have superior-level competence in both MSA and a spoken dialect and be able to switch between them on appropriate occasions" (Breiner-Sanders et al. [2000]). To the best of my knowledge, no native speaker of Arabic has superior-level speaking ability in both.

[4] Dormant skills have also been called "passive" and "receptive" skills.

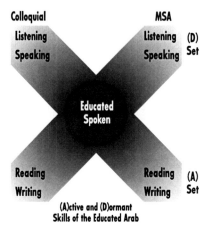

Figure 8.1

spontaneously and without obtrusive deviation from prevalent social or linguistic norms. D skills, on the other hand, are called upon in special and rare situations where the required skill is used haltingly and in deviation from prescriptive linguistic rules. Noncompliance with language norms in the case of D skills is tolerated and, in many cases, may even go unnoticed. Notwithstanding how frequently each set is used, both sets are important communicative tools; one does not substitute for the other. Teaching those skills must, therefore, be accomplished in situational context.

Active skills include, respectively, (1) speaking and listening in one's own geographical variety of L, and (2) reading and writing in the modern variety of H (MSA). D skills include, also respectively, (1) reading and writing in one's own variety of L, and (2) listening and speaking in MSA, with speaking located upon the lower reaches of the proficiency scale. Thus, MSA forms the main strand within the tapestry of the language skills of educated Arabs. Not only is it the main source for six of the eight skills of the educated (see Figure 8.1 above) but the remaining two, namely active speaking and listening, are, for educated native speakers, heavily influenced by MSA as well.

Suggested strategy for learning polyglossic Arabic

By the circumstance of their birth, Arabs learn L skills first, then they acquire those of H. Young Arabs encounter MSA formally at the age of five–six when they go to school. From that time onward, MSA takes over as the primary influence on their linguistic development, including L skills.

For the adult foreign learner of Arabic outside the Arab world, the road is less clear: in the absence of widely accepted, standardized criteria, the starting point in the long process of learning has been, in effect, left more or less to chance. Instructional programs vary greatly in this respect. Some begin with MSA, some with one or the other of the many geographical colloquials, and others with both at the same time.

However, the sociolinguistic situation of Arabic would suggest a starting point in learning Arabic opposite to that taken by native speakers. MSA, as a written variety and a language without a particular geographic bias, is most suited as the starting learning point for learning Arabic outside the Arab world. The adverse effect of the absence of a cultural milieu, in this case, should be minimal, while learning the colloquial varieties is best left until the learner arrives in an Arab country where its colloquial can be learned within its proper context of culture.

The position of reading as an important instrument in learning the totality of Arabic and as the main skill for learning Arabic while the learner is outside the Arab world should be clear. MSA is nearly exclusively a written language that is learned mainly through reading. Unfortunately, today's classroom emphasis on oral skills over written ones, an artifact of communicative approaches preferred for the teaching of European languages that have arisen in the wake of dissatisfaction with Grammar–Translation approaches, has distracted attention from features particular to polyglossic Arabic as an idiom heavily influenced by written MSA. The societal function of MSA requires that emphasis be placed upon training the learners in reading MSA aloud. Training students in speaking MSA in earnest, a role MSA does not play in Arab societies, would be a misuse of students' time. Speaking in the classroom, however, may be undertaken but only as a means of familiarizing students with the sounds of the language.

As for approaches to teaching reading, the more a learner reads, the more s/he learns. Since reading is largely a personal experience best performed on one's own, the development of independence and self-reliance is critical to the development of high-level reading skills.

The Center for Arabic Study Abroad (CASA) program

Organization

The CASA program was created in 1967 by a consortium of twenty American universities in order to provide instruction in Arabic at the Advanced level for college graduates who had spent a minimum of two years in studying Arabic, were registered in postgraduate programs in Middle East Studies, and had successfully competed for the national fellowships that provided fully funded study at the institute and represented the only gateway into the program. The program, which was for a number of years wholly supported by the then US Office of Education, aimed, in particular, at helping future academics gain the level of proficiency in Arabic necessary for using the language as an effective research tool. It was argued that the Arabic environment would aid students to break away from the learning plateau, vaguely labeled "the intermediate level," at which home universities seemed at that time to deposit learners. CASA was, and is still, the only program that teaches American graduate students Arabic at the Advanced level. The program is administered by a Stateside director, an American University co-director, and an on-site executive director. Students, as a result of selection via national competition, are highly motivated.

The reputation of CASA as the only program that offers American future academics effective training in high-level Arabic has become such that an applicant to an American university for a faculty position in Middle East subjects who has not had a CASA fellowship would have some explaining to do. In recognition of its contribution to the learning of Arabic in the USA, CASA, the longest surviving program for training Americans in a foreign language outside the USA, continues to receive US federal funding.

The CASA curriculum before 1970

The early CASA curriculum was not much different from what was common at the time in teaching Arabic in the West. In addition to materials for teaching colloquial Egyptian, the curriculum consisted of (1) a list of about 3,000 de-contextualized words for memorization, (2) a book of grammar-enhancing and short reading passages ingeniously contrived from the word list, (3) a grammar book at the Intermediate level, and (4) two authentic long texts.

The two long texts were (1) a treatise on the Islamic reform movement written in quasi-Medieval H and so far above the language level of the students that they were able to read only one paragraph during each class hour, and (2) the autobiography of the eminent belletrist, professor, and statesman, Taha Hussein, chosen for its literary value. Of the three-volume autobiography, the students were able to cover only thirty-five pages in the entire year. Impediments to greater accomplishments lay in the unsuitability of the text for teaching reading skills and a parsing-based approach to reading, quite popular at the time.

In November, 1969, students rebelled against the curriculum and teachers, and I was assigned to teach them on a part-time basis (three hours a week). It quickly became clear that the students, in spite of their seeming dependence on the teacher's guiding hand at every step of the way, were, in fact, ready for a large measure of independence, although neither students nor teachers believed that at first.[5]

[5] While there are some reasons particular to the teaching of Arabic for delaying the moment of declaring students teacher-independent, it is a well-known phenomenon in language teaching that teachers, like parents, are reluctant to let go of their wards.

As a result of the students' rejection of the existing program, a new position of curriculum advisor was created for the purpose of devising an alternative curriculum for the following year's group. At the heart of the new curriculum was a course for training the students in IR described below in the context of the overall curriculum.

The CASA curriculum 1970–1977

General

The overall objective of the new program, developed over a number of semesters and in consonance with faculty and student feedback, was, and still is, to help students reach an Advanced level of proficiency in Arabic much similar to what is now called Level 4+. Another, but subsidiary, objective was to familiarize each of the students with the language domain of his/her interests.

To enable them to reach the program objectives, students were gradually weaned from teacher and textbook. An IR course was designed for that very purpose.

The CASA full-year program was set into three successive semesters. Each had a specific sub-objective.

Eight-week summer program (first semester)

In addition to providing enrichment activities, such as singing, calligraphy, playing musical instruments, general lectures on aspects of Egyptian society past and present, and the like, the summer program equipped students with the linguistic tools necessary for living in Egypt, communicating with its people, and understanding, first hand, the society around them. To this end, they studied mainly (1) Egyptian Colloquial and (2) media Arabic, both printed (daily newspapers) and spoken (radio and television news bulletins). At the end of the semester, students were expected to know various Egyptian cultural institutions and to have gained insights into the cultural background of the Arabic language.

Fourteen-week fall program (second semester)

The fall semester was the heart of the CASA program. Its objective was for students to acquire proficiency beyond the Intermediate level in reading MSA and, to a lesser degree, in listening and taking notes in academic lectures and in writing reports. Upon completion of the fall semester, they were expected to read an Egyptian newspaper effortlessly, understand news bulletins, and have some facility with Classical Arabic. In Colloquial Egyptian, they were expected to gain fluency in speaking and listening and to read plays written in that medium; the program also introduced them to Educated Egyptian Colloquial. Of particular importance in the fall semester was the IR course, which fostered students' ability to read independently, served as the catalyst for building the overall confidence necessary for reaching Advanced proficiency levels, and activated students' dormant (receptive) reading skills. Amount of student progress was determined through the comparison of scores on written and oral tests administered by certified testers at the beginning and end of each semester.

Fourteen-week spring program (third semester)

In this semester, the program aimed at consolidating knowledge, raising skills to a definite stratum of Level 4, and putting to the test the skills activated and gained during the previous semester. The program centered around work in MSA and in the colloquial.

In MSA, each student took three graduate-level courses taught exclusively in Arabic by professors in specialized fields from Egyptian universities. The students chose the courses from a list circulated to them in the fall. They were free to add whatever subject they chose. Any subject chosen by a minimum of three students was automatically offered. Students were free to substitute one of the courses by a course of reading in a domain of their choice.

Evaluation of the students' performance at the end of this semester, particularly their facility with Arabic as a medium for acquiring knowledge and for self-expression (at various levels of sophistication including the academic level), was functionally carried out by the outside professors who were urged to evaluate their CASA students in comparison with their other students in the national universities. The CASA students who took the spring course at 400–500-level that I taught in Advanced Arabic Grammar with other Arab graduates always ranked among the top 25% in their overall performance.

Training students in Educated Spoken Arabic was carried out through a situation similar to that in which this medium is used, namely discussion of topics of high culture. Evaluation of this component was carried out by certified testers who compared the performances of the final semester with the recorded performances from the previous semesters. Generally speaking, a measure of the students' success in this final semester was their ability to read large amounts of Arabic materials independently.

The IR course

Development of the Independent Reading (IR) course required the identification of materials appropriate to anticipated tasks, an understanding of the students, the assignment and reorientation of teachers, the selection of reading texts themselves, the establishment of a teaching method (i.e., reading procedure), and a mechanism for evaluation.

Material selection

A Level-4+ reader should be able to perform a variety of reading tasks on linguistically and socioculturally complex texts: analytical (intensive reading), extensive reading, and skimming and scanning. The choice of text type that is culturally and structurally suited for each of the specific reading activities is crucial. By selecting the right type of material for the right type of reading task not only is the training more readily facilitated but also social norms associated with each of the various types of Arabic and the appropriate contextual functions they perform in the society are naturally brought home to the learners.

Arabic lends itself, quite naturally, to providing text types suitable to the training of each of the reading tasks. Texts from historical periods and certain texts from the contemporary period are molded, in style and thought, in the idiom of past historical periods; such texts would obviously be most suitable for training in intensive (analytical) reading. For training in reading aloud, on the other hand, Arabs themselves use literary texts: passages from the Koran, sayings of the Prophet Mohammed, speeches by historical figures, acts from classical plays, famous poems, and the like. For training in skimming, MSA newspapers are particularly suitable, and for developing extensive reading skill, plays work particularly well.

Intensive reading materials. Experience has shown that it is quite easy to find materials suitable for training in intensive reading. Contemplative analytical reading of a text, any text, is usually the method students of Arabic seem to acquire readily.

Extensive reading materials. It can be extremely difficult to amass a body of Arabic texts suitable in quality and quantity for structured training in extensive reading. This difficulty can be attributed to two phenomena: (1) the wide range of active vocabulary in written Arabic (thanks to the historical depth of the language), and (2) the complexity of the morpho-semantic system. It is usually difficult to find a sufficient number of texts sharing enough common vocabulary to facilitate reasonable passage from one text to the next.

The traditional training of students of Arabic adds to the difficulty. The old Orientalists' method still prevails and yields a typical Level-3 student who can identify, name, and number the verbal forms and their derivatives and derive morphological forms from a given root. Such students usually lack the ability to appreciate the semantic roles played by these forms within a given context. Such an ability can be acquired, not from compiling paradigms of Arabic words/forms and their corresponding English glosses, but from frequently meeting the various forms within the guiding confines of meaningful contexts in a multiplicity of texts.

Generally speaking, plays, by their nature as a genre employing mainly dialogue, are most suitable for purposes of extensive reading. In addition, Arabic plays are generally characterized by having a comparatively high degree of word and sentence redundancy, so that ideas, topics, issues keep bouncing among dialogue interlocutors for considerably long spans of time. In such exchanges, words belonging to the same morphological root appear time and again in different forms and with correspondingly different shades of meaning.

Many other features recommend plays for extensive reading. First, a play usually has a single theme; once the reader is acquainted with the theme of the play, it acts for him/her like a dotted line along which the action/plot proceeds. Second, plays are usually of moderate length, which facilitates measured work assignments; a learner is likely to feel more satisfaction from reading two 200-page books than from reading a single 400-page one. Third, plays also lend themselves to a multiplicity of language and real-life activities, including staging them. Attending a commercial staging or watching a videotape of any of the plays read in class adds to the students' overall language experience.

Novels, because of their narrative nature, have also been found to be suitable for extensive reading. However, because of the relative lack of dialogue in them, novels were introduced later in the semester. The more complex language of the novel provides an opportunity for naturally stepping up the level of reading required from students.

The language of the short story is usually complicated and condensed, mirroring in this respect the density of their themes. However, because they have the advantage of being short, they have been used for extensive reading activities. As a rule, short stories of various lengths were given in conjunction with the longer items in order to keep a balance between difficult and less difficult assignments from one week to the other.

One of the important considerations in selecting materials for extensive reading is the question of whether the literary value of a text or its linguistic features should have the greater weight. Extensive experience shows that, as teachers, we usually are influenced by the value of the content of the material. The old CASA program, for example, used only materials of high literary and academic value. The reconstructed CASA reading program gave preference to language characteristics over specific content for extensive reading. (Materials with high content value should, however, be included in the language program, but not necessarily for extensive reading.)

The assigning of texts during the semester was accomplished via a graded system of difficulty. With no valid vocabulary or grammar frequency lists, the selection and the ordering of the texts had to be based upon subjective knowledge of the students' level, the range of textbooks they studied in the USA before enrolling in the program, the results of enrollment and summer-term achievement tests, and, most important, personal knowledge of what is available in the Arabic library. (Knowledge of the literature can make or break a reading program of this nature.) To cater to student interests, alternative texts for each week at slightly different levels of difficulty were held in reserve.

The students

The CASA student body was elite, not only in the sense described above, as the highly motivated top candidates selected from a national competition, but also in proficiency level. Enrollment minimum was a tested Level 3, although not every student who gained acceptance was actually at the required level. Therefore, in the program students were divided, according to their proficiency levels, into three groups. Further sub-grouping occurred for particular purposes such as interest in a certain subject, a need for side instruction in a particular aspect of the language, and the like.

Typically, enrolling students displayed a limited range of vocabulary, particularly outside the domain of politics; a theoretical understanding of morphology with limited to no experience of using it to read authentic texts; and nearly no facility with semantics, although most were able to consult Hans Wehr's root-based *Dictionary of Written Arabic*. Many students also came to the CASA program having acquired bad reading habits in Arabic. Having bad reading habits in this case means being more focused on sentence structure, sentential components, and grammatical categories than on the message of the passage. Interestingly many of those who merely parsed their way through Arabic texts would not think of approaching a native-language (English) text in the same way. (While foreign language learners do tend to approach authentic texts with caution, it is our observation that Arab teachers of Arabic tend to instill parsing-based reading habits.) On the other hand, students often attempt to use English-language decoding strategies that are not fully suited to reading Arabic. Thus, they have to unlearn such things as the semantic role of punctuation, which has no counterpart in Arabic, punctuation marks having been borrowed into Arabic from French and playing more or less a "decorative" role.

Students at the beginning of the program were found to have fallen into the crippling habit of excessively using the Arabic–English dictionary. It goes without saying that the dictionary is an essential tool for the studying of languages. In the hands of some, however, and without clear guidance as to when and how to use it, the dictionary can become an obstacle to spontaneous and contextualized language learning. It has been our observation that frequent consulting of the dictionary, in fact, slows down the process of reading and quite often obscures the meaning of the text. After all, the full meaning of a word is nothing less than its total contextual occurrences within the language. Dictionary definitions and their illustrative examples cannot be expected to fully cover all the nuances of vocabulary items. The situation becomes more acute when one considers the average size of the standard dictionary in popular use. Haste in appealing to the dictionary for assistance deprives learners of the opportunity to decipher for themselves the meaning of words from living contexts. Even unsuccessful attempts to deduce meaning from context usually end in better understanding and retention. A meaning of a word quickly obtained from a dictionary is as quickly forgotten.

Students also bring their own objectives to the CASA program. Because they are registered in a graduate program, they are eager to acquire working facility in the domain of their studies. This interest is met in the final semester where taking university-level courses in Arabic serves, in addition to reinforcing the students' general language ability, to train each of them in the domain of their choice.

Proficiency aside, the greatest need the students were found to have at the time of enrollment was a change of attitude toward Arabic from that of a language they are being taught to one which they should start learning. In other words, the responsibility for improving proficiency passes from teacher to student while still in the classroom. (This is fully in keeping with other programs described in this volume, e.g., the LangNet option, some of the Chinese programs enumerated in Chapter 5, and others.)

The teachers

At the inception of this program, the need to reorient teachers became immediately clear. All teachers were graduates of language departments; some were from departments of Arabic. Some had higher degrees, but none had pedagogical training. (In fact, there was no academic program for training teachers in Teaching Arabic as a Foreign Language [TAFL] anywhere at that time. The first MA program in TAFL was established at the American University in Cairo in 1977.) However, experience in teaching Arabic to non-native speakers, knowledge of foreign languages, and, above all, sensitivity to the cultural and psychological needs of foreign learners living away from home in a society quite different from their own made these teachers valuable to the CASA program.

Misgivings were expressed about using some texts of no particular literary renown for intensive reading and also about including an extensive reading component, as well as the concept of Independent Reading. Teachers were not ready, for example, to entertain the possibility of Intermediate-level students reading a real play or novel without teacher assistance.

This reaction was to be expected. For the last fourteen centuries, Arab language planners have kept alive the linguistic features of Classical Arabic of the Koranic idiom, some of which, in fact, have become redundant as conveyers of meaning in MSA. The most far-reaching of those is the intricate system of case vowel endings. Educated Arabs are taught from early childhood to work out the case vowel endings for every word in the text in accordance with the grammar rules they, as students, have been diligently, if not successfully, taught. Thus, as they read, readers engage in a simultaneous mental analysis of the text (a task that often requires the reader to travel backward and forward along the sentence in order to readjust a conclusion prematurely reached). The attention necessary for carrying out such a task is usually so absorbing that it leaves little for the main purpose of reading, namely comprehension. Although the word order within the sentence, apart from the case vowel endings, is, by itself, quite sufficient for comprehension, it is not generally accepted by Arab educators as such.

The change of attitude toward the new IR course in the fall of 1970 was finally brought about through the students themselves. Having been assigned their first play for reading over the weekend and having been guided as to the procedure which they should follow in completing the task, the students, who were at first skeptical as to their ability to read an entire book on their own, surprised themselves with the results. The enthusiasm generated in the first few weeks for the IR program by the students swept away all resistance to it, and the reorientation of the teachers became a *fait accompli*.

The reading texts

Of the program's twenty contact hours a week, three hours (plus one hour for writing follow-ups) were assigned to the IR component.

Three items, one long (a play or a novel) and two short (combinations of a one-act play and/or a short story) were stipulated as the amount of materials to be covered in each of the fourteen working weeks of the semester. As the experiment progressed and the students' comments/reactions were gathered, particularly over the first two years, teachers discovered that generations of students did not react to the reading texts in the same way. Some took violent dislikes to texts previously well liked by others, and alternative texts had to be assigned to them. The reading list, as a result, had to contain additional titles that were made available to students as the need arose.

Texts were chosen in groups of at least three titles by the same author.[6] Also, each group of texts contained items escalating in difficulty to provide a continuum of graded readings. The lowest end of the scale had to be above the heads of the average students by a manageable distance, while the highest was determined as to be at a difficulty level far above where the students were at the beginning of the course. It goes without saying that the accessibility of the language of the first week's assignment was crucial for inspiring confidence in the students and the success of the experiment as a whole. Also, the appreciable difference in language difficulty between the top and the bottom of the scale

---

[6] Assigning multiple works in this way allowed students to become increasingly familiar with the linguistic structures and lexicon used by each author, allowing students to progress more rapidly from one work through the consolidation and deepening of a limited range of language – i.e., the language associated with that author (every author, every person has their own language "reserve") – as well as to transition to the idiom of other authors.

provided an added means of evaluating the amount of improvement achieved by course end.

Texts also had to be authentic, non-abridged, and written for the general native reader, preferably (but not necessarily) by leading literary figures and, as much as possible, have no extant English translations. (Compared with the time, effort, and cost of devising advanced language courses based upon short texts culled from copyrighted materials, the one-time cost of securing the materials for this course and the absence of copyright requirements were great advantages.)

However, it was a far cry from devising a number of specifications for selecting authentic materials for a language course to actually finding texts with such specifications, particularly when curriculum devisers were faced with the task of quantifying and qualifying what was "above the heads of the students by a manageable distance." An added difficulty at the time, and continuing today, was the absence of any reliable and up-to-date frequency listings of language features, particularly structure and vocabulary.

The selection of the actual texts, however, was made with the aid of the intimate knowledge of the students' language background and a long association with the genres from which the texts were to be chosen. Naturally, trial and error and the close monitoring of students' reactions, particularly during the first two years, played a significant role in weeding out unsuitable texts.

Four groups of texts comprised the assigned readings. Each reflected distinctive language features.

Group 1. Plays, both long and one-act, by the founder of Arab modern theatre, Tewfik Alhakim, were chosen in multiple quantity. In addition to the fact that Alhakim's style exhibits a notable degree of redundancy, the sources of his themes are generally familiar to students: Greek drama, Biblical stories, and Arab and world history. Also, his dialogue is lively, and his language is straightforward and deliberately chosen in order to be comprehensible to members of the general public, including those who have little knowledge of MSA. In fact, Alhakim prided himself for his choice of what he called "middle-of-the-way" language. For the above reasons, items from Alhakim's work, both long and short, were assigned during the first three crucial weeks. They proved to be a success.

Group 2. This group, which had to be a step higher on the scale of difficulty, came from the work of the journalist, novelist, and short-story writer, Ihsan Abdul Quddus. Unlike Alhakim, Abdul Quddus chose themes for his literary creation from social phenomena involving problems of the young, in particular in Egyptian society. Such themes are usually involved, and the language dealing with them often makes references to local customs and popular expressions, each of which causes Abdul Quddus's language to be less accessible than

Alhakim's. Also, the fact that novels and short stories lack the "relaxation" of the language brought about by the use of dialogues posits another plus for placing this group of texts higher than the last. Abdul Quddus's lucid, accessible, easygoing structure and, remarkably, controlled range of vocabulary further made the texts ideal for the second stage of the IR course. In addition, it was thought (correctly, as was proved later) that the problems of Egyptian youth should parallel those of young Americans and, therefore, be understandable to the CASA students, and the interest such subjects would generate for students should compensate for their added difficulty. (This formula of equating difficulty of language with general familiarity with content is a staple of many content-based courses, which, like the IR course, use challenging authentic texts [Stryker and Leaver, 1997b]).

Group 3. The reading of this group of texts started at the beginning of the eighth week. Texts were selected from the novels of the Egyptian novelist and short-story writer, Yusuf Idris. Idris wrote in an easy-flowing MSA style heavily interlaced with colloquial expressions, idiomatic usages, popular sayings, quotations from the Koran, and sayings of the Prophet. As is usually the case, understanding the general meaning of the text in which such language devices are used does not, particularly, depend upon understanding the meaning of those devices. On the contrary, the context of the narration itself provides sufficient clues for understanding the approximate meanings of quotes, in addition to providing authentic examples of the situations in which they can be used. Idris's writing also provided an example of the common ground where MSA and Educated, and even other types of, colloquials mesh. The calculated increase in language difficulty, particularly in so far as it was laden with references to social phenomena, was thus compensated for. Idris's writings provided a higher rung, suitably placed on the third level along the reading scale.

Group 4 (final). For this stage, individual items, not necessarily by the same author, were chosen. Balancing language features was no longer a consideration. Artistic value and special interests became the overriding considerations for item selection. In the final weeks, students read, for instance, *Algabal* ("The Mountain"), by the Egyptian novelist, Fathy Ghanem. This fascinating novel is narrated against the background of the never-ending battles between ancient tomb diggers, antiquity police, foreign buyers of stolen antiquities, and the romantic foreign lovers of Ancient Egypt. Also novels, other than his famous *Trilogy*, by Naguib Mahfouz were read during this stage in the semester.

Short items. One-act plays and short stories played a complementary role within the reading scheme. Because of their distinctive themes, narration technique, condensed language, and minimal length, short stories were mainly used for balancing the weekly reading assignments throughout the semester. A balance between length (which could be a few paragraphs) and language difficulty was the selection criterion for the short items.

The reading procedure

The course objective for the IR was defined as helping students develop an ability to read independently and in bulk printed Arabic materials in a wide range of genres – plays, novels, and short stories – without the immediate aid of language teachers and with minimal resort to the dictionary. In the process of achieving this goal, the students' command of the written language and their range of vocabulary, idiomatic usage, and structural knowledge would be enhanced. It was also envisaged that with facility in the language of these particular genres, which directly reflect the society in which they are written, the learner is likely to have an easier passage into the language of other domains, particularly the social ones.

The procedure was straightforward and simple. It was naturally centered around the students doing the major part on their own at home. The students were completely taken into the confidence of the teachers/supervisors as to details of what was to take place. As adult learners poised to start on their own, they had to be fully aware of all the details of the experiment and the philosophy behind it.

The weekly assignment (one long item and two short ones) was distributed to the students at the end of the week for reading over the weekend and the following days. For the first two weekly assignments, teachers prepared brief descriptions of the settings for each item.

The standing set of instructions given to the students for reading at home was the following:

- The most difficult part of a novel / play / short story is at the beginning where the setting is established and the reader is brought into what for her/him is an entirely unfamiliar situation. Bear with the text and be patient; things are bound to become clearer even if you do not follow everything at the beginning. Once you are on your way in the reading, you can go back to details of the settings for clarification, if you wish.
- Arabic writing, compared with English, has a notable degree of repetition and/or redundancy. Use this feature to your advantage: if you encounter a difficult word or a sentence, try the following ones for clarification; then you may go back, if you wish, to the offending part for matching purposes.
- Continue reading the text as long as you are able to make out a story/theme for yourself. There is no need to concern yourself with whether the story you are following is actually what the author has meant or not.
- If you encounter a word or part of the structure, the meaning of which you do not know and it stops you continuing with the reading, do not go for the

dictionary unless you fail to guess the meaning and you do not find someone at hand to ask.

- Mark the words you were able to do without, in following the general meaning of the narration, and the words whose meaning you were able to guess from context.
- Mark references to cultural features that you would like to have explained in class.
- Mark parts of the text, particularly expressions and grammatical constructions, that you would like to discuss in the class.

The procedure in the class was also simple and consisted mainly of making sure that the students had read the assignments and had followed the procedure at home. Students related the story (if necessary in English, particularly in the first weeks); then they presented the points they wished to discuss. Toward the end of the meeting the teacher, in turn, presented points, particularly related to culture, that the students had not brought up. One of the important class, and occasional home-assignment, activities was culling from the text the various derivatives of a joint root, each with its own distinguishing context, identifying the semantic and formal relations to the other derivatives and to the unifying root, most often using the *Hans Weir's Dictionary of Modern Arabic*. An important objective for this exercise for Arabic (and potentially for the learning of Hebrew as well) was familiarization with the unique "logic of Arabic" in deriving from a single concept/root various forms, since the semantic relation between each of them, as well as between each of them and the central root, is not universal or necessarily apparent to the foreign learner. For example, the root *K-T-B* includes derivatives meaning "to write," "to assemble," "to subscribe," and "to regiment." In discovering that the semantic domain connecting the derivatives of *K-T-B* is "gathering things together," the students' attention is directed to the semantic channels through which a message is conveyed in Arabic. The students' mastery of the derivational system and their retention of vocabulary items markedly increased through such exercises. (One note of caution, however: when this type of exercise is not used judiciously, it can result in a "semantic witch-hunt.")

The written follow-ups. Once a week the students accomplished writing tasks in class that were related to the previous weekly reading assignment. With the teacher circulating among the students in order to provide assistance on the spot, the students summarized the plots, explained idiomatic usage and other significant vocabulary items, discussed cultural phenomena, and gave their opinions on matters concerning the content of the text as a whole.

In their written replies, the students were at liberty to revert to English if and whenever they felt they had to do so. As expected of such a highly motivated group, very few availed themselves of this license and only for a short period.

The fact that they performed the writing task while the teacher was at hand meant the written follow-up sessions were welcomed by the students.

Weekly conference. The teachers, supervisors, and students met at a weekly conference in order to discuss details of the reading procedure, including levels of texts and their suitability as a whole. Students also related personal experiences, described difficulties, and exchanged discovered techniques. Culling students' experiences in those meetings contributed greatly to improving the reading technique and enabled students to benefit from each other's experiences. The theoretical foundations of the reading experiment were clarified during those conferences.

Evaluations

On the average, students read about 2,500 pages during the fourteen weeks of the semester. This average increased from one year to the next as the teachers and the students became more convinced of the validity of the course's postulates. Task-based evaluations at various levels were employed. The principal means of assessment were as follows.

• Arranging the reading texts in four groups of ascending equidistant levels of difficulty provided a built-in system for evaluating the progress of the students, the suitability of the materials, and the reading procedure as a whole. The ability of students to handle the very difficult texts of Group 4, when they finally reached that stage (texts that would have been impossible for them during the early weeks of the semester), demonstrated the validity of the experiment.

• At the middle and, particularly, the end of the semester, the students were asked to go over the texts they had already covered in order to review the items of vocabulary and parts of the structure whose meanings/function they had not understood at the time they read the text and which they had merely marked without consulting a dictionary, to discover for themselves what percentage of those items had become intelligible to them. The results (25%–40%) always surprised the students (and also the teachers at the early stages of the experiment). This vocabulary acquisition test, in particular, was important for demonstrating to the students the effectiveness of the procedure. Students always expressed doubt, at the beginning of the course, as to the possibility of learning unknown vocabulary through the reading of long texts without appealing to a dictionary.

• The primary evaluation, however, took place during the following (and final) semester. As stated above, the curriculum for that semester consisted of three graduate-level courses taught exclusively in Arabic. Demonstrable independent reading in the volume of materials related to those courses formed a significant portion of the course evaluation. Naturally, the skills demonstrated by the students in taking those courses were the function of the CASA program as a whole and not merely of the IR course alone. However, it would be fair to conclude that the students' independence and self-reliance and the reading in quantity would not have been as evident but for the IR course. This conclusion was also supported by the CASA graduates themselves.

Conclusions

The objective of the IR course was to activate what could be described as the dormant ability of Level 2–3 learners to read, on their own, authentic materials in the target language. In the process, however, the language proficiency of the students notably increased.

Although students gained direct facility in the specific genres of the Arabic play, novel, and short story, experience repeatedly showed that the abilities gained in the fall semester in independent reading in these genres was, without great difficulty, transferred to other genres and domains in the spring semester when the students had to take graduate courses in an assortment of other subjects.

There was also an indication that reading authentic materials in bulk (i.e., extensive reading) favors the writing skill as well. At the end of the reading course, teachers noted that students were producing in their writing chunks of Arabic cohesively structured in the ways of Arabic prose.

At the center of the experiment was the use of complete texts. Reading a whole book does to the morale of the learner at the Intermediate stage (and probably also to his/her proficiency level) much more than would the reading of several times the amount in mere extracts. It is not a matter of encouraging self-deception in the learner but of guiding them toward self-awareness.

In the IR course, materials from exclusively literary genres were used. The reason for selecting such materials, as explained above, was that in setting Intermediate learners to read authentic texts for the first time on their own, they had to be provided with self-monitoring devices to keep them on course. The theme of a novel, play, or a short story provides such a device. The depth and richness of the language of the literary genres is another important consideration. It is through the literary genres that the reader gains insight into the complexity of language expression and social phenomena in one package.

Criticism, however, has been made of this reading course because of the exclusive use of the literary genres. Not every learner likes to read such materials, it has been argued. In our experience with this course, no student has ever expressed such a dislike of the genre as a whole. Should there be learners who dislike reading literature to a point where they are unable to learn from it, then a different type of material together with a different type of approach should be found for them. The kind of text or set of materials that suits every adult learner has not yet been written. It is unlikely that it ever will be.

In connection with the above, it is notable that most of the materials used for training foreign language learners, at least in Arabic, seem to be of the narrowly defined political type.

In a seminar at the Beijing University of Foreign Languages held in 1988, the Head of External Relations of the Central Ministry of Education of China lamented the fact that in the eagerness to train as many translators as possible within a short time, literary material was excluded in teaching foreign languages in China as a whole. The result was, he said, that translators lacked a requisite depth of field.

Objective measurements in the studying of Arabic are difficult at present because of the absence of reliable statistical analyses of Arabic language features, particularly vocabulary and structure, and also because of the need to revise the Arabic Proficiency Guidelines to reflect Arabic-specific linguistic reality. At present, they seem to be more influenced by generic L2, rather than specific Arabic, features.

Reaching Level 4+ is achievable basically through the personal efforts of the learner with judicious assistance from teachers in the form and quantity the learner requires. No learner will ever achieve this level without gaining independence from teacher and textbook. Courses for training learners in reading independently, such as the one described above, should therefore be introduced no later than Level 2–3.

9 Teaching high-level writing skills in English at a Danish university

Tim Caudery

I do not believe that there can be any "quick fix" or magic formula for making students Distinguished-level writers in a foreign language. There is simply too much to learn. However, I do believe that developing an awareness of variety of voice, of different generic conventions, of the way that audience and purpose can dramatically shape text in different ways, is an area where many writers can make a major and necessary step. Activities can easily be devised to develop this awareness, and this chapter briefly describes a variety of these. Acquiring the language range necessary to transfer the benefits of awareness into greatly improved writing is likely to be a longer process, but one where even the smallest increment helps. If students are asked to tackle a variety of tasks which differ from those of "conventional" essay/self-expression writing courses, these should create a clear need for, and provide opportunities for teaching, language that will increase students' range.

This chapter describes the rationale behind a course taught at the English Department of the University of Aarhus, Denmark, and gives examples of activities used in the teaching. The course covers a variety of aspects of English in use but focuses particularly on written English and on writing skills in a non-literary context. One aim of the course is to help students over time to improve their own writing proficiency to a truly Superior or Distinguished level. Given that the course only lasts a year and that it is one of many courses that make up the students' program, it certainly cannot be claimed that all students could be described as Distinguished-level writers by the end of it. However, course instructors believe that it helps students make an important advance in writing skills by focusing on aspects of language and written communication to which they may previously have given little thought, and that it provides them with the tools to go on working independently at observing how texts work and incorporating the knowledge obtained from such observation into their own writing. Improving proficiency is only one aim of the course; it is also an academically oriented course in understanding how real texts "work" (or fail to work) as communication in given situations. Were writing proficiency the only aim of the course, no doubt it would include an even greater range of writing activities, among them perhaps some "free" or "creative" writing.

Background: university students in Denmark

Danes, in common with citizens of several other countries in Northern Europe, are often regarded – by themselves and by others – as having quite a high level of English language skills. There are a number of factors that might contribute to such a generally high level of proficiency.

First, as speakers of a Germanic language that is fairly closely related to English, Danes have the advantage of being able to draw on their L1 knowledge of syntax and lexis. They encounter a large number of Danish cognates in English. This relative linguistic closeness is further supported by the huge number of English loan-words which have entered Danish in the past half-century, a process which is itself promoted by the other factors mentioned here.

Second, there is massive exposure to English in everyday life in Denmark. With only around 5 million native speakers, Danish is one of the world's smaller national languages, and the population cannot provide the economic and human resources to have everything they might want produced in Danish. Particularly notable in this context is the import of movies, TV programs, and popular music. While larger countries often choose to dub imported TV programs and movies, Denmark uses subtitles, leaving the original spoken language of the media as it is – and, of course, that language is most often English. A considerable proportion of the programs transmitted on Danish TV are imported; Denmark would not have the resources to produce enough of its own soap operas, made-for-TV movies, etc., to fill the airtime available. TV and movies are not the only areas in which Danes encounter English-language materials, however. Popular songs are often foreign productions, with lyrics in English, and even songs by Danish singers may have English lyrics. As a nation with a large number of privately owned computers, many Danes have access to the Internet, where the greatest amount of information available is in English and where the amount of information in Danish is relatively small. Books and magazines aimed at the general public are produced in Danish, although many such books are translated from other languages; however, slightly more specialized publications are often available only in English. In the academic world, students studying beyond high-school level find that they have to deal with reading materials in foreign languages: it would be uneconomic to translate even all basic academic textbooks into Danish.

Third, learning at least one foreign language is a necessity for any Dane who wishes to have contacts with the world beyond the borders of the nation. Swedish, Danish, and Norwegian are more or less mutually intelligible, but these are all languages spoken in a very small area of the world. To understand or be understood in the vast majority of destinations, Danes traveling abroad are virtually compelled to speak another language, and the most useful language for international communication today is English. In the field of commerce,

Denmark has to be outward-looking and trade with its neighbors; English is increasingly the language of the international business world. There is even a trend for the larger Danish companies to make their internal company language English, allowing them to work more easily within a multinational network of parent and subsidiary companies and trading partners. Employees therefore have to use English, at least to some extent, in their daily work.

Fourth, English is the main second language taught in schools. The teaching of English begins at the age of around ten, and it receives high priority in the school program.

Fifth and finally, Denmark has a certain cultural affinity for Britain. This is difficult to identify in exact qualitative or quantitative terms, but one can point to a definite switch in cultural orientation as part of the outcome of the Second World War, when Denmark was invaded and occupied by its large neighbor to the south, Germany. However, the cultural links are much deeper and older than can be explained by a postwar reaction against things German, and perhaps it is not too fanciful to look back more than 1,000 years to the Danish invasions and settlement of the eastern part of England and the interaction between Britain and Denmark that has gone on intermittently ever since.

These factors are mutually supportive of one another and together produce a national culture in which the English language is encountered in some form or other at almost every turn. It is hardly surprising, then, that the majority of Danes can communicate orally in English with a considerable degree of fluency, if not always accuracy.

Given the generally reasonably high level of English in the population as a whole, it is perhaps to be expected that most university students choosing to major in English should have a reasonably high level of proficiency even before they begin their studies. Since this is indeed assumed by the universities to be the case, courses in the English Department at the University of Aarhus (and also at most other universities in Denmark) are all conducted in English from the outset, and virtually all books and written materials used are in English. In fact, however, there is very considerable variation in the level of English-language proficiency among students in the Department, and few could be described as having Distinguished-level written English skills at the start of their studies. The majority would be described as Advanced or Superior.

Many language teachers could feel a certain amount of envy of the teaching situation in Denmark, given the level of students' knowledge of English. However, this situation of reasonable general oral proficiency in a foreign language in the population as a whole and relatively high proficiency among many students starting to study the foreign language at the university level is far from being unique to Denmark. The same type of situation is found in many countries; the reasons for generally high levels of familiarity with an L2 may vary, but the end result is often similar. In yet more countries, the same general pervasiveness of the foreign language in the culture may not pertain, but there may still be high levels of oral proficiency among a smaller section of the population and among university students of the subject, thanks perhaps to periods of residence in the foreign culture being common for a select group of the population. In such cases, as in Denmark, one of the main areas in which students can make, and may need to make, a step from adequate to advanced second language skills is in the field of writing. The situation in Denmark shares some literacy issues with the heritage population described in Chapter 10 of this volume, although the discrepancy between oral proficiency and literacy may not be as great as it is among heritage speakers.

Answering the need for Distinguished-level second language writing skills

Students at Aarhus need good written and oral academic English-language skills in the short term, for use in their university studies. They are given a course in study skills in their first semester at the university, and this includes some brief training in writing academic papers, reading academic books, and so on. However, they also have a much longer-term need related to language skills in a wider context. There is a general expectation of university graduates in English that they will be able to produce good English in almost any situation – writing letters, producing information materials, representing their employers, teaching, and so on. Traditionally, many of our university graduates in English would go into schoolteaching as a career; now fewer than half of them do so, and the proportion is constantly diminishing. The others find employment in quite a wide variety of professions; the demands that will be made on their language skills are equally varied and rather difficult to predict. The Department of English feels a responsibility to give students a sufficiently good understanding of the way English is used in different forms of communication for them to make a satisfactory job of doing whatever may reasonably be asked of them.

Such needs for flexible, high-level language skills are, of course, not confined to university students. Second language skills are vital for many people today in both work and leisure contexts. They are certainly vital for the Danes, as noted above; their language is of little use for communication outside their own country, and there are times when it will not suffice even within their homeland. Spoken language skills may appear to be of primary importance. Ours is a world of fast and convenient long-distance travel, of face-to-face meetings, of the telephone, even of video and Internet conferencing; in these contexts, spoken language abilities are vital in achieving many goals – in requesting, in persuading, in making agreements, in complaining, and so on – as employees, citizens, and private individuals. Yet, written language skills are also very important and often in the most crucial of situations: the delicate and complex request, the information to be provided for permanent reference, the legal contract. Cope and Kalantzis (1993) identified writing skills as an area of empowerment; underprivileged children in Australian schools, they claimed, were being disempowered in society because they could not write in the forms accepted by the establishment (see also S. Gee [1997] for a concise account of ideas about teaching genres in Australia). The same is true for users of second languages. If they cannot write in a way that is effective and that is generally accepted as being appropriate, then they are likely to be disempowered in important areas of communication and interaction with people of other nations.

Writing and choice

The field of teaching second language writing skills (or first language writing skills, for that matter) is one marked by controversy and passionate disagreement with regard to teaching approaches and methods. Advocates of process approaches have been described as (and condemned for) displaying almost religious fervor in promoting their ideas (Horowitz [1986]), while in Australia many who embrace a genre-based approach to teaching do so almost as a reaction to process. Yet, there is at least widespread agreement that effective nonliterary texts are shaped by considerations of audience, writer/reader relationships, purpose, and occasion (see, for example, Tribble [1996, pp. 45–61]). Expert writers choose their content, their text structure, and their language in the light of these considerations.

This implies that writers make choices. Indeed, the writing process can be seen as a constant series of choices, of selecting what is most appropriate for audience, writer/reader relationship, purpose, and context. Choice of content and of the overall text structure may be seen in terms of selecting what is needful and leaving out what is not and in terms of presentation in a logical sequence that can be easily processed by the reader; yet there are also cultural and generic conventions to be observed in selecting the overall framework and coherence for the text (see Grabe and Kaplan [1996] on contrasts between rhetorical conventions in different cultures), and if these conventions are flouted, the text may seem odd or inappropriate to the reader. Choices of style and register (i.e., level of formality) have to be matched to the relationship between writer and reader; too informal a style implies a degree of familiarity and intimacy that may be considered insulting, whereas language that is too formal may seem off-putting and distant. Sentence structure and lexis need to be selected to convey meaning with precisely the degree of clarity – or on occasion ambiguity – which the writer considers desirable and conducive to conveying the message efficiently to the particular readership envisaged.

The choices discussed above are often very sophisticated in nature, requiring a careful calculation of the effect of the writing on the target audience and a high degree of awareness of the issues involved. Above all, such choices demand that there is a range of options open to the writer. If the writer's language is limited, then he or she may be pressed to find more than one way of conveying the message, and talk of choice then becomes meaningless, or at least refers solely to a lower level of choice – the choice of what is grammatically correct as opposed to what is incorrect, for example. Even the choice of whether to include or exclude a certain point may be governed in part by linguistic knowledge, since writers may decide not to include points that they find difficult to express. Similarly, if the writer is unaware of the importance of these choices, or of the different signals that are conveyed through making them, then simply knowing a wider range of vocabulary and syntactic structures may make little difference to writing effectiveness. One option may seem as good as another, and the writer may make selections between alternatives more or less at random. The kinds of lexical, structural, discourse, and sociolinguistic precision mentioned here are described in other chapters in this volume as essential for Superior/Distinguished-level proficiency.

At Aarhus University, first-year students often have written language skills that are adequate for the basic communication of a message but inadequate in range to enable them to make the sophisticated choices that would truly empower them in an English-language context. They continue to make language errors, of course, in the sense that they sometimes write sentences that are grammatically inaccurate or use words or phrases that do not have the meaning that they wish to convey. Errors like these can be gradually eliminated by a variety of methods, and the linguistic input that students receive through their reading and their various classes also contributes to gradual improvement in accuracy. However, simply improving the accuracy of their written English in these senses would not be enough to make students truly Superior/Distinguished-level writers. Beginning students seem to have only one voice in which they are comfortable. They write in a fairly uniform style that owes much to colloquial English. It is a style that would be generally appropriate to personal letters, for example. Confronted with a task such as writing a more formal letter such as a job application, they either produce exactly the same kind of writing or go "over the top" in attempting to use a formal style which they are unable to handle.

This is not an uncommon type of problem among second language writers all over the world. One approach to solving it is teaching fairly rigid patterns for specific types of writing. In British universities, for example, overseas students may be taught "academic writing." Because it is possible to identify a particular genre in which students will need to write – in this case, the academic essay – it is possible to work along the lines pioneered by Swales (1990) in analyzing essential features of this genre. These features can be detailed from paragraph and essay structure down to grammatical features and prefabricated phrases that are thought to typify the writing, and these features can be modeled and then taught by imitation through course books such as Jordan (1990). One can question the effectiveness of this approach on a variety of levels from considering whether it is really possible to identify common structure and language patterns for academic writing through to the question of how well learning to imitate models can make for successful, independent writers. In truth, however, in the short pre-session courses frequently offered by universities for potential students this may be the only viable approach, and learning to imitate models "because that's the way it's done" may be an effective survival kit for students who have to follow university studies in a foreign language. Using this type of formulaic approach, however, is unlikely to give students the flexibility they need to become truly Distinguished-level writers able to accomplish many different types of writing.

Process approaches to teaching writing have had great impact on the second language classroom since the early 1970s. The concept of "the process approach" has perhaps become increasingly diffuse as it has spread to different teaching contexts (Caudery [1995b]), but consideration of writing audience and purpose is a common theme. However, the essence of process approaches seems to lie in the teaching of the writing process itself – encouraging students to realize that "writing is rewriting." Could a process approach provide what is missing in our students' writing?

Process approaches may provide a useful teaching framework. Insofar as they can involve the teacher in the process of the creation of the text (see, for example, Hedge's description [2000, pp. 300–302] of the writing classroom, in which the teacher acts as a consultant on writing in progress), I believe that the insights of the process movement can be very relevant. Our students are, however, by definition, reasonably successful writers in L1; they have to be, in order to gain admission to university. There is ample evidence that L1 writing processes and habits, for better or worse, are likely to be transferred to L2 to the extent that the writer's knowledge of the L2 permits (e.g., Arndt [1987]; Cumming [1989]). Danish university students are certainly familiar with the concept of revision; indeed, many of them seem to spend too much time revising, with no great improvement in the end result. (Caudery [1995a] demonstrates that Danish students who are asked to redraft a text unaided may make many changes, from surface-level editing to total restructuring of their texts, but that such revisions rarely make any significant difference to the rated quality of their writing.) Teachers of Danish at high schools in Denmark are familiar with process approaches, and many encourage their students to seek peer feedback on their work; again, those students who find they like this way of working transfer the habit to their L2 writing at university. I suggest that writing process problems are not at the heart of the writing problems of the majority of our students. Instead, their problems relate to lack of linguistic and cultural knowledge.

Teaching approach at Aarhus

Concepts

Our teaching at Aarhus is founded on a number of straightforward ideas. These are:
- development of awareness of text types;
- clear specification of writing tasks;
- development of thinking techniques;
- focus on making conscious choices;
- development of linguistic sophistication and precision.

Development of awareness of text types

In order to reach Distinguished levels, students need to be made more aware of the characteristics of different types of text and of the importance of these differences in making the texts suitable for their purpose. In doing this, large numbers of fixed "rules" for writing texts of particular genres are not given, but rather explanations of textual features emanating from authors' choices regarding language and structure to suit audience, purpose, and context. This element of the course involves discussion of authentic texts of different types, and it is necessary to teach some terminology in order to analyze and discuss the characteristics of texts fairly precisely.

Clear specification of writing tasks

Students work on writing texts where writer's role, reader, purpose, and context are defined by the teacher and where students' efforts are directed toward making their texts appropriate in terms of these parameters. This is not a course in free writing where students decide for themselves what they want to write about or who they want to write for, and invention strategies are by and large not in focus. While this policy may seem anathema to teachers who view the encouragement of self-expression as central to a writing course, there are many advantages to specifying the writing tasks closely – including greater authenticity, since real-life writing is often a matter of meeting specific writing requirements rather than expressing one's innermost feelings. This is not to say that writing tasks do not require creativity, but rather that the creativity is channeled into problem-solving that requires both ingenuity and language skill.

Development of thinking techniques

Learning to write successfully does not mean copying a limited range of model texts or learning conventions and writing formulas for a small number of text types that students will themselves need to work with in later life. In part this is because teachers cannot predict what types of texts students will need to be able to write and so need to provide them with techniques that will enable them to think about the characteristics required of any text they might reasonably be asked or wish to create. It is also because truly Distinguished-level writers do not turn out texts shaped by templates; they write flexibly, creatively, and individually but nevertheless within a set of limits that are defined not only by the characteristics of the genre in which they are writing, but also by the characteristics of genres within which they are *not* writing. Thus, we do not ask students to follow models slavishly, but rather to use knowledge gained from examining authentic texts to write texts with slightly different requirements.

Focus on making conscious choices

A course premise is that students need to be aware of the choices they make in writing. Further, they should be able to discuss and explain these choices.

Development of linguistic sophistication and precision

Another course premise is that students need to learn more language – more vocabulary, more idiomatic expressions, more syntactic structures – in order to have alternatives that they can consider in writing.

Discussion

The aims of the course are thus very high, and what is achieved may often seem limited in relation to the ideal – creation of a sensitivity that many native speakers never achieve. The amount of knowledge of language and of conventions needed to make use of such sensitivity is itself vast. The process of moving from being an adequate if limited writer to becoming a Distinguished-level second language writer takes years, and no course can pretend to do more than get writers part of the way down the road. Yet even a few steps on the way can make a difference to the effectiveness of students' writing in the short term. In the long term, getting the students to think about their writing in new ways can provide a stimulus that will enable them to go on improving their writing skills over many years.

The principles above do not specify any particular teaching methodology. Post-feedback redrafting, peer feedback, and other patterns of teaching associated with process approaches are neither promoted nor precluded. These and other techniques, such as group writing, may be used from time to time as needed and desired by teacher and students. Typical techniques include students commenting on the choices they have made in their own work, teachers giving detailed written feedback on written work handed in, and discussing students' work in class.

It goes without saying that using written language to communicate effectively requires understanding of the culture of the target audience. Any course that deals with studying authentic texts, as this course does, involves discussion of cultural factors, but students do also attend courses in British and American history and society, as well as courses in British, American, and Postcolonial literatures. I would regard it as self-evident that Distinguished-level language students need to gain cultural understanding in order to use their target language successfully, but systematic teaching about English-speaking cultures does not form part of the course described here because it is covered in other parts of the university syllabus.

Some might question the exclusion of creative writing from our course. While all writing is "creative" in some senses, we have deliberately excluded any training in literary writing, as well as in the sort of creativity involved in writing, for example, advertising texts. We regard these areas as requiring separate and special abilities. The creative writer needs Distinguished-level writing skills, but the Distinguished-level writer is not necessarily a great novelist or poet and should not be expected to be.

Teaching materials and exercise types

Awareness of differences

The first aim of the course is to make students aware of the fact that texts differ from one another in more ways than simply content, and that differences can be related to writer, reader, purpose, and context (i.e., the type of writing).

The course often begins by looking at letters. There are a number of reasons for this. First, writer and reader are clearly defined. Second, there are very obvious differences in style and content between personal letters to friends and more formal letters, and these differences can be related to writer/reader relationships, the knowledge which the writer can presuppose the reader has, etc. Third, letters do very often have clear structures that lend themselves to analysis of the overall pattern of coherence. Fourth, there are generic conventions in letter layout which can be used to illustrate how conventions for some text types may simply have become established by historical happenstance, but which readers nevertheless expect to be observed. Fifth, letters lend themselves both to analysis and to writing exercises, so that it is easy to go on from awareness-building exercises to writing short letters of different types.

Although authentic materials comprise the bulk of course materials, a devia-tion is made in the case of letters where it is advantageous to construct parallel texts such as those shown in Figure 9.1. Such texts provide students with the opportunity and training to "spot the differences." (The illustrative texts are constructed texts that relate differences in writer/reader relationships to text content and style. In both cases, letters are on the company notepaper of a British firm of engineering consultants, and the letters are written in connection with a forthcoming visit to Australia by one James Finlay. He is writing to one

Letter A	*Letter B*
August 25th 1999	August 25, 1999

Mr William Hadley
J & P Machine Tools Inc
P O Box 2742
Melbourne
Australia
 	
Dear Mr Hadley,
    This is to confirm the arrangements made in our telephone conversation last Monday for my visit to J & P Machine Tools.
    My flight, Quantas QA 427 from London, arrives at Melbourne airport at 14:35 on Saturday, September 10th. I am most grateful to you for offering to meet me at the airport, and also for arranging my hotel accommodation.
    I leave for Brisbane on Saturday, September 17th at 18:15. I will therefore be available for five days' consultancy during the week September 12th–16th, with the possibility of continuing during the morning of Saturday 17th if absolutely necessary.
    I look forward very much to meeting you.
<div align="right">Yours sincerely,
J. W. Finlay
(signature)
James W. Finlay</div>
	Dear Bill,
	    It was great to talk to you again on the 'phone last week, and I'm really looking forward to seeing you and Joyce in September. Eight years is a long time!
	    As I said, my plane gets in at 2:35 in the afternoon on Saturday, September 10th. It's a Quantas flight, number QA 427 from London. What with the jet-leg and the eighteen-hour journey, it'll probably take me the whole of the rest of the weekend to recover from the trip, I'm afraid.
	    It's a shame this has to be a working visit! Still, I've managed to put off my flight to Brisbane till Monday morning (19th), so we'll have that weekend free. Do try not to overload me with problems, so that I can get through with everything by Friday afternoon!
	    Very best wishes to you, Joyce and the kids.
	<div align="center">Jim</div>P.S. Don't forget to let me know if there's anything special you want me to bring you from England.

Figure 9.1

of the people he is supposed to work with in Australia, William Hadley. In letter A, it is assumed that the correspondents have only had telephone contact; in letter B, the two are old friends who have not met for many years.)

In addition, the old device of writing letters in inappropriate styles (illustrated in Figure 9.2) highlights the features of more formal and less formal writing, i.e., the relative vagueness of informal language and precision of formal language. Students are asked to identify the inappropriate features of two texts. The first text (on the left) is a holiday postcard. The second text (on the right) is a letter

Apollo Hotel Apartments
Grivas Dighenis Ave
Larnaca
Cyprus
Wednesday, May 17th, 2000
Mrs Jenny Hargreaves
3, Birch Avenue
Salisbury
Wilts SB4 3RW
ENGLAND

Dear Mrs Hargreaves,

This is to inform you that my husband, James, and I have arrived without incident at our destination, Larnaca in Cyprus. The average maximum daily temperature at present is $28^{\pm}$ Celsius, and the average sea temperature is $18^{\pm}$. We therefore spend a considerable amount of time each day at the beach, where we swim and lie in the sun.

We judge the food served in restaurants here to be of a high standard, especially with respect to flavour, and also to be relatively inexpensive. Consequently, we dine out frequently, despite the fact that our apartment has cooking facilities. I regret that James usually becomes slightly inebriated at meals, being unable to resist indulgence in the low-priced local wines and spirits.

Yours sincerely,
F G Finchley
Freda G Finchley (Mrs)

Wednesday
Dear Joe,

Do you remember me? We had quite a long chat about six weeks ago when you dropped into our bookshop to order some stuff. Actually, you were a bit upset at the time about how little we'd got in stock and so on. I hope the Manager was able to explain everything to you alright?

Anyway, one of the books you ordered has come at last! It's that one by Anne Raimes, called 'Techniques in Teaching Writing', or something like that. Actually, I'm afraid the price has gone up a bit. We told you it would cost £5.30, but there's been a new price list come out, and they've put it up to £7.75! Shocking, isn't it? Well, I suppose that's inflation for you.

So, any time you like to come in, the book will be here waiting for you. Well, I say 'any time', but actually you're supposed to come and get it during the next two weeks, otherwise we have to send it back again, which would be a bit of a shame, really, considering.

It'll be wonderful to see you again when you come for the book.

All best wishes,
Sandra

Figure 9.2

from a bookshop informing a customer that a book he has ordered has arrived. There are other activities that can be accomplished with the texts. For example, students could also be asked to rewrite each of the letters.

However, other types of text can be used to make the same points equally clearly. Figure 9.3 shows an excellent parallel text notifying the public of a regulation. (London Transport used to display the first of these notices; they later changed to the second. Students should discuss the differences, the probable reasons for the change, and its effects.) Interestingly, some students feel that the

1
DOGS. Small dogs may, at the discretion of the conductor and at the owner s risk, be carried without charge upon the upper deck of double-deck buses, or in single-deck buses. The decision of the conductor is nal.

2
You can take your dog with you if it is a small one and the conductor agrees. It travels free, but at your risk. If the vehicle is a double-decker, you must both go on the upper deck.

Figure 9.3

change is not an improvement; the less legalistic text, while being more easily comprehensible, can give the impression of condescension because it may seem appropriate to word regulations in a legalistic way.

Another awareness-building exercise can be to take three- or four-line extracts from a variety of sources and ask students to suggest what type of texts they come from; if they can do this (and the extracts should be selected so that with a little prompting they *can* do it), then they can be asked to identify the linguistic signals that served as clues.

This work on awareness of the features of different text types is a recurring theme in the course. During the course, students develop a variety of tools for more precise analysis or description of texts. Lengthy text analysis, however, is avoided. Instead, students make brief commentaries on a variety of short and long texts – perhaps just discussion of a particular text feature. An example is a ten-minute class discussion on collocation and cliché, based on the inside of a British Airways lunch box. The inside of the box lid showed a picture of a farmer sitting by a pickup, with wheat fields stretching into the distance and displayed a text reading "Time for a snack. An elderly farmer takes a well-earned break from tending his crops before heading home at sunset." I blanked much of the text out, asked the class to suggest what went in the blanks, and then discussed what it was that had enabled them to do this, relating this to work on the importance of lexical phrases in communication (Nattinger and DeCarrico [1992]).

Awareness is further developed by asking students to comment on the texts that they themselves have written and the choices they have made in the process. This is a difficult thing for them to do, and they are not always particularly successful; many of their choices remain at a subconscious level! However, even the attempt does seem gradually to increase sensitivity to text features and to encourage students to make more deliberate choices.

Reading and text analysis

If students are to become aware of how texts "work," of the choices the text writers have made, they need to examine and discuss features of a wide variety of texts. For this, they need extensive input from authentic texts. The course concentrates on short texts, both for the sake of maintaining interest and in order to get through the maximum possible range of text types. Texts can be presented and discussed in a variety of ways – to the full class, using group work, with students preparing their comments on texts outside class, and so on. Students can occasionally be asked to find their own texts for analysis and comment. It should be noted that this is not primarily text work for the sake of explaining the meaning of new vocabulary, etc., though, of course, students do sometimes ask about unfamiliar words or expressions, or the teacher may draw the class's attention to some language item. By and large, though, the students are able to understand the texts more or less unaided, and can focus on considerations of the *way* they are written.

Students use a variety of tools for text analysis. Features discussed include levels of formality, patterns of textual coherence, cohesion, message functions, sentence structure, choice of lexis, selection of content, layout, and use of pictures. Among the text types are scripted speeches (particularly good for clear patterns of coherence and cohesive devices) and magazine advertisements, the latter selected because (1) professionally written advertisements make use of many different styles, often based on other genres; (2) they use many special effects as verbal "eye-catchers"; (3) in general they are written with great care and attention to detail; and (4) they are often fun and interesting. Students also analyze texts of types that they are expected to write (see below).

One type of analytic tool used – a simple scheme of message functions (adapted from Preisler [1997]) is shown below.

The terms shown here can be applied at both the macro (whole text or section) level and the micro (sentence or clause) level, and can reveal interesting points about the way texts work. For example, advertisements are nearly always regulative at the macro level (aimed at persuading people to act in a particular way, such as buying a product) but may contain very few explicitly regulative sentences.

Formality is one of the most difficult areas to discuss. For that, a four-level division is helpful: informal, neutral, formal, and frozen/legalistic. However, the features that distinguish these levels are by no means fixed, and one can only identify certain features which *tend* to make texts seem less or more formal. The list of such features includes use/avoidance of colloquial expressions, vagueness/precision, avoidance/use of long and syntactically complex sentences, avoidance/use of uncommon or longer words, avoidance/use of nominalization, use/avoidance of direct address to the reader, use/avoidance of personal pronouns, and use/exclusion of "redundant" material (especially that related to phatic communication).

While students might sometimes be asked to comment on *every* feature they can see in a text, attention is also often focused on particular areas of interest.

Tools for Analysis: Message Functions

These terms can be used to characterize both a complete text or section of text (macro function) and clauses. Note that these concepts do not represent watertight boxes; a single clause or sentence may have more than one message function, and not all elements of a text may be easily analyzable in these terms.	**The REPRESENTATIVE function** Purports to say something about how the world is, to *represent* reality objectively.	*Reportives:* Statements about the world which are presented as if their truth value could be immediately veri ed. *Assumptives:* Statements about the world which appear less easily veri able, e.g. generalizations, interpretations, statements about the future.
	The EXPRESSIVE function *Expresses* the speaker s subjective view.	*Estimatives:* Statements involving an estimation by the speaker, where the truth value of the statement depends on how one de nes the terms used (It depends what you mean by *x* .)
		Evaluatives: Statements which involve the expression of a positive or negative value judgment by the speaker.
	The REGULATIVE function Aims at altering the world, at *regulating* it by getting people to act in a certain way.	*Directives:* Language which aims to affect people s actions by ordering, telling, asking, advising, etc.
		Commissives: Language which aims to affect people s actions by promising, threatening, etc.

Figure 9.4

Examples include the structure of encyclopedia entries, the vocabulary of a feature article from a newspaper, and the layout of an informative leaflet.

Writing

Writing tasks are central to the course. The approach might be described as primarily a *problem-solving* one. Students are required to work on a particular communication problem – creating a text for a particular audience, a given context, and a given purpose. The content of the text is often provided in some form, though normally students will have to select exactly what is most appropriate to use from the source material provided. On other occasions, though, students would be asked to provide their own material – for example, if writing a movie review, they would select a movie they had seen recently to write about.

Students will normally have seen and discussed examples of other texts of the type they are to produce, but they will not be given a specific model to imitate. Alternatively, they may simply be asked to discuss the characteristics they think the text that will fulfill their task might have.

The following are among the text types students have written:

- Leaflets: informative, advisory, persuasive
- Brochures (extracts)
- Newspaper articles: features, reviews, columns, editorials
- Letters: personal, apology, request, complaint, etc.
- Encyclopedia entries, handbook/reference-book entries
- Instructions
- Reports (of various types)
- Book blurbs
- Lecture handouts

Note that text types are selected more for their practicality than because students will have to do these things later in life. It is simply not known what they may be called upon to write. The training given is in being able to reason out ways of tackling the task on the basis of context, purpose, reader, and writer. There is often a strong element of role-playing involved: students have to imagine themselves as writers in a particular role.

Frequently, the information students need to provide the content of the text will be in the form of a text in a different genre. They will thus need to think particularly about the differences between the two types of text. Such tasks are termed *text transformation tasks*. Newspaper articles are often good as source materials, but a variety of other sources can be used. On occasion, source texts are not authentic but specially created for the purpose of the exercise.

Here are some examples (selected from many) of text transformation exercises that have been used:

A newspaper feature article about a Malagasy tradition called Famidihana which involves digging up dead ancestors, wrapping them in new shrouds, dousing them with alcohol, telling them the local gossip, and reburying them *used as the basis for writing* an encyclopedia entry on Famidihana.

A diary entry about a disastrous attempt to get to a wedding (not authentic) *used as the basis for writing* a letter of apology.

Extracts from a handbook about birds *used as the basis for writing* a local-newspaper nature column about owls.

A magazine feature about child labor in the third world *used as the basis for writing* a leaflet persuading prospective buyers of handmade carpets to boycott products made using child slave labor.

A text from a nature guide about wolves *used as the basis for writing* an entry in a TV guide about a program for children.

Two opposing editorial comment columns (*USA Today*) about the advantages and disadvantages of photo radar speed traps *used as the basis for writing* a report to a city council on the advantages and disadvantages of installing such equipment.

A newspaper story about the need for a mass vaccination program against Hepatitis B *used as the basis for writing* a circular letter to parents of twelve-year-old schoolchildren asking for their consent to such a vaccination.

Students' own knowledge of their university *used as the basis for writing* a guide to campus eating facilities for exchange students from overseas.

These examples should suffice to give an idea of the range of task types that are possible. Academic essays generally do not figure in the list; students get practice in writing these in other courses. Nor is there much in the way of personal expression: it does not usually fit in particularly well with the philosophy and goals of the course. Instead, students are asked to select from and use information actually available to create a text that is "needed" in a given situation. This matches the type of requirement frequently found in real-life situations where writing is necessary.

Text transformation exercises challenge and stretch students through the specific text requirements involved. They provide opportunities for teaching language that will be needed in the task, either before students work at the task or after a first attempt has revealed a need.

Tasks need to be carefully specified, with clear instructions as to the writer's role, the purpose, the audience, and the context of the text to be created. It is important that students be told that they may only use information stated or implied in the source text (or provided by the teacher, if there is some key point the source text does not cover). Students may feel that they want to be able to invent extra details, but in practice this can create any or all of three problems. The first is that the details students invent are often not appropriate or realistic. The second is that, in effect, it is no longer the case that all students in the class are tackling the same task; being able to introduce other information changes the task. Finally, students can use this as an avoidance strategy, enabling them to ignore elements of the source material that they would find difficult to handle. Avoidance of difficulties is a factor that may be involved in freer writing exercises, where students can generally manage to stay on "safe" ground if they wish to do so; one major advantage of text transformation exercises is that they force students to attempt things which they would never otherwise try until they actually came to need to do them in "real life."

Most of the text transformation tasks listed above will produce written texts of 200–300 words in length, but shorter tasks are also useful. It can be just as helpful to thrash out the wording of a single sentence or short paragraph. For example, students can find a variety of ways of saying the same thing, and then select the most appropriate for a particular context. An example of this technique is to find a variety of ways (at different levels of formality) of expressing a message, such as "No smoking inside the buildings," and then select one to go into a conference program.

There are no set patterns for the process of writing course tasks. The task may be discussed in class first, often in the light of reading and discussing texts of the genre students are to produce; alternatively, students may be left to work things out on their own. Students may work on texts individually or in pairs or small groups – team writing is often rather hard, but discussing and justifying one's ideas in pairs or small groups is an excellent way of getting students to make their own thinking clear and explicit. Students may work in class, with the teacher advising if needed, or they may work at home. Students may get comment from the teacher or peers on a first draft, or they may simply hand in their final draft.

However, there are some regularly recurring features of the teaching. At some stage, students will usually see the work of at least some other members of the class. Since everyone has been working at solving the same problem, other people's efforts are usually particularly interesting, and can be appreciated in the light of one's own efforts. I often photocopy some students' finished work for distribution – not choosing especially "bad" or "good" texts, but trying to pick three or four that represent different ways of tackling the problem, and also of course ensuring that everyone gets a chance to have their work "published" in this way. There will also be other follow-up work – perhaps class discussion of common problems, or of other possible ways of solving the problem. Because everyone has worked on the same task, this type of follow-up is much more successful and useful than in classes where everyone has written about different things.

Another frequent feature is the use of students' commentary on their own writing. Sometimes this may take the form of an explanation of the way they have tackled the task, again with the aim of encouraging awareness of choices in writing. However, we also encourage students to begin the post-writing dialogue on their own texts, rather than waiting for the teacher to "render judgment." Students are encouraged to ask the teacher to consider specific points about their texts – for example, points where they were uncertain about what word or syntactic structure to use. In this way, they can begin to get the feedback on their text that they want, rather than the feedback that the teacher opts to provide. This useful approach was described in an article by Charles (1990).

Other activities

Discussing and writing texts is a major element of the course. However, activities not linked to any particular text transformation task can help build up students' range of writing options. These include the following.

Work with reference materials

Work with reference materials means learning to get the best out of a dictionary, thesaurus, grammar usage guide, etc., through problem-solving tasks.

Vocabulary-building exercises

These exercises are activities in which work may be done on words in a semantic field to distinguish between them, for example in terms of their collocations, semantic features, antonyms, related words, etc. An example of this might be to get students to list as many words as possible associated with laughing (smile, grin, chuckle, giggle, chortle, hoot, cackle, bray, snicker, etc.), add a few more to the list, and then work on the distinguishing features of the words. Numerous examples of vocabulary-building exercises – though generally at a lower level – can be found in Lewis (1996).

Sentence manipulation exercises

This (rather old-fashioned) type of exercise gets students to reformulate sentences in various ways, cueing them by giving another start to the sentence ("Jenny would have lost her job if Sue hadn't intervened. *But for...*"). These can remind students of ways in which they can introduce variety into sentence structure in their texts.

Writing to artificial rules

Stephen Keeler pioneered the use of the *Sunday Telegraph* "Minisagas" competition, in which writers have to produce a coherent and complete story in exactly fifty words, no more and no less, as a second language writing activity. It's great fun, and practices very precise control.

Learning strategy discussion and teaching could also form a useful element of a course.

All these activities are useful, and often motivating and entertaining as well. However, they do not form a coherent course, and no doubt readers will have their own favorite activities that can be used equally effectively to expand students' linguistic range. The point is not that these particular suggestions are any better than many other activities that could be used, but rather that the course should provide a range of activities to maintain interest and increase awareness.

Conclusion

This chapter has described ideas and principles. It is not intended as a presentation of a fixed teaching program (the course is adapted and improved from year to year), nor yet a rigid teaching methodology. No claim is made that the course covers all aspects of the writing skill or that it would answer all the needs of all students seeking to make the leap to the Distinguished level of second language writing competence – nor that the suggestions in the chapter, taken individually, are original. On the other hand, because the chapter contains a fairly loose set of teaching ideas, rather than a teaching "formula," teachers of many different Superior-level writing courses may be able to incorporate some of these suggestions into what they do and some of the thinking about advanced writing into their planning.

The course described here is concerned with texts in English but the ideas would be equally applicable for teaching in other second languages. Further, although the ideas described are discussed in the context of teaching Advanced- and Superior-level students, they could be advantageously adapted for inclusion in lower-level courses, preparing students, from the outset, ultimately to become Distinguished-level writers.

10 Heritage speakers as learners at the Superior level: Differences and similarities between Spanish and Russian student populations

Claudia Angelelli and Olga Kagan

Taking stock at the beginning of this new century, it is clear that educational systems, including foreign language classrooms, will have to address a new and growing segment of the population of the USA, the bilingual community.[1] According to the 2000 US Census information, almost 11% of Americans were born outside of the USA. In some states, the number is higher; for example, it is close to 26% in California. Due to migration, the processes of nationalism and federalism, the need for education, commerce, intermarriage, and other factors (Grosjean [1982]), languages in contact are becoming the norm rather than the exception, leading to increased bilingualism (Appel and Muysken [1987]).[2]

The student population: toward a description

Speakers living in households that use more than one language at a high level of proficiency are considered bilinguals – although the term, *bilingual*, has many definitions[3] and the concept of a bilingual individual as equally proficient in all aspects of two languages and cultures may be more myth than reality (Valdés [2000]). Various terms have been applied to bilingual L2 students. *Home-background speakers* and *heritage learners* are the terms used in this chapter to refer to those speakers who emigrated with their parents or were born to émigré families and who have a language of "a particular family relevance other than English" (Fishman [2001, p. 81]).

Since their schooling is usually exclusively or predominantly in English and linguistic interaction at home generally limited to face-to-face interpersonal communication, heritage learners typically perform well in the Interpersonal

---

[1] In this chapter, we discuss programs for heritage speakers living in the USA. However, many of the issues would be the same for heritage speakers living in any other country.

[2] Although languages in contact may also lead to the development of pidgins and creoles, this chapter focuses exclusively on the phenomenon of bilingualism.

[3] See Valdés and Figueroa (1994) for an overview of terms used and proposed.

mode (direct oral or written communication between two or more persons) but less well in the Interpretative (mediated communication via print and broadcast materials) and Presentational (oral or written communication for an audience without immediate possibilities of personal interaction) modes, as described in the National foreign language Standards (ACTFL [1999]). In other words, they are not experienced communicators at the Superior level across the full range of interactions.[4] Nevertheless, if compared with non-heritage students receiving instruction in a foreign language, heritage language speakers typically possess skills that require a non-native speaker hundreds of hours to acquire, including some skills that foreign language (FL) learners may never acquire at a native-like level, such as unaccented pronunciation, fluency in colloquial register, comfort with dialects, and sociocultural understanding (Brecht and Ingold [1998]).

For linguists, the focus in researching bilingualism has centered on the relationship between the majority and home languages themselves (Haugen [1978], cited in Fishman [1978]). This relationship is of interest to language educators, too, because of its sociolinguistic and sociocultural significance. Children who grow up in homes where a non-English language is spoken acquire some of the culture of their families and immediate communities. However, outside of the home they grow up within the context of the American educational system and public culture, becoming fully acculturated while their parents typically remain more comfortable in the non-American culture. Kramsch's (1993) notion of the combination of one's own culture (Culture 1) and the target-language culture (Culture 2) resulting in the acquisition of Culture 3 (a form of "interculture") does not apply to émigré children who live and function between the inside (home) and the outside (mainstream) cultures (Bermel and Kagan [2000]). How does one determine what constitutes Cultures 1 and 2 for such students? As with bilingualism, these speakers are bicultural to various degrees. Valdés (2000) and Polinsky (2000) address the issue of continuum in heritage speakers' linguistic ability. Since Superior-level proficiency includes sociocultural competence in the target culture as experienced in a country where the target language is spoken, even very proficient heritage speakers cannot be said to possess the full range of sociocultural competence.

Moreover, home-background speakers and second language learners differ in needs and motivation they bring to a language classroom (Valdés [1992]; Valdés and Geoffrion-Vinci [1998]). First, whereas non-native-speaking foreign language students need to acquire a linguistic system and the rules that help them make sense of it, in many cases home-background speakers already possess that system. Very often, they cannot explain or justify the rules (like most native speakers of any given language, for that matter), but they use them naturally. They may speak even better than the teacher who explains the rules

---

[4] The ACTFL Guidelines were not designed for home-background speakers (Valdés [1989]). Therefore, the terms, *Advanced* and *Superior*, are used here in an approximate way.

to them. Sometimes, while listening to teachers' explanations of some rules, they may even get confused (Valdés [1995]). Second, it is not uncommon for home-background speakers to want to forget everything they have learned at home so that "they can just learn it the right way." Many times they feel ashamed of the language variety they speak at home. They have heard that it is not the "right" kind of language. Often, they have been excluded in L2 classrooms and, therefore, often need teacher validation of their home usage (Valdés [1988]).

The status quo

Until recently, the special needs and benefits in developing the language proficiencies of heritage students were largely ignored. Now, however, education of these students is beginning to be viewed as safeguarding the development of a valuable national resource (Campbell and Peyton [1998]).

Gonzalez-Pino and Pino (2000) stress that "heritage students of Spanish are an ever-increasing consideration in education at all levels." The same statement can be made about heritage students of many other languages – Arabic, Armenian, Chinese, Korean, Persian, Russian, Thai, and Vietnamese, to name a few. Ever more heritage students view their home language as a valuable asset and an individual achievement and are willing to study the language if an appropriate program is offered to them (H. Reid [2000]).

The interest in heritage learning led to the formation of a new field: heritage language acquisition. Its establishment began formally with the first national conference on heritage issues in Long Beach, California, in 1999 and a subsequent conference (University of California, Los Angeles, Fall 2000), addressing issues of importance in teaching foreign languages to home-background speakers / heritage learners.

In this chapter, we describe three heritage language acquisition programs. We have chosen to compare two communities, Spanish and Russian, not because they are similar but because they are so unlike each other. The histories, composition, and patterns of assimilation are totally different. However, the needs of children growing up in bilingual families, their attributes, and the methodology for teaching them are similar. Therefore, what works for teaching and acquiring these two languages can inform other heritage language programs.

Although many heritage learners need instruction at lower levels of proficiency, in this chapter we describe only programs and courses at the Superior/ Distinguished (SD) level. Each of the presented programs enrolls heritage speakers whose language proficiency is at least at the Advanced level and whose goal is to reach the SD level. The designers of these courses have made two assumptions: (1) SD-level proficiency is a realistic expectation for heritage students and (2) SD-level proficiency can be developed through institutionally based direct instruction.

Programs for Russian heritage speakers at UCLA and Barnard/Columbia

The program for Russian heritage speakers at UCLA was established in the late 1990s. Prior to that, either heritage speakers were accommodated in the general Russian program, although that program did not necessarily meet their needs, or they did not elect to study Russian. The need for a separate program became evident in 1998 after a survey conducted among heritage speakers demonstrated that they were interested in maintaining their language proficiency, learning about Russian culture in its many manifestations, and reading Russian literature. The program subsequently developed took into account these expressed interests.

The program for heritage speakers at Columbia University / Barnard College was established in the early 1990s with the introduction of a two-semester course, Masterpieces of Russian Literature, that had as a prerequisite native or near-native proficiency in Russian. From that time until 2000, this literature course was the only one available that could challenge the heritage speaker audience. As a result of increasing numbers of heritage speakers with diverse levels of proficiency, in 2000 the Russian Department at Columbia University / Barnard College introduced several new courses. Among these was the course in Russian culture described below.

The program at UCLA

The UCLA program combines Russian culture, including literature, with language materials in the Interpretative and Presentational modes. The program for heritage students entering at the Superior or near-Superior level currently consists of three upper-division classes: 1) Russian National Identity, 2) Literature and Film, and 3) Special Topics (e.g., History of the Russian Language). The choice of the themes was prompted by the students' interest in Russian culture, history, and philosophy as ascertained via surveys conducted in 1996 and subsequent years at UCLA. The latest, conducted in 2001, showed similar results. These results are by no means unexpected: Zemskaya (2001) found that Russian families highly value Russian literature and are disappointed if their children do not read Russian authors. The program is taught over 1–2 years, the duration that experience has shown to be required for most enrollees to reach SD proficiency.

Course content

Students engage in academic reading and writing, as well as classroom discussions and formal presentations. These students are typically at the Advanced High or Superior level of proficiency in the Interpersonal mode (in speaking and writing), close to Superior in reading (but are rarely at the Distinguished level as they cannot always discern stylistic subtleties of texts), and Advanced in writing. Their writing displays linguistic accuracy but lacks in discourse competence (Celce-Murcia, Dörnyei, and Thurrell [1995]). In particular, their writing exhibits: (1) inappropriate use of short sentences and straightforward narration, rather than Russian academic syntax, which is characterized by complex sentences, embedded clauses, and participial constructions; (2) limited vocabulary with rare use of synonymous expression; (3) extensive and often inappropriate use of everyday nonacademic vocabulary; (4) missing or inappropriate transitions between sentences and paragraphs; (5) missing or incorrect punctuation; and (6) a tendency to use SVO word order, rather than Russian discourse, in which word order depends on the prior utterance or background knowledge of shared information.

Approaches to teaching

Three interrelated approaches to teaching are used. These include (1) a process approach to writing, (2) a communicative approach to development of oral skills, and (3) a content-based approach to syllabus design.

Process writing. Students write weekly essays that are peer edited. In editing and rewriting, students are required to replace several simple sentences with a single compound, complex, or compound complex one. Similarly, they are required to paraphrase in a stylistically appropriate register. They are also expected to give an explanation of why a sentence or paragraph does not appear to sound right and what improvements could be made. On the mechanical side, special attention is paid to the differences between Russian and English punctuation (e.g., the treatment of clause subordination or quotations).

Communicative activities. Oral presentation skills are developed through classroom discussion and preparation of formal presentations. Students are assigned readings and given discussion questions in advance. The discussion in class revolves around the content of literary works, with the emphasis not on literary analysis but on the reflection of Russian cultural identity. When speaking in class, students are expected (and taught) to use the vocabulary, intonation, and grammar appropriate for an academic setting. The approach used is a combination of linguistic training with content-based discussion – and a constant monitoring of students' linguistic behavior.

Content-Based Instruction (CBI). In our view, CBI is the most natural vehicle for academic language use. The content-based nature of these courses also responded to students' interests expressed in the surveys mentioned above. (Appendix A displays results from the 2000 survey.)

An example of a CBI course for heritage learners is the Russian National Identity course. The course goals, in descending order of priority, are to (1) develop a comprehensive understanding of Russian culture and self-identity;

(2) expand students' vocabulary reserve to the domains of culture, cultural history, and academic terminology; (3) develop age- and cognitively appropriate formal, academic oral expression; and (4) improve students' writing skills, as measured by portfolio assessment focusing on spelling, punctuation, and stylistics.

In 1999, the course was based on Lev Tolstoy's *War and Peace* and was team-taught by a language instructor and a professor of Russian literature.[5] The literature professor lectured weekly on Russian cultural history, while the language instructor led discussions, gave assignments, and graded papers. Extensive reading (about 100 pages) was assigned every week. Students wrote weekly short papers (2–3 pages) and a final term paper (5–10 pages). The students also gave a 20-minute final oral presentation. Its preparation required students to engage in independent research, and its completion required giving a presentation in a manner acceptable in a Russian academic institution. Since the majority of the students had never given academic presentations in Russian, they needed guidelines and practice in the norms of academic discourse, choice of vocabulary, syntax, intonation, and pace of the presentation.

Further, students were given specific guidelines as to the linguistic behavior expected during a research conference. The class engaged in discussion conducted in the appropriate register. The criterion for the selection of topics for the presentation and term paper was the identification of background information that would help other readers understand *War and Peace*. As in the course itself, the oral reports focused not on literary criticism but rather on the exploration of Russian cultural history. Representative topics included Russian Cuisine of the Nineteenth Century, Duel in Russia and in Other Countries, The Russian View of Death, Upbringing in a Russian Aristocratic Family, The Life of Women at the Beginning of the Nineteenth Century, and Balls as Part of Russian Aristocratic Life. Background reading was required. The grade for the oral presentation depended on (1) quantity and quality of new information obtained in the course of the research, (2) the interest the presentation stimulated, and (3) linguistic quality – appropriateness of genre and register.[6]

The program at Columbia University / Barnard College

A representative course from the program at Columbia University / Barnard College used a similar approach, i.e., a combination of lectures and discussion

[5] Team-teaching, in which a language instructor is paired with a content instructor, is frequently used in CBI and Languages Across the Curriculum courses and is one of several CBI / Foreign Languages Across the Curriculum (FLAC) configurations described by Shaw (1997).

[6] The Russian academic genre, referred to as "scientific style" in Russian, is characterized by participial constructions, long complex sentences, stylized syntax, domain-specific jargon and phraseology, abstract vocabulary, parenthetical expressions for citation and reference, first person plural narration, and an abundance of impersonal constructions that have no equivalent in English.

with written essays. Russia on the Hudson: Russian Culture in New York[7] introduced several aspects of Russian culture: ballet, opera, theatre, film, and visual
arts.

Each unit included a lecture by a specialist in the field, readings from a
number of genres, and writing and translations from and into Russian. Some of
the lectures were in Russian delivered by Columbia faculty or other specialists
who were native speakers of Russian; some were in English. Lectures were
recorded so that the students could listen to them again, and students were
asked to submit a written synopsis in Russian of each of them. The summaries
required use of SD-level vocabulary, grammar, and text structure, along with
writing in the academic genre.

The texts introduced in the course included literary criticism, opera libret-
tos, plays, and scripts. These provided students with source material for their
presentations at the end of the course.

Students made short (ten-minute) presentations at the end of each unit. They
were not required to conduct extensive independent research but rather to provide their own interpretation of a work of art, a short Balanchine ballet, an aria
from an opera, and the like. These presentations were followed by discussions,
in which opinions frequently varied.

SD elements common to the UCLA and Columbia University / Barnard College courses

Both the UCLA and Barnard/Columbia courses relied heavily on students'
background knowledge and strong proficiency in aural and oral modalities.
The primary goal was the development of content knowledge, accompanied
by an improvement in Russian-language proficiency, achieved through student
in-class interaction, the writing of papers, the making of presentations, and
the acquisition of the academic genre in writing and speaking. Even though
the instructors developed their courses independently, they adopted similar approaches. Common characteristics of the two courses included (1) the use of
authentic materials, (2) tasks that required students to synthesize information
from multiple sources, (3) attention to the development of a culturally appropriate yet personal style of written and oral presentation, (4) work on preliminary
steps before requiring a finished product, and (5) the encouragement of students
to be active researchers.[8]

Materials

Only authentic materials were used in both courses. Written texts were combined with video and lectures to expose students to all the modalities typically

---

[7] The authors are grateful to Mara Kashper of Columbia University for sharing her course design
and insights into her interaction with the class.
[8] These goals are similar to those set by Frodesen et al. (1997) in their introduction to a content-
based ESL course.

encountered by native speakers in an academic environment. Materials included a variety of genres and were lengthy and complex from the point of view of both content and language.

Instructional techniques

Instructional techniques differed from those used with lower-level learners and even somewhat from those used with Superior-level learners of Russian as a foreign language. Students were assigned large quantities of text and listened to academic lectures with some, but not extensive, language support. They were expected to cope with the large volume of authentic text mostly on their own. Whereas non-heritage students even at the Superior level need an occasional explanation of uniquely foreign grammatical concepts, such as verbal aspect or verbal government, heritage learners are mainly in need of stylistic improvement and register "fine-tuning."

Evaluation/results

Although no formal feedback was solicited, the students in both UCLA and Columbia courses expressed satisfaction with the materials, approach, and general content of the courses. They commented that the course improved their linguistic knowledge and cultural understanding.

Since one semester of instruction rarely results in measurable progress on a proficiency scale, even in the presence of evident improvement, portfolio assessment (Moore [1994]) in addition to (or instead of) more traditional testing was used in both courses. In keeping with principles of content-based instruction, the assessment was also based on the quality of the content of the final presentations and increase in topical knowledge.

Spanish for home-background speakers at Stanford University

Spanish occupies a unique position among heritage languages in the USA today. The increase of Spanish speakers in the USA, along with strong bonds maintained with the community/country of origin, often results in Spanish continuing to be a strong component of home-background speakers' identity. However, like all other heritage languages, Spanish struggles to avoid language shift, especially after the third generation (Veltman [2000]). Maintenance occurs in the midst of adversarial politics, such as the English-Only Movement.

Sometimes high schools, colleges, and universities offer separate tracks for bilingual Spanish students. Other times, non-native speakers and heritage speakers share courses and programs even when their needs and motivation may be clearly different. In 1995, Stanford University established a program of Spanish for heritage speakers called "Spanish for Home-Background Speakers"[9] in order to meet the needs of nearly 40% – a growing share – of the student population of the Spanish Department. (Stand-alone courses had been taught for fifteen years previous to that.) In creating this program, various elements were considered – among them entry mechanism, faculty, curriculum, and materials.

Enrollment mechanism

Enrollment was effected based on the results of a placement test specifically designed for home-background speakers. Students can take the test online at the Stanford home-background speaker home page (www.language3.stanford.edu).

The faculty

Instructors of the Spanish for Home-Background Speakers courses are native speakers of Spanish and whenever possible home-background speakers themselves. They represent the Spanish language variety spoken in various countries of Latin America (e.g., Mexico, Puerto Rico, Argentina) and in Spanish-speaking communities in the USA (e.g., Los Angeles and Miami). All the home-background-speaker instructors work closely with a full professor.

The curriculum

The program of Spanish for Home-Background Speakers at Stanford University is a comprehensive one. It consists of preliminary courses for home-background speakers not yet at the Superior level and several advanced courses. Only the latter are discussed here.

At the upper level are courses especially developed for bilingual students. Spanish Composition for Home-Background Speakers is an example. Students in this course exhibit unevenness in proficiency levels among speaking, listening, reading, and writing skills, or they may lack the ability to transfer their skills to an academic environment. This course, then, focuses on developing academic language skills to a level of use that parallels the ease with which they use less formal language.

Stanford University also offers courses that are open to both home-background speakers and Superior-level non-native students, e.g., CBI courses.[10]

---

[9] The creator of this program was Guadalupe Valdés, Professor of Spanish and Portuguese and Professor of Education.

[10] Here we are using the concept proposed by Leaver and Bilstein (2000) that CBI contains at least three kinds of courses: (1) Language for Special Purposes (LSP) courses that focus on the development of language skills while using content for a specific discipline, (2) Sheltered Content courses that simultaneously develop both language skills and content knowledge, and (3) Languages Across the Curriculum courses that focus on the development of content knowledge with accompanying readings, and sometimes discussions, in L2.

Some of these may be Language for Special Purposes courses geared for Spanish majors; examples include Spanish for Life Sciences, Spanish for Legal Professionals, and Spanish for Pre-Med Students. Others may be (Foreign) Languages Across the Curriculum (LAC) courses, examples being cultural courses in Latino issues such as Espaldas Mojadas, linguistic courses such as Spanish dialectology or sociolinguistics, and literature courses such as Chicano or Border literature.

The curriculum is based on the new National Standards (ACTFL [1999]), using objectives prepared for heritage speakers (Valdés *et al.* [1997]). These objectives represent three modes of communication: Interpersonal (requiring interaction with speakers from a range of sociocultural backgrounds), Interpretative (developing strategies to interpret and react to authentic texts), and Presentational (offering opportunities for oral and written formal presentations on abstract and challenging topics to academic audiences).

A sample course: Structure of Spanish

Heritage learners at the SD level typically need clarification of linguistic structure as well as the opportunity to acquire the specific terminology of their field of interest. Students may use clarification tactics discussed in Chapter 6 to request information on the metalanguage. In order to do that, however, they need a safe forum. Discussion in literary criticism courses where students have to (and want to) sound erudite requires that they already be able to make their points precisely and to use appropriate metalinguistic terminology to speak about language and literature. The acquisition of the metalanguage and the mastery of the mechanics and structure of the language need to happen elsewhere. These examples are just a few of the instances in which Superior-level students indeed benefit from traditional learning environments in, for example, the structure of Spanish. As has been discussed in Chapters 3 and 4, Superior-level students do not find answers to metalinguistic questions merely by exposure to native speakers. They need specific answers. A Superior-level course on the structure of language is one possible forum where metalinguistic questions can be addressed.

Structure of Spanish, a course developed by Angelelli (1996), provides home-background students with the metalinguistic awareness and the metalanguage necessary for success in courses that require strong competence in academic Spanish. Students enrolling in this course generally produce grammatically correct discourse but cannot justify the decisions they make in producing it. In advanced literary courses, sometimes the feedback they get entails comments using metalinguistic terms with which they are not familiar, for example: "El análisis es bueno pero está escrito de forma demasiado simple. No se ha usado ni una oración compleja, cuando las subordinadas constituyen la base del discurso español." (The analysis is good, but it is written in a simplistic style. There are no complex sentences in spite of the fact that subordinate clauses are the backbone of Spanish discourse.) Structure of Spanish, then, serves a dual purpose: it helps students acquire the metalanguage for Spanish, and it develops Superior-level grammatical competence.

Course objectives

Course objectives are based on the Spanish departmental objectives[11] conceptualized in response to the National Standards in Foreign Language Education Project (ACTFL [1999]). They are summarized in Table 10.1.

Course content and activities

Course content reflects the latest research available in the field of heritage language teaching (Valdés, Hannum, and Teschner [1982]; Valdés and Teschner [1999]). Through class discussions, informed by assigned readings and exercises, Structure of Spanish describes and analyzes the main points of Spanish grammar, such as simple and complex sentences, types of clauses, relative pronouns, verb aspect, mood, and tenses. Two oral assignments – one individual and one group – require students to present such topics as the use of *vos/tú/usted* (second person singular, subjective pronouns), use of articles, and different forms of *se*. For the group presentation, throughout the semester students work in small groups to prepare a topic. Two written assignments acquaint students with the process of writing a research paper in Spanish. Topics have included a comparison of the different forms of expressing the past in various Latin American countries, the use of past tenses in literary narratives and in news reporting, the use of diminutives and their variations in various countries of the Spanish-speaking world, linguistic markers in situational contexts, and analysis of the use of *tú* and *usted* in soap operas.

Students come to class having read about a topic and completed application exercises. In class, the instructor asks students to explain or suggest why traditional rules may not offer enough of an explanation for linguistic phenomena. Class is conducted in Spanish and, sometimes, contrastive analysis is used to illustrate topics. For example, students learn the different uses of the pronoun, *se*, in Spanish. At lower levels (Intermediate/Advanced), they have

---

[11] During the summer of 1997, Professor Valdés chaired a Stanford University committee to design the new Spanish objectives for home-background speakers and non-native speakers (Valdés *et al.* [March, 2000]). Angelelli was part of the committee that wrote the objectives and implemented them across levels.

Table 10.1

Interpersonal mode	Interpretative mode	Presentational mode
Oral Language Students exhibit growing competence in carrying out face-to-face interactions with same age, older and younger people in culturally appropriate ways. After successfully completing the course they will: • Identify levels of formality and informality in speech and react accordingly • Discuss and support perspectives with peers and/or speakers of Spanish on a variety of academic topics	Oral Texts Students exhibit growing ability to comprehend and interpret live and recorded extended texts such as academic lectures and documentaries. After successfully completing the course they will: • Take notes on linguistic and sociolinguistic issues • Problematize linguistic features according to different social settings	Oral Presentations Students exhibit growing competence in using oral language to present information to an academic audience. After successfully completing the course they will: • Present extensive reports on assigned topics to their class mates • More effectively monitor their oral production for non-academic language features
Written language Students exhibit growing competence in using written language for interpersonal communication in culturally appropriate ways in academic settings. After successfully completing the course, they will: • Feedback to peers via peer editing assignments • Have culturally appropriate e-mail exchange with peers	Written texts Students exhibit growing ability to comprehend and interpret written texts. After successfully completing the course, they will: • Research information on academic topics from Spanish sources • Demonstrate an increasing understanding of academic Spanish features	Written presentations Students exhibit growing competence in using written language to present information and state a position to an academic readership. After successfully completing the course they will: • Write research papers in Spanish • Edit their writing for style and register appropriate to written academic language

briefly discussed the use of *se* with reflexive and reciprocal verbs. Sometimes they have even addressed the frequency of *se* in the Spanish passive voice. In this class, students are able to explain how the construction of the Spanish passive form with *se* differs from the regular Spanish and English passive voice constructions. They also discuss other uses of *se* such as the "affective *se*" (*se murió mi perro* instead of *murió mi perro* ["my dog died on me" instead of "my dog died"]), or the *se* that diffuses responsibility. An example of the latter is *se me cayó el vaso* (the glass fell) instead of *dejé caer el vaso* (I dropped the glass).

Materials

Readings come from authentic materials. Some are from linguistic and sociolinguistic journals such as *Hispania*. Other readings include doctoral dissertations on topics related to students' interests. Still others are readings from periodicals brought in by students. Students are provided one textbook, *Gramática Española* (King and Suñer [1999]), which contains exercises and a self-scoring key. This textbook was chosen on the basis of the pedagogical approach to the teaching of grammar. (Unlike other grammar texts, King and Suñer offer extensive explanations on grammar points that are otherwise generally trivialized [e.g., defining and non-defining relative clauses]. They add sociolinguistic information that rarely appears in grammar books [e.g., use of second person pronoun in areas where "*vos*" completely overlaps "*tú*"]. The text does not prescribe a limited set of arbitrary rules but rather describes a linguistic system in its entirety.)

Evaluation/results

Structure of Spanish has been taught for six years. The success of the course is evident in the fact that for the last two years an additional section has had to be opened to accommodate the number of students who wanted to take this course. Students comment that the course provides them with the necessary concepts to understand the Spanish linguistic system as well as with the metalanguage to discuss it. In their course evaluations (Appendix B) students highlight the importance of reading about the language and illustrating issues discussed in the authentic materials, especially when they cannot be explained by applying the 'traditional" rules generally offered in language textbooks. They also find that they are able to present technical and abstract aspects of the language in front of an audience of peers. This is very rewarding for home-background speakers whose language variety has been often stigmatized in a classroom situation. In their evaluations, they stress the fact that they can not only make sense of the system now but also talk about it using appropriate terminology.

Discussion

In this chapter, we chose to discuss the approaches to heritage education in two languages: Spanish, with the largest numbers of heritage speakers, and Russian, with a much smaller number of speakers but a sizable presence in some, mostly urban areas. The two populations differ in as many as five ways. First, Spanish speakers come from a host of countries and cultures, representing a number of language varieties, whereas Russian speakers, even though they may come from different parts of the former Soviet Union, speak a fairly uniform language and share a standard lexicon. Second, the sheer numbers of Spanish speakers create numerous opportunities for communication outside of class while for Russian speakers such communication is limited to home and certain areas in the city/country. Third, while Spanish speakers, especially in some states, can regard Spanish as a non-foreign language, Russian speakers realize that Russian is an "exotic" foreign language in the USA. Fourth, even though issues of ethnicity and race that underlie many discussions regarding Spanish speakers are not relevant in the case of Russian heritage students, Russian heritage speakers still face the problem of teacher attitudes to their substandard, "kitchen" Russian; at the same time, some Slavic departments dismiss them as native speakers who do not need any instruction because of their oral/aural proficiency. Fifth, Spanish departments have been grappling with the problems of teaching heritage speakers of Spanish for the past twenty-five or so years, whereas the Russian departments have been dealing with this problem for less than ten years and are only now beginning to come to terms with this new student population. Unlike for Spanish, so far almost no commercially available Russian-language materials have been developed for these students.[12] This juxtaposition allows us to show the range of needs, as well as the range of possibilities, in teaching heritage speakers.

Program design

Although the two groups of heritage speakers presented in this chapter – Spanish and Russian – differ vastly, they share many traits, including, importantly for this chapter, their position as students within the university. Table 10.2 summarizes the similarities and differences between these students and traditional FL learners.

A comparison of the needs of non-heritage and heritage learners at the Superior level reveals similar needs in the areas of writing and speaking. For example, in working on academic topics in the Presentational mode, both groups need to acquire academic register in oral and written discourse. However, while both groups also need work on punctuation, heritage speakers are more likely to need work in spelling. The differences are especially noticeable in pronunciation, grammar, listening skills, and sociocultural competence. While heritage speakers typically have no need to practice intonation, non-heritage speakers may have a distinct accent, even at the highest level of proficiency. Superior-level non-heritage students, on the other hand, most likely have a solid foundation in grammar, in use as well as declarative knowledge. Heritage learners do not. The distinction between knowledge and skill in language proficiency (Bialystok [1981]) is nowhere as striking as it is in heritage speakers.

---

[12] The only available material, as of this writing, is a textbook, *Russian for Russians* (Kagan, Akishina, and Robin [2002]).

Table 10.2

Teaching domains	Non-heritage learners at the Superior level	Heritage learners at the Superior level
Pronunciation and intonation	In need of practice even at higher proficiency levels	Not an issue
Vocabulary	May need everyday lexicon in the absence of extensive time in C2	Need literary/academic/ specialized vocabulary
Grammar	Have solid declarative knowledge	May have little declarative knowledge
Reading	Need exposure to various styles, genres and registers	Need exposure to various styles, genres and registers
Writing	Need extensive practice in syntax, punctuation, stylistics	Need extensive practice in syntax punctuation, spelling
Speaking	Need Distinguished-level tasks (including formal presentational opportunities)	Need Distinguished-level tasks (including formal presentational opportunities)
Listening	May still need to work on listening comprehension	Not an issue
Sociolinguistic competence	Need to acquire academic register, as well as sophisticated understanding of appropriateness of other registers	Need to acquire academic register and raise awareness of lower-register occurrences in formal discourse
Sociocultural competence	Need to develop greater sociocultural competence, including literature, political, and historical allusions	Depending on home and community student may need to develop some aspects of sociocultural competence

To summarize, effective programs for heritage learners will both overlap with and differ from L2 programs for non-native speakers. Boyd (2000) identifies four critically important areas, all of them discussed further below:
1) an appropriate curriculum;
2) appropriate assessment instruments;
3) qualified instructors;
4) positive attitudes to heritage languages.

An appropriate curriculum

Programs for heritage speakers can take a number of forms. Courses designed specifically for heritage learners can be taught as stand-alone courses, presented as a sequence of courses in a specific "track," or form a comprehensive program devoted to home-background speakers. Stand-alone courses can be of various kinds, from purely heritage-language courses (Spanish, Russian, Vietnamese, etc., for Bilingual Students) to Presentational skills in writing (Composition for Bilingual Students), study of structure courses, and/or Content-Based Instruction (including LSP courses, such as Spanish for Lawyers and Russian for Business, among others). Comprehensive programs are definitely the best option but are only just appearing on the horizon across the USA. They need a large population of heritage speakers to justify their existence. They offer specially designed curricula, measurement instruments, materials, and other types of academic support (e.g., tutoring). The program at Stanford University is an example of a comprehensive program.

The Russian program at UCLA faced the challenge of designing an entirely new curriculum. The challenge resulted in a new methodology and a new textbook for heritage students of Russian because the field is so new that there are no commercially available materials or even in-house materials prepared by other instructors. Instructors of heritage-speaker courses must become researchers and course designers. This is different from most other language courses with extant materials and syllabi.

Appropriate assessment instruments

Valdés (1989) discusses the problems arising when ILR/ACTFL proficiency guidelines are applied to Hispanic bilinguals. Her careful analysis of the dimensions underlying the generic descriptions of the speaking descriptors shows how meaningless they can be when assessing the abilities of native speakers. One example of this is comprehensibility, a salient dimension in the Oral Proficiency Interview (OPI), regarded as a contributing factor to the accuracy construct. Valdés argues that comprehension "across regional and social varieties of Spanish is as much a test of the abilities and background of one interlocutor as of the other. This dimension appears to be meaningless for assessing language abilities of native speakers" (p. 397). She also argues that many of the abilities that are considered to be present in higher levels of proficiency for non-native speakers (e.g., the ability to function well in areas involving social exchanges) are present at lower ability levels in heritage speakers. Finding appropriate assessment instruments for heritage speakers continues to be a challenge. The assumption behind the "native" ranks informing most extant proficiency tests, such as the ILR and ACTFL scales is an educated native-speaker form. This reflects the "norma culta" and does not address the "norma popular" or "norma rural" often used by heritage Spanish students in the USA. The question, then, is how to measure such speakers' proficiency for placement purposes.

McGinnis (1996) cites the role the Scholastic Achievement Test (SAT) II, a widely used discriminator in college admissions, has played in developing accelerated programs for Chinese heritage speakers, aiding accurate placement and more homogeneous grouping of students. Unfortunately, such tests are not available in many languages, including Russian.

Even though standard tests are not available, students can be given diagnostic tests at the beginning of the course to be compared with exit tests at the end. A Superior-level test would consist of Distinguished-level material, i.e., test the understanding of complex aural and written texts which require considerable sociocultural, sociolinguistic, and discourse knowledge. An oral interview and a writing sample would both contain a task of an Interpretational and/or Presentational nature. Achievement tests during the course would ideally contain all the four modalities as well. At this level of instruction it is natural to suggest that any achievement test has elements of proficiency so, by necessity, the test becomes a prochievement test. We have also advocated use of portfolios at this level.

Qualified instructors

One of the crucial needs in a heritage program is for an informed and skilled faculty, aware of the different needs of heritage students, including theories in bilingualism and methods of teaching heritage speakers. Yokoyama (2000) points out that "[c]onsiderable leadership skills, tact, and confidence are necessary on the part of the instructor" (p. 473) when dealing with heritage students who share a classroom with their non-heritage peers. However, the same is true even when heritage students are in a special track. The instructor's role in a class for heritage speakers is not only to serve as a linguistic role model and a motivator but also as a link to the heritage culture at large. The tact Yokoyama refers to is extremely important when dealing with students who have regional and dialectal features in their speech. These deviations are often stigmatized, and the instructor risks making students regard their families as inferior because of these variations. The best way to deal with these differences is to put them in the context of informal versus formal/academic language.

When foreign language learners and heritage speakers share a class, the role of the instructor becomes crucial. As discussed earlier, non-native speakers have been exposed to rules and generally have studied the language in a classroom. They may lack exposure to many L2 nuances and registers. The home-background speakers, on the other hand, understand nuances and have been exposed to various registers of the language but not necessarily to an academic one. They do not necessarily know the rules that govern a language, but they can use them, and they do not make the type of mistakes that would identify them as non-native speakers. When it comes to writing, they need direct instruction in certain areas (such as spelling) that non-native speakers have already mastered in their first stages of language acquisition. The instructor, then, has to be able to balance students' needs in order for them to learn as they share experiences and to scaffold their learning process.

Linguistic issues. As mentioned earlier, Spanish faculty at Stanford University are, if possible, native speakers and, where possible, home-background speakers of Spanish. Among Slavic faculty, on the other hand, there is considerable debate regarding qualifications for teaching heritage speakers. Superior-level students can be taught by language instructors who are native speakers of the language and also by content faculty (e.g., linguists, historians, artists) who may or may not be native speakers but whose proficiency is at the Distinguished level. SD classes at UCLA are taught by both kinds of instructors. Classes can also be team-taught by a content specialist and a language teacher. Both models have been used at UCLA and at Columbia/Barnard. Experience with faculty has shown, however, that no matter how proficient faculty members are in the language, they succeed in instructing heritage learners only when they have given considerable thought to heritage issues and relevant pedagogy. It is important, then, to start preparing graduate students to teach heritage classes in general and at the higher levels of instruction in particular.

Training in methodology. The role of the teachers being a determinant of the success or failure of home-background-speaker classes (Draper and Hicks [2000]), Stanford University instructors specializing in teaching home-background speakers take a number of relevant courses in the Spanish Department as well as in the School of Education. Topics covered in these courses include Bilingualism (theories and issues), Methods to Teach Spanish to Heritage Speakers, Spanish Dialectology, History of the Spanish Language, Spanish in the Chicano Community, as well as curriculum design, syllabus writing, lesson planning, development of materials, and strategies and tactics to teach students to monitor their own production. Likewise, in the past several years, the Teaching Practicum in the Slavic Department at UCLA has included a discussion of the special needs of heritage speakers.

Positive attitudes toward heritage languages
Home-background speakers do not differ only in the linguistic needs they bring to the classroom. They also differ in affective needs (Valdés [1992]). Even though these needs may differ from language to language, in all émigré groups family and community relations are important. In fact, participants at the UCLA

research conference mentioned earlier agree that maintenance of a home language by children is a mental health issue (University of California at Los Angeles [2000]). It is essential that instructors capture the attitudes that home-background speakers have toward their own group and their own identity since often home-background speakers see the heritage language as unimportant or unnecessary – or blame the language for being an obstacle to acquisition of English. The classroom environment has to lead home-background speakers to value both their heritage and their language and to allow them to maintain and enhance the gift that they already have.

Teaching methods

Instructors of heritage learners can use any of a number of current and traditional teaching methods. The Russian programs described in this chapter use communicative and content-based courses as a vehicle for Superior-level heritage instruction. The Spanish program at Stanford University, an older and much larger program, offers a course in grammatical structure, taught communicatively, in addition to content-based and other language courses. The Russian Program at UCLA teaches a course in History of the Russian Language that will serve a purpose similar to the Stanford Structure of Spanish course. Based on experience at UCLA and Stanford University, we suggest that this combination of courses is needed in order to train heritage speakers to become Superior-level speakers, readers, and writers.

Communicative approaches

The question raised in the introduction to this volume – whether communicative teaching practices, while being effective at the lower levels, may be ineffective at higher levels – clearly needs to be addressed in regard to heritage speakers as well. Our experience with heritage language teaching indicates that the instruction needs to remain communicative (if communicative is understood as the ability to handle real-life texts, both aural/oral and written), but it also needs to include considerable declarative knowledge and consciousness raising (Valdés [2000]) as they pertain to dialects, speech etiquette, cultural knowledge, and language structure.

Communicative instruction is as appropriate for heritage speakers as it is for any student at a higher proficiency level. It is part and parcel of content-based and structure courses described in this chapter. The critical learning needs of heritage speakers fall into the areas of academic and professional forms of reading and writing, requiring them to recognize, select among, and use appropriate discourse types, forms of text and thought organization, register, and specialized formats. They need to be able to read between the lines and interpret intent (intensive reading) and write in ways that are both clear and, where useful, intentionally vague, employing *double entendre*, cultural (including historical, political, literary, and everyday) references, and genre-specific techniques. They need to develop endurance for extensive reading and the ability to separate the wheat from the chaff in the texts. They need to be able to do similar things in listening, exhibiting both perspicacity in understanding unspoken intent and endurance in listening at length. In speaking, they need to learn to adapt their speech to the audience and select the culturally appropriate (or subgroup-sensitive) arguments that will persuade their audience. Clearly, nothing short of communicative instruction will serve to develop these skills and abilities, although the form and content of communicative instruction, as well as the task and the materials, will differ considerably from the nature of communicative instruction at lower levels of proficiency and for non-heritage speakers.

Content-Based Instruction
CBI in any or all of its forms – LSP, sheltered content, and Language Across the Curriculum courses – serves as a vehicle that allows instructors to engage heritage students' interest and develop their language ability naturally – and even painlessly, as some students have claimed (Duri [1992]). Any foreign language department of a college or university wishing to implement a comprehensive program for home-background speakers at the SD level can benefit from interdepartmental collaboration. Offering an array of LSP courses, such as Spanish for Business, Chinese for Lawyers, or Vietnamese for Medical Personnel is always attractive for students who see the benefit of enhancing their knowledge of a language as they gain exposure to the content they will need in their future careers or intellectual development. If the home-background-speaker population is not large enough and a school can only implement isolated courses for these students, these courses would generally have to be broad enough to attract all home-background speakers regardless of the career interests. In this case, the courses would most likely be language courses with an emphasis on culture, including elements of CBI. No matter what discipline they are in, the knowledge of culture and literature of the language is necessary to get to the higher levels of proficiency. This argument is clearly stated in Chapter 5 of this volume regarding the role of ancient Chinese poetry in achieving Distinguished-level proficiency.

It is also conceivable that General Education courses could offer sections in several languages. For example, a course in Latin American or Russian history could have a discussion section in Spanish/Russian. Likewise, courses in other majors, such as history, sociology, journalism, psychology, and science can require readings, as well as offer discussion sections, in heritage languages. Such courses are becoming more and more popular on campuses across the USA for foreign language students and are known as (Foreign) Languages Across the Curriculum (LAC). There is every reason why the LAC movement should be expanded to include heritage speakers – and there should be no great difficulty in accommodating them in existing LAC programs. For example, in the spring of 2001 a course in Soviet history at UCLA had a discussion section in Russian. The "Russian" section read Soviet archival documents in the original, exploring the use of language and how it reflects culture in the Soviet Union in the 1930s under Stalin. This section was open to non-native speakers, but most students, as anticipated, were heritage speakers.

Conclusion

To help heritage speakers reach the Superior/Distinguished level, a program has to capitalize on students' strengths, most often displayed in an Interpersonal mode of communication, and address less developed areas, which are most frequently aspects of communication in the Interpretative and Presentational modes, in all modalities. Linguistic deficiencies cannot serve as the only area of improvement; so, a program cannot be based on error eradication (Valdés [1989]). Any program for heritage speakers should be broad-based and rich in cultural content that will provoke and hold students' interests and motivate them to continue on a path to lifelong learning. It should also contain elements of learner-centeredness and individuation as would any program at higher levels.

Many questions remain unanswered. What are the best approaches to teaching reading and writing to heritage students? Is there a transfer between writing in the dominant language and writing in the first language? What are the best testing instruments to determine the progress of heritage learners? Even though it is clearly possible to bring heritage speakers to the level of the Superior or even Distinguished proficiency, it may take some time and effort to determine the most efficient pathways in doing so. One interesting research and pedagogical question that is outside the scope of this chapter but nevertheless relevant for heritage-program curricular design is how fast and under what conditions heritage speakers whose oral/aural ability is Advanced but whose literacy is lower can achieve Superior- and Distinguished-level proficiency.

This chapter has presented programs in two languages that have been successful in helping heritage students reach higher levels of proficiency. Some of these results have been possible in spite of lack of answers to the above questions. In some cases, intuitive responses were acted upon in course development. In other cases, some decisions were reached through trial and error or research. While the programs described herein have been successful and can be emulated, it is the authors' hope that the questions that remain will be answered with time and will lead to even more effective, refined programs for heritage learners.

Table 10.3

Grades completed in Russia	1-4	5-8	9-11
Number of respondents	9	14	18
Reasons	**Responses**		
Family	6	8	2
To preserve Russian culture	6	14	11
To read Russian literature	7	15	10
Career	1	3	3
Other	1*	1**	5***
*self-education; in order not to lose language skills **I want to live and work in Moscow ***interesting lectures; personal; GE (General Education) requirement; to improve my GPA (Grade Point Average)			

Presentations and papers on language issues solidified understanding of course topics. (2nd-year Social Sciences, Spanish minor)

The textbook was quite good. A little challenging because it was all in technical Spanish but that is a good thing. Authentic materials were especially helpful for understanding the topics. (3rd-year Spanish major)

Assignments allowed for choice and creativity. Also teamwork and peer editing of drafts of papers were useful and educational and kept us from last minute work. Muchas gracias. (3rd-year Humanities, Spanish minor)

Even though there was a diverse range of ability in Spanish between Spanish students and heritage speakers, she made everyone feel comfortable about their abilities and truly treated everyone fair. This definitely helped the heritage speakers and the second language learners to learn from each other. (4th-year Engineering, Spanish minor)

11 Teaching Russian language teachers in eight summer Institutes in Russian language and culture

Zita Dabars and Olga Kagan

Leaver and Shekhtman (this volume) state that in the USA "few students achieve Superior and Distinguished levels of proficiency in any foreign language." Thompson (2000) finds in her sample of fourteen students that after five years of study 22% achieved Superior proficiency in speaking, 35.7% in reading, 14.3% in listening, and none in writing (pp. 264–271).[1] Clearly, time on task alone is insufficient for reaching the Superior/Distinguished (SD) level. What *is* needed, as noted by many authors in this volume, is direct instruction, cultural experience through in-country study or work or its equivalent, and attention to the development of specific aspects of the components of communicative competence.

Since teachers are the product of this educational system, it is safe to assume (and our personal experience bears it out) that teachers of foreign languages do not themselves always possess SD-level proficiency. That, of course, raises the question: what proficiency is sufficient to teach a foreign language? The answer varies, depending on the level taught and the approach used. Some teachers would argue that they have been able to meet the needs of their students, even though they themselves have never exceeded the Advanced level of proficiency. Such teachers are probably teaching in a traditional program, focused on developing students' knowledge of the Russian linguistic system. For example, in the traditional organization of American university foreign language departments (especially languages other than Spanish and French), faculty have often been linguists with mostly theoretical knowledge of the language, rather than with well-developed oral and aural skills. These latter skills, if taught at all, were developed in conversation courses, conducted by a native speaker of the language – either a professional instructor or someone who just happened to be available locally. While such an approach was typical in the 1950s and 1960s, it has gradually become less common, especially with the advent of the

---

[1] This excludes students taught in US government programs, where, for example at the Foreign Service Institute, 80–90% reach the Superior level in a ten-month intensive course (Leaver [1997]).

Proficiency Movement in the 1980s and the communicative approach in the 1990s.

Beginning with the 1980s, proficiency in the language became a *de facto* requirement for a language instructor because he or she now taught all aspects of the language: grammatical structure, conversation, reading, listening, and writing, as well as culture. An instructor was expected to be at ease with the current idiom, well versed in both small "c" and big "C" cultures, and competent to teach the grammatical system. Some changes specific to Russian language teaching were a matter of the Russian foreign language education field catching up with practices in commonly taught languages. Moreover, with the advent of *glasnost* and *perestroika*, followed by the demise of communism, student goals for Russian language study changed. Previously, students were unlikely ever to visit the USSR. Now students could look forward to living, studying, and working in Russia. Their professional and language-learning needs escalated accordingly, and teachers at the Intermediate and Advanced levels of proficiency, who earlier might have felt complacent, no longer had the skills to meet their students' needs. The main lacunae appeared to be in their ability to converse in Russian and their knowledge of culture. This assessed need led to the organization of intensive programs (or institutes) for training teachers of Russian in Russian language and culture, as well as in contemporary approaches to teaching.

During the course of the Institutes, it became apparent that teachers' deficiencies in these three areas undermined their effective performance in another way: they eroded their confidence. Teachers at lower levels of proficiency were less open to communicative approaches and defended using the grammar–translation method partly because they were familiar with it from their student days and partly because it permitted talking *about* the language rather than *in* the language, thereby avoiding that which they could not do successfully. Some of them were also in favor of the Audio-Lingual Method (ALM) with its dependence on drill, again because ALM reduces the need for free expression, a level of proficiency that they had not developed. Forcing the issue of teaching communicatively, using Russian as the medium of instruction had created a Catch-22: teachers needed a higher level of language proficiency to feel comfortable using Russian in the classroom, but their anxiety impeded their ability to improve their proficiency.

That raises a new question: what level of proficiency is sufficient to obviate teachers' anxiety and uncertainty? While much has been written about students' anxiety and uncertainty while studying a foreign language (Bailey [1983]; Horwitz [1988]; Horwitz and Young [1991]; Scovel [1991]), much less is known about the role anxiety and uncertainty play in a teacher's performance. So, the directors and faculty at the various Institutes had no choice but to use their own observations and intuitions in lowering participants' affective filters. As a minimum, they speculated that a teacher should have enough confidence in his or her language ability to (1) answer students' grammatical questions, (2) handle many questions about vocabulary usage, (3) convey basic aspects of the culture, and (4) admit lack of knowledge of answers to specific questions, along with showing willingness to research the answers. What follows explains how Institutes for teachers of Russian were organized and how they achieved the goals of proficiency improvement, with the accompanying lowering of affective filters, increased linguistic competence, and development of cultural knowledge.

The setting and the history

In response to the needs described above, eight nationwide summer Institutes in Russian Language and Culture were conducted by The Center of Russian Language and Culture (CORLAC) at Friends School of Baltimore, in collaboration with the American Council of Teachers of Russian (ACTR), from 1987 to 1989 and from 1992 to 1996. The Institutes were funded by the National Endowment for the Humanities (NEH) and were held at Bryn Mawr College. Faculty, staff, and participants were housed together for the duration of the Institute in one of Bryn Mawr's dormitories. The rooms were private; the common areas were shared, providing for daily living language use.

Fifty-eight faculty members, lecturers, and staff were involved in the eight Institutes, and participants came from schools and universities throughout the USA. Thirty-six states and the District of Columbia were represented.

The program

The goals

The published goals of the Institutes were to (1) enhance the language skills and cultural knowledge of Russian teachers, (2) inform participants of the latest methodological insights, and (3) assist teachers in adapting and/or developing supplementary teaching materials. A fourth goal – developing networks – emerged from the teachers during the Institutes as a natural result of the interactions of educators from many states and language programs, and a fifth goal was established as a result of faculty observations: a need to develop the field of Russian teaching.

Enhancing language skills and cultural knowledge

Non-native teachers, working in a communicative environment, need to have the greatest level of proficiency possible. Using information from the latest research as to the most efficient and effective ways of improving foreign language proficiency, the Institutes chose to use a content-based, total immersion approach, as described below.

Improving linguistic skills. Most Institute participants set the improvement of their linguistic skills above other goals. This goal was realized through: (1) improved accuracy, (2) increased fluency, and (3) development of cultural knowledge.

Improving accuracy. Improvement in breadth and precision of grammar and vocabulary was achieved through readings and interactions. In addition, a formal grammar lecture was presented twice a week.

Increasing fluency. Russian was the language of instruction in all seminars and the working language of the Institute. This immersion experience worked to develop the fluency component of participants' linguistic competence. In setting this goal, faculty adopted several practices to reduce the anticipated affective filtering; these are identified in the description of the various activities.

Developing cultural knowledge. An emphasis on culturally oriented materials was a natural, given the National Endowment for the Humanities as funding source for the Institutes. Moreover, high-level proficiency cannot be achieved without strong sociocultural competency.

Learning about the latest methodology
Until very recently, Russian has not been taught in a communicative mode. Many, if not most, teachers who attended the summer Institutes, had been trained in a very different way of teaching. Further, most of these teachers had few opportunities to become retrained in more contemporary teaching methods. The Institute provided a way to do this through a seminar on teaching methodology.

Assistance with adapting/developing supplemental materials
The purpose of the third goal was twofold. First, most of the teachers attending the Institutes were not skilled in developing their own supplemental materials. Learning the concepts of materials adaptation and development, then, would be immediately useful to them in their work. Second, commercial materials for Russian are much less extensive than those available for the more commonly taught languages. Therefore, through a materials development seminar, participants prepared valuable classroom materials, and the shared materials from each seminar helped to compensate for the lack of commercial materials.

Networking

Although it was never published as a formal goal, both faculty and participants understood that an important outcome of the Institute was the establishment of a network of professional contacts with colleagues, in both high schools and colleges, for the exchange of ideas on teaching and research in the fields of Russian culture and language. Since the Russian profession is small, many teachers work alone in their schools and even school districts. Meeting colleagues who were in the same situation, from other parts of the country, provided Institute participants with a network of professional contacts that many of them have maintained long after their participation in the Institute.

Development of the Russian field

Likewise, while not an official goal of the Institutes, the faculty and directors were well aware of the need to focus on field development for the Russian language-teaching profession. New programs needed to be developed and support needed to be extended to existing programs. This concern was of paramount importance to them as professionals and was among the major considerations in establishing the Institute and seeking funding.

The participants

A total of 171 Russian language teachers from elementary, middle, and secondary schools and colleges, and graduate students who intended to enter the teaching field participated in the eight four-week Institutes.

Applicants were selected based on a variety of criteria. Priority was given to full-time and part-time teachers of Russian at the pre-college level and secondarily to teachers of Russian from small colleges.

The application process included a telephone interview lasting 10–15 minutes of oral (and to a degree, aural) proficiency, conducted by ACTFL-certified testers. Group placement was determined by the proficiency level of the Russian language as reflected in the written application and this telephonic interview. About one third of the participants were placed into the Superior-level group.[2] These are the participants whose program is described in this chapter.

Institute overview

Each Institute provided four weeks of instruction, transportation to and from the participant's hometown, air-conditioned individual rooms, a meal plan in the Bryn Mawr Russian language residential house, and a stipend of $1,000. In

---

[2] Upon occasion, for specific purposes, a stronger student was placed into one of the lower-proficiency groups.

addition, each participant was supplied with a variety of materials for use at the Institute, as well as in their school programs upon return: scholarly books on Russian literature and culture, pedagogically oriented books, extensive photocopied materials, slides of Russian art, cassettes of classical Russian music, and cassettes of Russian bards, folk, and children's music. In return, each participant was responsible for obtaining his or her principal's or department chair's commitment to contribute $100 toward the cost of the Institute, becoming familiar with the Institute's course through reading selected items in advance, and participating full-time for all four weeks of the Institute.

The schedule

During the eight years of the Institute there were slight variations in the daily schedule, assignments, number of participants, and other details. In this chapter, we focus largely on the type of Institute that was arrived at eventually and existed the longest.

Each day at the Institute consisted of three seminars. Each addressed one of the three formal goals of the Institute: skills enhancement, methodology, and materials adaptation/development.

Skills enhancement

The first seminar each morning was Skills Enhancement through Authentic Readings on Russian Culture and Contemporary Society (henceforth referred to as Skills Enhancement). The SD group typically included 8–9 participants, who attended this seminar for ninety minutes daily and were taught by a native speaker of Russian.

The Skills Enhancement seminar was highly valued by the participants. In their evaluations, many suggested that this seminar be lengthened. Whether or not the participants could formulate it that way, a compelling feeling of professional worth may have made them value language classes over everything else. After all, language teachers are supposed to be proficient in the language, and few were as proficient as they thought they could be.

The goal of the Skills Enhancement seminar was to develop sociocultural, linguistic, discourse, and sociolinguistic competence in reading, speaking, listening, and writing, within a framework of humanistic literature / culturally oriented readings. Particular areas of focus were vocabulary enrichment, lexical precision and stylistics, complexification of expression, speaking fluency at a more sophisticated level, reading fluency, genre study, text organization, and idioms.

The readings for the Skills Enhancement seminar varied and were determined by their cultural value. The four themes (shown in Table 11.1) were chosen because they advanced the goals of enhancing the participants' knowledge of past and current Russian history, social mores, and cultural expectations, including family issues, the role of women, politics realized in the family (e.g., a novella and a poem about a mother whose son is caught in the indiscriminate KGB net), contemporary issues, and folk literature. Throughout the Institutes, participants repeatedly expressed a strong desire for reading authentic, contemporary sources. Indeed, following a tradition that was started in the nineteenth century with Russia's "thick journals," much of the most stimulating, culturally pertinent writing in Russia at the turn of the twenty-first century appears in the Russian press. In addition to the readings of the press, the children's literature week built sociocultural knowledge that teachers were not likely to get elsewhere. Such knowledge was considered important because these works are part of every educated Russian's upbringing and allusions to their characters and situations are encountered in adult literature and conversation.[3]

The Skills Enhancement seminar had an additional, metalinguistic goal: to provide a master class. Each genre by its nature required a different approach to teaching. The topical foci of the Skills Enhancement seminar reflected four of the main kinds of discourse associated with Superior-level proficiency, ranging from the language of childhood to high-level nonprofessional prose – a range of language that educated native speakers use freely. (Professional prose was, of course, a staple of the methodology seminar.) Institute participants observed the different ways in which the Institute faculty presented and discussed a large variety of materials. Teachers demonstrated a variety of techniques when dealing with a text and conducting a language class, and Institute participants noted and frequently analyzed the ways their instructors approached teaching. They were themselves the subjects and the ethnographers (Kramsch [1993]).

Table 11.1 provides a week-by-week comparison and overview of the contents and activities of the seminar. Each resource and each activity was chosen to develop specific skills, as described in the paragraphs below.

Vocabulary enrichment

Unlike beginning students who must acquire basic vocabulary, SD participants focused on expanding and enriching an extensive lexicon: using productive morphemes to form new words and expressions and determining the meaning of new words not by using context as much as by using an understanding of the Russian linguistic system, including morphemes, syntagms, and the correct implications of words with multiple meanings. In working with fairy

---

[3] Historically, teachers have been woefully ignorant of this aspect of Russian culture and unable to pass such knowledge on to their students. This lack of knowledge was due not only to the inaccessibility of Russian culture in the past but also to the traditional exclusion of such content from most university Russian-language programs.

Table 11.1

Week #	1	2	3	4
Topic(s)	Literature of life in Russia	History: Soviet Union under Stalin	Contemporary issues	Children's literature
Genre(s)	Everyday language	Historical narration; literary narration	Media	Folk tale; children's literature
Discourse	Social language and discussions	Narration; argumentation; persuasion	Argumentation; documentation; persuasion; opinion-writing	Fairy tale; children's discourse
Sources(s) / Sample readings	*Just Another Week* (Baranskaja); *I Am, You Are, He Is* (Tokareva)	Novella: *Sofia Petrovna* (Chukovskaia); Poem: "Requiem" (Akhmatova)	Magazines and newspapers; *The Glasnost Press-Ogonyok 1990* (Lekic); *Literary Newspaper*	Fairy tales; children's stories and poems
Activities	Group discussions; weekly composition	Textual explication; complexification of expression; weekly composition	Small-group work; individual presentations on linguistic features; complexification of expression; weekly composition; idioms, acronyms, language change	Identification of characters and situations commonly alluded to in other genres; weekly composition (create and write fairy tale, using appropriate devices)

tales, for example, special attention was paid to the twenty or so beginning and ending phrases that are typical of this genre, as well as frequent expressions that pepper Russian fairy tales, because they are so common in both literary and conversational use. The unabridged texts with their inclusion of obsolete words, idiomatic expressions, and colloquial speech allowed the instructor to work with a very advanced level of vocabulary mastery.

Participants started using vocabulary at an interpersonal level, relating their own life experiences, and moved into more abstract social themes, providing for a "graded" ascent into more academic discourse. It was interesting to note that while some of the participants had a lexicon suitable for abstract discussions, they lacked the vocabulary of "home and hearth." This presented an interesting contrast to the language of heritage speakers who were at approximately the same general level of proficiency.

Lexical precision and stylistics

Participants were not allowed to use strategic competence in lieu of linguistic competence, a tendency that Leaver and Shekhtman (this volume) consider an attribute of Superior-level speakers that creates a barrier to reaching the Distinguished level. For example, participants were asked to find in the text and explain the use of Russian equivalents for the verb "to speak." Such an assignment forces the learner to account for features of the language that could otherwise be neglected because they are easily understood. Russian verbs and expressions for "to speak" serve as an entrée to a variety of speech ranges and clearly indicate the difference between academic and less formal speech. Other assignments included providing synonyms and antonyms, explaining idiomatic expressions, and illustrating them as well as discussing their stylistic usage. The vocabulary development assignments thus had a heavy component of stylistics. Another register-development activity was a host of assignments requiring complex syntactic structures. For example, one exercise asked learners to combine a series of simple sentences together by using a variety of connecting devices, including participles and verbal adverbs that are typical of the Russian academic style.

Complexification of expression

Similarly, instructors used a large number of exercises that explored synonyms and antonyms, paid close attention to the usage of verbs in context, and asked for paraphrase and narration of specific scenes and events. This complexification of expression contributed to the development of many aspects of SD-level speech, e.g., supporting an opinion, developing an argument, making a hypothesis. Using the text as a departure point, instructors urged learners to go beyond the text, incorporating their own background knowledge and making cross-cultural comparison, arguing their views, and supporting a position against their beliefs. Participants were taught to use the stylistic devices appropriate for academic discussion.

Speaking fluency

The Superior-level group started most classes with individuals reciting tongue twisters and ditties, where rhyme, alliteration, and rhythm aided the participants to achieve lightning speed by the end of the Institute. This technique is one of the mechanisms for "hidden memorization" described by Leaver and Shekhtman (this volume).

Reading fluency

Extensive reading – or reading fluency – is a skill required at the SD level. SD students can be expected to exhibit endurance in reading for long periods of time and relative ease and speed in reading large amounts of materials. Participants read at least 20–30 pages of literary, newspaper, and professional texts in the Russian language each evening. Reading took place at home, and discussions of the texts were conducted in the classroom.

Genre studies

Genres ranged from short stories to poems, memoirs, folk and fairy tales, literary reviews, newspaper articles, editorials, letters to the editor, and expository articles in journals. Faculty introduced participants to as wide a range as possible during the short period of the Institute.

The language of the Russian press was challenging even for Superior-level participants. Discussion of press articles took second place to working on accurate reading of the text: discernment of humor, sarcasm, and allusions to historic events, literary texts, and facts of common knowledge that saturate Russian journalistic prose. Unlike their American colleagues, Russian journalists infuse news with opinion and rarely explain who or what they refer to. To be able to read at the Distinguished level one needs to be able to understand most, if not all, of these allusions, a task that is challenging even for native speakers living outside of Russia's changing political and cultural scene.

Close and accurate reading continued with exposure to Russia's folklore and other kinds of children's literature.[4] This activity was deemed important because literature that most Russians know from childhood plays a much more

---

[4] There was a practical reason for including such content in the Institute program. At the time, the American Council of Teachers of Russian had organized teacher and student exchanges. For the first time, American high-school students of Russian were able to spend time in Russian homes and schools, and Russian instructors came for a limited time to teach at American schools. The readings in children's literature that served to fill a gap in the teachers' education were especially important in view of these changes: students who were beginning to come face to face with Russians needed to understand the culture of their peers.

significant role in Russian nonfictional prose than it does in American writing of the same genre.

Text organization in writing

Class participants worked on a weekly composition in Russian. The writing topics provided participants with an opportunity to practice Russian text structure for various genres, review newly acquired vocabulary through repetition, develop lexical precision, use both simple and more elaborate grammatical forms appropriately, choose appropriate register and style, and make cultural references.

Idioms/acronyms

In reading the Russian press, attention was paid to idiomatic expressions and acronyms that had entered, or become more important in, the Russian language in the preceding ten years. That was the time of the beginning of a rapid change in Russian life that was reflected in the language of newspapers.

Methodology

The Methodology seminar met for ninety minutes daily. It was taught by specialists in teaching methodology who were native speakers of Russian, or in the last two years by a non-native speaker experienced in teaching methodology in Russian. Here, emphasis was placed on familiarizing participants with the latest ideas in foreign language education, in particular with techniques for teaching communicative skills, the use of authentic materials, the role and use of prelistening and pre-reading activities, and the content of the ILR/ACTFL Proficiency Guidelines (see Chapter 1). Lessons focused on current theory and practice in foreign language teaching and testing and individualized ideas for improving participants' own programs and classrooms. Of course, the specific content of the Methodology seminar changed over the years, as the field of foreign language teaching evolved.

Course content

During the first Institutes at the end of the 1980s, participants were introduced to the ideas of the Proficiency Movement that were only being developed at the time and were entirely new for the Russian profession. Participants in the Institute had an opportunity to familiarize themselves with current proficiency testing instruments in Russian. At that time, the ideas of proficiency and prochievement testing and the difference between such testing and a commonly used achievement testing were still new for the profession. Because of that, much time was dedicated to various kinds of testing, including oral interviews.

By the last two Institutes, the Methodology seminar had evolved to include four topics: learner differences, history of methodology, communicative language teaching, and testing. These topics gave participants the theoretical background and practical understanding needed for developing comfort in teaching via learner-centered, communicative approaches and in preparing appropriate materials for use with communicative approaches. Participants in the Institute also had an opportunity to familiarize themselves with current proficiency testing instruments in Russian. Associated with these topics, participants made individual presentations on such topics as teaching methods, techniques for teaching various skills, aspects of testing, and theories of methodology; presentations were followed by a general discussion.

Manner of instruction

The Methodology seminar was conducted in Russian. In the last two years, partly in response to participants' requests, the following format emerged: a short, interactive lecture, followed by small-group and pair work, in which the instructor interacted with each group, providing suggestions and support for completion of group tasks, after which each small group shared information about how they completed their task with the whole group. (Most often, tasks differed among the groups, adjusted for participants' learning styles, interests, and proficiency level.)

The interactive lectures in the methodological component of the syllabus did more than just acquaint teachers with contemporary teaching methods. They required teachers to use Russian for professional needs and learn specific new terminology typically expected at the SD level: participants made formal presentations, using professional vocabulary. These expectations, especially formal presentations, are typical of the activities used by a number of authors in this volume to develop SD-level proficiency (see, for example, Angelelli and Degueldre, Shekhtman *et al.*, and Angelelli and Kagan). The repetition of this vocabulary through reading it in the homework assignments, hearing it in lectures, and using it in oral and written presentations fostered participants' ultimate ease in using it. In short, the lectures in methodology served as both a content course and a language experience.

Materials

The materials for the Methodology seminars in the earlier Institutes were in English because no appropriate materials existed in Russian. Over time, it became clear that participants would benefit from materials discussing new developments in language teaching that were written in Russian. Attempts to use scholarly articles or books published in Russia were not successful because of the differences between teaching Russian as a Second Language (a thrust of publications by Russian scholars) and Russian as a Foreign Language, as well as the new approaches presented at the Institutes (proficiency philosophy and communicative approach). As a result, a set of materials exploring contemporary American foreign language teaching methodology was written in Russian by two of the instructors at the Institute.[5]

Materials Adaptation/Development

In the Materials Adaptation/Development seminar, which met for ninety minutes three times a week, the participants prepared materials that would be helpful at their home institutions. In this seminar, theoretical knowledge was combined with hands-on experience, as teachers adapted and/or developed supplementary teaching materials to enhance the basic textbooks they were using and to provide them with missing instructional tools.

Materials evaluation

In the first few days, participants were presented with guidelines for textbook and supplemental materials evaluation and acquainted with the range of Russian language-teaching materials available. They were then asked to evaluate various materials,[6] using the handout in Figure 11.1.

This comprised the task for the first week and enabled participants to prepare materials of their own. During this week, one of the seminar instructors ascertained participants' needs and desires for supplementary materials. On the basis of these specific needs, participants were paired with Institute faculty for mentoring and individual assistance with adapting and developing supplementary teaching materials.

Materials adaptation/development

As a subsequent task, participants were required to submit a project to be shared with other participants. This project was the megatask for the last three weeks of the Institute. Some participants arrived with an idea of what they would like to do. Others waited until arrival to decide. Participants who used the same textbooks in their teaching frequently joined forces to work on common projects. The projects went through a number of revisions. Before the final

---

[5] The materials were later developed and became a book that was published in Russia, *Uchimsya uchit'* ("We're Learning to Teach") (Akishina and Kagan [1997]).

[6] For the most part, participants evaluated versions of Russian *Face to Face* field-testing materials – textbooks, exercise books, tests that accompany these textbooks, and videos, and language learning cards that could be used with these materials – that were being produced by the Center of Russian Language and Culture and eventually were published by the National Textbook Company (now McGraw Hill), Kendall/Hunt, and Basil Products. Participants were asked to evaluate these materials in particular because they were in the process of development or refinement. The lower levels are the primary text materials available for teaching at the high-school level, while the more advanced-level materials are used in both high schools and colleges and lend themselves to questions of articulation.

SUGGESTED CRITERIA FOR EVALUATING TEACHING MATERIALS

- Is the book grammar driven? (Is the sequence appropriate?)

- How is the grammar presented? Throughout the lesson, at the end of chapters? Are the explanations adequate?

- Is the book communicative? Does it allow the students to speak about themselves? about people living in Russia?

- How is culture treated? Is there culture with a capital C (writers, composers, painters, history, architecture, religion, etc.) and with a small c (holidays, clothing, food, daily customs, etc.)? Is it given in Russian or in English?

- How is vocabulary treated? Is it given throughout the lesson, how is it treated at the end? Are the words given in alphabetical order? In the order that they appear in the lesson? By thematic categories? By grammatical terms? Which do you prefer? Which do students like the best?

- How is reading used in the textbook? Is it on an appropriate level? Is there enough of it? Too much? Is there reading for interest, pleasure, comprehension?

- Are photographs and illustrations appropriate? Are there enough of them? Too many? If you had an artist available, what kind of illustrations would you ask him/her to draw for the various lessons?

- When you look at the pages in the textbook, do you feel comfortable with the proportion of text vs. white space?

- Are there puzzles, fun things in the textbook? What fun things would you add?

- Might the textbook lend itself to working in pairs? in a group?

- Are there listening comprehension materials?

- What kind of learner (learning style) would do well with this book? What kind of learner would struggle? How could you help the latter?

Figure 11.1

version was photocopied and distributed to all participants and faculty, every project was read for accuracy by three Institute teachers.

At the first three NEH/CORLAC Institutes (1987–1989), participants created Culture Capsules – materials on topics such as Theatre, Sports, and The Russian Family. These Culture Capsules were written, compiled, put into the computer, illustrated by the participants, and made available at subsequent Institutes. At later Institutes, participants prepared materials that included cultural information, tests, vocabulary aids, communicative activities, and grammar exercises, to list just a few. At the 1996 Institute, several participants worked together to create cultural materials for the American Russian Spoken Olympiada.

After the first week, participants generally did not meet as a group, unless they were working on a small-group project. Rather, time was reserved for individual work on projects. Formally, the Institute co-director and the technology director co-taught the Materials Adaptation/Development seminar. In actuality, all faculty assisted with ideas and linguistic accuracy. Two professional artists illustrated participants' materials. Accompanying media was produced and distributed for free.

During the last three days of the Institute, oral presentations were made by the participants in which they explained the goals and methodology of their projects. With minor exceptions, these presentations were done in Russian – giving participants yet another opportunity to use their Russian language skills for the presentation of professional reports. As pointed out in many chapters of this volume, the ability to perform such tasks is an essential feature of foreign language proficiency at the Distinguished level.

Grammar lectures

Grammar lectures were conducted twice a week for ninety minutes. In earlier years, these were delivered by a native speaker of Russian. In later years, they were taught by a highly proficient non-native speaker.

The topics chosen were in response to concerns which, for many of the Institutes, were voiced the first time the group met. Some of the topics are familiar ones for anyone who has taught students – or teachers – of Russian: verbal aspect, the one-stem verb, Russian noun stress, verbs of motion, the use of aspect with imperatives – in short, those grammar features that have historically frustrated, annoyed, and confused speakers of English who are learning or teaching Russian.

For the 1996 Institute, a special attempt was made to coordinate the grammar presentations with the grammar that was focused on in the Skills Enhancement seminar. In addition, contextualized grammar study was used in conjunction with the video, *Peers* (Lekic [1994]). Participants viewed the video and analyzed the use of aspect in its unscripted conversations.

From time to time, participants in this seminar made short grammar presentations to the group. The presentations were followed by questions and commentary by the instructor. This exercise gave yet another opportunity for the participants to perform a professional task in Russian in front of a supportive audience.

Evening activities

Augmenting the themes of the Institute, the evening activities provided participants with the cultural knowledge they would need to teach not language alone but language and culture. In several cases, both materials and suggestions for teaching cultural topics were given to the participants.

On average, three evenings of each week were scheduled for required NEH/ CORLAC Institute activities. Films (all in Russian), as well as lectures (some delivered in Russian, others in English) on art, music, historical developments, economy, and architecture, broadened the participants' knowledge of Russian culture and contemporary Russian reality and served to develop participants' sociocultural and sociolinguistic competence – essential components of communicative competence for SD-level speakers.

The films reflected the themes of the reading assignments in the Skills Enhancement seminar. For example, when the participants were reading Akhmatova's "Requiem" and Chukovskaia's *Sofia Petrovna* about the Stalin years, the film version of *Sofia Petrovna* was shown, as was the documentary, *The House with Knights*. Both conveyed, each in its own manner, the hopelessness and terror experienced by many Russian citizens during the Stalin era. During the week in which the participants read children's literature, *Cinderella* and *Three from Prostokvashino* were presented. For all of the films, the teachers of the Skills Enhancement and Methodology seminars prepared handouts that focused on expressions and facts with which the participants might experience difficulty. After the films, optional discussions were held over soft drinks, wine, and cheese, providing participants with the opportunity to develop informal, social linguistic skills, another feature of SD proficiency. In the Skills Enhancement seminars the following day, the participants could express their reactions to the films and raise any concerns regarding comprehension.

Through the Cultural Evenings, the participants became acquainted with films that an educated Russian would have seen. In addition, the Institute staff, where appropriate, pointed out expressions from films that have become classics and of which anyone aiming for the Distinguished level should be aware. For example, after viewing *Cinderella*, all the participants knew that the expression "I am not yet a magician, I'm only an apprentice" entered the Russian language because of this film.

Distinguished scholars delivered lectures in their areas of expertise. For example, an English-language music lecture by a well-known specialist (held at several of the Institutes) taught participants how to listen effectively to Russian music and how to teach music to their students. (The participants also received audiotapes of the music played as examples at the lecture.) Similarly, two Russian-language lectures on Russian art served not only to instruct the participants, but also to enable them to share their knowledge with students. (Each of the participants received every one of the fifty-eight slides shown in these lectures, each individually labeled with painter, title, and date, as well as handouts with art terminology in Russian.) Lectures were almost always followed by an informal discussion with the lecturer. (Afterward, many a participant burned the midnight oil getting ready for the next day's classes!)

Technology

A secondary goal of the Institute – and a necessity – was to provide instruction in and access to various computer hardware (Macintosh, IBM) and software programs with both English and Russian word-processing and graphic capabilities. In addition, participants became familiarized with electronic mail and computer-assisted instructional programs.

Computer support, assistance, and training was made available to all participants who wanted or needed it. The goal, in many cases, was to expose participants to word processing in English and Russian, although some participants were already quite proficient in basic computer skills and were able to develop more advanced skills while at the Institute.

A suite of three rooms in the Denbigh dormitory and the room adjoining the instructor's quarters were the primary areas in which the participants used computers. The Computer Center was also available, and during the last two Institutes, when it had extended hours, was heavily used.

In the application to the Institute, applicants were asked what hardware and software they used. For almost all of the Institutes, there was not a single participant who had not by the end of the Institute prepared a project using the computer – this included a number of people who had never even used a typewriter prior to the Institute. This was especially significant during the early years when computers were not as prevalent as they are today.

Special events

During two of the Institutes, Bryn Mawr College was the site for conferences of the Presidium of the International Association of Teachers of Russian Language and Literature. Institute participants were challenged to understand lectures on a variety of topics pertinent to their profession – all delivered in Russian. At a banquet that included the international guests, as well as students and staff from Bryn Mawr College's Russian Language Institute and participants and staff from the NEH/CORLAC Institute, a happy cacophony of Russian was heard. As the banquet ended, the Project Director invited a number of the international guests to visit the Institute dormitory. There guests, participants, and staff mingled informally. (One of the tenets of the Institute was for no distinction to be made between Institute staff and participants. The latter were the staff's colleagues – we were all teachers. More than one Outside Evaluator commented that such an attitude fostered a caring, supportive atmosphere and did much to alleviate any anxiety that teachers may have encountered in using Russian.)

Evaluation

Assessment of the Institute's effectiveness was based on informal observations of intermediate results and formal evaluative instruments and activities used in qualitative analysis, including instructor observations, formal participant feedback to the Institute, formal participant feedback to NEH, and external evaluation. (Given the short duration of the Institutes, quantitative measurements of proficiency gain were not feasible.)

Instructor observations

Instructors observed that participants' command of the Russian language noticeably improved in areas of both fluency and accuracy. Their range of vocabulary and precision in word choice grew, as they became exposed on a daily basis to a wide variety of lexical domains: professional terminology, literary and media language, words of the hearth and home, and expressions needed for social interactions.

Computer literacy also noticeably increased. Unlike language proficiency, computer literacy was measurable by objective criteria. The fact that participants who had not used a computer before enrollment at the Institute word-processed their projects for the Materials Adaptation/Development seminar served as evidence of their improved skills.

Participants also became aware of the latest methodological insights in teaching. Their presentations in the Methodology seminar, along with the Materials Adaptation/Development projects, indicated an increased awareness of teaching for communicative competence.

The faculty considered the Institute a success, based on the criteria established as goals for the Institute and by the rapport established with the participants. Continuing use of the informal "networks" that developed also served as evidence of success.

Formal participant feedback to the Institute

Participants had three separate, scheduled opportunities to assess the value of the Institute's work to their individual professional needs and to evaluate the living arrangements. The first one took place two weeks into the Institutes, when the Project Director met with the participants with no staff present. Any concerns were shared with the appropriate parties and, where deemed possible, adjustments were made in the remaining two weeks of the current Institute.

On the last day of the Institutes, the participants filled out an anonymous five-page questionnaire. The questionnaire asked for participant feedback on the seminars, the lectures, films, other activities, and the organization of the Institute on a scale of 1 to 5. In addition, thirteen other questions were asked about suggested changes for the curriculum and scheduling for future years, about the availability of computers, and whether the Institute would make a difference in the way the participants taught.

Participants stated, without exception, that the Institute had met their expectations. Among the positive aspects, teachers identified an increased confidence in using Russian, acquisition of or improvement in computer skills, stimulating evening activities, experience in the preparation of curricular materials, and contacts they had made, as well as rating the Institutional organization as effective.

Specific areas in which participant feedback influenced subsequent Institutes included sending more materials to participants in advance of the Institute, increasing the amount of history studied, and a greater emphasis on concrete application of theoretical explanations in the Methodology seminar and Grammar lectures. The need for more time, especially for preparing projects, was a recurring theme but not one that was easily remedied in the short duration of the Institute.

Most participants indicated that they would significantly change their teaching methods. All were appreciative of copies of the projects and other teaching materials (such as slides, lyrics and audios of songs) that they were given free of charge to take home. Most teachers expressed gratitude for the opportunity to attend the Institute.

Formal participant feedback to NEH

Following the Institute, the National Endowment for the Humanities (NEH) solicited participant feedback. After deleting the name and institution of the responding participant, NEH forwarded the evaluations to the Project Director, who distributed them to the staff. The questionnaire contained two sections:

1) Summarize your overall assessment of this Institute experience, taking into consideration the director, contributing faculty, Institute colleagues, topics, organization, discussions, extra activities, and effect on your teaching and scholarship. Do you have any suggestions for improvements?
2) Evaluate the host institution, particularly with respect to hospitality, housing arrangements, and the suitability of library facilities.

In general, the feedback was highly positive. The results from the NEH questionnaire paralleled those obtained from the Institute's questionnaire, described above.

External evaluation

At each of the eight Institutes, an Outside Evaluator, renowned for scholarship on Russia, spent two days at the Institutes, during which time he or she observed the classes, met separately with the participants and with the staff, and wrote an evaluation of the Institutes. Representative comments made over the years by various evaluators are shown in Figure 11.2.

Assorted Comments (1987-1996) • "…stimulating lectures and reading"; • "…command of…Russian…improved, and they became aware of the latest methodological insights in teaching"; • "Computer literacy was greatly increased"; • "…aware of the latest developments in the Russian profession, especially as they impacted the future of …Russian teaching"; • "International as well as U.S. visiting scholars were introduced to the participants."	*October 4, 1995 (Grammar Seminar)* "These lectures have a twofold benefit for the participants. On the one hand, the information conveyed, complete with handouts, … addresses points essential to a good working knowledge of Russian that are not often covered in the coursework … On the other hand, the participants are exposed to a model of a non-native speaker of Russian who is genuinely fluent—a term that is unfortunately all-too-often misused and devalued in today's parlance … this model of what can be achieved by a non-native speaker, like the other models of excellent teachers … in the Methodology and Skills sections, and the example set by the director … is in itself of great importance to these participant/teachers. To continue to grow as a teacher, one must discover new incentives, be exposed to new challenges, become aware of higher goals. This, in addition to a new appreciating and understanding of Russian culture and language, is what this institute has also given the participants."
August 6, 1996 "By the time I arrived all of the participants were able to give presentations in Russian, to complete major pedagogical projects in Russian, and to speak publicly with excellent pronunciation and intonation, to say nothing of grammar and vocabulary … [participants] had made significant progress … at the Institute."	

Figure 11.2

Issues

Issues that were important in the conduct of the Institute fell into four areas: affective variables, time management, mixed levels of language proficiency, and mixed exposure to the Proficiency Movement. In addition, depending on the year of the Institute, participants needed more or less exposure to and practice in new methodologies and computer literacy. At all times, attention was to be paid to faculty staffing and participants' interaction with various faculty members. Each of these issues is discussed in greater detail below.

Affective variables

Faculty was attuned to affective variables and noticed that while all participants were highly motivated, many were frequently anxious. In some cases, participants were overwhelmed initially.

Motivation

Participants at the Institutes were highly motivated learners and not only because of the pledges that they had to make and the support they had to garner before attending. They saw the Institutes, and the time they would spend there, as an opportunity to improve their knowledge of language and culture to approach more closely the levels that they needed (or wanted) for professional and personal reasons. They also bonded with the faculty. Finally, they were genuinely interested in the language. Hence, their motivation was both integrated and instrumental (Gardner and Lambert [1972]), both intrinsic and extrinsic (Deci and Ryan [1985]).

Anxiety

Many of the Institute participants exhibited stress and anxiety, making the development of rapport between the faculty and the participants an important factor in the success of the Institutes. Faculty members not only provided information to but also learned from the participants, all of whom were experienced language teachers and learners. In fact, some of the participants had been teaching longer than their instructors and brought a wealth of experience with them. Further, communicative approaches were new and controversial in the Russian profession in the mid-1990s, and many senior participants felt threatened by new methodologies. It was vitally important for the Institutes' faculty to respect their experience and incorporate it rather than dismiss it out of hand. The instructors, for example, facilitated, rather than directed, the learning process. They continuously assessed the needs and desires of the participants through direct questioning. This "gauging" served several purposes: it alleviated some of the participant anxiety, allowed for program flexibility, and demonstrated effective teacher–student communication and teacher behavior. Participants were never referred to as students by the faculty, they were thought of as colleagues. Since one of the goals of the Institutes was to expose participants to new communicative methodologies, this learner-centered approach served as meal and vessel.

Time management

Closely associated with anxiety – and perhaps a cause of it – was the relatively small amount of time available to accomplish the relatively extensive assignments. This was especially true for the Skills Enhancement and Materials Adaptation/Development seminars.

Without exception, all participants, even the native speakers, found the assignments of the Skills Enhancement seminar challenging. Many, especially those who had not been in a classroom recently, simply had not been exposed to such extensive reading for years, if ever, and found the pace of the Institute quite demanding. It helped that the Institute faculty repeatedly stated that participants should do what they could – and were understanding of the emotional drain accompanying participants' hard work.

The participants of the Institutes could be justly proud of the teaching materials that they developed in the Materials Adaptation/Development seminar and their mastery of the mysteries of the computer. However, some participants experienced difficulty with time management in this area, too: some of the projects were so ambitious that they took up an extraordinary amount of participants' time.

Mixed proficiency levels and backgrounds

Addressing a large group with varying language ability from Intermediate Low to Distinguished was a demanding task for all the undivided seminars. However, it was a particularly daunting task for the Grammar lectures. There a decision had to be made whether to offer lectures that improved the participants' command of Russian or to concentrate on how to teach a difficult grammar point, such as the use of aspect or verbs of motion, to the participants' students. Each choice reflected a goal of the Institute – (1) to improve participants' grammatical competence, and (2) to demonstrate teaching methods – and a combined approach was used as much as possible. Although smaller groupings might have been desired, there is no evidence that sharing Grammar lectures with participants with lower levels of proficiency in any way adversely affected the increasing proficiency of the Superior-level participants.

Some Institutes had a few participants who were native speakers of Russian, educated in Russia. They were attending the Institutes to learn about new methodologies and did not need language practice. Their needs were handled variously, especially for the Skills Enhancement seminar. In some years, they were grouped with the most advanced section and served as sources of linguistic and cultural information while also observing the approach to teaching. One year, two native speakers served as assistants, assigned to lower-level sections where participants needed more individualized help and where the native speakers could acquire teaching skills. In all cases, they enhanced the atmosphere of the Institutes, providing extra native-speaker input.

Mixed exposure to the Proficiency Movement

As with the mixing of proficiency levels, mixing of knowledge levels (in this case, of teaching for proficiency, the basis of the methodology used at the Institute) created some anticipated difficulties. Typically, although not always, the senior, more experienced teachers were the least familiar with principles of teaching for proficiency, and many were reluctant to turn in their tried-and-true techniques for methods with a new promise. Additionally, a number of the affective issues and linguistic difficulties typical of such a senior group were present. What was significant overall, however, was the need to teach, in Russian, new teachers, experienced teachers, and heritage speakers with varying amounts of teaching experience and education together in one group with varying proficiency levels. This situation had the greatest impact on the Methodology seminar; it was handled best by having participants work in small groups, where like levels of linguistic proficiency and content knowledge could be combined advantageously.

Conclusion

The eight Institutes can be described as a total immersion content-based experience for adult professional learners. The Institutes resembled a venue where a native speaker might naturally find him/herself: a professional development seminar.

While it is unrealistic to expect that within a period of four weeks, however intensive, a learner could move to the next level of proficiency, there were, indeed, tangible results. Observable language improvement was noted by the instructors and the participants. Participants' increasing ease at table talk, discussions with visitors, and formal presentation provided some objective evidence of this. This increased proficiency was recorded by the Outside Evaluators, as well.

Moreover, the participants gained in confidence. Not only were they required to engage in professional discussions and formal presentations, but they were able to do so with increasing success – and this led to their increased self-confidence (which, in turn, led to even more language improvement).

In addition to intellectually meaningful exchanges on topics of professional interest, participants expanded their sociocultural understanding through interaction with texts, as well as in discussions with native speakers among their instructors. They analyzed their own teaching preferences and habits, deciding to accept or reject the new approaches offered in the course of methodology lectures.

Although the summer Institutes are no longer offered through CORLAC at Bryn Mawr College, they could be revived by other institutions. Similar institutes could be developed for other languages – particularly languages that share the problems that were extant in the Russian field in the mid-1980s and the mid-1990s: inaccessibility of the culture and country and a profession mired in teaching traditions of the past.

As for the eight NEH/CORLAC Institutes, there are many teachers in the Russian profession today who benefited linguistically, culturally, technologically, and in terms of classroom materials. Frequently, the participants wrote to the organizers that, following the Institutes, they were proud of the fact that they as teachers of Russian had ideas and materials that were of interest to French,

Spanish, and German language teachers in their schools. A number have used their improved skills to the advantage of the Russian teaching field as a whole, including becoming involved in national Russian organizations and projects, and many former Institute participants give papers at conferences. Through the generosity of the National Endowment for the Humanities many young teachers have been molded and more experienced teachers were able to enhance their professional confidence and acquire new insights into their profession.

Part III

Learners and users

12   Understanding the learner at the
Superior–Distinguished threshold

Madeline E. Ehrman

This chapter discusses second language acquisition at the Superior–Distingui-shed (SD) threshold from the point of view of language-learning psychol-ogy. Some important elements of learning psychology include linguistic fos-silization, learning strategies and strategic competence, individual differences, affective factors, learner autonomy, and relations among teachers and learners. Since the important elements of learner psychology at the SD threshold can best be understood in the context of actual programs, this chapter uses exam-ples of concepts as they have been realized or encountered in SD programs at the Foreign Service Institute (FSI).[1]

About the SD threshold

To talk about learners and learning at this level, it may be useful to summarize what the SD threshold entails. First, it represents the boundary between the Interagency Language Roundtable (ILR) 3 or 3+, at which a language user is capable of performing professional work and carrying out a social life but with considerable imperfection, and the 4 and beyond, at which there are few limitations on what a user can do with the target language. Byrnes (Chapter 2) points out that integration of language, meaning, and social context is essential for really effective Distinguished language use. Another way to view really high-level proficiency is as an expansion of choices and options, especially of register, or, more specifically, a maximization of sophisticated choices.

SD programs at FSI

The "Beyond Three" initiatives undertaken at FSI since the early 1990s and pro-grams explicitly aimed at helping students reach the ILR 4 have made a shift

---

The content of this chapter does not represent official policy of the US Department of State; the opinions and observations are those of the author.

[1] FSI is the training bureau of the US Department of State; it offers full-time intensive training in over sixty languages to members of the US foreign affairs community. Average student age is 41; approximately two-thirds are between 30 and 50 years old when they enter training.

of emphasis from traditional grammar and lexical activities to helping students learn to sharpen their focus on fine points, incorporate new learning in socioculturally appropriate ways, and maximize *aware* exposure to real language use.

The earliest of these programs (1984–1989) was an Advanced language program initiated in response to needs for Level 4 speakers expressed by the US Ambassador to Moscow. This six-month content-based program for Superior-level diplomats was designed anew by the students themselves with each iteration. In addition to selecting course topics, students served as peer instructors in their areas of specialty, augmenting their knowledge with research using authentic materials. In this course, the teachers served as language, not content, experts. Classroom work was augmented by student participation as presenters and interpreters in a public conference in Russian, "internships" that partnered students with émigrés for real-life language use, and professional seminars on diplomacy-relevant topics. Teachers helped students prepare for language use activities, debriefed them, served as language models, role-played Russian officials, and the like. Individual interests were used to target teaching and learning. Authentic reading and listening texts taught tactics, nuance, genre, and register (Leaver and Bilstein [2000]).

The demands of training diplomats to serve in newly opened missions in the states of the former Soviet Union prompted a renewal of the advanced Russian program in the early 1990s. Entering students were required to be at the Superior (ILR 3) level and preferably to have spent a significant amount of time in a Russian-speaking milieu. They began with a thorough grammar review – especially fine points and discourse structure – during the first weeks of the program. The remaining 44 weeks emphasized massive and diversified reading, including 13 long novels (eighteenth- to twentieth-century) and contemporary intellectual journals, classroom discussion of the readings, and a variety of short field trips with immigrants in the Washington DC area and immersion trips to Russian-speaking locales in the US, and ordinarily training immersions overseas. A highlight of this program was a week in a New York émigré community participating in literary salons and discussions with leading writers. As much of the training as possible took place outside the classroom – for example, going to an airport café to converse with a lot of ambient noise.[2]

The next initiative was "Beyond Three," part of an overall revision of FSI language training in 1994, that was initiated in French as the pilot language. The "Beyond Three" program, meant to help learners at the ILR Level 3 achieve Level 3+ or 4 proficiency, adapted some of the Russian SD innovations and

[2] The author thanks FSI program administrators James Bernhardt, Marsha Kaplan, Thomas Madden, and Natalia Lord, for providing essential and extensive information on the "Beyond Three" programs in Russian and French that has informed the description of those programs throughout this chapter. I am also grateful to the Distinguished-level speakers who took the time to share their experiences as language learners and the lessons they have learned about achieving very high language proficiency.

created approaches taking advantage of the relatively close relationship between French and English. Its students come, usually one at a time, with a tested ILR 3 in speaking cum interactive listening for 1–10 weeks of "refresher" training. They receive a highly individualized program that at the same time is intended to provide structure and enhance learner confidence. To reduce learner anxiety (often intense in the high-stakes FSI setting), the goals are better tools and comfort level rather than a specific proficiency level; the end-of-training test is made optional; and students set their own performance objectives, negotiated throughout the program as their needs change (Kaplan [1997]).

Three tools provide focus and structure in "Beyond Three": learner diagnostics, a learning contract, and self-assessment. The diagnostic exercises in the first few days pinpoint learning needs and provide objectives. The contract, negotiated between the learner and the teaching staff on an ongoing basis, is the "backbone" of the program (1997), and students indicate that the process is more useful than the actual document. Finally, students constantly self-assess: comfort level in a given activity, need for focus or review, accomplishments, and ideas about how to follow up. Among areas of student focus are public speaking, press statements (and fielding questions), informal consecutive interpreting and note-taking, representational interactions, coping with provocations, managing meetings, and telephone talk (e.g., proper requests for appointments). Attention to register pervades these programs (1997).

"Beyond Three" has expanded to other languages, such as Greek and Polish. Its principles are adapted on an *ad hoc* basis in a variety of other languages for learners at the ILR 3 level or above. Additionally, FSI has been providing training to Level 4 for years at its overseas field schools in Beijing, Seoul, Taipei, Tunis, and Yokohama (where the usual mission is to enable students to go from the ILR 2 to the ILR 3 or 3+). Madden (1989), who has directed both of the Chinese field school programs, notes that because learners at the SD threshold usually arrive one or two at a time, these programs have been highly individualized, in terms of both language needs and professional goals.[3] Students are given four or five hours daily of individual instruction, relevant and challenging materials, and teachers who work well with very advanced students, as well as support for Chinese language, culture, and personal contacts

---

[3] Professional needs listed by Madden (1989) include listening, reading, and speaking tasks. Listening tasks are used with face-to-face discussions (gathering specific information), speeches, presentations at professional meetings, radio and television broadcasts, overheard conversations at social gatherings, monitoring development of third-party discussions, and monitoring an interpreter. Reading tasks are used with materials from the local press, local government documents and legislation, source materials for preparation for interviews on specific topics, contemporary literature, official documents, handwritten documents, and correspondence/translations (with these, a monitoring task is used for ensuring the accuracy of local staff). Speaking needs include opening and closing face-to-face encounters, interviewing and exchanging information, making presentations, leading or moderating discussions, formal negotiating, socializing, supervising local employees, and informal interpreting.

in which the program is embedded. Deep exposure to culture and literature is an important emphasis of the program.

Online reading maintenance courses are a recent innovation in FSI's "Beyond Three" language instruction. Targeted to State Department officers with R-3, 3+, and 4 level proficiency in reading, their goal is to help officers maintain and refresh their reading proficiency throughout their careers and while stationed in posts around the world. The course is taught through the Department's Intranet, with mentoring by a trained teacher through e-mail and online conferencing software.[4]

The first such course was the Russian Reading Maintenance Course; the program is now available too in French, Spanish, and Portuguese. The Russian course consists of six self-paced units, each of which features two authentic readings of 2–6 pages each about cultural analyses and Russian–American relations. Readings are supplemented by vocabulary glosses, brief cultural and historical commentaries, interactive comprehension, grammar, vocabulary, and discourse exercises with feedback. There is a wide range of suggested online language references and resources as well. Participants post responses in Russian or in English to open-ended interpretive questions on an electronic bulletin board. The mentor probes responses, facilitates discussion, and provides a supportive learning environment. Linguistic issues are generally taken up privately with the mentor via e-mail. The French, Spanish, and Portuguese courses are similar.

The State Department has been experiencing increasing need for speakers who can use language at the Distinguished level. In response, FSI has recently begun an initiative to ascertain what is involved in learning to this level for its students, building on what is known from previous programs. Among the criteria that have already been noted in the beginning of the needs assessment are an extraordinary breadth of topics with which the individual can cope at a high level of accuracy, extensive sociocultural competence, speed and stamina in reading massive amounts of material accurately, and, above all, flexibility and versatility. Former Ambassador to the USSR Jack Matlock indicated that he needed a speaker who could cope equally well with visits to fisheries, steel mills, and hospitals as well as the usual political and economic business of diplomacy (James Bernhardt, personal communication, May 23, 2001). Before him, Ambassador Hartmann noted that he needed a Level-4 speaker once every 2–3 months. Such conditions require language that does not disappear with only occasional use. Many teachers have noted such stability as a characteristic of Level-4 proficiency over years of working with refresher students: although all language skills become latent with disuse but available with sufficient refresher,

---

[4] The author is indebted to Marsha Kaplan for providing the description of the Russian On-line Maintenance Course.

Level-4 skills are much more rapidly recovered (e.g., David Argoff, personal communication, March 10, 1999).

Fossilization

Fossilization, which has long been considered an obstacle in moving beyond lower levels of proficiency (Higgs and Clifford [1982]), is indicated in this volume as a key problem for SD learners. Heritage learners present a unique variation of this phenomenon, inasmuch as their fossilization is in register and lexicon more than in the basics of language.

There seem to be several varieties of fossilization. These include (1) functional (including structural and morpho-semantic), (2) instruction-fostered, (3) domain restriction, (4) affective fossilization, and (5) arrested strategic development.

Functional fossilization

This well-known type of fossilization (Selinker [1992]; Gass and Selinker [1994]) is defined as the continued use of incorrect or limited linguistic forms, structures, and semantic domains that may be functional but not precise, usually as a result of ability to function satisfactorily and consequent lack of motivation for continued linguistic development. Remediation of this kind of fossilization is a top priority in many, if not most, SD programs, among them the FSI "Beyond Three" courses and overseas field school programs. Superior-level learners have learned compensation strategies that have served them well for the tasks they have needed to perform at the lower proficiency levels, but higher-level tasks demand a level of lexical, structural, sociocultural, and semantic precision of which they may not be aware (Kubler, this volume). Angelelli and Kagan (this volume) address the fossilization that takes place among heritage learners, whose language fails to develop beyond that characteristic of earlier ages or social relations within their settings of origin and suggest that its remediation is an important focus for heritage learner programs.

Instruction-fostered fossilization

Linguistic fossilization may also be the result of overly compliant interlocutors, teachers and non-teachers, who adapt to the learner's errors. The term, *iatrogenic illness*, means illness caused by a doctor's efforts to cure disease. This kind of fossilization is a kind of "iatrogenic" effect, the result of well-meaning but perhaps misfocused efforts to help students learn. Countless FSI student end-of-training questionnaires speak of how much teacher efforts to "push" them were appreciated; effective "Beyond Three" teachers are rigorous about lexical, structural, discourse, and sociocultural precision.

Domain fossilization

Another form of linguistic fossilization comes from narrow language use, for example the routinizing of language that often affects consular diplomats, whose work consists largely of issuing visas, or a secretary in an international organization answering phones and routing calls. An explanation suggested by interviews of students who have participated in FSI's Language Learning Consultation Service is that repeated use of stereotyped language is likely to result in withdrawal of the attention to differences that leads to continued linguistic development. This kind of fossilization results from too narrow a definition of language task needs by learners. (Another possible explanation, of course, is that this is fossilization of the first kind: students perceive no need to go beyond what they already know.)

Affective fossilization

A fourth type of fossilization can be called affective fossilization. It is related to the sense of self-efficacy as learners that is essential to a long, difficult task like learning languages to a high level. Very goal-oriented students can tune out what they think is irrelevant, and some students limit themselves in order to minimize the risk of being corrected. Students may fear being criticized overtly by teachers or covertly by classmates; still more, they may fear their own self-criticism for not living up to their expectations of themselves (see Stevick [1980]). In short, students may avoid expanding their proficiency because they are protective of their self-esteem and self-image. Reduction of this kind of self-limitation is one of the goals of the Rogerian (Rogers [1968]) psychology-based learning approach of Counseling Learning (Curran [1972]). In the FSI "Beyond Three" courses, for example, every effort is made to enhance students' sense of freedom to learn, including the mutually negotiated (and negotiable) contract based on needs analysis drawn up with the student, and presentation of the program as if it were a "consulting firm" to the student rather than a directive, judgmental course.

Strategic fossilization

Finally, fossilization can appear in the use of strategic techniques (such as global comprehension that ignores what is not known) that work well at the lower proficiency levels but can lead in the case of some students to lack of attention to distinctions important at the higher levels. Without developing attention to the complex relations among language form, meaning, and context, learners find it difficult to cross the SD threshold (see Byrnes [this volume]).

In addition, Superior-level learners often have schemata about how to learn firmly in place – a kind of "cognitive" fossilization, especially if they have been successful with a specific classroom method. For example, during the transition at FSI from audiolingual methodology to a more communicative approach in the 1970s and early 1980s, it was commonplace for students who had reached the Superior level in audiolingual classrooms to express considerable doubt about the changes they encountered on returning for "refresher" training or training in a new language.

Learning strategies and strategic competence

Learning strategies have been among the most discussed topics in educational psychology for years (Dansereau [1988]; Pask [1976]; Riding and Rayner [1998]; Schmeck [1988]; Weinstein, Goetz, and Alexander [1988]), as well as in second language education (Chamot and O'Malley [1994]; Cohen [1998]; Ely [1989]; Oxford [1990]; Wenden and Rubin [1987]). Strategic competence is often associated with levels of proficiency lower than the SD threshold because the best-known example of strategic competence is compensation strategies, ways of working around what one does not know, that are in fact vital at lower proficiency levels. When the balance of known to unknown changes, as noted throughout this volume, compensation strategies become not only less useful but, as indicated by Leaver and Shekhtman (this volume), potentially counterproductive. Strategic competence does not, however, consist only of compensation strategies.

What kinds of strategic competence, then, would characterize the SD threshold? There are a number described in the preceding chapters. Leaver and Shekhtman (this volume) suggest that teachers can encourage the student in developing strategies

to use what they already know and . . . how to "sell" their language and themselves in communicating, . . . how to fill pauses, how to avoid direct translation of their native language into foreign language, how to paraphrase, how naturally to elicit help in comprehending from a native speaker in unnoticeable ways that do not impede the flow of thought, how to become linguistically an equal partner with native speakers.

They also mention such tactics as appropriate entrance into and exit from native-speaker conversations. Kubler (this volume) urges focus on "processes and strategies (e.g., how to learn, how to use Chinese in Chinese society) as well as on inventory (e.g., vocabulary words, grammar patterns)."

Additionally, a key strategy in language learning is focusing attention on what is not known, rather than ignoring it, and interpreting it in the light of increasingly sophisticated understanding of the context in which the target language is used, consistent with the shift in the ratio of known to unknown. This "tactic" is one of the highlights of the specific activities in Chapter 6; most of the other tactics that Shekhtman *et al.* describe, such as using questions to continue a conversation or "islands" of mastered language, contribute to the development of a sophisticated form of strategic competence as part of managing communication. Closely related is developing attention to fine distinctions of meaning or register, a skill often neglected because of the necessity to gain the basics at earlier levels (see Leaver and Shekhtman, this volume).

Seeking increasingly challenging opportunities for language use is an example of high-level strategic competence that can be used at nearly any level of proficiency. For example, the diplomat on the visa line could seek rotation to other responsibilities or join community activities in the city where s/he is posted; another instance for university learners could be making use of opportunities to read or listen to difficult material outside their immediate fields. FSI SD learners are encouraged to develop hobbies that entail interaction and potential formation of social relationships – anything will do, from Chinese porcelain through children's sports to the salsa dancing and consequent friendships that took one learner over the SD threshold in Japan (Woo Lee, personal communication, July 2, 2001).

Continuing exposure to language in real-use settings promotes development of the rich associative networks that contribute both to grasp of nuance and to emotional competence – the ability to be oneself in an authentic way for the target language and culture (Eshkembeeva [1997]). Receptivity to the surrounding culture and sociolinguistic milieu is needed for truly Distinguished-level functioning. The FSI "Beyond Three" programs are able to simulate partial real-life "emotional" settings by virtue of using only native speakers as instructors. The FSI field schools, of course, are in the best position to shape the development of emotional competence since they are located in-country.

Metacognition is a key factor in self-directed, autonomous learning at all levels, but nowhere more than in successful achievement of Distinguished-level proficiency. Metacognitive considerations comprise a consistent explicit and implicit theme in many, if not most, SD programs. In the "Beyond Three" French programs at the FSI, for example, learners are encouraged to observe their own language behaviors and to develop realistic assessment of their own progress. The contract learning process, and the periodic reviews of the learning–teaching contract, foster this kind of constructive self-examination.

Metacognition also applies to the concept of Communicative Focus (CF) introduced by Leaver and Shekhtman (Chapter 1). Use of the balance between CF and the need to attend to matters of linguistic form – Linguistic Focus (LF) – to conceptualize teaching and learning at the SD threshold can serve as a base for teacher and student metacognition in two ways. First, CF can contribute to decisions about what to focus on in a class session or even from moment to moment, based on what is affecting the learner's ability to communicate with appropriate precision. Second, a self-aware student can also make use of

CF to make decisions about learning activities. Metacognitive strategies are developed in the "Beyond Three" programs at the FSI in several ways: joint needs analysis in which the student participates in determining learning goals, extensive student participation in the development of the learning contract, constant ongoing self-assessment with program guidance at first, and active student participation in renegotiations of the learning contract in response to changing circumstances.

Personality variables in learning

The programs in this volume, including those at the FSI, indicate that much of the learning and teaching for crossing the SD threshold is done in response to individual needs. Student proficiency profiles, interests, and professional needs, of course, are a common source of individualization.

Personality is frequently mentioned by program managers and teachers at the FSI as a factor. Tom Madden, who has headed Chinese field school programs for many years, writes: "The efficacy of [a formal program aimed at the 4] is too heavily dependent on having a student with innate talent (not just a lot of previous training), a gung-ho attitude, [and] an outgoing personality" (Madden [1989]). Another personality characteristic, tolerance for ambiguity (Ehrman [1996]; Ely [1989]), plays a role in overcoming strategic fossilization (overdependence on generalizing learning techniques like ignoring what is not known) or in gaining greater experience with language *in situ* and especially in interactions. Students who do not bring these qualities with them may need different kinds of program support.

A number of studies have addressed the difference between students who are active initiators of language use and learning opportunities (Seliger [1983] called them "High Input Generators"), and those who are not, indicating a clear learning advantage for the former (Naiman [1996]; Seliger [1983]). Goodison (1987) at the FSI reported similar findings with respect to later improvement and attrition of students who completed FSI Russian courses at the Superior level. Type A students, like Seliger's High Input Generators, who tended to improve while assigned to overseas posts, were intrepid and willing to take a variety of risks in language use. Type B students, whose language ability declined, were extremely focused on accuracy over fluent language use and tended not to take conversational risks. These differences showed up in the classroom and were magnified when students were at post: Type As used the language, and Type Bs tended to avoid it. These findings parallel the conclusions reached by researchers using a longitudinal database of the in-country study and family living experiences (and language gain) of students participating in the study-abroad programs of the American Council of Teachers of Russian from the mid-1980s to the mid-1990s (Brecht, Davidson, and Ginsberg [1993]).[5]

Affective factors: motivation, anxiety, self-efficacy

Motivation

Language learning is driven by various forms of motivation, the topic of innumerable papers in the second language acquisition field. One important distinction is that of extrinsic and intrinsic motivation (Deci and Ryan [1985]). The former is something done for rewards outside of oneself; the latter because it corresponds with the learner's sense of self and enjoyment.

Motivation for students at the SD threshold can, like those at lower levels, be both extrinsic and intrinsic. Learning may be driven by demanding task expectations or, as is often the case in the US Foreign Service, by generous monetary incentives. Career issues are likely to be salient for university students, whether they hope to join the professoriate or enter the business world. Alternatively, motivation may well be a matter of desire to assimilate to a new society, especially for those who expect a long-term stay in the culture where the language is spoken. More personal factors such as need for achievement, perfectionism, narcissistic drives, or sheer pleasure in the learning may also motivate the aspirant to Distinguished-level proficiency. More than anxiety, motivation varies widely by individual. Classroom instruction at the SD threshold may well afford a kind of interpersonal motivation through relationships with native-speaking teachers, especially when outside the area where the target language is spoken, and, of course, in-country, greater or lesser desire to integrate with the people there can be a powerful motivator. All these kinds of motivation show up in SD classrooms at the FSI.

Anxiety

Teachers and administrators of FSI programs have found that anxiety can play a negative role, even at high levels of language learning. Anxiety can arise, for example, when students are taught by teachers who do not adapt to student expectations for classroom conduct, i.e., Western student-centered teaching approaches (Kubler, this volume). The affective, then, is as important as the linguistic for informing instructor selection and roles (Angelelli and Kagan [this volume]).

---

[5] One of the analyses of data from this database (Brecht, Davidson, and Ginsberg [1993]) also pointed out at least two additional areas of interest: (1) the better the grammatical control before students entered study-abroad programs, the greater the gain, and (2) males improved more than females, perhaps, according to the researchers, a matter of the Russian society being more open to the kind of social assertiveness that permits language use in a wider range of venues, on a wider range of topics, at greater length, and with more visibility on the part of men than of women.

Although lower-level learners are often made anxious by fear that they may not be able to cope (Horwitz and Young [1991]; Reid [1999]), the student at the SD threshold is likely to be confident of coping ability in most situations. Instead, the SD learner is likely to be concerned about appropriateness of language and behavior for given cross-cultural interaction because the ability to tailor language to the situation is essential for successful accomplishment of high-level tasks (see Leaver and Atwell, this volume). At every level, learners can feel overwhelmed by the amount still to learn; at the Superior level, the amount and range of subtle language and cultural background to be mastered may seem to have multiplied exponentially from the grammar rules and basic vocabulary of the earlier stages. In these cases, Madden (1989) emphasizes the importance of high motivation to establish contact with the target-language people and culture as a "key success-predicting factor."

Anxiety is also characteristic of many heritage learners. Since they often experience themselves as outsiders or as socially stigmatized and may have serious difficulty with literacy, they may be more subject than "mainstream" learners to various kinds of anxiety at all levels of proficiency. Their atypical profiles can put them out of step with their classmates, leading them to focus on what is wrong with them rather than what is right, including shame about their backgrounds and the language they bring with them. They are vulnerable to stereotype threat (Steele [1997]): people from stigmatized groups perform worse in those settings when they believe that in some way their performance is likely to reflect on them as group members.

Self-efficacy

Teacher selection can play an important role in helping students to develop self-efficacy. Cross-culturally aware teachers who understand affective issues as well are essential for validation of heritage learner home usage (Angelelli and Kagan, this volume) and for making available the academic "secondary discourse" that leads to greater social choices (Byrnes, this volume). The comments of students in the translator–interpreter program described in Chapter 3 of this volume highlight this: they considered the professors to be the key to program success. These professors functioned as individual coaches and group facilitators, a typical mechanism used to develop self-efficacy. In FSI "Beyond Three" programs, student self-efficacy is enhanced by the substantial empowerment of the learner and regular confirmations of progress.

Learner autonomy

Learner autonomy has been discussed in the literature for some time, both in general educational psychology (Deci [1992]; Schunk and Zimmerman [1997];

Winne [1995]) and in second language acquisition (Aoki [1999]; Benson and Voller [1997]; Dickinson and Wenden [1995]; Ehrman [1996, 2000]; Ehrman and Dörnyei [1998]; Rubin and Thompson [1994]; Ushioda [1996]; Wenden [1991]). The literature addresses both learner autonomy – ability to learn on one's own – and learner self-regulation – ability to manage one's own feelings and cognition while learning whether in or out of a classroom, as well as the role of teacher–student relations in formation of self-regulation. Self-regulation is foundational for learning autonomy.

An increasingly desired outcome of formal instruction is development of the ability to continue improving language proficiency through self-instruction and experiential forms of learning (Benson and Voller [1997]; Dickinson and Wenden [1995]). According to Holec (1981), learner autonomy depends on these principles: (1) there is no one ideal method; (2) the teacher is not the source of all methodological expertise; (3) knowledge of the mother tongue is a useful resource for learning a second language; (4) experience gained as a learner of other subjects can be transferred at least partially; (5) learners can make valid assessments of their performance. I would add that (6) learners can make valid decisions about what and how to learn.

On the other hand, there are limits to absolute learning autonomy. Most human beings find it difficult to be fully objective about themselves, and need outside feedback, especially when they have been using sophisticated, functional language to meet most of their needs. They may have withdrawn attention from linguistic and sociolinguistic specifics to focus more intensively on their tasks. It would follow that a truly autonomous learner knows when to seek feedback and assistance. Indeed, Pemberton *et al.* (1996) point out that such a learner is at liberty to opt for teacher feedback or direction. Thus, autonomy is not total freedom from outside influence; instead, it is an increasingly sophisticated balance of internal decision making and external effects.[6] This point is especially relevant to the role of formal instruction in crossing the SD threshold. Making use of a resource to reduce the amount of time a learner would need to accomplish this task is not a reduction in learning autonomy; instead, it is an example of autonomous informed choice and a venue for increasingly effective self-regulation.

Many foreign language learners at the FSI have strong potential for crossing the SD threshold; however, conversations and surveys sent to students after they have been at their overseas posts for some months indicate that many of them experience trouble with linguistic precision once they leave their classrooms

---

[6] In this vein, Esch (1996) clarifies what autonomy is not: (1) autonomy is not self-instruction/learning without a teacher; (2) it does not mean that intervention or initiative on the part of a teacher is banned; (3) it is not something teachers do to learners; (4) it is not a single easily identifiable behavior; (5) it is not a steady state achieved by learners once and for all (p. 37).

(most leave at the ILR 3 level). They indicate a desire for continuing classroom training at their overseas posts of assignment because they have difficulty learning structure on their own. A variety of factors could affect them, including lack of attention to the specifics needed for precision, inability to use inductive strategies to generalize from the examples around them, or lack of self-regulation. The "Beyond Three" programs in French and other languages have taken initial steps to increase the self-management skills of their learners through encouraging self-observation and promulgation of effective strategies for noticing and practicing subtleties of language use.

The importance and role of teachers at the SD threshold

What happens in classrooms and between learners and teachers affects the success of learning. This section, therefore, takes a brief look at teachers, classrooms, and student–teacher relations.

What is the place of formal instruction? As many of the chapters in this book indicate, most students at the SD level seem to require, or at least benefit from, explicit instruction where it has been available (Leaver and Atwell, this volume). Surveyed learners have also reported real-life interaction with the target-language society to be a crucial element in their success (Belcher and Connor [2001]). Both of these processes entail attention to and awareness of both linguistic and sociocultural features, which can be aided by teachers who have extensive cross-cultural experience, not only by pointing these out but also by giving a time and place away from society for controlled practice.

Many Distinguished-level language users report that simply being in the country where the language is spoken is not enough to achieve a level beyond 3+, nor, according to these learners, are good observation skills and well-developed strategies for autonomous learning. In a classroom, these former students point out, it is possible to learn in a short time – hours, weeks, or a few months – what takes a few, if not many, years of immersion, in-country work and study, and extensive real-life interactions (e.g., Thomas Miller, personal communication, June 15, 2001; William Davney, personal communication, July 6, 2001).

The classroom can serve as a safe place to make mistakes. The nature of the mistakes may vary by proficiency level, but the potential for miscommunication and misunderstanding does not. The higher the linguistic level of the learner, the more is likely to be expected, especially in the way of sociolinguistic sophistication. For example, many FSI teachers speak English very well; they can operate effectively in many situations. As a result, their mistakes may be attributed to incompetence or even bad character when in fact they are functions of well-disguised deficiencies in their English language and/or culture skills. *Mutatis mutandis*, the same applies to increasingly proficient learners of foreign languages. It is much better for this kind of miscommunication to take place in the sheltered environment of a classroom than for a learner to lose an important sale or miscommunicate a crucial concept.

Many Superior-level learners do not realize how much improvement they need to make to get "Beyond Three" (Kubler, this volume). An important role for the teacher is to establish the kind of relationship that makes it easy for learners to accept imperfections that may come as a surprise to them, especially if they have experienced themselves as effective and have taken pride in their prowess as language learners. The expectation that the instructor will not think less of them because they still need formal training makes it easier to make needed repairs and achieve complex new learning for transitioning from "cross-cultural" to "intracultural" communication, to use Kubler's description.

At every proficiency level, the relationship between learner and teacher plays a key role in learning. At higher proficiency levels, the teacher–student relationship may well be one of relative equals, especially when the student knows more than the teacher about the subject-matter and has strong linguistic competence, though the teacher knows even more of the language. At this level, however, the situation is complicated for the teacher by the very fact that the student is so much closer to being an equal. Curran (1972) pointed out that when the learner is very advanced and knowledgeable, the teacher may feel threatened by the possibility of no longer being needed. Such anxieties on the part of the teacher of an SD student may lead to defensive behaviors like rigidity, avoidance, or excessive *laissez faire*. The role of the learner is thus complicated in turn by the necessity to assure the teacher that he or she is still needed and help the teacher make the transition to more knowledgeable companion. Most of this dynamic is unconscious, but effecting this change in relationship can nevertheless be one key to successful learning at the higher proficiency levels, especially when the "teacher" is a native speaker in an informal relationship with the learner (Ehrman [1998]).

In conclusion

None of the students in these programs will remain in formal training. Even at the linguistic stratosphere of the SD threshold, all that a learner can expect of a formal program is to provide a certain amount of content, awareness, and level-appropriate strategies for continued learning, and, as Caudery (this volume) notes, this is all that teachers should expect of themselves. One of the most important outcomes of successful language programs at any level is an individual who is equipped to keep learning at the appropriate level without fossilizing after leaving the classroom. The equipment needed by the SD learner to accomplish this goal is different from that needed at lower levels, both because of the much greater knowledge brought by the learner to the task and because of the linguistic and sociocultural demands of what a person with truly Distinguished language can be expected to accomplish.

13   Preliminary qualitative findings from a study
      of the processes leading to the Advanced
      Professional Proficiency Level (ILR 4)

Betty Lou Leaver
with Sabine Atwell

Most of the chapters in this volume focus on the practices of language teaching at Levels 3 (Professional Proficiency) and 4 (Advanced Professional Proficiency[1]); a few focus on theory of language learning at this level. This chapter takes a slightly different direction; it reports on the purpose and nature of a highly comprehensive examination of the processes involved in achieving Level 4 (Distinguished or Advanced Professional Proficiency) and higher levels of proficiency that is being conducted through the joint efforts of the National Foreign Language Center (NFLC) and the Defense Language Institute (DLI).[2] The researchers have interviewed in great depth language users at several US government agencies and in academia who have developed one or more language skills to Level 4 and beyond and asked them what did and did not help at various points in their language-learning careers. The purpose of the investigation is to examine the nature of Level-4 language from the perspective of those using it in their daily and professional lives, to assess the behavioral aspects associated with Level-4 proficiency, and to determine the most important factors that contribute to reaching that level.

The NFLC-DLI Superior/Distinguished Language User Study began in July 2001, is still in progress, and the full range of conclusions possible will not be available for some time. While it is too early to report definitive results, some trends do emerge from the data. This chapter reports on behaviors, attributes,

---

[1] The Interagency Language Roundtable (ILR) uses the labels 3 and 4 and the terms, *Professional Proficiency* and *Advanced Professional Proficiency*. The ACTFL scale uses the term, *Superior-level proficiency* (Breiner-Sanders [2000]), for both levels, but at one point had proposed the term, *Distinguished* (ACTFL [1986]), for the upper level. Since very few language learners ever reached Level 4, in time there appeared to be no need for separating the highly proficient from the near-native. The US government does have a need to make this distinction; in this chapter, we will be using the ILR terminology.
[2] We thank the DLI and the NFLC for supporting this study and assistance in its conduct. Thanks are also offered to the interviewees for their substantive participation in the study and feedback on early versions of the interview guide. Special thanks are given to those interviewees who provided detailed narratives.

260

experiences, and opinions that are shared by at least 75% of the interviewed population.

Methodology

The study described here is based principally on quasi-experimental methods, sometimes called grounded theory. Using theoretical sampling, the researchers collected qualitative and quantitative data through in-depth, open-ended interviews, then coded the quantitative data and those qualitative data that could be quantified into categories that were suggested by the constant comparative method of data analysis. In this method, the researcher simultaneously codes and analyzes data in order to develop concepts (Glaser and Strauss [1967]).

Data collection

The study began with a research focus – the 3+/4 threshold and its crossing – and a plan of action – in-depth interviews of previously tested language learners who had successfully crossed that threshold in one or more skill (although the preliminary results reported reflect only speaking data). As with other qualitative studies (Bogdan and Biklen [1992]; Taylor and Bogdan [1984]), the research design has evolved in accordance with emerging findings.

The data is being collected, so far, by two researchers, the authors of this article. We both were previously tested by the DLI to be at Level 4 in multiple skills in one or more foreign languages and are very familiar with all ILR levels, to include Level 4, as well as with the parallel levels established by the American Council on Teaching Foreign Languages (ACTFL). While a certified examiner at the Foreign Service Institute and an Outside Evaluator for Molink (Washington–Moscow "Hot-Line") translators, Leaver conducted more than 1,000 proficiency tests, including many at the Advanced Professional Proficiency level; she also led the effort at the American Councils for International Education to design a space-related specific proficiency test for NASA. Atwell is a certified and currently active proficiency tester and tester trainer for the US government; in the past, she has trained testers for ACTFL. Both are experienced classroom teachers and language program managers. This background has aided the interview process, both in the design of an interview guide (our practice interviews of each other resulted in significant revisions) and in being able to obtain the most information possible from interviewees in terms of quantity and insight.

We, however, have been careful not to use our personal experience to influence or prompt interviewees; for this, the interview guide has proved to be very helpful. Most interviewees do arrive at the interview having seen the guide and having responses in mind. Often, they have firmly held ideas about how learning takes place at the 3+/4 threshold.

The interview guide, which was developed with the assistance of the DLI Research Division,[3] contains descriptive, open-ended questions, as well as an empirical questionnaire, incorporated into the body of the guide. Since the various skills involve differing, albeit, in many instances, overlapping variables, the interview guide has five sections: demographics, speaking, listening, reading, and writing. The demographics section is used with all interviewees. The other sections are used as pertinent, based on test scores. (The interview guide, consisting of some thirty-five pages, is too long to include here; however, it is available at www.mindsolutionsinternational.org.)

Information is collected via in-depth interviews, e-mail responses (followed by interview) to the questionnaire, and solicited or proffered narratives (following interviews). As is typical of qualitative research, as new questions and trends appear, prior responses from earlier interviews are clarified with those interviewees; answers to such follow-up questions are obtained from interviewees via e-mail or phone. Member checks are achieved by giving interviewees the written interpretation of their responses for comment.

For the full study, data will be collected in more than 100 categories per skill (reading, writing, listening, and speaking) and in 28 demographic areas. The theories by which the study is informed include general second language acquisition (SLA) theory and psychological theories of individual variables in information acquisition; data about the latter are still being evaluated.

To date, interviews have not been taped; a number of interviewees have expressed hesitancy about being recorded. However, the interviewers have kept interview journals that are transcribed and presented to interviewees for confirmation. Some interviewees have also chosen to prepare in advance and have brought with them some typewritten thoughts that have been discussed during the interviews. Plans also call for presenting interpretation of the data to the interviewees for comment.

Interview

Interviews are conducted in person with either one or both of us questioning one participant. Group interviews, a possibility for follow-up interviews, have not been held to date, although since both interviewers are Level-4 language users, we, in essence, form a small group with each interviewee.

---

[3] We received substantial assistance in research design from John Lett, Director of the Research Division of the Defense Language Institute, along with Gordon Jackson and Ward Keesling, also of the DLI Research Division. Others who provided research design assistance and feedback were John Thain and Marzena Krol of the DLI Research Division and Gary Buck, Director of the DLI Testing Division.

The speaking proficiency portion of the interview lasts from one to four hours (the range in time reflects learner differences, with reflective learners taking longer and, on some occasions, more than one meeting). Interviews are followed up with transcripts, which are also discussed with the interviewees. New questions that emerge during the study and are added to the interview guide are subsequently asked of previous informants, thus increasing the amount of time spent with each interviewee. Teachers have been the most skilled at providing direct data; from non-teacher, non-tester language learners, some data has been indirect. Interviewees have been very willing to reflect at length and in detail about their learning experiences. Most have reached a level where their language proficiency is taken for granted, compliments are no longer forthcoming because they are not perceived as foreign, and their multi-year efforts seem to be of interest to no one but themselves – or so a number of them have told us; the opportunity to be interviewed was found to be "the most interesting thing I have done all week," in the words of one interviewee.

Written narrative

A number of the interviewees prepared written narratives that contain much detail, as well as insight into philosophy and theory related to their learning experiences. They are the beginning of a collection of case studies that can be used to inform further the interpretation of data.

The participants

Participants in the part of the study presented here are a subset of all the participants interviewed to date; the larger group includes anyone with a test score of 4 (or Distinguished) on any proficiency test. The subset is composed of those (1) with a tested Level 4 in speaking on a noncompensatory[4] proficiency[5] test, (2) whose test scores could be confirmed by existing records, and (3) who considered their test scores to be an accurate reflection of their proficiency. (In general, interviewees' tested proficiency levels are a matter of institutional record, and their positions and some biographical information are a matter of

---

[4] There are at least two kinds of scoring mechanisms in use by the various testing agencies and organizations: compensatory and noncompensatory. The former allow an averaging of subcomponents to determine the overall level of performance. The latter require all subcomponents to be at the higher level of proficiency in order to award the higher score. The DLI uses the latter, and, therefore, although data collection has taken place on a much wider scale, for the purposes of determining preliminary findings that we consider unambiguous, we have restricted the group upon which we have based this report to those whose test scores were awarded by the DLI.

[5] Proficiency tests have had two general intents: (1) to test global language skills and (2) to test potential performance. We refer to the latter as performance tests, rather than proficiency tests. In this chapter, we are using interviewees who have been tested and scored on a proficiency test of global language skills.

public record.) The rationale for separating the subset from the larger group was to avoid comparing unlike groups.

Source of participants

Names of potential interviewees were obtained initially through three sources: (1) those personally known to the authors of the study, regardless of institution or source of test score, (2) those available from Defense Language Institute testing records (other agency records not being available to us for obvious reasons), and (3) referrals from other interviewees. (Without a national database of Level-4 language users and given the paucity of such a human resource in general, one of the most difficult tasks of this study has been to locate appropriate individuals.) Identification of additional interviewees occurred in two ways: (1) through asking colleagues and associates for names, and (2), as mentioned above, through names provided by interviewees during the interview process. These potential participants were contacted; approximately 80% were willing and available to participate in the study. Although a number of the interviewees have been known to one or the other of the interviewers, few have been known to both of us, and that has controlled experimenter bias to the extent possible.

Proficiency of participants

The description for Level 4 was that defined in the ILR proficiency descriptors (see Leaver and Shekhtman, this volume). All participants held test scores of Level 4 or higher in speaking. Many also had test scores of Level 4 and higher in other skills; however, those skills are not the focus of this chapter.

General characteristics of participants

To date, all of the participants have been adults; most have been over the age of 40. If younger examples of Level-4 users can be found, they will be interviewed. So far, however, most of those who have been identified have not reached Level 4 until age 30–50, in some ways disproving the myth of the older learner as less able.

None of the participants to date have been taught with communicative methods. This is clearly a matter of the era in which they undertook their initial study.[6]

All of the participants have lived abroad and have had the opportunity to acquire language and culture in context, although none were exclusively self-taught. Many have personal ties to the countries where their foreign language is

---

[6] This experience parallels that of another study of near-native language learners: in this case, those who use L2 for academic writing (Belcher and Connor [2001]). It may be some time before the communicative generation of learners produces language users at Level 4 and, therefore, some time before the relative effectiveness of the two distinct approaches for ultimate language achievement can be adequately compared.

spoken, such as a spouse, children, or very close friends, and visit those counties on a regular basis. More than two-thirds of the participants grew up in bilingual or multilingual families or communities. (One might note that this is also typical of individuals with well-developed academic writing skills in L2 [Belcher and Connor (2001)]).

Nearly all the interviewees are working in positions that require use of their language skills in some way. Among them are translators, interpreters, foreign language educators (teachers, teacher-trainers, curriculum developers, and proficiency testers), administrators, and cross-cultural consultants.

It is particularly interesting to note that all have studied more than one foreign language. Some have studied several languages to Levels 3 and 4. Foreign languages at Level 4 in this group include Arabic (1), Croatian (1), English (10), French (5), Russian (5), and Serbian (1). Native languages of English learners were German (2), Greek, Hungarian, Norwegian, Russian, and Turkish (2). Native languages of other language learners were Arabic (2), Bulgarian (2), English (8), Farsi (1), Greek (1), and Turkish (1).

Hypotheses

A number of hypotheses that could be falsified and investigated empirically emerged from the earliest data collected in this study; some are reported here, and others will be investigated over time. The findings reported here relate to those hypotheses (and in some cases, widespread assumptions or research at lower levels of proficiency) that have clear and strong reflections in the data collected to date and lend themselves to unambiguous interpretation. Two sets of hypotheses were used: (1) hypotheses developed prior to interviewing and (2) unanticipated hypotheses developed during and as a result of the interview process.

A priori hypotheses were related to motivation, components of communicative competence, and the role of direct instruction (including changing needs across the proficiency spectrum). They included:

(1) the most successful language learners are motivated in integrative (attraction to the culture) and intrinsic (interest in language study, love of learning) ways;

(2) critical factors for reaching Level 4 include sociocultural and sociolinguistic competence;

(3) Level-4 language users have unified personalities (not dual ones) in both L1 and L2 cultures (emotional competence); and

(4) self-study and social interactions (i.e. comprehensible input) have a greater impact on language acquisition at higher levels than does direct instruction.

Unanticipated hypotheses developed during the interview process were related to multiculturalism, short-term memory load, skill integration, authenticity, and changes in native-speaker attitudes toward language learners. Questions were added to the later interviews, and earlier interviewees were reinterviewed on these topics, in order to test these hypotheses. They included:

(1) multicultural experience is important for high-level language achievement;
(2) short-term memory capacity increases with automaticity, and a strong ability to hold new information in long-term memory while communicating is typical of Level 4;
(3) skills are integrated, with literacy contributing more than speaking practice to achieving Level 4 in speaking;
(4) access to authentic materials is critical to reaching high levels of proficiency; and
(5) attitudes of native speakers toward language learners change as proficiency increases.

Statistical analysis and manner of data interpretation

No statistical analysis has been done to date. Coding is beginning, but a larger sample size is anticipated before undertaking a statistical analysis. For the purposes of this early report, percentage statistics (rounded to the nearest whole number) have been calculated for qualitative data that could be readily quantified.

Preliminary results

The results reported here have proved to be strongly characteristic of this particular group of language users. The researchers are not yet ready to generalize them to all Level-4 language users and will continue to test the hypotheses related to them. Table 13.1 lists those attributes, experiences, factors, and opinions that characterize at least 75% of the population.

Motivation

We considered two kinds of categorizations of motivation: instrumental vs. integrative and intrinsic vs. extrinsic. Our initial hypothesis, in keeping with research on foreign language students at lower levels of proficiency, was that integrative motivation would be the strongest (Gardner and Lambert [1972]), and that intrinsic motivation would be high. The interviews, however, revealed a very different situation. Less than half of the Level-4 language users reported integrative (38%) or intrinsic (48%) motivation. Further, none of the interviewees reporting intrinsic motivation described an achievement orientation; rather, they were polyglots with a genuine interest in foreign language study.

The overwhelming majority (82%) reported, instead, instrumental motivation. For the most part, the motivation was to acquire a skill needed to

Table 13.1

Attributes of Level-4 speakers	
Polyglotism	100%
Instrumental motivation	82%
Use of authentic texts in preparation	100%
Check presentations with native speaker	77%
Want feedback	80%
Unified bicultural personality	75%
Focus on sociolinguistics in speaking	90%
Loading of short-term memory	94%
Experiences of Level-4 speakers	
Bi(multi)cultural childhood	100%
Foreign degree	77%
Native speaker attitude change	89%
Factors contributing to proficiency	
Direct instruction	100%
In-country experience	86%
Informal conversations with NS	100%
Improved grammar	80%
Improved vocabulary	80%
Improved sociocultural competence	95%
Training in reading	86%
Training in writing	92%
Training in listening	77%
Extensive independent reading	95%
Improvement in formal language	83%
Opinion re study at 3+/4 level	
Very different from lower levels	85%
Can/should be taught	77%

accomplish a specific job. At least one interviewee commented that if his only purpose in learning a foreign language was to integrate with the culture, he could have stopped learning at Level 3.

We did observe a language-specific trend: American learners of Russian and Arabic were more likely to exhibit extrinsic or instrumental motivation, whereas European learners of English were more likely to report integrative motivation. As the study continues, this trend will be further analyzed to determine whether it is unique to this group or more widespread.

Sociocultural competence

We expected sociocultural competence to be an important factor in reaching Level 4. This expectation was based on our own language-learning experiences, as well as input from a symposium on Level-4 reading held by the NFLC in May 2001 (see Ingold [this volume] for a description of the factors – Generic Learning Profiles – for Level-4 reading that were developed at that seminar).

The results were as anticipated. Included on the list of twenty (exclusive of the category, "other") pre-identified, potential factors critical to reaching Level 4 were the seven components of communicative competence described in other chapters of this volume (see Leaver and Shekhtman; Ingold): linguistic competence (grammar and vocabulary), sociolinguistic competence, discourse competence, sociocultural competence, strategic competence, emotional competence, and social competence. Of these, sociocultural competence was rated by interviewees as the most important factor in reaching Level 4. It was rated as critical by 95% of the interviewees, compared to refined grammar (80%) and improved precision of lexis (80%).

These results were obtained not only through the rating of suggested factors. Sociocultural competence was mentioned without prompting by interviewees themselves in the open-ended questions. All interviewees noted the need for cultural appropriateness in informal speaking and in tailoring their presentations to the cultural background of their audience.

Sociolinguistic competence

Similarly, we expected sociolinguistic competence to be an important factor, based on our own language-learning experiences, input from the NFLC Level-4 reading symposium, and the description of Level 4 in the ILR standards. As expected, sociolinguistic competence, especially register, figured strongly in the interviews. While a slightly lower percentage of the interviewees (74%) rated register as an important factor in reaching Level 4, most (90%) said that in speaking they focused principally on sociolinguistics and the social appropriateness of the intercourse, as opposed to mechanics (21%), ideas (26%), or simultaneous processing of content and mechanics (53%). This concern for social appropriateness may be one of the components of the attribute that Kramsch (1996) calls "politeness": switching behavioral genres to match C2 (i.e., foreign culture) social norms. A number of interviewees described specific instances in which they found it necessary to tailor language to particular individuals or circumstances.

Emotional competence

Emotional competence – being able to express one's own personality and emotional states in culturally appropriate ways – is a newly suggested component of communicative competence (Eshkembeeva [1997]) and may be another component of politeness – the pragmatic-linguistic decision to follow or flout social norms for affective goals. Although there is a widespread assumption in the foreign language field that a bifurcation of personality accompanies language gain – i.e., that a proficient L2 speaker has a different personality in C1 than in C2 – based on our own language-learning experience we expected a unification of personality across cultures. In our experience, at very high levels the two personalities elide, and we based our hypothesis on this.

The results confirmed the hypothesis: only 5% reported no change in personality. Likewise, very few (20%) reported a "dual" personality, one per culture. Rather, the majority (75%) reported a unified, bicultural personality. A number reported going through a process from single personality to dual to bicultural; for the most part, they noted that it was at Level 4 that the elision occurred. They considered very important the ability to express their personality in C2 in such a way that they would be perceived by native speakers of C2 similarly to the way in which they are perceived by native speakers of C1, be that for purposes of persuasion, argumentation, manipulation, deception, insinuation, seduction, intimidation, expressions of anger or joy, or any other affective motive. Beyond negotiation of meaning, they were able (and wanted) to use words, gestures, and behaviors in telic ways.

Role of direct instruction

In keeping with current learning theory, we expected self-study and social interactions (i.e., comprehensible and personalized input) to have a greater impact than direct instruction (Krashen [1985]; Pienemann [1985]), anticipating that nonsystematic variability would be regularized and systematized through in-country and at-work intensive exposure (Towell, Hawkins, and Bazergui [1993]). In this hypothesis, we were probably also influenced by our knowledge that 15 of the 20 interviewees had not had formal instruction in L2 at the 3+ level.

The results from this group of interviewees, however, did not support that hypothesis. In fact, 100% of the interviewees considered direct instruction essential to reaching Level 4. Although all of the interviewees learned their L2 through a grammar–translation approach, the teachers in the group were split in how they currently teach. Some continue to use the traditional methods that they consider worked for them; others prefer communicative methods.

Most interviewees noted that the instruction was early in their language-learning careers and provided an essential base upon which communicative experiences later built. Although only five had had instruction at Level 3+ (and considered it essential), 77% of the remaining interviewees felt that a class at this time, appropriately tailored, would have cut down on the many years it took most to reach Level 4; 85% felt that such a class should look very different from classes at earlier levels. Specific activities that they suggested include:

(1) combining classroom work with interaction in the C2 community, with the classroom providing structure and sociocultural–sociolinguistic information needed to accomplish specific tasks and feedback on *faux pas*;

(2) reading very sophisticated materials that are highly embedded with culture: ideas that are often understood but rarely put into writing directly, idiosyncratic expression of thought, unusual authorial intents, uncommon erudition, connotative meanings that differ from denotative ones, and the like;

(3) watching contemporary films and explaining the nonlinguistic behavior, register, and sociocultural phenomena encountered in them;

(4) writing academic papers and articles for publication, as well as, where appropriate, creative writing;

(5) tailored, content-based instruction that focuses on the specific professional linguistic needs of individual students, such as work with the discourse, grammar, and vocabulary to be used in the preparation (or rewrite) of treaties and ongoing negotiations;

(6) practicing the mechanisms for successful persuasion and argumentation;

(7) making formal oral presentations (as preparation and rehearsal for a public presentation to native speakers);

(8) analysis of the language used for various registers, including acquisition of words that are "not in the dictionary": slang, obscenities, kitchen talk, dialects;

(9) stylistic analysis and production of creative works that emulate the styles of various authors;

(10) development of a greater reserve of cultural knowledge (including the stories and games learned as children) and political history and the language that accompanies it;

(11) interpreting nonverbal behavior and learning to use it appropriately;

(12) learning how to be a good observer of linguistic and cultural behavior, i.e., learning how to learn from the authentic environment (as opposed to simply coping with it).

Moreover, though this population could be considered near-native, they continued to want correction. Since they were perceived as friends and colleagues, rather than as foreigners and language students, by representatives of C2, the 80% that wanted native speaker feedback complained they rarely received it, even when they asked for it, except when they asked for specific proofreading of outlines, slides, or other materials related to a pending formal oral presentation.

Multiculturalism

Since early demographic information showed these high-level language learners to have some kind of multicultural background, we quickly developed the hypothesis that early multicultural experience is important for high-level foreign language achievement. The venues in which this experience occurred were home, school, community, and workplace, and we, therefore, proposed to examine each of the venues as a factor in achieving Level-4 language proficiency. In total, 100% of the interviewees had had multicultural experience of some sort before the age of twenty.

More than one-third (35%) came from families where more than one language was spoken. Two-thirds (66.67%) grew up in bilingual or multilingual communities. (In some cases, the languages of the family and/or community were not the same as the Level-4 language for which the interviewee was being interviewed; in these cases, they reported that the influence of the family or community was a broadening of their understanding of communication – that it can take many linguistic and cultural forms – and this prepared them for any language study.)

Most interviewees travel abroad on a regular basis (57%). Even more (62%) had worked abroad or married a native speaker of their foreign language (48%).

In keeping with what has been learned from studies of study-abroad gains (Brecht, Davidson, Ginsberg [1993]), we hypothesized that authentic experience is important. We, therefore, expected to find much study-abroad experience in the group. Quite surprisingly, only two interviewees had studied abroad in programs for foreign students. (We are not yet ready to try to explain the significance of study-abroad experiences; we have no information whether this group is typical or atypical of Level-4 language learners in its absence of study-abroad experience.) Alternatively, 76% had earned a foreign degree, typically an advanced degree. They reported that being in the foreign educational system together with native speakers and without the support system typically offered to foreigners was a very important contribution to their language proficiency and cultural understanding. (One mentioned that he was required to attend a speech therapy class for two years together with students with speech defects because of his accent; he now has no foreign accent when he speaks, although he first started language study postpuberty.)

There was a small subset of learners who had reached Level 4 with very limited time in the foreign country. When we explored how they managed to reach this level without authentic experience, it turned out that all were very actively involved in the expatriate/immigrant community at home. In short, not one learner reached Level 4 in cultural isolation. (This could, of course, be either a cause or an effect.)

Short-term memory load

In interviewing Level-4 language users, one characteristic appeared time and again for which we did not even have a label. This was the ability to hold new information (vocabulary, structure, content) in short-term memory while continuing to interact in the language and ultimately acquiring and using the new information on the spot. We labeled this attribute short-term memory load, although we might have labeled it as a form of automaticity, as well. We hypothesized that this ability is critical to Level-4 language use, and 94% did, indeed, describe this attribute. From a purely psychological point of view, it is unlikely that the memories of these individuals improved. Rather, as the processing of language and meaning have become automatic, there is no longer competition for cognitive resources when new linguistic information comes in while talking or interacting.

Skill integration

There is a widely held assumption that one learns to speak by speaking. We considered that a given, but we collected data, anyway, especially once evidence of the importance of skill integration, not separation, began to appear early in the interview process. Our new hypothesis, then, contradicted traditional thinking. We considered that perhaps one learns to speak less by speaking and more by reading and writing.

Reading and writing skills may become increasingly more important as proficiency improves. Although all of the interviewees considered informal conversations with native speakers (including a wide representation of social classes) to be essential to reaching Level 3 (thereby providing a platform for continuing on to Level 4), only 25% considered this kind of language and activity essential to reaching Level 4. Rather, most (83%) considered formal aspects of language – writing (92%) and reading (86%) – more important. Almost all (95%) read "promiscuously," to use the words of one interviewee. When questioned directly, many stated that once they had reached Level 3/3+, reading and writing improved not only their reading and writing proficiency but also their speaking proficiency, even without additional oral practice. Some of them (77%) felt that listening also helped, but not quite as much.

Authenticity

Another hypothesis, in keeping with current SLA theory, was that authentic materials are critical to reaching high levels of proficiency. This hypothesis was confirmed. Not only did interviewees report talking to a wide range of native speakers and reading a wide range of text types, but they also preferred the use of authentic materials to references and dictionaries in preparing formal presentations. Authentic materials – articles downloaded from the Internet and books on related topics – were the resource of choice for 100% of the interviewees. Only 47% – typically translators and interpreters – reported using dictionaries and more traditional aids, whereas 77% preferred to check with native speakers (that figure was higher for those with test scores of Level 4, and lower for those with scores of 4+ and 5 – the latter tended to trust their own language skills and typically checked with neither reference nor native speaker).

Change in native-speaker attitudes

We had not originally thought to consider changes in native-speaker attitudes toward foreign language learners. This was another topic that emerged from the first interviews. Early on, then, we added the hypothesis that native speakers' attitudes toward language learners do change as proficiency moves from Level 3 to Level 4. As it turned out, 89% confirmed that hypothesis.

Many noted that at Level 4, they have been treated like just any other native speaker "with all the good and bad implications of that," to cite one interviewee. For 77%, that meant that they were more readily accepted into the culture. One interviewee related that his French relatives began to "let their hair hang down" when he reached Level 4. Another interviewee related that she was simply expected to know things that come with growing up in a culture: once she had found herself reciting a ditty in the center of a child's circle game with teachers from C2, and another time was handed a guitar at a party with people she had just met with the expectation that she would be able to play a C2 folk song (and she, fortunately, could).

What many have noted is that the compliments on their language skills become fewer and even, in some cases, disappear. As one interviewee stated, if an interlocutor pays a compliment, it means that s/he is aware that the language user is a foreigner. Actually, for 41%, "compliments turn to criticism," in the words of one interviewee, as any *faux pas* is interpreted as intentional behavior, cultural misunderstanding is considered to be intent to offend, and linguistic error is met with surprise and, sometimes, irritation. This seems to vary by language, with Russian language users most frequently reporting instances of criticism and Arabic language users least frequently. This is an area that needs greater exploration.

Discussion

Given that this study is in its very initial stages, we are reluctant to make many claims in relation to what we have found. There are, of course, concepts and findings for speaking, as well as for the other three skills, that we have not included in this chapter simply because they are not yet clear, i.e., not confirmed by at least 75% of the interviewed population. (Other hypotheses are still being tested.) As a maximum, at this point in time, we feel confident in stating only that important roles are played by literacy, direct instruction, and authenticity and that issues of motivation (the research findings that have now become a matter of assumption in SLA) might well need to be reexamined. We would also suggest that reaching Level 4 might be a different process than reaching Level 3, and that teaching to Level 4, as Leaver and Shekhtman (this volume) contend and other authors in this volume illustrate, is not more of the same.

Role of literacy

Foreign language instruction does not often include the development of literacy skills, except in the case of heritage learners. In fact, with the advent of the communicative approaches, speaking has been given priority in many classrooms, perhaps unwisely (Byrnes, Chapter 2, this volume). Writing is not only rarely instructed, but very few materials exist in any language with which to teach writing skills – especially of the kind needed to reach Level 4: ability to write within the framework of various genres and an understanding of L2 written discourse. However, the experiences of the Level-4 language users in this study point to a critical role for literacy even for the development of oral skills at highly advanced levels; perhaps the segregation of skills (or at least, the distancing of the writing skill) that has taken place in communicative classrooms needs to be revisited. When the teaching of literacy should begin is a topic for another article and one that may require considerably greater research. Nonetheless, literacy clearly must be achieved by the time a student approaches the 3+/4 threshold.

Role of instruction

The importance that Level-4 language learners placed on direct instruction is very likely a surprise for most proponents of communicative approaches to learning – or at least for those who advocate a "Natural Approach" (Krashen and Terrell [1983]) or a natural order of acquisition (Pienemann [1985]). What those who made it to near-native levels are telling us is that they did not do it alone, that teacher input was essential, and that it did not even matter that the teacher decided the order of presentation and required rote work. This will not be surprising for some. Schultz (2001) questioned more than 600 students and teachers in Colombia and the USA and found that the majority of students in both countries wanted various aspects of direct instruction; teachers, too, considered grammar instruction and most, but not all, kinds of error correction essential. Robinson (1997) found that automaticity of second language forms occurred more regularly and more quickly when students were encouraged or allowed to focus on form.

Instruction can take many forms, however, and the feedback from the Level-4 language learners in this group, all of whom cut their teeth, so to speak, in grammar–translation classrooms, raises more questions than it answers. Would, for example, a communicative approach in their Novice years have allowed them to reach higher levels faster? Or is time on task an inevitable adjunct to direct instruction at this level? We will not know until we can identify and interview a group of Level-4 language learners who began their cross-cultural journey in communicative programs.

Was it the classroom drills that allowed the learners in this study to develop the automaticity needed to hold information in short-term memory and communicate at the same time (parallel processing)? Or was it simply practice time and time on task? The interviewees were almost evenly split in their view of the role that grammar played in their language acquisition. While most felt that a refined knowledge of grammar was essential, some achieved it through grammar practice, others through drill, and yet others through explanation alone and observation. DeKeyser (1997), in agreement with the first two subsets of the population in this study, suggests that automaticity is built gradually through practice. He also suggests that automatic control does not auto-develop: "The ability to comprehend or produce sentences in a second language is not necessarily acquired through the implicit mechanisms of a separate mental model (as is generally accepted for first language acquisition)" (pp. 211–212). He characterizes automaticity as a reduction in reaction time and error rate and diminished interference from focusing on mechanics when simultaneously completing other tasks. In most cases, interviewees in the study reported in this chapter describe their own language processes in ways that DeKeyser would label automatized, and we would note that the teaching framework described by Shekhtman et al. (this volume) is based, in part, on the development of automaticity. Robinson (1997), in agreement with the third subset in this study (those who learned through explanation and observation), suggests that there is actually a complicated interaction between automatization and rule-based generalizability that depends on the conditions of learning – implicit, incidental, enhanced, or instructed – and that memory-based implicit knowledge is fast but limited in generalizability and other learned knowledge may be slow but more generalizable. His conclusion is very much in keeping with the opinions of the Level-4 learners in this study: "Instructed learning of rules results

in generalizable knowledge and fast decision-making about new sentences"
(p. 246).

If, then, direct instruction (including explanation and supervised language
practice) is critical, at what level is it most important? That, too, is unclear.
All interviewees had direct instruction at beginning levels, and all insisted that
dispensing with instruction is simply not possible if one aspires to Level 4. One
quarter of the interviewees also had instruction at the 3+/4 boundary, and all
of them thought that instruction at that level was important (although several
without that experience did not consider that the experience would have made a
difference). A larger sample size and more in-depth questioning will be required
in order to explore further whether instruction at Level 3/3+ will reduce the
length of time required to reach Level 4 and higher. (We would note, however,
that various authors in this volume make a convincing case for the usefulness
of direct instruction at this level.)

Role of authenticity

Authenticity in all its forms – locale, native speakers, materials – clearly is
a critical and, apparently, irreplaceable component in learning programs for
students aiming at Level-4 proficiency. There are many aspects of authenticity
to be explored. There is a qualitative difference between teachers providing
students with articles from newspapers to read and parse or to use for assigned
tasks in the classroom and language learners seeking representative articles
from the foreign press to serve as a template for their own professional writing.
There is also a qualitative difference between study abroad in a classroom for
foreigners and studying in C2 high schools, colleges, and graduate programs
alongside native speakers. Is the latter required, as this group of interviewees
would indicate, or is the former an acceptable substitute? Again, data needs to
be collected from a larger group of Level-4 language learners.

What is clear from this group is the very strong influence that authenticity had
and has on their language proficiency. They have graduated from dependence on
dictionaries (although nearly half still do use them at times – both monolingual
and bilingual dictionaries) and prefer to use articles and books published in
C2. Clearly, a part of this preference is that an article provides the full discourse
model, whereas a dictionary supplies little more than a missing word. Given
that few L2 programs teach discourse competence, perhaps these language
learners are learning text structure of various genres through a form of self-
study – which they can accomplish because they already possess the linguistic
system and, to a great extent, the cultural code of L2–C2. (This is perhaps
not unlike the native speaker who must produce a document in an unfamiliar
genre; it is not uncommon in such cases for a native speaker to ask for a
sample.)

Reevaluating motivation

Given the surprising response in the area of motivation, we suggest continuing research into the kinds of motivation that will take a student from Level 3 to Level 4 – to determine whether that differs from the kind of motivation that propels students to achieve Level 3. After all, many people who use language professionally work their entire lives without surpassing Level 3. Can this phenomenon be explained, in part, by differing kinds of motivation? Have we, for too many years, underrated the strength of instrumental motivation? One interviewee, who reported an exclusively instrumental motivation, stated that the language was interesting but the culture "unsavory." Several interviewees spend as little time as possible in C2 – and some have not been back since achieving Level 4 – because of a strong dislike for the culture, yet they reliably serve as cross-cultural consultants, sometimes in very important positions, and remain abreast of cultural change through expatriates, television broadcasts, and newspaper articles. Is perhaps the kind of motivation to some extent predicated on C1–C2 political relations or the extent of differences in cultural values? In other words, is it possible that the kind of motivation that results in successful language acquisition will vary by language? Would one learner have a different motivation in learning L3 from that in learning L2? In some instances in this study, that is, indeed, the case. However, there are not enough instances to report even a "finding" of this nature, let alone generalize it. Further investigation, not only with additional learners, but with learners with Level-4 proficiency in multiple languages, is needed.

Recommendations for teachers

Most of the recommendations fell into the sociocultural and sociolinguistic domains, and, to a lesser extent in the areas of emotional, discourse, and linguistic competences. Whether it happens in a classroom or in some other venue, one thing is clear: even at Level 4, language users desire feedback. Most want correction, and when it is not naturally forthcoming, they seek it out. They want their *faux pas* explained, and they want to make sure that their oral performance, especially in formal situations, is as close to that of the educated native speaker as possible – and they check their presentation materials and outlines with native speakers. They are not looking for correction of errors that interfere with meaning; that does not happen very often at this level. Rather, they are looking for correction of language that is imprecise, not *à propos*, or lacking in erudition. Many of the recommendations made by interviewees are very much in line with the contents of the programs described in earlier chapters of this volume, and we would refer readers to those chapters for ideas in establishing their own programs at Level 3+/4.

Conclusion

For too long, teaching methods have been informed by the paradigm of the moment – usually influenced by current educational policies in areas other than foreign language, reactions against previous methods that "did not work" in the minds of the current crop of teachers, advances in linguistic and psychological theory, and research on students in beginning programs. Few researchers, if any, have explored what Level-4 language proficiency is and how individuals achieve it. Yet, that understanding would seem to be a very important base upon which to build a language program – especially if, as some evidence appears to suggest, some of the students who struggle early in the language-learning process actually reach the highest levels.[7] Such highly proficient learners have much they can reveal of value, if we can appropriately formulate the questions to ask them.

This study has many questions to be answered. What, for example, are the factors critical for reaching this level? How many are generalizable? One multi-literate writer contends that "every bilingual and multilingual person will have a highly personal and idiosyncratic linguistic past" (Belcher and Connor [2001, p. 59]). Does that mean, though, that there will not be at least some common elements? We think that there will be – ones that can be defined and even some that can be taught. We have seen this so far in this study. In analyzing the uniqueness of each learner's path to Level 4, we would ask about the role played by learning style, personality type, or other individual variables. Also, how much difference does early onset of language training really make? Many of the interviewees in this study took their first language lesson in their L2 as an adult, but those who started earlier did not reach Level 4 until adulthood, and some who started as children reached it no younger than those who started as adults. Is Level 4, by definition, "adult language"? What is the range of attributes associated with Level-4 behavior? The ILR provides a general description, not a detailed one. Is there a set of language aptitude factors that define who will be a successful language learner at higher levels that differs from the traits displayed by successful learners at lower levels? (We have some evidence of this, but not enough yet to report on it.) These questions and dozens more are being addressed in this study. Only a few have been reported in this chapter; only

---

[7] There is some evidence from a multi-year study of Russian students conducted at the FSI in the 1980s (Leaver [1986]) that indicates that individual differences that advantage a learner in the beginning stages of language learning (such as right-brain dominance and more global learning) can, in turn, disadvantage them in achieving higher levels, and that some of those who struggle at lower levels (especially, left-hemisphere-dominant and analytic students who often do not tolerate ambiguity well) may blossom and outperform their peers in a tortoise vs. hare fashion once they have passed Level-3 proficiency. Correlation of early data on such attributes as learning style and tolerance of ambiguity with interviewee feedback indicates that teachers' typical characterization of the traits of the "good learner" in pre-3 classes does not fully match the traits that we are finding in the Level-4 population. That, too, of course, awaits further elucidation.

a few have shown clear trends. Many answers, instead, have raised additional questions and suggested topics not previously considered.

This study has several limitations, some of which will disappear with time and an increasing pool of interviewees. First, all findings are preliminary; more time and a larger population may change the results. Second, the pool is small – not just the pool of those we have interviewed, but the pool of Level-4 language learners in general. Third, locating Level-4 speakers is difficult. Except for US government testing records, no lists of such learners are kept on file anywhere. Thus, in sampling the population, we do not know what percentage of the total population we really have sampled. Further, we need Level-4 speakers of multiple languages – even more rare – to determine what attributes are pertinent to one individual or to one language and which are generalizable. Fourth, in some cases, similar interviews need to be taken with Level 3+ speakers to identify the behaviors that separate the Level-4 speakers from lower levels; we have begun to do this. Fifth, not all Level-4 interviewees have understood the proficiency scale. Therefore, when we asked interviewees to identify changes in their behavior from Level 3+ to Level 4, not all could do that easily. Sixth, we have not yet been able to control for the variable of language distance. The early data from the interviewees here, who represent all categories of language difficulty, indicate that language distance issues have disappeared by this level, but will that trend hold with a larger group? We will need a much larger population, and one balanced among language categories to be able to comment on the importance (or lack of importance) of language distance.

We will be seeking answers to these questions and testing a large number of additional hypotheses with many more language users. Our goal is to reach a sample size large enough in each language that we can be confident that the results are representative of that language. When that goal is achieved, we should be able to present findings that are firm, not preliminary.

Nevertheless, the findings from this study, for which we have been unable to find a precedent, can do much to inform teaching practices at the 3+/4 level. We have found that there are stories to be told by language learners at this level, and those stories are varied, rich, and well worth the several hours of listening time it takes a language user to relate his or her experience. The findings, while only able to be considered as trends and preliminary at the moment, confirm assumptions and hypotheses in some cases and are quite surprising in others. Most important, the results, when ready, promise to provide reliable guidance in establishing programs and otherwise assisting proficient language users to become advanced professional users – to aim for that elusive "near-native" goal that is talked about frequently and achieved rarely.[8]

---

[8] Updated information about this study can be obtained at www.mindsolutionsinternational.com.

References

ACTFL. 1986. *ACTFL Proficiency Guidelines.* Yonkers, NY: American Council on the Teaching of Foreign Languages, Inc.

——— 1999. *Standards for Foreign Language Learning in the 21st Century.* Lawrence, KS: Allen Press.

Akishina, Alla, and Olga Kagan. 1997. *Uchimsya uchit'* ("We Learn to Teach"). Moscow: RAN.

Aliev, Nizami N., and Betty Lou Leaver. 1994. *A New Age in Two Lands: The Individual and Individualism in Foreign Language Instruction.* Salinas, CA: The AGSI Press.

Allott, Robin M. 1989. *The Motor Theory of Language Origin.* Sussex: Book Guild.

Angelelli, Claudia. 1996. "The Education of Translation/Interpretation Trainers: A Pedagogical Dilemma." Paper presented at the 37th Annual Conference of the American Translators Association in Colorado Springs, CO.

——— 2000. "Interpretation Pedagogy: A Bridge Long Overdue." *ATA (American Translator Association) Chronicle*: 40–47.

Aoki, Nacko. 1999. "Affect and the Role of the Teacher in the Development of Learner Autonomy." In *Affect in Language Learning*, ed. Jane Arnold. New York: Cambridge University Press, 142–154.

Appel, René, and Pieter Muysken. 1987. *Language Contact and Bilingualism.* London: Edward Arnold.

Arndt, Valerie. 1987. "Six Writers in Search of Texts: A Protocol-Based Study of L1 and L2 Writing." *ELT Journal* 41(4): 257–267.

Atkins, Paul B., and Alan D. Baddeley. 1998. "Working Memory and Distributed Vocabulary Learning." *Applied Psycholinguistics* 19(4): 537–552.

Bachman, Lyle F. 1990. *Fundamental Considerations in Language Testing.* Oxford: Oxford University Press.

Badawi, Elsaid. 1985. "Educated Spoken Arabic: A Problem in Teaching Arabic as a Foreign Language." In *Scientific and Humanistic Dimensions of Language: Festschrift for Robert Lado on the Occasion of His 70th Birthday on May 31, 1985*, ed. K. Jankowsky. Philadelphia: J. Benjamin, 15–22.

Bailey, Kathleen M. 1983. "Competitiveness and Anxiety in Adult Second Language Learning: Looking at and through the Diary Studies." In *Classroom-Oriented Research in Second Language Acquisition*, ed. H. W. Seliger and Michael H. Long. Rowley, MA: Newbury House, 67–103.

Bakhtin, Mikhail M. 1986a. "The Problem of Speech Genres." In *Speech Genres and Other Late Essays*, ed. Caryl Emerson and Michael Holquist. Austin: University of Texas Press, 60–102.

1986b. "The Problem of the Text in Linguistics, Philology, and the Human Sciences: An Experiment in Philosophical Analysis." In *Speech Genres and Other Late Essays*, ed. Caryl Emerson and Michael Holquist. Austin: University of Texas Press, 103–131.

Bazerman, Charles. 1988. *Shaping Written Knowledge. The Genre and Activity of the Experimental Article in Science*. Madison, WI: University of Wisconsin Press.

Becker, Alton L. 1995. *Beyond Translation: Essays toward a Modern Philology*. Ann Arbor: University of Michigan Press.

Beebe, Leslie M. 1988. *Issues in Second Language Acquisition: Multiple Perspectives*. New York: Newbury House.

Belcher, Diane, and Ulla Connor. 2001. *Reflections on Multiliterate Lives*. Buffalo: Multilingual Matters.

Benson, Phil, and Peter Voller, eds. 1997. *Autonomy and Independence in Language Learning*. Harlow: Longman.

Berkenkotter, Carol, and Thomas N. Huckin. 1995. *Genre Knowledge in Disciplinary Communication*. Hillsdale, NJ: Lawrence Erlbaum.

Bermel, Neil, and Olga Kagan. 2000. "The Maintenance of Written Russian in Heritage Speakers." In *The Learning and Teaching of Slavic Languages and Cultures*, ed. Olga Kagan and Benjamin Rifkin. Bloomington, IN: Slavica Publishers, 405–436.

Bernhardt, Elizabeth B., and Michael L. Kamil. 1995. "Interpreting Relationships between L1 and L2 Reading: Consolidating Linguistic Threshold and the Linguistic Interdependence Hypotheses." *Applied Linguistics* 16(1): 15–34.

Bialystok, Ellen. 1981. "The role of Linguistic Knowledge in Second Language use." *Studies in Second Language Learning* 4(1): 31–45.

Bialystok, Ellen, and Kenji Hakuta. 1994. *In Other Words: The Science and Psychology of Second-Language Acquisition*. New York: Basic Books.

Birdsong, David. 1992. "Ultimate Attainment in Second Language Acquisition." *Language* 68(4): 707–755.

ed. 1999. *Second Language Acquisition and the Critical Period Hypothesis*. Mahwah, NJ: Lawrence Erlbaum.

Bloom, Benjamin S. 1956. *Taxonomy of Educational Objectives*. New York: McKay.

1968. *Learning for Mastery*. Los Angeles, CA: University of California, UCLA-CSEIP Evaluation Comment.

Bloomfield, Leonard. 1933. *Language*. New York: Holt, Rinehart and Winston.

Bogdan, Robert, and S. K. Biklen. 1992. *Qualitative Research for Education: An Introduction to Theory and Methods*. Boston: Allyn and Bacon.

Boyd, Rossana R. 2000. "Attitudes of Teachers of Spanish as a Foreign Language Toward Teaching Spanish to Hispanic Students." Ph.D. dissertation. Baton Rouge: LA State University.

Brecht, Richard D., Dan E. Davidson, and Ralph B. Ginsberg. 1993. *Predictors of Foreign Language Gain During Study Abroad*. Washington, DC: National Foreign Language Center.

Brecht, R. D., and V. M. Frank. 2000. *Impact of In-country Study on Language Ability: National Security Education Program Undergraduate Scholarship and Graduate Fellowship Recipients*. Washington, DC: The National Foreign Language Center.

Brecht, Richard D., and Catherine W. Ingold. 1998. "Tapping a National Resource: Heritage Learners in the United States." In *ERIC Digest*. Washington, DC: ERIC Clearinghouse on Languages and Linguistics.

2000. "Literacy, Numeracy, and Linguacy: Language and Culture and General Education." *Liberal Education* 86(4): 30–39.

Brecht, Richard D., and William P. Rivers. 2000. *Language and National Security in the 21st Century*. Washington, DC: Kendall Hunt and National Foreign Language Center.

Brecht, Richard D., and A. Ronald Walton. 1993. *National Strategic Planning in the Less Commonly Taught Languages. NFLC Occasional Papers*. Washington, DC: National Foreign Language Center.

1994. "The Future Shape of Language Learning in the New World of Global Communication: Consequences for Higher Education and Beyond." In *Foreign Language Learning: The Journey of a Lifetime*, ed. Richard Donato and Robert M. Terry. Lincolnwood, IL: National Textbook Company.

Breiner-Sanders, Karen E., Pardee Lowe, Jr., John Miles, and Elvira Swender. 2000. "ACTFL Proficiency Guidelines – Speaking. Revised 1999." *Foreign Language Annals* 33(1): 13–18.

Brod, Richard, and Elizabeth Welles. 2000. "Foreign Language Enrollments in United States Institutions of Higher Education, Fall 1998." *ADFL Bulletin* 31(2): 87–93.

Brown, H. Douglas. 1994. *Principles of Language Learning and Teaching*. Englewood Cliffs, NJ: Prentice Hall Regents.

Bygate, Martin, Peter Skehan, and Merrill Swain. 2001. *Researching Pedagogic Tasks: Second Language Learning, Teaching and Testing*. London: Longman.

Byrnes, Heidi. 1996. "The Future of German in American Education." *Die Unterrichtspraxis* 29(2): 251–259.

1998. "Constructing Curricula in Collegiate Foreign Language Departments." In *Learning Foreign and Second Languages: Perspectives in Research and Scholarship*, ed. Heidi Byrnes. New York: MLA, 262–295.

1999. "Meaning and Form in Classroom-Based SLA Research: Reflections from a College Foreign Language Perspective." In *Meaning and Form: Multiple Perspectives*, ed. James F. Lee and Albert Valdman. Boston: Heinle and Heinle, 125–179.

2000a. "Languages across the Curriculum – Intradepartmental Curriculum Construction: Issues and Options." In *Languages across the Curriculum: Interdisciplinary Structures and Internationalized Education*, ed. Maria-Regina Kecht and Katharina von Hammerstein. Columbus, OH: The Ohio State University Press, 151–176.

2000b. "Of Standards, Articulation, and Curriculum: Finding a New Narrative." *ACTR Letter* 26(4): 1, 3–5, 23–24.

2001a. "The Dialogism of Meaning, the Discursive Embeddedness of Knowledge, the Colloquy of Being." In *Hermeneutical Philosophy of Science, van Gogh's Eyes, and God: Essays in Honor of Patrick A. Heelan, S. J.*, ed. Babich E. Babette. Dordrecht: Kluwer, 409–420.

2001b. "Reconsidering Graduate Students' Education as Teachers: It Takes a Department!" *Modern Language Journal* 85(4): 512–530.

Byrnes, Heidi, Cori Crane, and Katherine A. Sprang. 2002, in press. "Nonnative Teachers Teaching at the Advanced Level: Challenges and Opportunities." *ADFL Bulletin*.

Byrnes, Heidi, and Susanne Kord. 2001. "Developing Literacy and Literary Competence: Challenges for Foreign Language Departments." In *SLA and the Literature*

Classroom: Fostering Dialogues, ed. Virginia M. Scott and Holly Tucker. Boston: Heinle and Heinle, 31–69.

Calvin, William H., and George A. Ojemann. 1994. *Conversations with Neil's Brain.* Reading, MA: Addison-Wesley.

Campbell, Russell, and Joy K. Peyton. 1998. "Heritage Students: A Valuable Language Resource." *ERIC Review* 6(1): 31–35.

Canale, Michael, and Merrill Swain. 1980. "Theoretical Bases of Communicative Approaches to Second Language Teaching and Testing." *Applied Linguistics* 1(1): 8–24.

Carroll, Mary. 1997. "Changing Place in English and German: Language-Specific Preferences in the Conceptualization of Spatial Relations." In *Language and Conceptualization*, ed. Jan Nuyts and Eric Pederson. Cambridge: Cambridge University Press.

——— 2000. "Representing Path in Language Production in English and German: Alternative Perspectives on Figure and Ground." In *Räumliche Konzepte und sprachliche Strukturen*, ed. Christopher Habel and Christiane von Stutterheim. Tübingen: Niemeyer, 97–118.

Caudery, Tim. 1995a. "Multiple Drafting and Second Language Writing Skills." Unpublished doctoral dissertation, University of Aarhus, Denmark.

——— 1995b. "What the 'Process Approach' Means to Practicing Teachers of Second Language Writing Skills." *TESL-EJ* 1(4): A3. http://www.jyotosu.ac.jp/ information/ tesl-ej/ej04/a3.html.

Celce-Murcia, Marianne, Zoltán Dörnyei, and Sarah Thurrell. 1995. "Communicative Competence: A Pedagogically Motivated Model with Content Specifications." *Issues in Applied Linguistics* 6(2): 5–35.

Chafe, Wallace L. 1998. "Language and the Flow of Thought." In *The New Psychology of Language: Cognitive and Functional Approaches to Language Structure*, ed. Michael Tomasello. Mahwah, NJ: Lawrence Erlbaum, 93–111.

Chamot, Anna Uhl, and J. Michael O'Malley. 1994. *The CALLA Handbook: Implementing the Cognitive Academic Language Learning Approach.* New York: Addison Wesley.

Chaput, Patricia. 2000. "Fifteen Common Errors in Language Teaching; Assumptions and Strategies." In *Twelve Years of Dialogue on Teaching Russian: From the Front Pages of the ACTR Letter 1988–1999*, ed. Betty Lou Leaver. Washington, DC: ACTR/ACCELS Publishing, 283–299.

Charles, Maggie. 1990. "Feedback in the Writing Process: A Model and Methods for Implementation." *ELT Journal* 44(4): 286–293.

Child, James R. 1987. "Language Proficiency Levels and the Typology of Texts." In *Defining and Developing Proficiency: Guidelines, Implementations and Concepts*, ed. Heidi Byrnes and Michael Canale. Lincolnwood, IL: National Textbook Company, 97–106.

——— 1990. "Language Skills and Textual Norms across Languages." Paper presented at the annual meeting of the American Association of Teachers of Spanish and Portuguese, Miami, FL.

——— 1998. "Language Skill Levels, Textual Modes, and the Rating Process." *Foreign Language Annals* 31(3): 382–391.

Child, James R., Ray T. Clifford, and Pardee Lowe, Jr. 1993. "Proficiency and Performance in Language Testing." *Applied Language Learning* 4(1 & 2): 19–54.

Christie, Frances. 1989. "Language Development in Education." In *Language Development: Learning Language, Learning Culture*, ed. Ruqaiya Hasan and James R. Martin. Norwood, NJ: Ablex, 152–198.

———. 1999. "Genre Theory and ESL Teaching: A Systemic Functional Perspective." *TESOL Quarterly* 33(4): 759–763.

Clines, Frances S. 2001. "An Archipelago Called Russia." *New York Times*, April 8, Travel Section, 10, 18.

Cohen, Andrew D. 1998. *Strategies in Learning and Using a Second Language*. New York: Longman.

Collins, Allan, John S. Brown, and Susan E. Newman. 1989. "Cognitive Apprenticeship: Teaching the Craft of Reading, Writing, and Mathematics." In *Knowing, Learning, and Instruction: Essays in Honor of Robert Glaser*, ed. Lauren B. Resnick. Hillsdale, NJ: Lawrence Erlbaum, 453–494.

Cook, Vivian. 1992. "Evidence for Multicompetence." *Language Learning* 42(4): 557–591.

———. 1999. "Going Beyond the Native Speaker in Language Teaching." *TESOL Quarterly* 33(2): 185–209.

Cope, Bill, and Mary Kalantzis, eds. 1993. *The Powers of Literacy*. London and Washington: The Falmer Press.

Coppieters, René. 1987. "Competence Differences between Native and Near-Native Speakers." *Language* 63(3): 544–573.

Corin, Andrew. 1997. "A Course to Convert Czech Proficiency to Proficiency in Croatian and Serbian." In *Content-Based Instruction: Models and Methods*, ed. Stephen B. Stryker and Betty Lou Leaver. Washington, DC.: Georgetown University Press, 78–104.

Council of Europe Modern Languages Division. 2001. *Modern Languages: Learning, Teaching, Assessment. A Common European Framework of Reference*. Cambridge: Cambridge University Press.

Cowie, Anthony Paul, ed. 1998. *Phraseology: Theory, Analysis, and Application*. Oxford: Oxford University Press.

Crookes, Graham. 1986. *Task Classification: A Cross-Disciplinary Review*. Honolulu: University of Hawaii at Manoa, Social Science Research Institute, Center for Second Language Classroom Research (Technical Report No. 4).

Crookes, Graham, and Susan M. Gass, eds. 1993. *Tasks and Language Learning: Integrating Theory and Practice*. Clevedon: Multilingual Matters.

Cumming, Alister. 1989. "Writing Expertise and Second-Language Proficiency." *Language Learning* 39(1): 81–141.

Curran, Charles A. 1972. *Counseling Learning*. New York: Grune and Stratton.

Damasio, Anthony R., Hannah Damasio, D. Tranel, and J. Brandt. 1990. "Neural Regionalization of Knowledge Access: Preliminary Evidence." *Cold Spring Harbor Symposia on Quantitative Biology* 55: 1039–1047.

Damasio, Anthony R., and Norman Geschwind. 1984. "The Neural Basis of Language." *Annual Review of Neuroscience* 7(14): 127–147.

Dansereau, Donald. 1988. "Cooperative Learning Strategies." In *Learning and Study Strategies: Issues in Assessment, Instruction, and Evaluation*, ed. Claire E. Weinstein, Ernest T. Goetz, and Patricia A. Alexander. Orlando, FL: Academic Press, 103–120.

Deci, Edward L. 1992. "The Relation of Interest to the Motivation of Behaviour: A Self-determination Theory Perspective." In *The Role of Interest in Learning and Development,* ed. K. Ann Renninger, Suzanne Hidi, and Andreas Krapp. Hillsdale, NJ: Lawrence Erlbaum, 43–70.

Deci, Edward L., and R. M. Ryan. 1985. *Intrinsic Motivation and Self-Determination in Human Behavior.* New York: Plenum.

DeKeyser, Robert M. 1997. "Beyond Explicit Rule Learning: Automatizing Second Language Morphosyntax." *Studies in Second Language Acquisition* 19(2): 195–222.

1998. "Beyond Focus on Form: Cognitive Perspectives on Learning and Practicing Second Language." In *Focus on Form in Classroom Second Language Acquisition,* ed. Catherine Doughty and Jessica Williams. Cambridge: Cambridge University Press, 42–63.

Dew, James E. 1994. "Back to Basics: Let's Not Lose Sight of What's Really Important." *Journal of the Chinese Language Teachers Association* 19(2): 40–41.

Dewey, John. 1938. *Experience and Education.* New York: Collier Books.

Dickinson, Leslie, and Anita Wenden, eds. 1995. "Autonomy, Self-direction and Self-access in Language Teaching and Learning." Special issue of *System,* 23(2).

Doughty, Catherine. 1998. "Acquiring Competence in a Second Language: Form and Function." In *Learning Foreign and Second Languages: Perspectives in Research and Scholarship,* ed. Heidi Byrnes. New York: MLA, 128–156.

Doughty, Catherine, and Jessica Williams. 1998. "Pedagogical Choices in Focus on Form." In *Focus on Form in Classroom Second Language Acquisition,* ed. C. Doughty and Jessica Williams. Cambridge: Cambridge University Press, 197–261.

Draper, J., and J. Hicks. 2000. "Teaching Heritage Learners: The Road Traveled." In *Teaching Heritage Language Learners: Voices from the Classroom,* ed. John B. Webb and Barbara L. Miller. Yonkers, NY: American Council on Teaching Foreign Languages, 303–306.

Duri, Jayne. 1992. "Content-Based Instruction: Keeping DLI at the Cutting Edge." *Globe* 5: 4–5.

Ehrman, Madeline E. 1996. *Understanding Second Language Learning Difficulties.* Thousand Oaks, CA: Sage Publications.

1998. "The Learning Alliance: Conscious and Unconscious Aspects of the Second Language Teacher's Role." *System* 26(1): 93–106.

2000. "Affect, Cognition, and Learner Self-Regulation in Second Language Learning." In *The Learning and Teaching of Slavic Languages,* ed. Olga Kagan and Benjamin Rifkin. Bloomington, IN: Slavica Publishers, 109–134.

Ehrman, Madeline, and Zoltán Dörnyei. 1998. *Interpersonal Dynamics in Second Language Education: The Visible and Invisible Classroom.* Thousand Oaks, CA: Sage.

Ehrman, Madeline, and Betty Lou Leaver. 1997. "The E&L." Unpublished learning styles test.

Ely, Christopher. 1989. "Tolerance of Ambiguity and Use of Second Language Strategies." *Foreign Language Annals* 22: 437–446.

Esch, Edith. 1996. "Promoting Learner Autonomy: Criteria for the Selection of Appropriate Methods." In *Taking Control: Autonomy in Language Learning,* ed. Richard Pemberton, S. L. Edward, Winnie W. F. Or, and Herbert D. Pierson. Hong Kong: Hong Kong University Press, 35–48.

Eshkembeeva, Ludmila Vladimirovna. 1997. "Emotional Competence." Paper presented at MAPRIAL (International Association of Teachers of Russian Language and Literature) International Congress, Moscow.

Ferguson, Charles. 1959. "Diglossia." *Word* 15: 325–340.

Fillmore, Charles J. 1979. "On Fluency." In *Individual Differences in Language Ability and Language Behavior*, ed. Charles J. Fillmore, D. Kempler, and W. S.-Y. Wang. New York: Academic Press, 85–101.

Finlay, Ian. 1971. *Translating*. Edinburgh: The Edinburgh University Press.

Fishman, Joshua A., ed. 1978. *Advances in the Study of Societal Multilingualism*. The Hague: Mouton.

2002. "300-Plus Years of Heritage Language Education in the United States." In *Heritage Languages in America: Preserving a National Resource*, ed. Joy K. Peyton, Donald A. Ranard, and Scott McGinnis. Washington, DC: Delta Systems and Center for Applied Linguistics.

Freedman, Aviva. 1999. "Beyond the Text: Towards Understanding the Teaching and Learning of Genres." *TESOL Quarterly* 33(4): 764–767.

Freedman, Aviva, and Peter Medway, eds. 1994a. *Genre and the New Rhetoric*. London: Taylor and Francis.

1994b. *Learning and Teaching Genre*. Westport, CT: Heinemann.

Frith, James R. 1980. *Measuring Spoken Language Proficiency*. Washington, DC: Georgetown University Press.

Frodesen, Jan M., Christine Holten, Linda Jensen, and Lynn Repath-Martos. 1997. *Insights 2*. Ed. Donna M. Brinton. New York: Longman.

Gadamer, Hans-Georg. 1976. "The Nature of Things and the Language of Things." In *Philosophical Hermeneutics*, ed. David E. Linge. Berkeley: University of California Press, 69–81.

Gardner, Robert, and Wallace E. Lambert. 1972. *Attitudes and Motivation in Second Language Learning*. Rowley, MA: Newbury House Publishers.

Gass, Susan M., and Larry Selinker. 1994. *Second Language Acquisition: An Introductory Course*. Hillsdale, NJ: Lawrence Erlbaum Associates.

Gee, James P. 1986. "Orality and Literacy: From *The Savage Mind* to *Ways with Words*." *TESOL Quarterly* 20(4): 719–746.

1990. *Social Linguistics and Literacies: Ideology in Discourses*. London: The Falmer Press.

1998. "What is Literacy?" In *Negotiating Academic Literacies: Teaching and Learning across Languages and Cultures*, ed. Vivian Zamel and Ruth Spack. Mahwah, NJ: Lawrence Erlbaum, 51–59.

Gee, Smiljka. 1997. "Teaching Writing: A Genre-Based Approach." In *Writing in the English Language Classroom*, ed. G. Fulcher. Hemel Hempstead: Prentice Hall Europe ELT, 24–40.

Gerver, D. 1976. "Empirical Studies of Simultaneous Interpretation." In *Empirical Studies of Simultaneous Interpretation*, ed. R. W. Brislin. New York: Gardener Press, 165–207.

Gile, Daniel. 1995. *Basic Concepts and Models for Interpreter and Translator Training*. Amsterdam: John Benjamins.

Givón, Talmy. 1993. *English Grammar: A Function-Based Introduction*. 2 vols. Amsterdam/Philadelphia: John Benjamins.

Glaser, B. G., and A. Strauss. 1967. *The Discovery of Grounded Theory: Strategies for Qualitative Research.* Chicago: Aldine.

Gläser, R. 1998. "The Stylistic Potential of Phraseological Units in the Light of Genre Analysis." In *Phraseology: Theory, Analysis, and Application*, ed. Anthony Paul Cowie. Oxford: Clarendon Press, 125–143.

Gonzalez-Pino, Barbara, and Frank Pino. 2000. "Serving the Heritage Speaker across a Five-year Program." *ADFL Bulletin* 32(1): 27–35.

Goodison, Ronald A. C. 1987. "Language Training and Language Use – The Uncertain Connection." Unpublished manuscript.

Grabe, William, and Robert B. Kaplan. 1996. *Theory and Practice of Writing.* London and New York: Longman.

Grosjean, Françoise. 1982. *Life with Two Languages: An Introduction to Bilingualism.* Boston, MA: Harvard University Press.

Halliday, M. A. K. 1985. *An Introduction to Functional Grammar.* London: Edward Arnold.

1993. "Towards a Language-Based Theory of Learning." *Linguistics and Education* 5(2): 93–166.

2000. "Grammar and Daily Life. Concurrence and Complementarity." In *Functional Approaches to Language, Culture and Cognition. Papers in Honor of Sydney M. Lamb*, ed. David G. Lockwood, Peter H. Fries, and James E. Copeland. Amsterdam/Philadelphia: John Benjamins, 221–237.

Halliday, M. A. K., and James R. Martin. 1993. *Writing Science: Literary and Discursive Power.* London and Washington: Falmer Press.

Hancock, Charles, and Edward Scebold. 2000. "Defining Moments in Foreign- and Second-Language Education during the Last Half of the Twentieth Century." In *Reflecting on the Past to Shape the Future*, ed. Diane Birckbichler and Robert Terry. Lincolnwood, IL: National Textbook Company, 1–18.

Hasan, Ruqaiya. 1995. "The Conception of Context in Text." In *Discourse in Society: Systemic Functional Perspectives: Meaning and Choice in Language: Studies for Michael Halliday*, ed. Peter H. Fries and Michael Gregory. Norwood, NJ: Ablex, 183–283.

1999. "The Disempowerment Game: Bourdieu and Language in Literacy." *Linguistics and Education* 10(1): 25–87.

Hayward, Fred M. 2000. *Internationalization of US Higher Education: Preliminary Status Report 2000.* Washington DC: American Council on Education.

Head, Henry, Sir. 1920. *Studies in Neurology.* Oxford: Oxford University Press.

Hedge, Tricia. 2000. *Teaching and Learning in the Language Classroom.* Oxford: Oxford University Press.

Heelan, Patrick A. 1998. "The Scope of Hermeneutics in Natural Science." *Studies in the History and Philosophy of Science* 29A(2): 273–298.

Heelan, Patrick A., and Jay Schulkin. 1998. "Hermeneutical Philosophy and Pragmatism: A Philosophy of Science." *Synthese* 115: 269–302.

Higgs, Theodore V., and Ray Clifford. 1982. "The Push toward Communication." In *Curriculum, Competence, and the Foreign Language Teacher*, ed. Theodore V. Higgs. Skokie, IL: National Textbook Company, 57–79.

Hirsch, E. D. 1987. *Cultural Literacy: What Every American Should Know.* New York: Vintage Books.

Holec, H. 1981. *Autonomy and Foreign Language Learning*. Oxford: Pergamon. (First published [1979], Strasbourg: Council of Europe.)

Horowitz, Daniel. 1986. "Process, Not Product: Less Than Meets the Eye." *TESOL Quarterly* 20(1): 141–144.

Horowitz, Elaine K. 1988. "The Beliefs about Language Learning of Beginning University Foreign Language Students." *Modern Language Journal* 72: 283–294.

Horwitz, Elaine K., and Dolly J. Young. 1991. *Language Anxiety: From Theory and Research to Classroom Implications*. Englewood Cliffs, NJ: Prentice-Hall.

Howarth, Peter. 1998a. "Phraseology and Second Language Proficiency." *Applied Linguistics* 19(1): 24–44.

1998b. "The Phraseology of Learners' Academic Writing." In *Phraseology: Theory, Analysis, and Application*, ed. Anthony Paul Cowie. Oxford: Clarendon Press, 161–186.

Huckin, Thomas N. 1995. "Cultural Aspects of Genre Knowledge." *AILA Review* 12: 68–78.

Hymes, Dell H. 1971. *On Communicative Competence*. Philadelphia: University of Pennsylvania Press.

Hyon, Sunny. 1996. "Genre in Three Traditions: Implications for ESL." *TESOL Quarterly* 30(4): 693–722.

James, Dorothy. 1989. "Re-shaping the 'College-level' Curriculum: Problems and Possibilities." In *Shaping the Future: Challenges and Opportunities*, ed. Helen S. Lepke. Middlebury, VT: Northeast Conference, 79–110.

Jones, Janet, Sandra Gollin, Helen Drury, and Dorothy Economou. 1989. "Systemic-Functional Linguistics and Its Application to the TESOL Curriculum." In *Language Development: Learning Language, Learning Culture*, ed. Ruqaiya Hasan and James R. Martin. Norwood, NJ: Ablex, 257–328.

Jordan, R. R. 1990. *Academic Writing Course (New Edition)*. London and Glasgow: Collins ELT.

Kagan, Olga, Tatiana Akishina, and Richard Robin. 2002. *Russian for Russians*. Bloomington, IN: Slavica Publishers.

Kaplan, Marsha. 1997. "Very Advanced Language Learning: 'Beyond-Three' and Refresher Training." Unpublished manuscript.

Kern, Richard. 2000. *Literacy and Language Teaching*. Oxford: Oxford University Press.

King, Larry, and Margarita Suñer. 1999. *Gramática Española. Analisis i Practica*. Boston: McGraw Hill.

Kintsch, Walter. 1988. "The Role of Knowledge in Discourse Comprehension: A Construction-Integration Model." *Psychological Review* 92: 163–182.

Klee, Carol A., and Diane J. Tedick. 1997. "The Undergraduate Foreign Language Immersion Program in Spanish at the University of Minnesota." In *Content-Based Instruction: Models and Methods*, ed. Stephen B. Stryker and Betty Lou Leaver. Washington, DC: Georgetown University Press, 140–171.

Knowles, Malcolm S. 1990. *The Adult Learner: A Neglected Species*. Fourth edn. Houston, TX: Gulf Publishing.

Koike, Dale L., and Judith E. Liskin-Gasparro. 1999. "What is a Near-Native Speaker? Perspectives of Job Seekers and Search Committees in Spanish." *ADFL Bulletin* 30(3): 54–62.

Kramsch, Claire. 1993. *Context and Culture in Language Teaching*. Oxford: Oxford University Press.

1996. "Proficiency Plus: The Next Step."*ERIC Digest* ED402789.

1997. "The Privilege of the Nonnative Speaker." *PMLA* 112(3): 359–369.

Krashen, Stephen D. 1985. *The Input Hypothesis: Issues and Implications*. London: Longman.

Krashen, Stephen D., and Tracy Terrell. 1983. *The Natural Approach: Language Acquisition in the Classroom*. San Francisco: Alemany Press.

Kubler, Cornelius C. 1985. "The Five-Minute Lecture." *Journal of the Chinese Language Teachers Association* 20(2): 65–69.

Lado, Robert. 1964. *Language Teaching: A Scientific Approach*. New York: McGraw Hill.

Langacker, Ronald. 1987. *Foundations of Cognitive Grammar. Vol. 1: Theoretical Foundations*. Stanford: Stanford University Press.

1988a. "An Overview of Cognitive Grammar." In *Topics in Cognitive Linguistics*, ed. Brygida Rudzka-Ostyn. Amsterdam and Philadelphia: John Benjamins, 3–48.

1988b. "A View of Linguistic Semantics." In *Topics in Cognitive Linguistics*, ed. Brygida Rudzka-Ostyn. Amsterdam and Philadelphia: John Benjamins, 49–90.

Lange, Dale L. 2001. "Postlude to the Dialogue on Articulation and Curriculum: Should It Never End! Part II." *ACTR Letter* 27(4): 1–3, 24–25.

Leaver, Betty Lou. 1986. "Hemisphericity of the Brain and Foreign Language Teaching." *Folia Slavica* 8: 76–90.

1997. "Content-Based Instruction in a Basic Russian Program." In *Content-Based Instruction in Foreign Language Education: Models and Methods*, ed. Stephen B. Stryker and Betty Lou Leaver. Washington, DC: Georgetown University Press, 30–54.

1998. *Teaching the Whole Class*. Dubuque, IA: Kendall Hunt.

Leaver, Betty Lou, and Paula M. Bilstein. 2000. "Content, Language, and Task in Content-Based Programs." In *Languages Across the Curriculum*, ed. Maria-Regina Kecht and Katharina von Hammerstein. Columbus, OH: Ohio State University Press, 79–118.

Leaver, Betty Lou, and Melina Champine. 1999. "Beginning a Journey: The Choice to Study a Foreign Language." In *Passport to the World: Learning to Communicate in a Foreign Language*, ed. Betty Lou Leaver, Inna Dubinsky, and Melina Champine. San Diego, CA: LARC Press, San Diego State University, 1–15.

Lee, James F., and Diane Musumeci. 1988. "On Hierarchies of Reading Skills and Text Types." *Modern Language Journal* 72(2): 173–187.

Lekic, Maria. 1990. *The Glasnost Press – Ogonjok 1990*. Lincolnwood, IL: National Textbook Company.

Lekic, Maria, Nadezhda Nitkina, and Tatiana Kirsh. 1994. *Rovesniki/Peers*. Washington, DC: ACTR/ACCELS Publications.

Lewis, Michael. 1996. *Implementing the Lexical Approach*. Hove: Language Teaching Publications.

Lipson, Alexander. 1968. *A Russian Course*. Cambridge, MA: Slavica Publishers.

Logan, Gordon. 1988. "Toward an Instance Theory of Automaticization." *Psychological Review* 95: 492–527.

Long, Michael. 1988. "Instructed Interlanguage Development." In *Issues in Second Language Acquisition: Multiple Perspectives*, ed. Leslie M. Beebe. New York: Newbury House, 115–141.

1998. "Focus on Form in Task-Based Language Teaching." *University of Hawai'i Working Papers in ESL* 16(2): 35–49.

Lotman, Yuri M. 1988. "The Semiotics of Culture and the Concept of a Text." *Soviet Psychology* 26(3): 52–58.

Luus, C. A. E., and G. W. Wells. 1991. "Eyewitness Identification and the Selection of Distracters for Line Ups." *Law and Human Behavior* 15: 43–57.

Madden, Thomas. 1989. "Advanced Chinese Language Study." State Department cable sent to the Foreign Service Institute.

Maly, Eugene. 1993. "Task-Based Instruction from the Teacher's Perspective." *Dialogue on Language Instruction* 9(1): 37–48.

Martin, James R. 1985. "Process and Text: Two Aspects of Human Semiosis." In *Systemic Perspectives on Discourse*, ed. James D. Benson and William S. Greaves. Norwood, NJ: Ablex, 237–274.

1992. *English Text: System and Structure*. Philadelphia: John Benjamins.

1999. "Mentoring Semogenesis: 'Genre-Based' Literacy Pedagogy." In *Pedagogy and the Shaping of Consciousness: Linguistic and Social Presses*, ed. Frances Christie. London: Cassell, 123–155.

McGinnis, Scott. 1996. "Teaching Chinese to the Chinese: The Development of an Assessment and Instructional Model." In *Patterns and Policies: The Changing Demographics of Foreign Language Instruction. AAUSC*, ed. Judith E. Liskin-Gasparro. Boston, MA: Heinle and Heinle, 107–121.

McLaughlin, Barry. 1987. *Theories of Second Language Acquisition*. London: Edward Arnold.

McNamara, Tim F. 1996. *Measuring Second Language Performance*. London/New York: Longman.

Miller, C. R. 1984. "Genre as Social Action." *Quarterly Journal of Speech* 70(2): 151–167.

Miller, John P., and Wayne Seller. 1985. *Curriculum: Perspectives and Practice*. New York: Longman.

Ministère de l'Education Nationale et de la Formation Professionelle. 1998. *L'apprentissage précoce des langues . . . et après? Innovation et recherche pédagogiques.* ("Early Language Learning . . . and Then? Pedagogical Innovation and Research.") Luxembourg: Ministère de l'Education Nationale et de la Formation Professionelle.

Mitrofanova, Olga Danilovna, ed. 1996. *Porogovoj uroven': Russkij jazyk: Tom I: Povsednevnoe obshchenie.* ("Threshold Level: Russian Language: Volume 1: Everyday Communication.") Moscow: Sovet Evropy Press.

Moore, Zena. 1994. "The Portfolio and Testing Culture." In *Teaching, Testing, and Assessment: Making the Connection. Northeast Conference Reports*, ed. Charles Hancock. Lincolnwood, IL: National Textbook Publishers, 163–182.

Naiman, Neil. 1996. *The Good Language Learner*. Clevedon: Multilingual Matters.

National Foreign Language Center. 2001. *LangNet Procedures Manual*. Working document.

Nattinger, James R., and Jeanette S. DeCarrico. 1992. *Lexical Phrases and Language Teaching*. Oxford: Oxford University Press.

New London Group, The. 1996. "A Pedagogy of Multiliteracies: Designing Social Futures."*Harvard Educational Review* 66(1): 60–92.

Nunan, David. 1988. *The Learner-Centered Curriculum*. Cambridge: Cambridge University Press.

Oxford, Rebecca L. 1990. *Language Learning Strategies: What Every Foreign Language Teacher Should Know*. New York: HarperCollins.

Oxford, Rebecca L., and Betty Lou Leaver. 1996. "A Synthesis of Strategy Instruction for Language Learners." In *Language Learning Strategies Around the World: Cross-Cultural Perspectives*, ed. Rebecca L. Oxford. Honolulu, HI: University of Hawaii East-West Press, 227–246.

Pask, G. 1976. "Styles and Strategies of Learning." *British Journal of Educational Psychology* 46: 128–148.

Pawley, A., and F. Syder. 1983. "Two Puzzles for Linguistic Theory: Nativelike Selection and Nativelike Fluency." In *Language and Communication*, ed. Jack Richards and Richard Schmidt. London: Longman, 191–226.

2000. "The One-Clause-at-a-Time Hypothesis." In *Perspectives on Fluency*, ed. Heidi Riggenbach. Ann Arbor: University of Michigan Press, 163–199.

Pellegrino, Valerie. 1999. "Plunging In: Taking the Risk of Learning a New Language and Culture." In *Passport to the World: Learning to Communicate in a Foreign Language*, ed. Betty Lou Leaver, Inna Dubinsky, and Melina Champine. San Diego, CA: LARC Press, San Diego State University, 111–129.

Pemberton, Richard, S. L. Edward, Winnie F. F. Or, and Herbert D. Pierson, eds. 1996. *Taking Control: Autonomy in Language Learning*. Hong Kong: Hong Kong University Press.

Piaget, Jean. 1967. *Six Psychological Studies*. New York: Random House, 111–130.

Piaget, Jean, and Barbel Inhelder. 1973. *Memory and Intelligence*. New York: Basic Books.

Pienemann, Manfred. 1985. "Psychological Constraints on the Teachability of Languages." *Studies in Second Language Acquisition* 6(2): 186–214.

Polinsky, Maria. 2000. "A Composite Linguistic Profile of a Speaker of Russian in the US." In *The Learning and Teaching of Slavic Languages and Cultures*, ed. Olga Kagan and Benjamin Rifkin. Bloomington, IN: Slavica Publishers, 437–466.

Preisler, Bent. 1997. *A Handbook of English Grammar on Functional Principles*. Second edn. Aarhus: Aarhus University Press.

Readings, Bill. 1996. *The University in Ruins*. Cambridge, MA: Harvard University Press.

Reid, Helen. 2000. *Survey of Heritage Languages Teaching at UCLA, Fall 1999*. http://www.humnet.ucla.edu.flrc/.

Reid, Joy. 1999. "Affect in the Classroom: Problems, Politics and Pragmatics." In *Affect in Language Learning*, ed. Jane Arnold. Cambridge: Cambridge University Press, 297–306.

Reiser, Morton F. 1991. *Memory in Mind and Brain*. New Haven, CT: Yale University Press.

Riding, Richard, and Stephen Rayner. 1998. *Cognitive Styles and Learning Strategies*. London: David Fulton Publishers.

Riggenbach, Heidi, ed. 2000. *Perspectives on Fluency*. Ann Arbor: University of Michigan Press.

Robinson, Peter. 1997. "Generalizability and Automaticity of Second Language Learning Under Implicit, Incidental, Enhanced, and Instructed Conditions." *Studies in Second Language Acquisition* 19(2): 223–247.

2001. "Task Complexity, Task Difficulty and Task Production: Exploring Interactions in a Componential Framework." *Applied Linguistics* 22(1): 27–57.

Rogers, Carl. 1968. *The Interpersonal Relationship in the Facilitation of Learning.* Columbus, OH: Merrill.

Rubin, Joan, and Irene Thompson. 1994. *How To Be a More Successful Language Learner.* Second edn. Boston: Heinle and Heinle.

Schemo, Diana Jean. 2001. "Use of English as World Tongue is Booming, and So Is Concern: In Washington a Lack of Linguists to Take Key Security Jobs." *New York Times,* April 16.

Schleppegrell, Mary. 1987. *The Older Language Learner.* Washington, DC: ERIC Clearinghouse on Languages and Linguistics.

Schmeck, Ronald R., ed. 1988. *Learning Strategies and Learning Styles.* New York: Plenum.

Schneider, Alison. 2001. "A University Plans to Promote Languages by Killing Its Languages Department." *Chronicle of Higher Education.* March 9, A14–15.

Schultz, Renate A. 2001. "Cultural Differences in Student and Teacher Perceptions Concerning the Role of Grammar Instruction and Corrective Feedback: USA-Colombia." *Modern Language Journal* 85(2): 244–258.

Schunk, Dale H., and Barry J. Zimmerman. 1997. "Social Origins of Self-Regulatory Competence." *Educational Psychologist* 32(4): 195–208.

Scovel, Thomas. 1991. "The Effect of Affect on Foreign Language Learning: A Review of the Anxiety Research." In *Language Anxiety: From Theory and Research to Classroom Implications,* ed. Elaine K. Horwitz and Dolly J. Young. Englewood Cliffs, NJ: Prentice Hall, 15–24.

Segalowitz, Norman. 2000. "Automaticity and Attentional Skill in Fluent Performance." In *Perspectives on Fluency,* ed. Heidi Riggenbach. Ann Arbor: University of Michigan Press, 200–219.

Seliger, Herbert W. 1983. "Learner Interaction in the Classroom and its Effects on Language Acquisition." In *Classroom-oriented Research in Second Language Acquisition,* ed. Herbert W. Seliger and Michael H. Long. Rowley, MA: Newbury House, 246–267.

Selinker, Larry. 1992. *Rediscovering Interlanguage.* London: Longman.

Shaw, Peter. 1997. "With One Stone: Models of Instruction and their Curricular Implications in an Advanced Content-Based Foreign Language Program." In *Content-Based Instructions in Foreign Language Education: Models and Methods,* ed. Stephen B. Stryker and Betty Lou Leaver. Washington, DC: Georgetown University Press, 261–282.

Shekhtman, Boris. 1990. *How To Improve Your Foreign Language Immediately.* Rockville, MD: Specialized Language Training Center.

Shohamy, Elana. 1998. "Evaluation of Learning Outcomes in Second Language Acquisition: A Multiplism Perspective." In *Learning Foreign and Second Languages: Perspectives in Research and Scholarship,* ed. Heidi Byrnes. New York: MLA, 238–261.

Skehan, Peter. 1998. *A Cognitive Approach to Language Learning.* Oxford: Oxford University Press.

Slobin, Dan I. 1996a. "From 'Thought and Language' to 'Thinking for Speaking.'" In *Rethinking Linguistic Relativity,* ed. John J. Gumperz and Stephen C. Levinson. Cambridge: Cambridge University Press, 70–96.

1996b. "Two Ways To Travel: Verbs of Motion in English and Spanish." In *Grammatical Constructions: Their Form and Meaning,* ed. Masayoshi Shibatani and Sandra A. Thompson. Oxford: Clarendon Press, 195–219.

1998. "Verbalized Events: A Dynamic Approach to Linguistic Relativity and Determinism." Working paper for the LAUD Symposium, March 1998.

Soudakoff, Steven. 2001. "Developing 3+/4 Reading and Translation Skills for Presidential Needs: A Summary." *ACTR Letter* 28(1): 1–3.

Spolsky, Bernard, ed. 1978. *Approaches to Language Testing.* Arlington, VA: Center for Applied Linguistics.

Sprang, Katherine A. 2002. "Vocabulary Acquisition and Advanced Learners: The Role of Grammaticization and Concept Formation in the Acquisition of German Verbs with Inseparable Prefixes." Unpublished doctoral dissertation, Georgetown University, Washington, DC.

Steele, Claude M. 1997. "A Threat in the Air: How Stereotypes Shape Intellectual Identity and Performance." *American Psychologist* 52: 613–629.

Stevick, Earl W. 1980. *Teaching Languages: A Way and Ways.* New York: Newbury House.

1996. *Memory, Meaning, and Method.* Boston: Heinle and Heinle.

Stryker, Stephen B. 1997. "The Mexico Experiment at the Foreign Service Institute." In *Content-Based Instruction: Models and Methods*, ed. Stephen B. Stryker and Betty Lou Leaver. Washington, DC: Georgetown University Press, 174–199.

Stryker, Stephen B., and Betty Lou Leaver. 1997a. "Content-Based Instruction: From Theory to Practice." In *Content-Based Instruction: Models and Methods*, ed. Stephen B. Stryker and Betty Lou Leaver. Washington, DC: Georgetown University Press, 2–27.

1997b. "Content-Based Instruction: Some Lessons and Implications." In *Content-Based Instruction: Models and Methods*, ed. Stephen B. Stryker and Betty Lou Leaver. Washington, DC: Georgetown University Press, 282–309.

Swaffar, Janet K. 1991. "Articulating Learning in High School and College Programs: Holistic Theory in the Foreign Language Curriculum." In *Challenges in the 1990s for College Foreign Language Programs*, ed. Sally Sieloff Magnan. Boston: Heinle and Heinle, 27–54.

Swales, John. 1990. *Genre Analysis.* Cambridge: Cambridge University Press.

Talmy, Leonard. 1991. "Path to Realization: A Typology of Event Conflation." Paper read at Proceedings of the Seventeenth Annual Meeting of the Berkeley Linguistics Society.

Taylor, Charles. 1991. "The Dialogical Self." In *The Interpretive Turn*, ed. David R. Hiley, James F. Bohman, and Richard Shusterman. Ithaca, NY: Cornell University Press, 303–314.

Taylor, Steven J., and Robert Bogdan. 1984. *Introduction to Qualitative Research Methods: The Search for Meanings.* New York: John Wiley and Sons.

Teliya, V., Natalya Bragina, E. Oparina, and I. Sandomirskaya. 1998. "Phraseology as a Language of Culture: Its Role in the Representation of a Cultural Mentality." In *Phraseology: Theory, Analysis, and Application*, ed. Anthony Paul Cowie. Oxford: Clarendon Press, 55–75.

Terrell, Tracy. 1986. "Acquisition in the Natural Approach: The Binding/Access Framework." *Modern Language Journal* 70(3): 63–76.

Thompson, Irene. 2000. "Assessing Foreign Language Skills: Data from Russian." In *The Learning and Teaching of Slavic Languages and Cultures*, ed. Olga Kagan and Benjamin Rifkin. Bloomington, IN: Slavica Publishers, 255–284.

Towell, Richard, Roger Hawkins, and Nives Bazergui. 1993. "Systematic and Nonsystematic Variability in Advanced Language Learning." *Studies in Second Language Acquisition* 15: 439–460.

Tribble, Chris. 1996. *Writing*. Oxford: Oxford University Press.

Turnbull, Miles. 1999. "Multidimensional Project-based Teaching in French as a Second Language (FSL): A Process–Product Case Study." *Modern Language Journal* 83(4): 548–568.

University of California at Los Angeles. Fall. 2000. *Heritage Language Research Priorities Conference Report*. http://www.cal.org/heritage/.

Ushioda, Ema. 1996. *Learner Autonomy 5: The Role of Motivation*. Dublin: Authentik.

Valdés, Guadalupe. 1988. "The Language Situation of Mexican Americans." In *Language Diversity: Problem or Resource?*, ed. S. McKay and S. Wong. New York: Newbury House, 111–139.

1989. "Teaching Spanish to Hispanic Bilinguals: A Look at Oral Proficiency Testing and the Proficiency Movement." *Hispania* 72(May): 392–401.

1992. "The Role of the Language Teaching Profession in Maintaining Non-English Languages in the United States." In *Languages for a Multicultural World in Transition (1992 Northeast Conference Report)*, ed. Heidi Byrnes. Lincolnwood, IL: National Textbook Company, 29–71.

1999. "Nonnative English Speakers: Language Bigotry in English Mainstream Classrooms." *ADFL Bulletin* 31(1): 43–48.

2000. "The Teaching of Heritage Language: An Introduction for Slavic-Teaching Professionals." In *The Learning and Teaching of Slavic Languages and Cultures*, ed. Olga Kagan and Benjamin Rifkin. Bloomington, IN: Slavica Publishers, 375–404.

Valdés, Guadalupe, and Richard Figueroa. 1994. *Bilingualism and Testing: A Special Case of Bias*. New York: Ablex.

Valdés, Guadalupe, and Michelle Geoffrion-Vinci. 1998. "Chicano Spanish: The Problem of the 'Underdeveloped' Code in Bilingual Repertoires." *Modern Language Journal* 82(4): 473–501.

Valdés, Guadalupe, Thomasina Hannum, and Richard V. Teschner. 1982. *Cómo se escribe: curso de secundaria para estudiantes bilingües*. New York: Charles Scribner's Sons.

Valdés, Guadalupe, and Richard V. Teschner. 1999. *Español escrito*. Upper Saddle Back, NJ: Prentice Hall.

VanPatten, Bill. 1998. "Cognitive Characteristics of Adult Second Language Learners." In *Learning Foreign and Second Languages*, ed. Heidi Byrnes. New York: MLA, 105–127.

Veltman, C. 2000. "The American Linguist Mosaic: Understanding Language Shift in the United States." In *New Immigrants in the United States*, ed. S. L. McKay and S. I. Wong. Cambridge: Cambridge University Press, 58–93.

Vigil, Needy A., and John W. Oller. 1976. "Rule Fossilization: A Tentative Model." *Language Learning* 26: 281–295.

Way, Denise P., Elizabeth G. Joiner, and Michael A. Seaman. 2000. "Writing in the Secondary Foreign Language Classroom: The Effects of Prompts and Tasks on Novice Learners of French." *Modern Language Journal* 84(2): 171–184.

Weinert, Regina. 1995. "The Role of Formulaic Language in Second Language Acquisition: A Review." *Applied Linguistics* 16(2): 181–205.

Weinstein, Claire E., Ernest T. Goetz, and Patricia A. Alexander, eds. 1988. *Learning and Study Strategies: Issues in Assessment, Instruction and Evaluation.* New York: Academic Press.

Wenden, Anita. 1991. *Learner Strategies for Learner Autonomy: Planning and Implementing Learner Training for Language Learners.* Englewood Cliffs, NJ: Prentice-Hall.

Wenden, Anita, and Joan Rubin. 1987. *Learner Strategies in Language Learning.* Englewood Cliffs, NJ: Prentice Hall.

Wertsch, James V. 1990. "Dialogue and Dialogism in a Socio-Cultural Approach to Mind." In *The Dynamics of Dialogue,* ed. Ivana Markovà and Klaus Foppa. New York: Harvester Wheatsheaf, 62–82.

Winne, Philip H. 1995. "Inherent Details in Self-Regulated Learning." *Educational Psychologist* 20(4): 173–187.

Wirt, John. 2001. *The Condition of Education 2001.* Washington, DC: National Center for Education Statistics, US Department of Education, Office of Educational Research and Improvement (NCES 2001–72).

Yokoyama, Olga. 2000. "Teaching Heritage Speakers in the College Russian Language Classroom." In *The Learning and Teaching of Slavic Languages and Cultures,* ed. Olga Kagan and Benjamin Rifkin. Bloomington, IN: Slavica Publishers, 467–475.

Young, Richard, and Agnes W. He, eds. 1998. *Talking and Testing. Discourse Approaches to the Assessment of Oral Proficiency.* Amsterdam/Philadelphia: John Benjamins.

Zemskaya, Elena A. 2001. "Umiraet li jazyk russkogo zarubezh'ja?" ("Is the Russian Language Dying Out in Russian Communities Abroad?") *Voprosy Jazykoznanija* 1: 14–30.

Zifonun, Gisela, Ludger Hoffman, Bruno Strecker, *et al.* 1997. *Grammatik der deutschen Sprache.* 3 vols. Berlin and New York: De Gruyter.

Subject index

Aarhus University, 182
academic reading, 200
academic writing, 72, 104, 107, 182, 183, 264, 265
accent, 41, 105, 210, 271
acculturation, 198
accuracy, 6, 18–19, 21, 24–26, 35–38, 40, 44–45, 51–53, 56–57, 65–66, 79–80, 82, 91, 98, 100, 109, 115, 127, 179, 182, 201, 212, 222, 232–233, 236, 248, 253
acronyms, 147, 229
ACTFL, *see* American Council on Teaching Foreign Languages
active listening, 78, 80, 87, 89, 94
ACTR, *see* American Council of Teachers of Russian
adaptive performer, 81
adult learning, 14, 17–18, 35, 38–39, 41, 49, 55, 97–98, 113, 156–157, 159–160, 172, 176, 225, 241, 264, 278
Advanced proficiency, *see* Interagency Language Roundtable, Level 2
aeronautics, 30
affective variables, 16, 21, 31, 55, 64, 67, 81, 86, 154, 214, 220–222, 238, 240, 245, 249, 250, 254–255, 269
agriculture, 100
allusion
    cultural, 147
    historical, 228
    literary, 115
American Council of Teachers of Russian, 221
American Council on Teaching Foreign Languages, 5, 12, 32–34, 36, 41, 61, 83, 142, 145, 148, 150, 152, 159, 198, 212, 223, 229, 260–261, 280
American Institute in Taiwan (AIT), 99, 100, 103, 112, 118
American University in Cairo, 156, 168

anxiety, 16, 73, 76, 220, 235, 239, 247, 254–255, 258
Arabic, 142–143, 153, 156–176, 199, 265, 268, 273
architecture, 232, 234
argumentation, 76, 269–270
art, 101, 203, 224, 233–234
articulation, 143, 231
assessment, *see* testing
Associated Colleges in China (ACC), 99, 118
attention, 21–23, 45, 54, 56, 69, 89, 127–128, 140, 147, 149, 173, 190, 250–252, 256–257
attentional focus, 147
Audio-Lingual Method, 9, 79, 107, 157, 220, 251
aural skills, 219
authentic
    culture, 3
    language, 119
    materials, 10, 14, 16, 20, 29, 31, 85, 93, 170, 175, 186, 203, 209, 218, 229, 246, 266, 273
    task, 14, 56, 119
    text, 14, 29, 61, 71, 136, 167, 171, 175, 184–185, 190, 204, 206
authorial intent, 29, 152, 270
automaticity, 5, 8, 24, 124, 126, 130, 136, 266, 272, 275
automatization, *see* automaticity
autonomy, *see* learner autonomy
awareness, 3, 51–54, 56, 62–63, 65, 69, 121, 175, 177, 182, 184, 186, 189, 194–195, 257–258

Barnard College, 200, 202–204, 214
Beijing Language and Culture University, 100–101
Beijing University of Foreign Languages, 176
"Beyond Three" courses, 99–100, 103, 150, 245–247, 249–250, 252–253, 255, 257–258

Author index

CPSIA information can be obtained at www.ICGtesting.com
Printed in the USA
BVOW011623020413

317078BV00010B/167/P